GUARDIAN OF THE
EAST INDIA COMPANY

'There are roads in solitude and rivers in the
desert, but there are no roads and no rivers in
a man who is always mixed up with other men.'
[Paurvels & Bergier]

GUARDIAN OF THE EAST INDIA COMPANY

The Life of
Laurence Sulivan

By

George K. McGilvary

Tauris Academic Studies
LONDON·NEW YORK

Published in 2006 by Tauris Academic Studies, an imprint of
I.B.Tauris & Co Ltd
6 Salem Road, London W2 4BU
175 Fifth Avenue, New York NY 10010
www.ibtauris.com

In the United States of America and in Canada distributed by
St. Martins Press, 175 Fifth Avenue, New York NY 10010

International Library of Historical Studies (Vol. 34)
ISBN 1 85043 856 0
EAN: 978 1 85043 856 4

A full CIP record for this book is available from the British Library.
A full CIP record for this book is available from the Library of Congress.

Library of Congress catalog card available

Printed and bound in Great Britain by T. J. International Ltd., Padstow,
Cornwall from camera-ready-copy edited and supplied by the author.

To
Margaret
Ever constant

Contents

Preface

This is the life of a man whose career was centred in London's eighteenth century business world. He worked from India House in Leadenhall Street, headquarters of the East India Company, but with a place reserved for him at the highest levels of national government.

The book concentrates upon what went on in London and from the perspective of the Company's leader. It is not a recitation of what happened in the Indian sub-continent – although Sulivan's policies with regard to India and reaction to events and other particulars originating there do come into play.

As well as management of all manner of domestic business, he and his fellow Directors had to deal with the impact made by events taking place abroad. The cataclysmic eruptions overseas, beginning with war in 1756, invariably affected the Company as well as the 'City' and Parliament.

This life at the heart of business in London, and at the centre of power in the Company (as often as not its chief spokesman) led Sulivan into deep involvement in the nation's affairs. Consistently, he was caught up in many of the major developments and controversies of the time. Some of these crises and events in which he was involved have already been subjected to analysis by others, but lack the 'Sulivan' dimension.

The most arresting feature about Sulivan was the extent to which he lived just for the East India Company. It dominated his waking and sleeping hours. He was a living encyclopaedia upon its affairs, forever up-to-date regarding business, home and abroad. He was the Company's guardian angel, continually striving to ensure that it would suffer no wrong.

Assumption of such an all-knowing role sprang from natural ability and length of service, but he also wanted to don such a mantle. Whether in or out of the Company's executive at India House he found himself resolving things or having to make decisions. Invariably he did so almost single-handed, although working within the bounds of committee structures and factions.

For great swathes of time Sulivan controlled India patronage, so much so that within public and private circles he was known as a 'king maker'. He was also an arch politician, a negotiator and manipulator. If the Company was involved in any way, he was the man who just had to be consulted. In or out of executive office he served as a human interface, enabling Company servants, Directors and Proprietors to come together; with whom Parliamentary interests and commercial entrepreneurs found common ground; and where developments in India, attendant problems, upheavals, and all else, found an understanding mind.

During a century of change, he was energetically involved at the centre of power. He is to be found planning and executing naval and military strategies; commanding and supplying adequate manpower, equipment and supplies for war and other emergencies; while running everyday concerns and liaising with Governments. His aims and achievements were to impact upon countless individuals, and affected British society then and in future years. The ramifications of much that he was engaged in reached outwith British shores. His exploits also shed additional light on the lives of many of those he was involved with, such as Chatham, Clive, Hastings, Burke and Pitt the Younger. The qualities and abilities he displays are breathtaking.

Sulivan regarded himself as a public man (and was looked upon as such) although strictly speaking he was a London business man, a director and proprietor of a private monopolistic Company. The fact of the matter, however, is that he was part of the governing nexus, shaping the future direction of events in the Indies and in Britain; and his role was crucial at a time when the Company's new relationship with the state was being re-defined.

He is certainly important enough to justify the in-depth treatment given here. Moreover, in analysing why he sought such power over the East India Company in the first place, and why he fought so stubbornly for the Honourable Company's interest and survival against individuals and governments alike, a very human story emerges. Not least, in this respect, are the implications of his financial tragedy, for himself and his family and the others it touched, such as the Burkes.

A striking fact to emerge is how very well known Sulivan was during his years of complete control of the East India Company, a feature that is more marked when contrasted with today's woeful ignorance. He was regarded as something of a phenomenon then. In London, from 1757 to 1786, he was the subject of gossip, newspaper comment and pamphlet war. His name was as well known to contemporaries as that of other public figures from all walks of life. He was always to be found showing the way at India House, whose Courts and committee rooms he graced for 31 years.

His achievements were many and the following list signifies some of the specific and striking claims that he can lay claim to:-

- He was the accepted leader of the largest and most powerful private Company on earth at that time.

- In all probability he was the most able individual ever to be involved with East India Company business and its most astute servant. No one else approaches him in stature.
- He ranks beside Clive and Hastings in East India Company history; and figures large in the story of Britain's imperial ventures.
- Sulivan was mainly responsible for eventual success in the East Indies against the French and their allies. He (not Chatham) orchestrated Company forces operating in the east; and he was responsible, in particular, for success in the Indian theatre of the Seven Years War.
- Clause 11 in the final treaty of peace was every word his own.
- He was on hand again from 1778 to 1784, helping the Company through the chaotic war situation in the Carnatic.
- While in Bombay he fearlessly exposed fraud and corruption, at every level; and initiated reforms in Customs, and the collection of revenues. These improvements and alterations he later implemented in every Presidency.
- Following his struggle to gain control of the Company, beginning in 1757, he initiated and carried through the financial rescue of 1758/59, saving the organisation from bankruptcy.
- By increasing exports of materials and goods to India, while cutting back in specie, he commenced a revolution in commerce.
- He completely overhauled and reorganised the Company's secretarial structure at India House to meet the new demands put upon it.
- He resolutely resisted moves towards autonomy in India, particularly Bengal, maintaining control from India House.
- He was the creator, champion and guardian of Warren Hastings – who he deluged with proposals and detailed plans.
- In London he organised and led the defence of the Governor-General against ministerial attack, whether or not this was understood at the time by his friend in Bengal.
- He was largely responsible for the appointment of Lord George Macartney as Governor of Madras; and for the appointment of many others to high position.
- He was a more than adequate adversary of his one time friend and business colleague, Robert Clive, in the feud that developed from 1759 onwards.
- He and Edmund Burke conducted an increasingly serious quarrel after prior joint-business adventures left them both impoverished.
- Their enmity was conducive to Burke's alignment with Clive; so much so that despite his Lordship's death, his struggle with Sulivan transformed into one of Burke/Francis versus Sulivan/Hastings. All of this had a bearing on the subsequent impeachment of Warren Hastings.
- Much of Sulivan's thinking is reflected in the India Act of 1784. From as early as 1757 he began planning reform of the Company at home, and of its settlements abroad. Over the years ministerial bureaucrats such as

Atkinson and Jenkinson clandestinely sought his advice and expertise. Finally he was asked for and placed his suggestions and essential details for reform before Robinson and Dundas. Much of what he said contributed to Pitt's Act.

In the years since his death he has been all but forgotten. Today there is an almost general ignorance of what he accomplished. Although somewhat puzzling, this is perhaps not altogether surprising, because the world of the Honourable Company remained quite impenetrable for a long time. Not much of its inner workings were known about by ordinary citizens during his lifetime; and until fairly recently the East India records remained a rather daunting area of study. The workings of the Company were tortuous, and its relationship with the state particularly so. However, modern scholars, like Professor Marshall, have added to the work of Namier, Sutherland and Philips, to name but a few, in clarifying much of this. More recently, a flurry of articles and Ph.D.s dealing with problems that involved the Company, have cleared away some mystery and confusion.

All of this might go some way to explain why until now there has been no major analysis of Sulivan's career. He has only figured within the context of other studies; or is mentioned in passing and in part, elsewhere. A limited biography of him exists in the *History of Parliament* (two pages); he appears in the *Dictionary of National Biography, Missing Persons,* published in 1993; and in the *Oxford Dictionary of National Biography* of 2004. The other published in-depth treatment is to be found within the structure of the late Dame Lucy Sutherland's, *East India Company in Eighteenth Century Politics.* There are some mentions in specialised histories – especially those eulogising Clive – and in a few academic treatises, such as my own examination of the early part of Sulivan's life.[1]

His particular significance was remarked upon by at least four eminent historians: L.S. Sutherland, K. Feiling, C.H Philips and A.M. Davies.[2] They all agreed that his life must be understood in order to determine many of the developments at the heart of British political, economic and imperial affairs between 1757 and 1786; and to bring into focus several questions that remain unanswered. So much began with him, passed through his hands or was affected by his thoughts and personal objectives that understanding him is pivotal to much else. Hopefully, this work makes the pattern clearer.

Acknowledgements

A great many people, knowingly or otherwise, have contributed towards this book finding life. In the beginning I enjoyed both inspiration and advice from the late Dr. James N.M. Maclean and from Professor Emeritus Victor G. Kiernan. Many others include: Dr. Angus Calder, Dr. James G. Parker, Owen Dudley Edwards, John Riddy, and the late Father Thomas Walsh. I have been honoured by the generosity of Laurence Sulivan's descendants, in particular Mrs. B.E. Baumer, Dr. J. H. Baumer, Mr. Martin de Bertodano, Lady Rosemary Griffin and Mrs. Diane Morrison.

As the bibliography will make clear, I owe an immense debt of gratitude to the staff of libraries, record offices and private collections the length and breadth of Britain and Ireland. These are too numerous to name individually, but I thank them, each and every one.

Of course, any new work owes much to the labours of scholars who have gone before, and to that of contemporaries; little of significance could be produced otherwise. In this respect I have benefited enormously and pay my due respects.

Lastly, I thank my wife Margaret for her patience and encouragement, together with her determination to see that I brought this work to a conclusion.

The form and spelling of Indian words used are based on the *Handbook of Oriental History,* edited by C.H. Philips, 2nd edition, London, 1963. Round brackets encompass words I have introduced that were omitted in the originals, or they have been inserted to make the meaning clear.

1

Bombay and Origins
1713-52

1

Portraits of Laurence Sulivan in mid-life suggest that when Elizabeth Owen first set eyes on him she beheld a lively young man, bursting with energy. Of small-to-middling height, around five feet six or seven, he must have bewitched her with his expressive blue eyes, arching eyebrows and fair hair. He possessed a strong, well-proportioned build. From later accounts, it seems his voice was of an even modulation. His attire and whole manner said he was a gentleman. He had a stamp of quality, of authority and awareness. He must have appeared different, interesting, exciting.

By her portraits, she was of a similar height and build to her husband-to-be. Her slightly long, well-proportioned face and general air of languor balanced one another; while her eyes were large and calm. Auburn hair framed the whole countenance. It was an appearance that bespoke natural repose.

They were married on 20 August 1739 in the Anglican Church, Bombay. He was twenty-six years old, she twenty-five. The wedding was a formal affair, the ceremony according to the rites of the Church of England, to which his wife belonged. From his many negative words on the subject, Sulivan went along with the church ritual since it was expected of him. Later in life he constantly described himself as 'an infidel'. Elizabeth Owen, on the other hand, remained a devout Christian all her days.

Despite the heat, flies and general discomfort of an Indian midsummer, the ceremony was subject to the formal protocol and strictures that governed everything in the English East India Company's Presidencies. Even during this most personal of occasions, pride of place went to the Governor, Stephen Law, and his spouse Martha; then to ex-Governor John Horne followed by Members of Council and their wives. The marriage was solemnised by the Reverend James Chapman. It must have been a severe trial, and it can only be hoped that the subsequent banquet was more relaxed than the actual ceremony.

The notification in the Bombay records of his wedding to Elizabeth Owen is the first indication anywhere that Laurence Sulivan existed. That he was born on 24 April 1713 is only known from a letter written by him in January 1782. The date he arrived in Bombay is a mystery, but he was there no earlier than 25 November 1738. Governor Stephen Law authorised a census of European inhabitants in Bombay reaching that far back and he does not appear. Nor is he present among Company servants in the factories; or in the lists of European inhabitants, free merchants and itinerant travellers in Bombay, Surat, Tellicherry, Madras or Calcutta.

The facts regarding his future wife are a little more copious. She appears from January 1738 onwards, among the European inhabitants in Bombay as a single woman. She had applied to join her brother Edward Owen, a covenanted servant, formally employed in the Bombay treasury where he 'weighed off the treasure that came from England – counted and packed the money to the Factories and signed the notes for the land marine paymasters.'[1]

It seems likely that Sulivan worked alongside Edward Owen, and that this led to an introduction then romance with his sister Elizabeth. Their father was possibly Richard Owen, Master of the *Bombay Merchant.* He was a free merchant* at Bombay and Surat in 1720. An Edward Owen, a Director* of the Company (and one of its accountants) was probably an uncle. He died in London in 1729.

Elizabeth Owen's family did not welcome Sulivan as a suitor. His own words to his son on the matter are clear enough, 'Your mother's relations all loved me as a friend and intimate, but dreaded and strongly opposed the union. And it was pronounced that your mother would be unhappy.'[2]

He would appear to have been the sort of rake young ladies travelling to India were entreated to beware of. They were to be 'Careful of their conduct...to guard against the ruin of their reputation...and in all things, to show prudence.'[3] He admitted as much later, saying that prior to his marriage he was 'wild, dissipated and a favourite with both sexes'.[4] Certainly, his conversation seems to have been very entertaining; and he was doubtless then an amusing, perhaps slightly disorientated, young man.

His inheritance must have been small for him to be in India at all: a few contacts, certainly a good education and a bright intelligence. However, he would not have been considered a good match and in all likelihood was known or presumed to have few possessions and even less prospects. On the other hand, he was looked upon as a gentleman and accepted as such. His speech, good manners, dress and deportment had to convince his superiors – not to mention his wife-to-be, of a certain status.

The speed of their courtship was remarkable by English standards, although perhaps not by those of Bombay, where the unhealthy climate and peculiarities of such a closed world bore down heavily. Nevertheless, the Governor's permission had to be sought. Weddings within the European community in Bombay were not too plentiful in the years 1738 and 1739. Apart from her own and that of her brother Edward to Ann Tolson in 1738, which had occasioned her visit to Bombay in the first place, there were only three others. Theirs was to be a match that lasted until death separated them.

For Laurence Sulivan everything changed with marriage. The vagaries of his previous existence ended. He set about forging a completely different approach to life. It might have been triggered by his new responsibilities; or perhaps the fact that his Owen relations did not consider him good enough stirred him to do something.

He admired what he later termed his wife's 'prudence, discreetness and sagacity...in some few instances...perhaps carried too far, yet 9 times in 10 she will be found on the right side'.[5] She was to be his main support throughout his life; and he nearly always asked her opinion of his ideas and decisions. The immense trust and affection she was held in is identifiable in all his correspondence.

Elizabeth Sulivan certainly worked a profound change in her new husband. She reached into the depths of his being to such an extent that he could not bear the thought she might think him unworthy. With his wife's total trust and support, he saw the path he must tread. That being said, his new awakening and kindling ambition were kept well hidden: 'My line was marked, unknown to all, and its success depended upon resolution and perseverance.'[6]

Marriage was hugely important to the development of Sulivan's career because of the determination it bred in him. He also had the respectability and security personified in Elizabeth Owen. Although a picture of the young Sulivan remains a little hazy, a clearer image begins to emerge by 1740, shown most distinctly in the way he approached his work. He now spent every morning at his official employment and every afternoon on his own affairs. He 'shut out every other temptation', broke all former habits, and severed all connection with those comrades of his former life.[7]

2

In the absence of irrefutable evidence of Sulivan's life before he arrived in Bombay, the conclusions reached must rest on inference. It is only possible to detect some echoes of an early life from later interests, by taking account of his skills, the travels he made, suggestions culled from later correspondence, and assorted gleanings. These, the attitudes he struck, duties performed in Bombay, and what he seemed comfortable with, tell quite a lot. Everything hints at a general legal and accountancy background, such as would be familiar to a notary public. He was almost certainly connected in some way with shipping and cargoes.

This practical acquaintance with activities peculiar to shipping and trade included particular skills like ship insurance, and the lading of cargoes. He knew about the transfer of mercantile goods and money; and was thus aware of the intricate relationships involving ships' captains, entrepreneurs and merchants. He was expert in measuring profit margins from freight transfer, of assessing shipping costs and other associated distribution dues. This training and knowledge is reflected in his own private records; and is signified by his intimate knowledge and understanding of the problems faced by the Company's marine service. A close connection with its shipping interest* was maintained throughout his life.

That he received this early training in Cork is suggested by some exceptional coincidences during his years in Bombay, concerning people who hailed from there and must be thought of as relations. The first of these was a Commander John Sullivan (or O'Sullivan) from Cork, who was involved in the country (coastal) trade,* especially at Bombay and along the Malabar Coast during the years Laurence Sulivan was there.[8] Also, a Commander James Irwin, again a probable relation, and also from Cork, appears on these shores at this time.[9]

Later in life he helped members of their families to a quite extraordinary degree. Contemporaries regarded their various offspring as his kinsmen, often referring to them as such. Help and opportunity in the first instance, therefore, possibly came to young Sulivan through these men. Captain Irwin was probably the prime mover. Dating from the early 1730s, he had been a free trader in India. Earlier he was at St. Helena before becoming involved with the East India Company. Irwin sailed on a brig called the *Mary* during these early years.[10]

This ship, or at least a ship called the *Mary,* appears significant. It is perhaps too coincidental that on 27 July 1708, by an 'Instrument of Attestation', a Captain Robert Irwin was Commander of the ship *Mary*, of Dublin, 'burthen about 64 tons'.[11] This vessel could have sailed from Ireland to the Indies in order to participate in the country trade.

From 1736, and earlier, Captain James Irwin (perhaps a relation of Commander Robert Irwin) traded along the coasts of India, being in Madras that year, acting as a Supercargo,* not in the Company. In 1737 he was working the Madras coast, still on board the *Mary*, but now in the Bengal service. By 1739 he had become part-owner and Master of the *Mary*. The other title holder was an Anthony Upton. It is perhaps no coincidence that in 1739 this same man was President of the Mayor's Court Bombay, when Laurence Sulivan served as an Alderman. Sulivan also remitted money for him.

Sometime between 1743 and 1751 Captain Irwin married a Sarah Beale in St. Helena.[12] He was to die in Bengal on 20 June 1752. Before his demise he had bought the estate of Hazeleigh in Essex, a clear sign that he had managed to accumulate a sizeable fortune. A great intimacy existed later between Sulivan and all members of his family, but especially with his eldest son, Eyles Irwin.[13] All Irwins of the next generation, who were the offspring of Captain James Irwin, were patronised by Sulivan and given good positions in the Company's various services.

There were quite a number of private ships from Britain involved in the country trade; interlopers who were there in defiance of the monopoly. They swelled the so-called 'separate stock' of Company ships licensed at the end of the seventeenth and early eighteenth centuries and let out for private trade. It might be the case, therefore, that sometime during 1737 or early 1738,

Sulivan sailed east on board the *Mary*, perhaps then owned by Anthony Upton, accompanying his kinsman, Captain James Irwin, at that time a Supercargo.

On board, Sulivan would have acted as his assistant. It is probable that around 1738 Commander John Sullivan (O'Sullivan) of Cork City, whose mother was Elizabeth Irwin (Mrs. Philip O'Sullivan), also captained the *Mary*. He and Captain James Irwin were probably brothers-in-law. Laurence Sulivan can be envisaged learning the duties of a Supercargo under the supervision of these men, en route to India.[14] But no matter how he arrived in eastern waters, he was certainly employed in a private capacity. Working on board such a coastal vessel, he would rapidly learn the avenues open to exploitation. Another discovery would be that in the layered society of the European settlements free traders held an inferior rank. Company servants were regarded as superior, and had more rights and privileges.

Some deductions regarding his Irish origins are possible. Evidence, including that relating to Commanders John Sullivan (O'Sullivan) and James Irwin, points to his being very closely related to Benjamin Sulivan of Cork, son of Philip O'Sullivan and his wife Elizabeth Irwin.[15] Benjamin and Commander John Sullivan (O'Sullivan) were brothers. Laurence and Benjamin were the only ones, however, to spell their surname with one 'l', and dropped the 'O'. This might signify their choice of Benjamin's mother's Protestant religion. Benjamin was a lawyer and conversion was required to practice in Ireland. Laurence Sulivan had some legal training.

What is more, the O'Sullivan More coat of arms (with a few minor differences from the traditional) formed the right half of Laurence Sulivan's seal. On the left was a rampant lion crowned with a coronet.[16] He and his son continued throughout life to use these heraldic arms, which were eventually granted on 13 July 1801 to Sir Benjamin Sulivan, Knight, eldest son of the above Benjamin Sulivan of Cork.

The interest shown by Laurence Sulivan in the family of Benjamin Sulivan of Cork was striking. He helped them all, and particularly the three older sons: Benjamin, John and Richard Joseph Sulivan. He launched them into life via the East India Company and set them on their way to riches and firm establishment in English society. He also helped the youngest son Henry Boyle Sulivan until his early death, and the sisters too.[17]

In the eyes of contemporaries Laurence and Benjamin Sulivan were very closely associated, though Laurence would only admit they were 'relations', and 'a family connection'. In London in the early 1760s, the two of them spent hours in social chat. The mystery arises from Laurence stating many times that Benjamin's family was connected to him, but saying no more; and in his non-appearance in all pedigrees traced.[18] Benjamin senior arrived in London in 1761 or just after, and in all probability it was Laurence Sulivan's dazzling leap to prominence that attracted him to the city. He died and was buried there in 1767.

The contact between the families is best illustrated by Laurence Sulivan's patronage of Benjamin's sons, though in the early 1760s he also lent

Benjamin between £200 and £300. In a letter, written some time later to John Sulivan (the second son), he said: 'Having in a former letter desired you to pay what your father owed me to Col. Wood, the death of that gentleman obliges me to request this money may be paid to Mr. Roger Darvall.'[19]

Laurence Sulivan also helped Philip, the only son of Commander John Sullivan (O'Sullivan), Benjamin Sulivan's brother. The youth was provided with a post in the Company's military branch, reaching the rank of Captain. Sulivan said to his son Stephen in 1778: 'Be kind to Philip O'Sullivan if he merits your attention.'[20] His other connection was with the family of Captain James Irwin, whose son Eyles Irwin was helped enormously. It is very likely that Captain James Irwin, of the ship *Mary*, was related to Elizabeth Irwin, wife of Philip O'Sullivan (mother and father of Benjamin Sulivan), and that in some way both were related to Laurence Sulivan. Like Captain James Irwin, Elizabeth Irwin stemmed from Counties Cork and Roscommon.

Sulivan never seems to have said who his parents were, where he was born or made any mention of his childhood and upbringing.[21] The reason why can only be guessed at; but he stemmed from an older, Anglo-Norman, Catholic and perhaps even Jacobite background. Prejudice against the Irish was rife, and he would not want contemporaries to dwell on his name, although many might have entertained suspicions of him.[22]

Despite declared adherence to the King, Constitution and religion of England, a prerequisite for his position, his enemies would have attacked without mercy. Perhaps he concluded that it was best to blank out his origins. He never mentioned ancestry or lineage, certainly not in writing. No family connection ever stated just what the relationship was, either by salutation or by inference. Naturally, such a course of action would require great care and a kind of grim determination by him and by others in the know. However, it is certainly plausible; secrecy was a central plank with Sulivan, allowing his career to go ahead, unhindered.

Logic, which (apart from the occasional but deadly mad gamble) seems to have always predominated with him, would have dictated that he must close and utterly forget the early chapter of his life, and merge with the English code. This might have influenced his marriage and entry to the Company. He wanted to become a high-ranking member of the established order, and in effect this is what he did become.

3

When he first appeared in Bombay, the English Company was competing successfully against the entrenched Portuguese, Dutch and French, though these were only fringe struggles in a subcontinent dissolving into chaos. The Mughal Empire, weakened and corrupt, was falling apart. Real power was being wrested from the emperor by his feudal vassals, primarily the Nawabs of the various regions. Warring tribes like the Marathas wreaked havoc. Skirmishes at sea against the Dutch and Portuguese were common.

Although its commerce continued to increase, Bombay remained the third ranking Presidency in terms of size and popularity. This might suggest that it was reliance on his relations that determined Sulivan would go to there; although the country trade along the Malabar Coast was good at that particular time. This freight (mostly Asian) was carried in British vessels; partly explained by superior British seamanship and navigation skills. A boom occurred in the period 1700 to 1742; and English shipping involved in the country trade doubled from 3,000 to 7,000 tons. With it came a demand for more mariners.

Bombay was always the unhealthiest Presidency; few children survived (as Sulivan would know all too personally). Society, for the most part, retained an English character, superimposed upon that of the native Indian. There was an easy understanding and tolerance. However, all understood that there was only one sovereign power, the English one. A stiffness and hauteur attended every public function; position and seniority governed social standing. This labelling was even reflected at worship in Bombay cathedral.

The settlement also had its wilder side; there was a great deal of intermarriage and concubinage. The Mayor's Court* records show ample evidence of this. Gambling was the pet vice. All kinds of card games were played. The taverns dealt with the huge demand for backgammon and billiards. Drinking, especially of heavy red wines, was widespread.

Slavery was practised, something the Company considered almost solely in economic terms. If Sulivan felt anything, he kept quiet. At the very least, he would have known of the profitable returns to be made from this vile commerce. He would have been aware too, of other dubious activities going on in this area, associated with piracy. Ships belonging to all the European trading nations were plundered. The most fearsome was the Maratha Admiral, Kohanji Angria. At the same time the brilliant horsemen of the Maratha confederation controlled inland routes; to such an extent that Governor Stephen Law had the main gates to the city strengthened and a constant watch kept. This accounted for Bombay expenditure rising to £26,338 in 1736, then to £37,500 by 1744. It also led to Law's recall in 1742 by a non-comprehending Court of Directors.

Sulivan could get to India only by sea – the overland route was not in operation until much later. Also, he had to do a job, fulfil some duty. He was not a seaman, nor a medical man; but very soon after his first appearance in Bombay, working in a private capacity, he was to become a successful businessman – as well as an excellent Company servant. This hints at prior knowledge and training. Yet he said little of this or of his travels. He made mention of only one occasion:

> I borrowed my ideas not only from reading but an instance which will never depart from my memory,...the Dutch deposit all their power with their Governor General...A certain habit with a truncheon proclaims his office. After the dreadful massacre of the Chinese at Batavia, Baron Imhoff held the truncheon until he had saved and secured that important settlement from destruction.[23]

This eyewitness account shows that he was on the island of Java during the initial part of Baron Gustav Wilhelm Von Imhoff's period of service as 'Raad' (Ruler) of the Dutch East Indies. The Baron reached Batavia in March 1740. By this time Sulivan was married to Elizabeth Owen, but it probably typifies the sort of commercial voyages he had already been involved in. This journey was almost certainly his last before entry to the East India Company's service.

4

Although it is only during Governor Stephen Law's tenure of office that Sulivan appears in the Bombay records in an official role, he had served his predecessor, Governor Horne, in a personal capacity for some time. There is no doubt, however, that Stephen Law becoming Governor in April 1739 was a fortunate and significant occurrence for him. As well as becoming his immediate master, Law assumed the position of patron; and then friend and confidant.

His place of work was Bombay Castle, in a room right next to that of the Governor. From him he learned much that had nothing to do with tiresome accounts. He became aware of the subtle undertones of Bombay society; and developed a thorough understanding of relationships with the local native powers and rival European trading nations. Most of all, he was given an insight into the usage of power. The art of exuding authority (if it can be taught at all) was learned from Governor Law. He and Sulivan were friends for life.

Ironically, in view of his later importance within the organisation, Sulivan's entry into the Company's service was extremely inconspicuous. On 17 March 1740, faced with a shortage of men, Law asked for three covenanted servants to help him. When they were not forthcoming, he called upon the Council to allow Sulivan to be his assistant, on a temporary basis. He was to be paid 80 rupees per month, the sum his predecessor, Governor Horne, had paid him out of his own pocket for also being his assistant.

The Governor did not have the authority to take Sulivan into the service, he could only advise such action to the Directors. His recommendation to this effect was included in the Bombay General Letter* that went to England on board the *Harrington*. After clearance from India House and a security of £1,000 paid in London by ex-Governor Horne and a Thomas Waters, he was formally entered in the records. As well as his duties for Law, Sulivan was employed clearing up the mess of Horne's personal affairs, abandoned on his return to England. Almost all of these were bound up with the country trade.[24]

The appointment was backdated to 1 January 1740, the date he had actually commenced the duties spoken of in March 1740. Also, although theoretically merely a personal secretary to Law, he obviously already had experience of the various branches of public business. He could not otherwise have been able to cope with what had been the work of three covenanted servants. It is almost certain that from April 1739, when the

Governorship changed hands, until January 1740, Sulivan worked in the morning on Company business in the new Governor's office. In the afternoon he would be busy with ex-Governor Home's private affairs. He would have received payment from both. During the course of the four years he worked there, from 1739 to 1742, he applied himself with great diligence.

His initial appointment on 13 February 1741 was as 'assistant to the President', with the rank of Factor. As a covenanted servant he received a good deal more than a salary. He was provided with free food, quarters and servants; and bought wine at special low rates. Remuneration was used more for pocket money than for maintenance. Wages were paid at six monthly intervals. The experience beside Governor Law provided him with telling insights; and enabled him later, when a Director of the Company, to deal with problems which were beyond the grasp of most Directors and Proprietors,* who had spent no time in India.[25]

Disaster struck, however, with Stephen Law's recall in November 1742 for over-spending. John Geekie, senior member of the Council, became acting Governor until William Wake arrived eleven days later. Geekie had no love for Sulivan, nor did Wake trust the disciple of the man he had replaced; although he continued to use him in a capacity similar to that established by his predecessors.

There is a hint of the unhappiness this change brought in a letter to his son, written many years and a lifetime of experience later: 'Take a little pains to be well... show an affected openness...but be close...watch...narrowly...it was not my practice and I suffered for it. I knew myself honest and thought caution unnecessary, which made me the dupe of many a fool.'[26]

Wake neglected him, and there was nobody in England with sufficient influence to speed his promotion; Stephen Law was not yet established. Nevertheless, Sulivan was determined to build a career within the Company, and gain financial independence. He also wanted knowledge and experience of every aspect of business. As his life would show, he was not the sort of man to quit easily.

5

Sulivan became fully immersed in the life of the settlement. On 20 December 1739 he was elected an Alderman in the Bombay Mayor's Court, at a time when the President of the Court, Anthony Upton, was away from the island. He remained an Alderman until 1743, attending Court regularly. Here, at first hand, he was involved with Indians in their own arena, with all the noise and fractious behaviour associated with life at street level. It was a joyous kaleidoscope, a seething world of heat, smells and sounds.

He handled wills, administrations and cases involving legal wrangles over commerce, on behalf of Asian and European alike. As suggested, his involvement in such work – from his very first appearance in Bombay – points to him being already skilled in legal and notary public techniques. He also acted for others in business and legal affairs, carrying their warrant of attorney. He was honest, thorough and had a sound knowledge of procedures, of the intricacies of the coastal trade and of local commerce. Unsurprisingly, many lawsuits were against ex-Governor Horne. Sulivan's four years of attendance suggests that real ability and knowledge were brought to bear.

Those of the Owen family still alive in Bombay could hardly be expected to have foreseen this complete change of character and lifestyle that Sulivan achieved so soon after marriage. He was happy with domestic life, and showed blinding devotion to his wife and son Stephen, born on 22 October 1742. The child was the second born, named after Governor Stephen Law. Two other children died: Martha, born 18 October 1740, died 12 November 1740; and Laurence, born 6 June 1745, died April 1748. The death of this little boy, when almost three years old, was particularly heartbreaking. In addition, he and his wife were to care for the widow and two surviving daughters of his wife's brother, Edward Owen, who died around 1745. These nieces, Elizabeth ('Betsy') and Anne ('Nancy') Owen were born on 24 October 1741 and 14 September 1743, respectively.

So many deaths prompted him to send Stephen to Britain around 1748. His nieces appear to have accompanied the boy. Later, in 1752, Adriana, the wife of his friend and follower, John Spencer, hoped that on arrival in England the Sulivans would be 'blessed with finding in Master Stephen the satisfaction you have so long wished for'.[27] It is very likely that the children joined Stephen Law, who occupied a house on the west side of Queen Square. Later, Sulivan too would have a long association with this particular neighbourhood.

The desire to get rich carried most Europeans to the Indies; but it took a long time if no patronage was available, to propel a young man into one of the more lucrative positions. Even though there were many perks, the Company paid a miserable salary. Servants were expected to barter and trade to better their lot and spent a great deal of their time so employed.

Money was made through recognised channels: private trade, money-lending and also accepting presents and perquisites from wealthy and important Indians, although this was something Sulivan always frowned upon. Nevertheless, he was adept at all other means of accumulating wealth. During the years in Bombay he was active in pursuit of riches, though not to the detriment of public duties.

His sharp business acumen was put to great use; and his skill helped amass a moderate fortune, which was all that he desired. His personal business ventures were launched while in Governor Horne's employ. He was markedly busy in the country trade, both on his own and on the Governor's behalf. His employment along the same lines in private work for Governors Law and Wake is witnessed by his name appearing on many and various papers; such as that on a bond of November 1739 concerning the goldsmith, Servaji Dharmseth.

These activities as a private trader were important then and for the future. Here he made his connections, and many became close business colleagues. That his maritime connections were numerous is confirmed by the many references to deals with ships' commanders. He dealt with sets of certificates, such as those 'on account of a Captain Thomas Brown'; and others 'on account of Captain Charles Foulis'. He handled President Wake's freight charges for goods going on the *Salisbury* to Gombroon.

It was during these years that he developed a close partnership with Captain Samuel Hough, Captain Thomas Lane and John Spencer, which was referred to later as 'The Marine Society'. The activities of this group, after his arrival in England, assumed even more importance. These men became special business friends. Spencer was to uphold the India end of the triple business enterprise. Captain Hough was an important figure in the Bombay navy.[28] Captain Thomas Lane developed into Sulivan's closest confidant and his man of business. Sulivan would later use him as a cover for his own hidden machinations at Leadenhall.* He arrived in England a year ahead of him, sailing from Bombay in December 1751.[29]

They were only three of a legion of friends and business acquaintances he was assembling, who would be central to his future success in London. The most important, apart from those mentioned, were Commander (later Sir) William James and Commander James Barton. The list of his friends among Company servants, 'Country' Captains and free traders is just as impressive. To these can be added many who later gave their support in England.[30] Of course, he made enemies too: Governor Wake, Charles Crommelin, William Price and perhaps Henry Savage, fall into this category.

There were other activities by which Sulivan acquired wealth, in doing so securing even more friends and business acquaintances. For nearly all of his time in Bombay he acted as an attorney and administrator, executor and trustee, for his colleagues – distinct from his duties in the Mayor's Court. He was involved to such a degree that he either displayed a new, exceptional skill, or (as indicated in his Mayor's Court duties) came to Bombay already qualified for such work.

In 1741 he was involved (together with Edward Owen and a John Lambton) as an attorney on behalf of ex-Governor Horne. Sulivan was required to make the goldsmith-cum-financier, Servaji Dharmseth, pay to the Company money that Horne had stood security for. He had to be as shrewd in understanding the minds and business habits of native Indian merchants as he was in his handling of Europeans.

Dealing with the estates of others gave him further room for manoeuvre. In December 1751 he and Hough bought bills in Bombay for the estate of Benjamin Lowe, deceased. On 8 December 1752 they did the same again, this time for the estate of an Alexander Fogue also dead. The money involved totalled £5,241-4-6, which was to be paid through the 'current account' in London. Nobody was specified, but as attorneys for the estates Sulivan or Hough picked up this money. This type of activity continued almost until the day of his departure. On 12 December 1752 he and a John Sewell were defendants in the Mayors Court for a Wifran set Savajee, against an action brought by William Sedgwicke. Then on the same day, together with Thomas Byfield, he and Sewell represented Savajee against a similar action brought by Brabazon Ellis and Francis Pym.[31]

6

In January 1747 he was promoted Junior Merchant; but no Company duties of significance came his way until October 1748, when he was created Provisional Collector of Rents and Revenues. It was an important and profitable post; confirmation came in July 1749, and was combined with the position of Mint Master. It was as Collector that Sulivan made his mark on Bombay; and developed models and methods that he carried to London. He was also to portray fraud on a large scale. What he created (and uncovered) was of great significance then and later.

Two months later, he was promoted Senior Merchant and made Deputy Accountant and assistant to a George Scott. He and Sulivan commenced chasing one another in and out of Company posts over the next four years. This office automatically meant a place as Deputy Accountant, the functions were so linked.

The duties that he had to perform as Collector were endless. The island of Bombay was five miles across at its widest and, according to Sulivan, nourished 20,000 people. It required to be surveyed minutely as to both value and extent. Everything produced in Bombay was farmed, that is, let out in return for a payment or rent to the Company. A detailed register was to be kept of all farms. He was to ensure that the soil and vegetation were not spoiled; and appointed and advised inspectors who made a weekly round, reporting to him.

In addition, it was his duty to adjust and settle all accounts, receive all moneys and make the necessary disbursements. He was to deliver his financial statement and the money every three months to the Governor and Council. Regular books were to be kept; and he was required to explain reasons for any increases or decreases in the sums received. The information was eventually relayed to India House.

Yet Sulivan had no power to lessen the amount of money expected by the Company, even in the event of famine or any other calamity. He could only represent the situation to his superiors and plead the hardship of the renters. Nor could he judge who should receive the farms; they were auctioned, and completely under the control of the President aided by his Council. For cases of glaring criminality, he had no jurisdiction. The Collector had to gather a variety of dues: rent from the growing of coconut, cultivation of tobacco and the production of arrack; rent from Bombay pensions; and money that stemmed from various privileges. He also collected money from salt sales, quit rents and batta* grounds. Similar collections were also made at Mahim, the Company settlement in the north of the island.

Coconut growing gave the biggest return. A few opulent merchants dominated this. They were given the whole crop for a number of years to work or sublet as they wished. These few merchants had combined to create a monopoly situation that could not be broken. As a result, the Company never received a fair price for the crop since this was always rigged.

Sulivan changed things. He created ten distinct divisions of the coconut grant with sixteen plots within each division. Each lot was leased by the Company, which now had direct ties and records dealing with every lot. The results were astonishing. A twenty-five per cent increase in revenue took place following the first of these new leases; fifty per cent following the second issue, with a continually rising yield thereafter. He increased the amount gathered from 8,177 rupees in December 1748, to 13,510 rupees in April 1749. This success encouraged him to enforce the system over the whole range of farms rented out by the Company.

From these fiscal reforms Sulivan was able to relieve some of the social distress inherent in the existing structure. The system of farming out operated by the Company had led to the under-tenants and labouring people becoming very dependent and open to persecution and oppression. The Company Collector, before Sulivan's time, was generally someone of Council standing. Part of his remit was to guard his charges from all threats; and he was duty bound to correct misbehaviour, enforce payment of dues and receive and judge petitions of complaint from renters or dependants. All these petitions and judgements would be registered in the Company books that they might be produced in the event of further appeals to the President and Council.

The Collector was, therefore, in a powerful position and could command the use of force (a body of sepoys*) to secure rents due. Theoretically, his role in this respect was only to assist the farmer, and he ought to have taken such action only when appealed to by him. Instead, the Collector took the initiative and the 'cruel, impolitic and oppressive practice of demanding money with menaces' was the order of the day. Sulivan stopped all this.

His efficiency in the Collector's office reflected upon the need for improvements in the Company's commercial administration in India; and showed how well equipped he was to make the necessary changes. He demonstrated that awareness of financial and administrative detail that later was to give unrivalled comprehension of the intricacies of the Company's financial system.

Evidence of the zeal and honesty that he brought to his new office of Collector was not long in finding its way into the Company records, doubtless just as he planned. His incorruptibility is so startling when compared to what went on among his colleagues that the question of a completely different morality seems to enter the equation.

In a letter to the President on 4 March 1749, a mere six months after assuming his post, he gave a comprehensive survey of one particular farm, the Mazagon estate. What he had uncovered constituted a first-class outrage. His aim was to justify the Company's right to all salt, fishing and other revenues from the estate; and he desired the authority of the President and Council to collect these. He quoted from the Company's own records to justify his arguments, going back to 1674 to do so; and he was quite truthful in his assertion that he had 'spared no pains to obtain a true knowledge'.[32]

The Governor and Council agreed with his findings but did nothing. On 16 May 1749 he again brought the affair before them, because the inhabitants of the Mazagon estate were not only still paying taxes to those who claimed possession of the farm on the estate, but had been taxed double. Governor Wake then formed a committee to enquire further. On 20 May it was adjudged that the Company owned the land, as Sulivan had said, but that the various so-called 'owners' of the farm also had good claims. The committee, therefore, turned down Sulivan's plea that no more taxes should be paid by the tenants, and argued that custom and usage had established the principle of payment at a 'fixed and fair rate'. A similar compromise, one that corrected nothing, was reached over fishing rights and disputes, such as those over the collection of brushwood and weeds.

Although unsuccessful up to this point in his efforts to remedy things, these details depict an awareness in Sulivan (unusual among those who occupied the office of Collector) of the predicament of the poorest Indian workers in Bombay. He seemed to be trying to combine humanity with efficiency. His work reflects this, as well as the delicate handling required.

From December 1749 onwards his thoroughness and unwillingness to waive his scruples over this affair earned him the displeasure of Governor Wake. His revenue books for the year ending July 1749, together with abstracts of the rents and revenues collected by himself and his predecessors from August 1747 to July 1749, were ordered to lie on the Council table, and remained there following their first scrutiny.

On 8 December 1749 they were finally remarked upon. The Governor began by praising Sulivan and noted that before his advent to the office the Collector's books had been kept in a very irregular manner. He was commended for creating order out of chaos. The Governor also noted that recently there had been an increase in salt sales compared to former years. Sulivan was able to answer that more salt had been sold by the Company because he had not disposed of it privately, so the whole profit had gone to the Company. Wake's response was that Sulivan, like his predecessors, had received five per cent on the sale of private salt.[33]

Further comments were passed on the nature of the private sale of salt, noting Sulivan's particular criticism of the profits made by his predecessors, Byfield and, to a lesser extent, Dorrill. Sulivan had shown in his abstracts of the collections made by these two that they made unjustifiable private profits. The Governor had no alternative but to agree, but hinted that his hands were perhaps too clean. Sulivan also took pains to point out where the unjustifiable increase in charges had occurred. Wake maintained that the sum involved was not unusual; that increases in costs had been unavoidable because of the exceptionally bad circumstances operating in 1748. He was not very convincing.

Now alarmed, the Governor took steps to cover all traces of his complicity. The details Sulivan had brought into the open would appear in a bad light to the Directors. He wrote, therefore, of Byfield and Dorrill as servants of the Company who had appeared to him both honest and above board. Yet, reluctantly and with many evasions and justifications, he conceded that the figures brought to light by Sulivan proved their abuse of office. He naturally portrayed himself as innocent of any intention of reducing the amount of salt to be sold through the Company.

His major defence was that Sulivan himself had 'kindly' depicted in his researches that if (as Governor) he had helped Byfield towards such extensive profits it was unintentional. Wake also appealed to the fact that Sulivan had handled his personal affairs from the moment he set foot on the island, and could verify that there was no evidence in his private accounts of any intention to defraud the Company.

After causing so much trouble for him, Wake took the post of Collector away. From internal evidence, he was suspended from 8 December 1749. By 2 January 1750 George Scott had taken over. There is little doubt that Sulivan had uncovered a state of affairs that said little for the senior Company servants in Bombay and even less for Governor Wake. It is also very probable that his purpose was to depict to the Directors, his part in clearing out the corruption that infected the collection of salt revenues. Nor did he allow dismissal from office to deter him from bringing forward evidence of yet more corruption in salt revenue collections.

Sometime before October 1750 he informed the President and Council that he had uncovered further abuses in the Collector's office. Wake accordingly convened a committee of councillors to examine the state of the salt revenues. What happened next appears like deliberate deception by Wake. The figures that Sulivan had given to Sedgwicke and a committee in his letter of 27 October 1750, were used misleadingly by the Governor against him in two sets of despatches to England. Those by the *Boscawen* stated that the revenues (those Sulivan was complaining about) for 34 measures of salt had been illegally collected by Sulivan and not by Byfield. The despatches by the *Salisbury* repeated the error, saying that Sulivan and not Byfield had been responsible for the collection. This time the salt mentioned had risen to 38 measures.

On 13 November 1750, four days before the new Governor, Richard Bourchier, took office, Sulivan was transferred to be Chief at Mahim. Wake wanted him out of the way. He was aware of Sulivan's smouldering resentment, and disgust at the loss of his post of Collector and shabby treatment he had received. It appears too much of a coincidence that he should be absent from Bombay when the new Governor arrived, it allowed Wake to misrepresent the situation when he handed over all settlement affairs to Bourchier.

Aware that everything would change with the new Governor, Sulivan timed his next letter on corruption in the salt revenues for delivery on 16 November 1750, the day before Bourchier took over. Again, as per Company law, a committee was forced to convene to enquire into this. Naturally, the new Governor wanted to start his term of office on a sound note and intimated how necessary it was to get to the heart of the matter.

Despite this, it was December before the issue was taken up once more; and again only due to Sulivan's insistence, even though he was still at Mahim. When asked to give exact details of the offences committed in the Collector's office, he took the opportunity not only of doing this, but of recounting the whole sorry history of events. He produced a copy of his letter of 27 October 1750, showing the misrepresentation by Governor Wake in the despatches to India House. He also asked that this letter be allowed to appear in the Public Consultations to vindicate his character. This was done.

Sulivan was to remain at Mahim until 10 May 1751. Re-arriving in Bombay, he once more took over the Collector's office from George Scott. This was Governor Bourchier's decision. Not only was he convinced of Sulivan's honesty, but wanted him to clear up suspicions he now entertained of further fraud, again in the salt revenues. By 28 May Sulivan had made a preliminary examination of the matter, enough to satisfy the President and Council that their worst fears were correct. Joseph D'Souza, the suspected ringleader, was taken into custody. Sulivan found subsequently that he was solely responsible for the fraud.

Meantime, he had also completed an inventory of the Customs House at Mahim and handed over control to Alexander Douglas. Now he could concentrate on the Collector's office at Bombay. The position afforded many opportunities for private trade, so he made a speedy return to the main settlement and lost no time in picking up the threads where he had left off.

7

He spent only a few months in the Collector's office, however, because on 24 October, as part of a committee, he was despatched upon an important mission, to settle a crisis at Surat involving Company officials and native powers. Surat was ruled jointly by representatives of the Mughal dynasty and the Marathas. A struggle had developed involving the forces of the Maratha leader, Naik 'Allam Khan, and his ally Atchund, against Safdar Khan, in alliance with Sidi Ma'sud, the Governor of Surat. This was a follow-up to troubles of earlier years, especially those of 1748.

The essence of the problem was that Naik Allam Khan was determined to subdue the surrounding province as well as the city of Surat. He did not propose to keep the city, but intended 'that it should remain in the hands of the Moors...(led by Atchund) that he will not place any person in the government of Surat without our concurrence and therefore desires that some person may be sent up'.[34]

There was some dithering whether to call the party 'Envoys' or send a committee representing the President and Board. The latter was decided upon. It comprised a Major Mackenzie, Henry Savage and Sulivan; who immediately begged the Board's permission for a few days to consider it all. It is possible that he did not relish the thought of the company he would keep, the dangers he would face or the neglect of his private interests. He had also become Warehouse Keeper. Bourchier was repaying him for uncovering the frauds. However, this also made it impossible to refuse the mission. Again he provisionally transferred the office of Collector to George Scott, while John Hope took over as Warehouse Keeper.

On 21 December 1751, armed with their instructions, the committee sailed for the Surat bar on board the *Bombay Grab*. Their principal objective was to secure peace. They were given ample powers for: 'Transacting all affairs in settling the government of Surat as if we were present ourselves.'[35] In the end Major Mackenzie failed to accompany the committee all the way. The Board then appointed Lt. Daniel Draper.

The commission was also charged with recovering large sums of money lost or spent by the Company at Surat; with recovering the full enjoyment of its privileges there; and with re-establishing the Company factory. It was to ensure the safety of Company personnel, particularly that of Mr. Lambe, the factory Chief, and of the military force. Two members of staff, Messrs. Pym and Hunt, were prisoners in the Dutch factory. They were to be freed. Another aim was to reverse the role of the fiercely hostile Dutch who would allow no goods to be shipped to and from Surat. Above all, the committee was to assume absolute command.

On the voyage north the Company force sailed into the Maratha pirate, Kohanji Angria fleet. They were taken and detained at Versora. The pirates kept some Company ships, and an Andrew Price was first despatched to Tannah and then Bassein to get other vessels. Astonishingly, the brigands then acted as a protective convoy as far as Surat.

The committee reaching Surat on 31 December 1751, took property from all inhabitants except the Europeans, and blocked the harbour. An attempt to take control of the besieged Surat castle where Atchund was holding out came to nothing because of the 'shameful disorder' of the Company's military force and its supply of ammunition. After consultations designed to dispel military ineptitude, it was decided again to try and reach the castle, when word was received that Atchund was preparing to give up the position. News followed that the forces of the Sidi were already in the fortress, forestalling their military plans. The struggle was at an end without the committee actually being involved at all.[36]

Devoid of bargaining power, Savage and Sulivan could only treat with Atchund and Sidi Ma'sud as best they could; but to get the best settlement for the Company, they resorted to any leverage that could be mustered. They took command of the river; resolved to prevent all trade; were determined that no 'insolent Dutch would pass without search'; and that they would commandeer as much property as possible. Neither held out much hope of success stripped as they were of alliances and burdened with problems.[37]

On 11 January 1752 the committee informed Bombay there was no change in the situation and that they were awaiting overtures from the enemy. Although they suffered small harassments, like the efforts to prevent them from getting fresh drinking water, this was certainly the best course of action they could have taken, and it soon began to show results. First though, James

Lambe was dismissed from his post of Chief at the Surat factory. This was done to convince their enemies of the powers the committee possessed. Savage and Sulivan then focussed their displeasure on the Dutch whose 'insolence will lead to seizure of one of their councillors as reprisal'.[38]

At the end of January there was tense concern over the arrival of the Maratha fleet in the Surat roads. Then the appearance of a large ship from Batavia gave the Dutch a temporary ascendance. Fortunately, both dangerous situations passed without mishap; and at once the struggle was carried to the Dutch who were made responsible for the whole situation.

They were also helped in that cracks were appearing in the hostile and intransigent attitude held by Sidi Ma'sud. A meeting was arranged aboard the *Defence*. Steps were then taken to bring all the principals together for peace negotiations. The situation was made easier because the local Asian merchants complained ceaselessly that business was suffering. Their lobbying reached sympathetic ears; a poverty-stricken Surat gave no advantage to anyone. There was an immediate emphasis by the committee on the needs and requirements of freight and other business. Bales were loaded on the *Hector* right away.

By 19 February the committee was certain of having achieved the end it set out for, securing peace. The President and Council at Bombay were urged to send the men who would replace Lambe, Pym and Hunt. With successful completion of the mission, Savage and Sulivan wanted to depart as soon as possible 'because the season advances apace and as we both intend for England by the first ships we shall barely have time sufficient to adjust our own private concerns'.[39]

Sidi Ma'sud signed the articles of peace on 25 February and on 5 March Charles Crommelin was appointed the new Chief. The Board expressed its delight, and approved of the initiative taken by Savage and Sulivan in advising the Court of Directors of the peace, although they had not consulted Bombay first. They had no wish to have their own roles diminished in a report issued from Bombay. The treaty with Sidi Ma'sud was finally concluded on 17 March, by which time Crommelin had arrived and was deemed acceptable. Savage and Sulivan chose this as the moment to depart. By 27 March the two were once more in Bombay.

8

Although Sulivan had intimated a wish to leave Bombay for England, upon his return from Surat he resumed his duties. On 31 March 1752 he again became Collector; then on 10 April, provisionally, Customs Master. During his absence he had been made ninth in Council, and took his seat on the Board. The amount collected in rents and revenues, now paid into the Company's treasury was astonishing after three months' absence. It paid tribute to the reliable system he had introduced. His books could, and did, balance.

The last serious thought given to Collector duties concerned some disputes between the Company and the inhabitants of Bombay; and particularly those concerning a certain Ramseth who had rented from the Company the right to plant all vacant spaces in Bombay and in Mahim. The Company had said that it would pay half the value of such improvements to the amount of 11,000 rupees. But it could not be decided whether or not damage done to trees and to wells and waterways was due to neglect and abuse by the renters. Upon this decision depended the Company's duty, or otherwise, to repair and pay for the damage. Sulivan was asked to evaluate the extent of the harm done and determine responsibility.

He spent from August to October in research and taking evidence on oath. He costed every conceivable item, and gave many sound reasons for the inability of the renters to account properly for either what they owed or were due. These ranged from property being seized by the raiding Maratha General Damaji, to the effect of the monsoon. Company records were searched for proofs of lease and terms offered. Unsurprisingly, it was Sulivan who found a 'mistake' had been made by Governor Wake's Secretary, which provided the farmers with an unusual demand on the Company allowing them a total of 23,155 rupees for 'improvements'.

He brought forward evidence that suggested a great deal of fraud; with lack of precedent for these advantageous terms. No comment was made at the time, by those in Council, upon the unique nature of the lease. An examination of Secretary Price's writing also showed that the clauses permitting such unusual profits had been put in afterwards.

This was clear indication of corruption at the highest level; and Sulivan made sure Governor Bourchier did not miss the point that Governor Wake was ultimately responsible for this chicanery, and had attempted to defraud the Company. He indicated this had to be the case because every written article required explanation by the Governor in Council, and this had to be understood by the merchants. He had completed his revenge on Governor Wake.

9

Avenues by which money made in India could be realised in England were always needed. Sulivan became a master of all this, knowing how cash could find its way home with as little loss in real value as possible. He perfected a few tricks using the Company treasury. For example, advantage was taken of fellow servants with no wish to remit money home yearly. Bills were paid into the funds in Bombay made out to such a colleague's account. These were endorsed that payment was to be made to a specified agent in England, supposedly that of the colleague, but in fact Sulivan's man.[40]

The ways of remitting India money were not to change very much throughout the eighteenth century. Thus, the guidance he later gave to his son gives perhaps the best description by an expert. These channels excluded bills drawn upon the English East India Company.

> From Madras to China money is frequently wanted by persons going thither…The next are remittances thro. the Dutch to their Company in Holland… A third is with the French…The last

> method is by diamonds…always advise me in time that I may
> insure. If any of our India Captains should want money for their
> ships, use; and will grant you bills upon the Husband…Formerly
> the Commanders and Agents of His Majesty's ships took money at
> an high exchange and gave their bills upon the Navy Ordnance or
> Victualling boards.[41]

The variety and number of these channels discloses his ingenuity. He
continued to be engaged in such activities when he reached England in 1753.
For an unbroken eighteen years, from 1740 until 1757, and fitfully beyond
this, he continued in this pursuit. Other more dubious enterprises in
common use were: borrowing money from the treasury; using Company
ships; not paying interest on sums borrowed from the Company; and lending
to Asian agents, without interest, in return for private favours.

Unfortunately, Sulivan was not averse to taking risks; best summed up in
advice to his son: 'Remember, you never have money lying dead in your
chest.'[42] He probably took this too far. As he ruefully commented later in life,
'From a strong propensity in my nature (which you inherit) I began early to
risque my fortune in lending money and standing security.' That this had
proved a rather painful occupation encouraged him to advise his son,
'positively and peremptorily be security to no man'.[43]

What these activities do portray are the systems Sulivan was capable of
developing, and the temperament he possessed. These were some of the
skills that would help him in the years ahead. His first maxim was:

> Enter into no schemes before you have perfectly digested them,
> traced every material circumstance, and are clearly satisfied you can
> confide in the person you may connect with. Habituate yourself
> not to a ridiculous but a suitable reserve. Be ever master of your
> affairs.[44]

There are also interesting glimpses of his attitude towards the Asians he
worked with: 'Black clerks and Dubashes are in general a set of artful,
plausible scoundrels… however, at the same time, under a proper curb, with
care that you are drawn into no scrapes, they may often be extremely
useful.'[45]

The feature, however, which more than anything else enabled him to
amass his fortune and build his career, was the strict method and regularity
he applied to his affairs. He said to his son:

> Ever bear in mind these truths that method and regularity ensures
> you ease and satisfaction, that irregularity and neglect constantly
> involves you in trouble and perplexity, that method and order in
> accounts, apportioning your time to invariable habits is so essential
> that upon it will depend the permanence of every good
> resolution.[46]

He stressed the necessity of laying down rules and following them into habits. This would 'be of infinite more consequence than you can at present possibly conceive'.[47] These were the techniques Sulivan instilled into the fabric of his being when in Bombay. As he said, 'it procured me a character with the Company and with individuals such as I trust my son would not be ashamed to possess.'[48]

He also kept a record of every conceivable thing. His methodical approach brought order, enabling instant reference to any subject at any time. Of prime importance was his 'Cash Book'. A second, equally significant to him, was an 'Account Current Book' containing a record of ongoing balances, and notes on people with whom he had ever conducted business. A third was his 'Letterbook'. It held copies of all correspondence ever entered into. A fourth was an 'Inventory Book', with details of the family's attire and other property. The fifth was for 'Miscellaneous Observations'. Over the years he had not faithfully entered up this book and came to regret it.

He can be pictured every morning at his post, and then 'all afternoons, when Public Employ admitted, were appropriated to my private affairs, accounts and business. And almost every evening of my life with my family.'[49] This order and regularity were the hallmarks, not just of his first career in Bombay, but of his later, illustrious one in England. With them came personal satisfaction as well as success.

10

On Wednesday 29 November 1752, accompanied by Henry Savage, Captain Hough and their families, and given a 17-gun salute from the shore batteries, Sulivan and his wife set sail for England on board the *Streatham* commanded by Captain Charles Mason. As one of the Bombay Council he was permitted five tons of baggage; and an Indian servant girl attended his wife. He had been granted his request for passage to England on the grounds of ill health. This was a familiar ploy, by which the Company paid for the trip, excepting personal expenses. He also received a gift of £100 from the Governor; and he and Samuel Hough shared £2,000 from 'the running cash'.[50]

For the first part of the journey they were protected from pirates by a flotilla of Company ships. It was a fairly uneventful voyage, however, as far as St. Helena, where they stayed for nine days. There was a shortage of drinking water before reaching the Scilly isles and they were limited to three pints each per day. He and his wife enjoyed the trip, remarking later in life that they had 'received distinguished marks of kindness...from the crew, much to the great mortification (of) the other passengers, Hough, Savage & Co. who, because of their familiarity were despised and ill-treated'.[51]

While at sea, he would have celebrated his fortieth birthday. He was wealthy and in the full flower of life, with a successful career behind him and a sound reputation. Should he wish, he no longer needed to discipline himself so severely; the future for his family was secure. Nor had the years in India affected his health too much, probably because of the self-control that dated from his marriage. He was set ashore in England on 7 June 1753, to be reunited with his son. He never saw India again.

It might have appeared to his fellow travellers that Sulivan contemplated a quiet semi-retirement. That this did not happen was entirely due to his ambition and passion. Instead, he was to become embroiled in issues of great controversy and in intense struggles written large upon the public stage. Traces of a ground plan that led to such a scenario are just visible: in the duties he performed, and in his assimilation of what was important and needed. Such a pattern is discerned in his making certain that any important work was known at Leadenhall. The nourishment of friends and adherents, and the favours he obliged many with suggest the same.

These years developed in him endurance and an ability to recover from severe setbacks; although in all probability he was already inured to tragedy and loss in a harsh age. His obsession with power perhaps took root in circumstances prior to arriving in the Indies; probably from an Irish background, but this can only be speculation. In Bombay, however, the driving ambition within him developed, even riches, came second; and he faced up to the long climb necessary. He wanted authority at India house; but kept his ambition well hidden.

He had evaluated his own strengths and weaknesses, assessing his fitness for the road ahead. Through application and unstinting prosecution of the Company's business he became an accepted authority. He had refashioned himself and practised 'method, regularity and constantly measuring...time in habitual but commendable pursuits'.[52] This systematic approach to life was developed; experience gained; contacts made; and caution learned. These lessons appear in the advice he would give to his son: 'Be guarded in delivering your opinion of man or parties, abroad as at home, it's always dangerous and may injure you.'[53] This acquired knowledge of human nature helped lay the basis for Sulivan's future supremacy. It was learned in the testing ground of Bombay.

2

London and India House
1753-63

1

As the carriage rolled into London in June 1753, Laurence Sulivan would have cast his eyes upon the colourful exciting London described by Swift and Pope, Dryden and Goldsmith, Johnson and Boswell, where peoples from every corner of Britain and most of the known world congregated. The carriage almost certainly took him to Queen Square, to be welcomed by his friend and patron Stephen Law. He and his wife were reunited with their son, and nieces.

In typical fashion, he was well prepared for his own arrival, with a home ready. It was a rented house in East Street, off Red Lyon Square, Bloomsbury.[1] The next move, in 1758, was to Mile End Green in the parish of Stepney. Sulivan had commenced the process of buying the house from the Chandler family in 1755; finally purchased on 15 July 1756 for £630.[2] Mile End was an excellent residential quarter for an East India Company Director, which Sulivan became in 1755, because of its proximity to both Company headquarters in Leadenhall Street and to the Company's shipping. The principal docks were at Blackwall.[3]

His friend Thomas Lane lived there, as did many other Directors, Proprietors and Captains of EastIndiamen.[4] He was soon in contact with quite a few of his neighbours. For example, 'on 26th November 1762…Stephen Martin Leake, Garter King of Arms in 1754, who lived in Mile End old town, recorded that he paid two shillings to "Mr. Sullivan's man for bringing a Fillet of beef".'[5]

His daily routine can be followed quite readily; it did not vary much from that of Bombay. After breakfast he worked in his study; went to the 'City' by coach; and after 1755 to India House. The midday meal was invariably taken at Leadenhall – paid for by the Company if he was in the Direction; for which he also received an annual salary of £200. Supper was with his family. Scarce an evening passed without answering messengers, followed by more work, and perhaps a glass of Madeira before bed. The house in Mile End Green was a substantial one; and the very survival of the documentation indicating the time and money spent on it, tells of a special fondness.[6] From the outside the house would have been quite striking, since Sulivan had the building white-washed, from the level of the bottom windows upwards. The original tiling, from base window level to the ground, was retained.[7] Inside it had a 'great staircase and hall'[8]

Apart from furniture, he drew up inventories of every conceivable article to do with the premises, its occupants and expenses. The methodology involved was typical of him. Lists were ranged under general headings; within these, individual categories, such as 'house expenses', were collated via a range of sub-titles. What he called 'Mrs. Sulivan's branch', when catalogued, came to over thirty-four items, ranging from butcher and baker expenses to the cost of mustard seed, lemons and tarts.

He paid eleven bills annually in respect of house-rent and taxes. These included payment of his pew, the parson and rector, the watch, the scavenger, and the poor rate. He paid for coals and for 'posterage charges'; and even for a sermon by a Bishop Coneybear – the parish church of St. Dunstan's Radcliff was only a few hundred yards from the house.[9] House and contents were fully insured with the *Sun Fire Insurance Company*.[10] He governed his household in a paternalistic manner, leading a well-ordered life; and became a respected member of the merchant community, living in a style befitting a prominent citizen with business in the City.[11]

This was necessarily a settling-in period; and he and his family had to adjust to the mores of conduct usual for returned Company servants. He spent liberally to keep up appearances. Infinite time, patience and money were used to gain the best possible advantage, and to be seen to be doing well.

His greatest expense, however, centred upon his own person. Sulivan took great care of himself. This is reflected in accounts with the apothecary, and with a barber: 'to shave me every day and powder my wiggs at 15 shillings a quarter'. His footman, called 'William', had also to shave him, 'no card money, no clothes but what I please'.[12] Sulivan knew it was important to put on a good show; and this is reflected in the extra care given to internal health and external appearance. Even his watch received an annual spring clean.

The master of the house very carefully specified every item of his own apparel. It might suggest a vanity with regard to his person. On the other hand, he did have to maintain the appearance of a man of substance; and he was appearing regularly in public. However, the particular relish which accompanied his description of each item smacks of self-satisfaction. These garments vividly portray his personality. He cut a striking figure in his crimson satin waistcoat, blue velvet coat and breeches trimmed with lace; his black silk stockings, gold garters, gold buttons, wig, and gold-laced hat with matching shoes.[13]

During this period of adjustment to life in London, he maintained a number of servants. He had a cook, a housemaid, a footman and a

coachman; and also kept an Indian girl as a servant for the first year of his
return from India. It was the coachman and footman who seem to have
caused him most trouble; and there would seem to be reason to doubt
Sulivan's ability to keep on good terms with his staff.[14] He was a cultured
man and kept abreast of opinion, paying his subscriptions to arts and science
foundations and to societies; attending plays. A voracious reader, he took
newspapers, magazines and reading-books; and was a member of a
circulating library. He was also building up 'Maitland's History', in numbers.[15]

   What excited him was meeting people, coming across new ideas, novelty.
His family, the Company, shipping and the life of the river interested him.
Court and country life bored him. He found relief from pressure within his
home, so different from the business world he frequented. Good
conversation washed down with an excellent vintage was perhaps his main
indulgence. His accounts speak of 'Liquors taken this day.' He kept an
excellent cellar. A pinch of snuff now and then was another luxury, but there
is no mention of tobacco.

   His hobbies and pastimes were little different from those of others. Apart
from reading, he would play cards, especially whist. Visits were made to spas,
such as those at Bath and Tunbridge Wells, where he and his wife
participated in the customary promenading. He took carriage rides, and
visited the West Country a lot, staying with friends in Taunton, Ashburton
and elsewhere. They took great delight in entertaining company, in calling
upon acquaintances and in going to the theatre.

   There is not much in his letters referring to enjoyment of these social
engagements; nor is there much in the way of family news or intimate detail.
Common gossip or behaviour was seldom mentioned. He gives no
description of inanimate objects, items of beauty or of possessions that might
have meant something in a sentimental sense. Only occasionally did he
mention the fact that in a will some friend had left him a ring, for
remembrance sake.

   The impression these manuscripts create are of a man always on his guard.
The colour that does appear, and it is powerful, is found in his narration and
superb use of language. He made wonderful use of imagery to put something
across; as in a letter to his niece Betsy: 'You must remember me always busy
about nothing;' or to his son, 'I never more will build castles.' In reality he
had few pursuits, the Company was his life.[16]

2

Sulivan's choice of home, suggests that he had no intention of retiring, and
intended to have a public commercial life. The first consideration, quite
understandably, was the remittance of his fortune; and he kept open all
channels and contacts that might lead to mercantile opportunities. His home
was to be the base for all his operations.

   The two years from 1753 to 1755, when he entered the Direction, were in
many respects critical in that he had to speedily forge and then consolidate

those connections in the metropolis necessary for his advancement. He must quickly pick up the thread of affairs. It was especially important to maintain contact with men who had been his friends and business acquaintances in Bombay, those now returned, and others continually visiting London. It was necessary too that he become familiar with men of importance, who could be useful and who held positions of rank in social circles as well as business. He was aware that advancement would depend upon projection of his own talents.

Ship expenses were notorious, so there would have been limited funds on arrival. Money from India would have to be speedily realised. It was essential, therefore, that he make swift contact with those acting as agents for him, probably Thomas Lane, or even Stephen Law. At no time is there mention of either Sulivan or Owen relatives.

At first there would be no opportunity or need to develop the associations required for any other line. He relied on friends already made. By confining his activities to what he already knew and had practiced in Bombay; and by keeping the affairs of the East India Company foremost in his mind, there would be little time lost. Sooner than it would have been possible in any other sphere, he was able to display on a wider stage those qualities already shown in India.

As a financial and commercial centre and as a focal point of world trade, London was immense. To Sulivan the metropolis would have been fascinating. He fell in love with everything he saw; it became his spiritual home, where he experienced exhilaration and a zest for life. Yet the sheer size of the place and multitude of activities re-emphasised that he must restrict himself to what he knew best.

The financial world he entered was undergoing what amounted to a revolution. A credit expansion was underway, particularly in the mobilisation of commercial capital. Those in the City he found interesting were the families of merchants, goldsmiths, assurance companies (particularly mercantile and fire insurance) and marine underwriters. Importers and exporters came to be included, as well as ship builders, ship owners and ships' captains. Bullion financiers, gentlemen speculators 'from the west of Temple Bar' and the casual investor, were all attached, from time to time.

From the transactions of people 'in the alley' and in the coffee shops of the capital in the 1750s emerged the stock exchange of the 1770s. Established centres such as *Jonathan's*; the stock-jobbing coffee house, *Lloyds*; and the *London Assurance Company,* among others, came to the fore. Such groups inter-connected through the market with the great monopoly trading companies, like the South Sea and East India Companies; and with the Bank of England and the Treasury. The needs of Government put an ever-increasing reliance upon the various institutions that collectively made up the market. Financiers from Amsterdam, Paris and other European currency centres were increasingly tempted to invest there because of steady and high return backed with security.

Britain was also gaining a position in world bullion distribution. The 'City' was taking over from Amsterdam because, apart from Jamaican and West Indian bullion, Portugal, which with Spain controlled the South American bullion sources, traded with Britain, and paid in gold from Brazilian mines. This was fed into the expanding English trade network, especially in the Far East and East Indies. The Bank of England and the London exchange market, and especially the monopoly companies, made greatest use of this specie.[17]

Specialists, like ships' husbands* assumed greater importance. Commanders of EastIndiamen had certain valuable powers as well. With their perpetuity of command* and control over appointments, they held a monopoly. Such rights had translated through time into property and vested right in command, and from there to sale of this. Private trade and smuggling made such posts even more precious. These pursuits could render an average profit of £4,000 per annum to a Commander in the 1750s.

Shipping insurers and shrewd directors of the great companies, especially the East India Company, were encouraged to become deeply versed in particular mercantile subjects. Similarly, the committees of finance, shipping and warehousing in an organisation like the East India Company were steadily absorbed into the booming commerce.

In realising his own wealth and remitting that of returned Company servants and ships' captains, Sulivan was provided with every opportunity to transact other pursuits in the City proper. Soon he was acting as a go-between, advancing the East India Company, its shipping, and many of its servants and their businesses, more and more into the London market. He came to terms with as many important men as he could within the City; and was engrossed in the mushrooming banking, credit and other monetary activities. He would deal in many spheres, but showed exceptional skill when handling anything that touched upon the Company.

He brought to bear on the commercial life of London great ability and much detailed information of what was going on abroad. Looking after the business concerns of others had also endowed him with objectivity. Armed with his own strict schedule he again worked industriously, a habit, as he said, which had 'fixed so strongly as to accompany (me) to England'.[18]

He had an exceptional grasp of how India House operated, of its affairs and financial structure. Stephen Law, Thomas Lane and Edward Owen, his late brother-in-law, had seen to that. Owen had been an accountant at India House for four years before going to Bombay. To some degree this knowledge helped prepare him for the launch of his remittance agency. The private occupations practised in Bombay were taken up again, but in a bigger way. He became involved in cargo and its insurance; in banking; and in speculating upon the stock exchange, as his careful notes on current stocks and bonds show.

Once more he acted as an attorney, fulfilling the executor and trustee tasks that this demanded. He also indulged in money-lending and notary work, since remittance and insurance activities for and on behalf of people with an

East India Company interest, made this unavoidable. He was embroiled with shippers and with the Company shipping interest;* and although increasingly absorbed in the affairs of the Company proper, even after he became a Director in 1755 his private activities continued. He helped link together individuals and agencies with the various arms of the money-market.

In his remittance work he acted as a receiving agent, converting into sterling the wealth flowing from the Indies in the form of bills, exchange notes and diamonds. To begin with, this mainly concerned returned Company servants and ships' captains. Such work triggered the functions of trustee, executor, or attorney, when authorised to act for clients.

The degree to which he placed his own affairs in good order and the propriety with which he handled the business of others is exemplified in one of the homilies he was fond of delivering: 'It is a true and trite observation that the man who neglects his own concerns is unfit to manage the affairs of others.'[19] His career demonstrates that he did abide by these rules. His appetite and faculty for dealing with rates of exchange, acting as a financial adviser and general factotum, soon made him a much sought after City figure.

The number of his friends within the Company's shipping interest ensured a sound foundation for his London agency. These included the ever-present and ever-active Captains Thomas Lane and Samuel Hough. He was helped too in that his good name had been carried to London prior to his arrival. Ex-Governors Horne and Law, Commanders Hough and Barton and Company servant Waters had seen to that. He had a very good platform upon which to build a business and attract associates.

Remittance work was easy for him, he was so steeped in such activity. It also involved granting loans. He was well versed in discounting bills and issuing promissory and 'drawn' notes, which allowed his money to be used by others. He became involved with scriveners, brokers and merchants. The agency was based on acquaintance and interest. In fact it was the extension of his web of contacts made in India that secured such work in London. He sometimes worked alone and at other times in partnership. Yet, as far as this particular activity was concerned, he had complete faith in only Commanders Lane, Barton and Hough.

In his private ventures with Sulivan, Captain Hough acted as the principal co-ordinator in the eastern hemisphere for all remittance activities. Agents holding powers of attorney on behalf of their clients acted through Hough and were channelled to Sulivan. Hough could provide ways and means of remitting Indian funds through confidants among his fellow captains – and via his position as Superintendent of the Company's Marine.

Robert Clive used Sulivan's remittance system quite extensively, employing Henry Vansittart and Robert Orme as his agents. They too worked through Captain Hough. In the course of making thirteen remittances in 1758, Clive paid the money to Captain Barton for bills 'at 180 days sight on Messrs. Sulivan and Boulton (Henry Crabb Boulton)'. By this means, the Colonel was able to send home a tremendous amount.[20] When he returned to England in

1760, he even paid a personal visit to Sulivan at his home in Mile End Green; perhaps only one of many.[21] The other members of the clique in India, all of them involved with Sulivan in remittances, were John Walsh in Calcutta, Robert Palk in Madras and John Spencer in Bombay. Clive knew Captain Samuel Hough and John Spencer, from the Bombay Council of 1756. Sulivan's agency was the London base for this triangular affiliation.

A principal concern in the 1750s was the partnership formed with his friend and Company servant, John Spencer – in his role of private merchant in Bombay. Sulivan in London and Spencer in Bombay formed a fixed axis for freight and mercantile insurance activities. Captain Hough joined them, caring for in-transit shipping freight and associated goods. James Moffat, a Scottish insurance broker of Lombard Street, acted with Sulivan from the London end, underwriting the ventures and bringing in extra capital. Captain Thomas Lane, a ship's husband as well as Sulivan's right-hand man, personified the tie that this consortium had with the immensely important Company shipping interest.

They formed a tight-knit body: Sulivan, Spencer, Hough and Lane – forging even stronger bonds with their business interests. James Moffat was an excellent business colleague and his many connections served them well. The presence of his brother Robert in the Bombay Presidency had created the link; and James Moffat himself enjoyed a particular friendship with Captain Hough.

The main outlet for Sulivan's funds was undoubtedly shipping and freight, particularly in association with these friends. Between 1755 and 1762 his business ventures involved him with at least eight ships in European and Indian waters; all noted in his India account with Hough. Debts in India, payments to ship owners, agents and customs dues were all entered. The books reflected a healthy state of affairs, typical of his business from 1753 onwards, which would remain steady into the early 1760s.[22] John Spencer provides an illustration of how long this particular line of business continued. As late as February 1766, he instructed Sulivan, 'You will please to continue the management of my concern in the 'Havannah' Captain Madge.'[23]

The middle of the eighteenth century was a period when specialists in a variety of financial fields were emerging. Assurances in general, and shipping or marine insurance in particular, were no exception. A bonus, as far as Sulivan was concerned, was its necessarily close connection with the Company's shipping. The firm formed by Andrew and James Moffat was one of an ever-increasing number of brokers, and the one he dealt with most. Sulivan's link was with James Moffat, the senior partner, who put him in touch with William Braund. He also used the firm of *Barclay, Amyand and Staples.*

Firms dealing in ship insurance functioned in an intermediary fashion. On the one hand there were merchants, brokers and men with landed wealth who would underwrite a risk. On the other were groups sharing ownership and the freight of ships. Such parties included Sulivan and Spencer, together with ships' husbands like Thomas Lane and ships' commanders such as Samuel Hough, who all required insurance.

The Moffats handled all types of gambles, but marine assurance interested them the most. James Moffat was also a director of the *Sun Fire Insurance Company*, with whom Sulivan had insured his house. This Company illustrates how interlocking were the many organisations in London. Sulivan and Thomas Lane were friends of the Moffat brothers; while the shippers, Peter and Joseph Godfrey, Charles Raymond and William Braund were all underwriters for the same firm. Since they were also ships' husbands, they were already intimately connected with Sulivan and Lane. Sulivan's close friendship with John Hyde, the Governor of the *London Assurance Company*, (whom he introduced to the First Minister, the Earl of Bute, in 1762) was doubtless also due to these incestuous relationships.

Insurance companies were important sources of ready cash in the market. Thus, as a Director of the *London Assurance Company* (since 1754) Thomas Lane was a pleasing channel for access to such money, or even the dispersal of personal funds. By acting as Sulivan's 'man of business', he allowed the great man to keep out of sight. The reason for such furtiveness Sulivan (later) put neatly into words: 'It is not (thank heaven) from a consciousness that my actions will not bear the strictest scrutiny but even an appearance unaccompanyd with the true spring and motive would be a triumph to my enemies.'[24]

Through Thomas Lane, he shared in the large sums lent out at interest by the *London Assurance Company*; and it was also invested, used or otherwise cared for on his behalf by the same man. John Dorrien, another who was close to him, and who dealt extensively with this company, would have been similarly employed. Other evidence displays the connection of insurers with his friends among Company shippers and Directors. All were close to him then and later, and associated with the Company at that time and in the years ahead. Many filled dual roles of insurance specialist and/or men with capital, or held seafaring positions or commercial employment.[25]

Bankers in the City were useful to know because of their capital; and they too were assuming a new importance just at the time Sulivan was making his mark. Financial houses were mushrooming, and in the 1760s and 1770s Sulivan was to have extensive dealings with firms such as the *Baring Brothers*; *Boehm, Amyand and Goslings*; and *Devon and Child*; but there is evidence to show that these connections began in the 1750s.

It was probably his friendship with James Moffat that led to contact with *Child's* bank; while the *Amyand* bank belonged to yet another acquaintance. In the intimate London commercial world, these bankers were also insurance brokers or directors of insurance firms with an interest in Company shipping. With his connections Sulivan was in close touch with these financial houses; and just how well he knew the banking business is illustrated in his later correspondence.[26] Also, his accounts for 1755-6, and 1759, speak of his early interest; while 'Bank of England annuities' for 1751, 1756 and 1757; 'Bank annuities consolidated' for 1756 and 1759; and 'Bank circulation at par', tell where some resources were parcelled out.

As a Director, from 1755 onwards, the importance of banking connections becomes even clearer. The letters to his son in 1778 display how much he understood developments in the application of money that had taken place over the years. The manner in which he urged his son to take action echoed his earlier habits, 'Every person returning to England whom you can influence, endeavour to engage that he takes my recommendation of a banker to keep his cash, as this often strengthens my interest.'[27]

Much of his money lending, executor, trustee and notary work was associated with, or came about because of his other lines of commercial endeavour or sprang from his involvements abroad. He linked his lending with this notary work, doing so at a time when demands for discounts and loans on mortgages were on the rise. It was a relatively open field in which the Bank of England had only a token interest.

His Bombay grounding gave him an advantage; and the City contacts he made following his return supplied ready funds. Success depended on the nature of the individual concerned. Sulivan had to be: 'A man of integrity, trusted by all, the self-evident executor and trustee for his whole family.'[28] This description, applied to William Braund, more than adequately describes how Sulivan was regarded. He was quite obviously an outstanding person, the one to depend upon, as far as his close family of friends were concerned. This is testified by the wills of Captain Samuel Hough, John Spencer, Governor John Horne and countless others who trusted him to carry out their last wishes.

The duties of an executor fitted well with Sulivan's special skills. Countless opportunities arose for what he and his contemporaries considered acceptable business practice. These advantages would appear during the payment of the deceased's debts, distribution of property, and the right to sue in law and receive any legacy.[29] His quasi-legal activities are best illustrated in a petition that reached the House of Lords in 1785, and was not to be dismissed until February 1787, that is, after Sulivan's death.[30] The matters considered were thirty years old, and concerned Samuel Hough's estate. Sulivan was a co-executor of Hough's will, together with James Moffat and the deceased's wife, Martha Hough. He was also co-executor in England of John Spencer's will, acting with the Reverend Edward Norton and Thomas Lane.

Sulivan and Moffat possessed themselves of Hough's estate to a great amount; according to the petitioners 'more than sufficient to satisfy all the testators' debts and funeral expenses'. They, in turn, coveted all the proceeds from the joint trade and private India accounts; that is the £3,598-12–9 Spencer owed Hough in 1763, plus £23,000 owed him through the joint trading account, with compound interest in full. Sulivan and Moffat maintained, on the other hand, that Hough had obtained further money and that this account was still open and unadjusted.[31]

They also countered the compound interest argument put forward by the petitioners, and specified that of the credit claimed, over £13,000 was interest, and over £6,000 consisted of compound interest. They had also renounced execution of Spencer's will. The decree of the Court of Chancery of 31 October 1785 upheld Sulivan's argument. No interest was allowed on either the private trade or joint trading accounts. Nor were any costs given to the petitioners. The petition was dismissed.[32]

This legal struggle lays bare the kind of transactions he was involved in; and illustrates sharpness in business practice. Moffat and he would have shared around £6,000. His hard-headed business acumen is apparent in other ways too. Items in his accounts for 1756 indicate that on 19 September 1753 he received 10,630 rupees; and on 1 January 1756 a further 1,913 rupees, to hold in trust for his ward, Louisa Barton. He invested this money in a manner beneficial to himself as well as his client.[33] There were several other instances of this kind. In yet another he was a trustee to a marriage settlement, whch resulted in a decree being brought against himself, Robert Palk and Henry Vansittart.[34] On 21 June 1757 he:

> Executed a bond to Thomas Rammet Esqr. and Mary Reynolds his sister and himself for and in consideration of £300 paid me by said Rammet. I engage to allow him and his sister during their natural lives the sum of twenty five pounds per annum to be paid half yearly, first payment of £12.10. to commence the 2 Decem. next, the second do. The 20th June l758.[35]

This type of risk illustrates the nature of a great deal of his work during the 1750s. The bond would scarcely ruin him, even if he should pay for many years. The cumulative result of similar transactions would prove lucrative.

Buying Government securities was another of his schemes. They were 'purchasable at a heavy discount redeemable at par and yet bore interest'. It is almost certain too that as well as holding Government and East India Company stocks and bonds, Sulivan invested in the *South Sea Company* and in insurance societies.[36]

His connections within shipping circles were particularly striking. This came to involve him in freighting activities, and he developed further his numerous contacts in the Company's marine service in general. He also formed several partnerships: The most important again involved Spencer and Hough, operating from Bombay; John Walsh in Bengal; and Robert Palk in Madras. Yet another involved James Moffat.

As far as his future intentions in the Company were concerned, it was the inroads made into the Company's shipping interest* that proved most important.[37] Sulivan identified closely with these men; he shared their views and promoted them in the years ahead. The shippers were to form a large part of what he was wont to term his 'natural' interest. Like them, he was dedicated to the independence of the Company and against state intervention. From the 1750s he and this interest were as one; and his support for them was well known. Even in 1764 John Walsh, writing to Clive, referred to it: 'and he (Sulivan) has obliged many (ships' husbands) I am satisfied in that channel'.[38]

Sulivan was one of a number of 'Charter Parties',* as appears from his 1755-6 accounts. He developed a deep understanding with (Sir) Charles Raymond and John Durand, both powerful ships' husbands.* They, together with the Godfreys, Thomas Lane and others of his friends, monopolised control of shipping. Invariably, these same men are to be found sitting upon the Committee of Shipping in the Company, dealing with the hiring of the special kinds of vessels needed, and ensuring a continuity of supply.

Again it was a closed society. Husbands of 'permanent bottoms',* masters holding 'perpetuity of command'* and Company Directors were almost as one. Such homogeneity gave the shippers tremendous political weight. The 'combinations' of husbands who controlled the Company's shipping had a big voting strength in the Court of Proprietors and a strong interest in the Direction. It is unlikely that Sulivan ever exerted much control over this close-knit body. Luckily for him, alliance with its leading personalities was enough. The shippers were capable of excluding rivals and of coercing the Company. Yet there were only about 30 really important persons, interrelated through business and marriage.

Another factor blocking any control over the shippers was that two years before Sulivan arrived in London, an owners' organisation came into being, whose shipping policy was approved by the then Direction. Thus, from 1751 to 1761, he was bound by a document he had no part in forming.

There were numerous networks linking him with the shipping interest. Stephen Law, already active on his behalf within the Company, brought interesting introductions. Messrs. Hough, Barton and Lane each introduced contacts. The connections Sulivan was bringing about between shippers and mercantile insurers helped to create closer links. In this manner James Moffat and Andrew Moffatt became firmly cemented into the Company shipping through him. The people for whom the Moffats acted as brokers were, in turn, usually in shipping, such as William Braund and his brother Samuel.

His pre-eminence among the shippers blossomed fully after 1755. Again Walsh hearkened to this tie-up: 'His (Sulivan's) interest is pretty strong in the shipping, among the husbands of ships and he has obliged many.'[39] Thomas Lane was of immense importance in the development of this. As a ship's husband, and through contacts with other husbands, who formed an elite, he could make strong representation. A remittance partnership with Henry Crabb Boulton also paid dividends, giving another connection with this interest.[40] However, the best evidence of these links lay in his friendship and business collaboration with the Godfrey family, and especially with Peter Godfrey. All of the Godfreys were involved with Sulivan and Stephen Law in remitting money from Bombay and elsewhere.[41]

For example, Messrs. Watts and Orme remitted money to Peter and Joseph Godfrey and to Sulivan in the 1750s; in June 1757, bills from Bombay worth £13,700 were made out to Sulivan, Law, Peter and Joseph Godfrey. In another instance, a warrant dated 14 September 1757 said that Sulivan, together with Peter and Joseph Godfrey, were to be paid a further £13,700. Using Company channels only, they remitted a total of around £30,000. In addition, Sulivan and Edmund Godfrey were trustees for a Bombay colleague, Timothy Tullie; and were joint executors of his will.

What was to prove most important was that Edmund and Thomas Godfrey influenced his initial entry and further progress in the Company. The Court Book for 3 November 1756 shows them acting on his behalf, alongside other shippers: Captain John Purling, Charles Raymond and Frederick Pigou.

Despite his success, there are signs that Sulivan knew he could only be satisfied working in the executive branch of the Honourable Company. There he could be his own man. The thought of becoming a Director was certainly not new in 1755, but it was brought forward as a practical reality in the lead-up to the April election of that year. Indeed in many ways, the period from his disembarkation in 1753 until entry to the Direction in 1755 was really one of preparation.

During his transactions in the money market, he consciously cultivated the image of being an expert on anything appertaining to the East India Company. Everyone who mattered in business and in politics was made aware that he knew what he was talking about in this field. He was helped by the dearth of first-hand knowledge of India among the Directors. Incredibly, experience of what was going on in the east was looked upon by many there as having little relevance. It was a situation Sulivan helped change; but first, he would take advantage of it.

3

In 1755 Sulivan stood on the threshold of events that would change his life forever, and would send his career on a dizzy upward spiral. Only in 1739 had he realised it was crucial for his own sense of identity that he participate in some way on the world stage. The obvious first step was to work for position and responsibility within the Company, which was to be the route to high office and perhaps fame. He had understood that he could only be 'in the game' if operating there, and amounted to very little outside it. He also found peace of mind. This organisation was all he would ever need for fulfilment. The bonuses were that it provided security, stability, nourishment and wealth.

It might also be the case that from 1739 to 1755 he developed a Confucian belief in how he would conduct his life. As far as possible, he behaved in a principled manner, emphasising personal virtue, devotion to family, and justice. He seemed to want to improve his moral character during these years; this developed into a desire to influence and change things for the good in the wider world. He had realised, however, that only upon a public stage could he do anything worthwhile. His wife would have sympathised, and perhaps influenced such traits. She understood him.

Gambling was almost certainly part of the dissipated life he once led. In 1739 he was a reformed gamester, but only in the sense that he ceased to take on crazy odds; but the volatile swings that accompanied such behaviour – even though well under control for much of the time – could affect his judgement. With the risks came the possibility of self-destruction. Of course, this all had to be hidden, and by and large it was. The image he wanted to project had to be worked at and then protected. He must be seen as the very model of stability, a man with a sure touch, a winner.

From this perspective, it really was not strange for him to say so little about his former life. He was making a new beginning. It could also explain why he left nothing much of his early years in his correspondence. It was only in 1778, when the father feared he would never again see his only child that some of the deliberately forgotten life came out. Nor did anything he ever wrote to others (other than to Stephen) indicate this propensity to dice with fate. But the termination of some first career in 1739, hints dropped during his second, illustrious one, and the imagery he used, gives the game away. His life was to be conducted in as secretive a way as possible - for someone who might become an eminent public figure. Everything was to be a mystery. The approach fitted nicely with the need for concealment, and suited his nature perfectly.

Between 1753 and 1755, probably at frequent intervals, his curiosity would have brought him to India House in Leadenhall Street, to the main doors of the Honourable Company trading to the East Indies, and upstairs to the 'Strangers Gallery'. The narrow front of the building that opened to the main street was quite unpretentious. But it hid a vast grandeur within, with a public hall and a Proprietors committee-room scarce inferior to anything of like nature in the City. It stood out as 'the most remarkable contemporary edifice of commercial capitalism'.[42]

As in all else up to that time, it was probably his patron and adviser Stephen Law, himself a Director, who would have attended his first step through the portals of this building that housed all his dreams; and he who conducted him through the Courts and minor committee rooms. Law would have led him along its corridors, showing him the labyrinth of warehouses and antechambers that lay between Leadenhall Street and the Thames.

On 25 February 1755 he purchased £2,000 of Company stock, which qualified him to become a Director. By then he was familiar with India House and the way it worked, knew many of the Proprietors and Directors, and had more than a reasonable knowledge of the problems the Company faced. By this move he clearly signified where he was now to concentrate his energies; and had taken the next step in a course probably planned before leaving Bombay. Much of the groundwork needed to bring about his rise from Director in 1755 to Chairman of the Company in 1758 was in place.

The lead was taken by that group of friends headed by Stephen Law, known as the 'Bombay Squad' or 'Bombay Faction'. They were backed up by the influence of the shipping interest and the support of the business contacts he had made in the City, especially in insurance and banking. The

'Squad' was willing and drilled enough to give him its combined strength in his push towards control. It was in their best interests to do so; a first move in securing their man an important office in the Company's executive, commanding patronage that would benefit them all.[43]

Sulivan understood the aspirations of his supporters and had much in common with them. It would have been perfectly natural to him and to those ex-Bombay colleagues that he should use their friendship. Nevertheless, he was the vanguard of a new presence in Leadenhall politics with this 'Indian' interest. It marked a new development. Until then the executive function of the Company had been firmly controlled by old City families.

Acquaintance and dealings with bankers and insurers helped; and he had extended his general Company expertise, paying a lot of attention to shipping connections. He was right in doing this, because it was probably the backing of the shipping interest, although deeply submerged, that served as the foundation for his climb to power. Fortunately, Sulivan was aspiring to the Direction at a time when this interest was 'searching for commercial ends by use of political means'.[44] The Godfreys, especially, made it their business to promote him.

This phalanx was to remain the bedrock of his support for years; so much so, that John Zacchary Holwell wrote to John Payne on 17 March 1759, 'For what have we not to fear from so malignant, powerful and inveterate a conjunction as Messrs. Law, Sullivan and Godfrey.'[45] Sulivan was able to marry his own interests to those of the shippers, at times subordinating his own desires to fulfil theirs, only to achieve what he wanted later by and through this important body.

He was sure of strong advocates, therefore, when he bid for a place on the Company's board. The only question was whether Stephen Law and he had assembled a power base that would carry the day. The support of Law was crucial. He, in turn, was most probably fulfilling a long-term objective of challenging the groups that controlled the Company. In 1732, while in India, he had learned from a Robert Adams of others making such an attempt.[46] After his unjustified recall from Bombay in 1742, this thought would have burned ever more brightly.

Law was a Director from 1746 to 1749, from 1751 to 1754, and would be again, finally, in 1756. It is not difficult to understand why he gave Sulivan all the help he could. It is doubtful whether the Bombay ties could ever be broken. He wanted to see his friend succeed; and also knew that if Sulivan prevailed he could only benefit. It was a legitimate ambition then for anyone involved in public service to make a comfortable fortune in the public employ and establish those he was associated with.'[47]

Governor Law would have advised Sulivan of the opportune time to take out the qualification to be a Director. His influence also meant his protégé would be placed on the 'House' (or Directors') list. In an effort to influence the electors, the outgoing Directors drew the 'House' list up each year. Direct canvassing, normally based on terms of personal friendship, was carried on. Everything suggests that a well thought out plan was being implemented. Co-option of such a new Proprietor was quite unusual. The very speed of his election to the executive office, just over a month after taking out qualification, and done without rancour, suggests as much. Other factors helped: the absence of serious party divisions within the body of Proprietors; the uncertainty brought about by the rapidly changing situation in India, and rumble of troubles ahead.

At the election in April 1755 his new share-holding commercial associates welcomed him and he was returned. The Proprietors had confidence in Stephen Law, and would know enough about Sulivan to satisfy them. It ensured there would be little or no resistance to his candidacy. Almost certainly his good sense and sound advice had already been noted. Potential leadership qualities would have played a part; and undoubtedly he was found to be a vital force, though he might have appeared a rather mysterious figure to many.

With his suitability guaranteed by the shippers and with the unstinting support of the 'Bombay Faction', he had found success. Once in the saddle he was very capable of staying there. His unopposed election, nevertheless, was a formidable achievement. He stood on the threshold of a new chapter in his career, a Proprietor and Director of a powerful institution. He also had something to prove, to himself mainly, but also to others who really knew him.

3

The Court of Directors
1755-58

1

What demands explanation is why, after only entering the Direction in 1755, Sulivan could so quickly become Deputy Chairman in 1757, then Chairman of the Company in April 1758. It was an extraordinarily short time. Why, too, did this mark the start of a new era, and be seen as such by contemporaries?

There are several answers to why he rose to the top so soon. They include his hunger for power and sense of opportunism; his natural abilities; and a lack of quality or the talent needed to oppose him. His strength of will, however, was unbelievable. He also had luck, and a formidable body of support. Significantly perhaps, the increasingly bedraggled state of the Company's affairs at home and abroad, which cried out for a change of direction, helped him. The threat of full-scale war with France (and possibly with the Dutch in alliance with unfriendly Indian Princes) was never far away.

His fellow Directors could not be expected to know that he was working to a different agenda from them. To him the Company was not just to be abused, of which he had first-hand experience. He held an ideal picture of the organisation's stature and grandeur, of its immense power and the central place it occupied in the fabric of the nation. Preservation of the rights and liberties, enshrined in its Charter from the Crown, lived with him from the very beginning.

There is little doubt though that prior to and following the election of 1755, Sulivan worked in what might be termed a conspiratorial manner towards achieving control. Within the Company Stephen Law worked in close harness with him. From 1756 he provided advice and information within the Direction and on the Committees of Accounts, Shipping and Private Trade. Sulivan used networks of contacts and a variety of approaches among his fellow Directors, shippers, returned Bombay servants and friends in the City. The aim behind all of this was to project himself.

This need for prominence and exposure pushed him to make as many friendships as possible. It is what also lay behind his membership of the Royal Society of Arts. He was gathering support for a bid for greater office. The importance of keeping in touch with influential contemporaries and the possibility of making new contacts are both reflected in his entry to that body. He was proposed by Dr. Manningham; a relation (and probably father) of his friends and business colleagues of that name, resident in London and Bombay.

The Royal Society of Arts might even have had a hidden agenda in that era, operating as a quasi-political club, possibly Whig orientated, such was its membership. It was popular because titled wealth and the landed gentry could meet there with the lower orders on common ground: the pursuit of knowledge and of new developments in science and the arts. Stephen Law had joined the Society shortly before and was obviously the inspiration behind Sulivan's move. Law was accepted as a member in May 1755, Sulivan in June of that year.

This manoeuvre did help his acceptance at the highest level, and within the city's business community. It eased his rapid ascent by ensuring a sound position in London society, helping his private business in the City and, most important of all, improving his standing with Company Directors and Proprietors alike in the shortest possible time. It was one of the soundest steps taken by him and his benefactor Stephen Law.[1]

It seems more than coincidental too that a 'Mr. Clive' was present at a Society meeting on 26 March 1755, at a time when Robert Clive was in London, and in very close collaboration with Messrs. Manningham. The Royal Society of Arts (and the Manningham family in particular) might even have provided the background for the early friendship of Sulivan and Clive, 1755 being a year when both attended meetings. Their mutual friend, Charles Manningham, son of Sir Richard Manningham, was fourth in Council at Fort William by April 1758. He was the agent in India for his relatives and had business connections with both Clive and Sulivan.[2]

Yet it must also be said in his defence that membership of this society was not all about politics. He did have a strong interest in Indian culture and had brought many pieces of Indian craft home; the Royal Society of Arts was an excellent institution for discussions of such topics. He also encouraged the artist Tilly Kettle to proceed to India and paint portraits of Asians as well as Europeans.

Sulivan found the Society useful because it provided a web of connection stretching from London to India. He had social capital to exploit here too, in that there had to be an underlying informal set of values or norms shared with those he encountered that encouraged co-operation. As a member of a group, those in it would expect that he was like them. They trusted one another, they would trust him. He deliberately identified with a group or groups wherever he went: fellow Bombay servants, 'City' businessman, Commanders of East Indiamen, Company shipping groups, shipping insurance people, and ships' husbands. He expanded his circles all the time, maintaining contact with all previous groups if he could.

His thinking on economic matters displays how suitable he was to be head of this Company. Basically he was pre-enlightenment, pre-Bentham in outlook. He was heir to the tradition that had grown among Britons trading in India, which said bullion had to be kept in reserve; excessive war was detrimental to trade - that it increased costs and multiplied the expense of bringing commerce onto a stable footing. Unfortunately for him, he faced an ever-growing need for military and naval activity; and was aware of the attack being mounted against its chartered rights, although not yet sharpened and honed by Adam Smith.

In 1755 Sulivan appreciated that he was in an age of compromise, where the views of Government ought to harmonise with the Company's commercial interests. Preserving this harmony was to be one of the overriding and lasting considerations of his life. His efforts at negotiation with leading Governmental figures in order to hold on to privileges and chartered rights, is one of his most worthy achievements. Perhaps more than most, he understood the delicate balance between the requirements of Administration and private interest.

His own superior qualities shone all the brighter throughout the period 1755 to 1758 because previously the quality of those in control was so indifferent. A languid approach to affairs characterised the executive; and commercial interests were suffering because there was nobody of real weight on board, and few with first-hand experience of India. He was helped by the continued and concerted push of his friends; largely the same groups and individuals who backed his entry to the Direction.

Probably even more important in explaining his rise to power was the threat to the Company's possessions in India, growing since the hostilities with France had re-opened in 1740. These apprehensions over possible war worked on his behalf when in 1756 open war with France broke out. Knowledge of the Indian theatre was needed.

It is too easy, however, to ignore Sulivan's talents. He had initiative, could seize an opportunity and possessed powers of persuasion and perseverance. Although approachable, he also had a genuine superior attitude; he oozed confidence at all times, and would use this commanding presence in his executive role. He understood perfectly when to tack in the face of opposition; and was able to bounce back from adversity. All these qualities he combined with dogged hard work; he pored over the minutest detail of Company's business. He was aided by experience of how things actually functioned, but even so, to reach the top required intricate planning.

It would be clear to many during the years leading up to 1755 that here was a man destined to make a mark. It might even have appeared that he was being groomed for the purpose. Such immediate recognition of his abilities was apparently the case within the Court of Directors where his skills were quickly and thankfully received. His name immediately appeared on several committees: accounts; private trade and a standing Committee.

With the Court of Directors Sulivan found the arena which suited him best. It is probable that no other man made its executive machinery more his own. It was to be the scene of his greatest triumphs and disasters. A somewhat hostile colleague during his later years, Richard Atkinson, was absolutely correct when he said, 'I think the ruling passion with him is the vanity of being supposed the head of the India Company'.[3] A good proportion of men in the years 1755 to 1758 and onwards saw him as the man of the moment; the one best suited to face growing problems. As far as Company affairs were concerned, he was ahead of his rivals in understanding men and systems; and from the beginning he was to show indications of planning ability.

Sulivan was under no illusions whatsoever that ultimate authority in the Company rested with the holders of India stock assembled as a Court of Proprietors or, as it was more generally known, the General Court. On the surface at least, it appeared a very democratic body for the age. Few were barred from it; and no one excluded on the grounds of sex, religion or nationality. The General Court voted by ballot for the Company Directors.

Although subject to the Company's shareholders gathered as a General Court, the executive, or Court of Directors, thus constituted, controlled the Company. As a body the twenty-four Directors made all appointments home or abroad and held ultimate responsibility for most things. In reality, however, authority was apt to gravitate to quite a small number of principals, some with remarkable acumen and grasp of what was going on. Sulivan quite quickly became one of this number. Mervyn Davies supplies an excellent picture of these individuals and of what generated their authority:

> The Directors were men of substance and great self-importance. They liked to surround themselves with ceremony and to exact ample respects from the Company servants. When the officers of the Company's ships appeared before the Court they had to wear full dress. The Directors lunched and dined at the Company's expense and always in great style, their banquets at the *London Tavern* in Bishopsgate Street on state occasions being famous for their lavishness and magnificence...What made their office highly sought after was the prestige and patronage; particularly the patronage, which was extensive and extremely lucrative.[4]

Dame Lucy Sutherland confirms this picture: 'Their position gave them many opportunities for personal advantage.'[5]

Certainly Sulivan stood to gain in various material ways as a Director; but with his conscientious nature he would have felt keenly another pressure from occupying the office. He had to deal with a conflict of personal and public duties in an age when there was no real standard of public morality.

No financial necessity propelled him into the Direction; he wanted to be there, to be accepted as if in his rightful place. It is even possible he deliberately shouldered the greatest burdens and took on board an inordinate volume of work to fulfil what was fundamentally a psychological need.

Yet he did not want to be a mere titular head. Instead, he set out to lead, to cut out new avenues of thought, action and inspiration, and apply these. The minutes of the Court of Directors form the best memorials to his endeavour and genius. He was present on 62 occasions between April 1756 and April 1757. This earned him the confidence of the shareholders. Nor did the exclusive and self-perpetuating appearance of the Company's executive appear to be threatened by him.

When, the Proprietors considered the Company's fortunes in India, they were not at all reassured. The English feared the French and the Maratha tribesmen in the Bombay area. They were scared of a French alliance with the Nawab of Bengal; and shuddered at the French presence in Madras, where they supported the Subahdar of the Carnatic, while the English clung to his feudal vassal, the Nawab of Arcot. The fears were reflected in a fall in credit and declining exports. The total bullion exported to India to promote trade fell from £668,893 in 1754 to £620,378 in 1756; merchandise exports dropped from £259,602 to £221,131 in the same period.[6] It would have been clear to some that something had to be done and a responsible leader chosen.

2

Coincidental with Sulivan's entry into the Direction, sporadic outbreaks of fighting in India were overtaken by the onset of the Seven Years War. Hostilities were officially started again in 1756 between the rival French and British companies, with further calamitous impact on business in London. Sulivan's knowledge of Indian affairs now made his opinions even more valued. The unstable position in India meant the Proprietors were even more fidgety and a general feeling of inadequacy prevailed.

He understood, however, what had to be done. Having just come from the sub-continent he was up-to-date with needs and responsibilities there. He knew that the anxiety and pressure in the settlements, engendered by fear and defensive preparations, required urgent relief. The despatches he helped shape sent to all the Presidencies, displayed his perception and understanding. Sound knowledge of the Company's possessions, not just those of Bombay, is revealed in his maps and plans. He was prepared for war.[7]

He was given added insight through the friends he had made in Bombay who were still there; and others in Madras and Bengal. His trading partners, such as John Spencer and Samuel Hough provided information to augment that coming from the Governors and Councils. The detailed answers, comments and instructions, show an aptitude and capacity for comprehending difficulties; and are evidence of his grinding industry. He also had the capacity to relate complications overseas to important and influential people in Government. It was a skill that was to prove vital to himself, to ministers and for the good of both country and Company in the dangerous years ahead.

Such tremendous application had its reward. On 6 April 1757 he again became a Director, taking the oath before his shipping friends Peter Godfrey and Charles Gough. He was then elected by motion to the Deputy Chairman's place. This put him in position to be a real driving force in the Company. Nor would there be any lack of supporters when he made his charge to the top, eight of the 'Bombay Squad' accompanied him into the Direction. The rest, led by Stephen Law, acted on his behalf in the General Court.[8]

So it was merit as well as the solidarity of the 'Bombay Squad', shippers and other supporters that brought him so quickly to the position of Deputy Chair. (The terms 'Chair' and 'Deputy Chair' were commonly used.) Thus, a mere two years after entering the Direction, he had taken a major step in gaining control of the Company and achieving his dream. He never forgot, however, how necessary it was to have a body of support, preferably hidden from the eyes of political enemies.

As Deputy Chair, Sulivan was a recognised public figure, important in the eyes of Company servants at home and abroad. The minutes show that it was he who now took the important decisions, not the Chairman John Payne, who was incapacitated and absent. He began to dominate the important Committees of Secrecy, Correspondence and Treasury, where detailed work was delegated before going to the full Court. In fact, his touch was felt everywhere as he was drafted, ex-officio, on many Committees.

The minutes also demonstrate that he was handed an almost impossible task, given the distances and time lag. He had to fight a war yet keep a tight rein on finances; and faced a rapidly deteriorating situation everywhere. His knowledge was called upon constantly, particularly in the Company Accountant's office; and he passed regulations governing the office of Collector of Rents and Revenues for all the stations. This, on a grander scale, was based on the post he had held in Bombay and had reformed so successfully.[9]

He complained of servants being undisciplined. In another he grumbled that the Madras Council was not providing sufficient information. His document, *Observations on the Bengal Establishment with such Alterations and Amendments as appear Absolutely Necessary,* was sent everywhere. It was perhaps the first evidence in England of the care and thought he could bring to bear upon Indian problems; a conscientious survey of troubles arising in this part of the world. A major work, it served as a template for constructive planning.[10]

Two months after Sulivan entered the Direction a chain of events took place in Bengal that would irrevocably change the Company's whole future. On 4 June 1756 the new Nawab of Bengal, Siraj-ud-Daula, attacked and took the Company's factory at Cossimbazar; he then took Calcutta where he allegedly perpetrated the atrocity of the 'Black Hole'. However, by January 1757 an expedition from Madras, under Robert Clive, recovered the city.

News of the outbreak of the Seven Years War, which reached Calcutta in January 1757, also helped conclude matters; and a treaty was signed on 9 February 1757. The immediate result of this for the Company was a confirmation of its privileges, such as the imperial grant (called the *firman*[*]), which confirmed the right to trade; the restoration of all plunder; the authority to coin rupees; and the fortification of Calcutta. On 14 March the English then attacked the French at Chandernagore, and the French surrendered on 23 March. What had transpired amounted to the first stage in a revolution regarding the Company's status in India. It was completed by the Battle of Plassey on 23 June 1757 and the negotiations that followed.

The expedition launched from Madras in 1756, with Clive in command (supported by Admiral Watson), was, therefore, of the greatest significance for the Company's future. It was to be of equal importance for Robert Clive. The Madras Council had invested him with a Squadron of the Royal Navy and a King's Regiment. He enjoyed complete military independence, contrary to all Company custom. A despatch from the Directors to the Governor of Madras, George Pigot, on 3 August 1757 condemned this precedent. It was written by Sulivan.

The new Nawab, Mir Jafar, faced a crisis hinging on lack of finance. He was forced to hand over land in lieu of money to the English Company in return for military help. In this way 'a mere trading corporation acquired territorial interests and ambitions. Its servants became king-makers.'[11] It was Clive who had made Mir Jafar; and to establish him he rid Bengal of the French. Mir Jafar's authority was nominal, however; his prestige completely undermined. Clive set about the strategy of 'rendering military assistance to the Nawab on a subsidiary basis, combined with his policy of affording protection to his prominent chiefs and officers'.[12]

Sulivan's entry into the Company also coincided with a crisis in the affairs of the Madras Presidency. The straightened circumstances in the Carnatic, from December 1755 to March 1758, seemed just as alarming overall as those which shook Bengal. They created just as much panic in London and the combination of troubles there as well as Bengal helps again explain his rapid rise.

From India House he took steps to guard Madras by having the defences in the settlements strengthened, and military instructions were forwarded. He was in close liaison with the ministry over naval movements; and made skilful use of the Company's Secret Committee. Constructive administrative measures were designed and set up, modelled upon those of India House. They were also implemented at Calcutta and Bombay.

In the end, the Carnatic war left the Madras Presidency struggling for its continued commercial existence. It reduced the Company dividend from eight to six per cent. The Select Committee at Madras was censured because of a show of power that almost signalled independence. The withholding of vital information was severely criticised. Again 'astonishment, regret and apprehension' was expressed over the complete power that had been given to Clive on his expedition north to Bengal, even though this had resulted in the retrieval of Calcutta.[13] They were told to slash costs because 'the Company's capital was bleeding almost to death upon the coast of Choromandel'.[14]

His list of advice was endless: on shipping; the making of gunpowder and ammunition; plunder regulations; the repair of fortifications; and the security of the Company cipher. All the groundwork required for these instructions appears in Sulivan's own scrawl in the records. It was certainly a critical time, as the despatches of 23 December 1757, 27 January 1758 and 15 February 1758 show. Fifty chests of treasure were sent to Madras, together with naval stores and recruits. Then two and a half chests of gold (equal to thirty chests of silver) were despatched on the *Pitt*.

In London, Sulivan was able to build a great deal of credit for himself from all this. He was at least trying to do something. John Payne's continuing incapacity was not well received. Sulivan's style was exemplified in his reply to Dutch accusations that the English Company unjustly brought troops into Bengal following the seizure of Calcutta by Siraj-ud-Daula in June 1756:

> The English did not commence war against Surraja Dowla. He came down upon Calcutta, destroyed it and murdered many valuable men, their blood called upon them to seek vengeance against him, as we should in like case against the Mogul himself had we the power – Our privileges were certainly part of the quarrel for he had taken them all away and drove us out of the country.[15]

This was an answer that most fitted the sentiments of Director and Proprietor alike. It incorporated patriotism and Company interest; and constituted a blunt response to the allegations of the hostile Dutch. It was well received.

While Payne's suspicious illness continued, Sulivan dominated the Direction. He made strenuous efforts to comprehend what was going on in India, as extracts from the many papers he gave the Company historian, Robert Orme, illustrate.[16] He stood on the grounds that the February 1757 treaty confirmed the Company's territorial claims to areas around Calcutta, first granted in 1711. But he understood the change created 'by men at the head of a victorious army and that this army still kept the field'.[17]

The news, from Bengal in particular, produced other developments, none of them beneficial to the Company in the end. The suggestion of fortunes to be plucked quickened interest in India; reports were hurried to friends and relatives. The rush for favours increased dramatically; and those holding influential positions were swamped with applications. Many Directors and Proprietors basked in the glow of attention, revelling in the patronage-inspired power they held.

Intelligence of the successful turn of events in Bengal during 1757 relieved tension somewhat in London and in Madras. The supposedly overflowing Fort William treasury was to supply the other two Presidencies. The upshot was that thirty chests of silver were diverted to China because of this belief. However, by the close of l757 Madras had still received a colossal amount of gold from home; by Sulivan's calculations, equal to £795,000.

The total worth of all the bullion, goods and stores despatched to India in 1757 was £1,108,430. Yet Sulivan realised that despite this help the crisis in the Madras funds would continue until the Presidency had built up sufficient money to ensure a profitable Investment* over several years. With the war against France still in progress he could not foresee this happening. It was this ability to build a precise picture of situations, and make forward projections that helped make him pre-eminent. It was based on endless hours of work which few, if any, of his colleagues could or would match.

The memorandum, in his hand, written sometime in 1757, stating that because of the Chairman's illness he was caring for the Company's affairs in Bengal, was something of an understatement. It was a staggering load, and although he was a willing workhorse, too much, when the startling events in India were interwoven with the factional strife growing within the Company. The evidence of his personal endeavour is overwhelming. Reams of correspondence in his handwriting exist on every concern imaginable, and are relative to all settlements, to the Company's personnel and to wharves and warehouses, home and abroad.

He wrote most of the General Letters to the Presidencies himself; the originals are in his handwriting. More able and knowledgeable than the bulk of his colleagues, he perhaps reached the peak of capability during these years. Later in life he maintained that: 'From 1757 to 1763 at the India House my power was absolute for this plain reason the vessel was sinking and no man had courage (or to my son I may say ability) to take the helm.'[18]

Everything points to this being true. As Deputy Chair, and with the Chairman absent, he was responsible for all major decisions; and there is nothing to contest his view that he now exerted total control. Despite being only one of the twenty-four who constituted the Court of Directors, he operated as the chief executive or managing director. His views on what had to be done seldom encountered any opposition, until Company politics turned ugly.

3

Sulivan's level of skill and energy were rare in the Direction, and such was his prestige following election to the Deputy Chair it seemed a foregone conclusion that he would become Chairman in 1758 with a minimum of fuss; it was also customary. Ordinarily, the Deputy Chairman one year would become the Chairman the next. This had been the case in 1753 and 1754 and again in 1756 and 1757. That such a progression did not readily occur, but required the 'first of the great contested elections' was a symptom of the effect events abroad were having in India House; and in particular, over who would control the amazingly rich field of patronage that had opened up.[19]

The fact was that while in an administrative sense his ability was accepted, his power, in the shape of political control of the Company, was not. The Chairman, John Payne, and his friends were determined to thwart him because of the enhanced value of service in India.[20] The struggle that developed for the Chair and with it political control of the Company, was simply the determined efforts of one group to keep the reins of patronage and that of another (Sulivan and friends) to rip these from their grasp.

That Sulivan's automatic promotion was to be challenged also suggests that his appearance had stimulated some (albeit stifled) adverse resentment. His success was probably viewed after the event as the result of calculation and opportunism. Belatedly he was to be prevented from becoming in name, what he already was, the supreme power in the East India Company.

The course of the struggle can be briefly sketched. Sides were taken over the future of Roger Drake, Governor of Bengal, and several members of Council, following their flight from the Nawab of Bengal's attack on Calcutta in June 1756. This transformed into the fight˜ for control within the Direction. Apart from deciding who would take charge in Bengal, the contest also decided what structure the government would take there; whether a rotation system, or a return to the President and Council format.

From the beginning Payne wanted John Zacchary Holwell to be Governor, superseding other Councillors. Sulivan favoured Charles Manningham and upheld the principle of seniority.[21] At the outset, the split in the Direction over the issue was roughly even, with Payne apparently enjoying a slight majority.[22] Holwell, a member of the Bengal Council who had remained in Calcutta during the attack, had scrambled back to England. Sulivan was particularly suspicious of his exploitation of proceedings. His dislike hardened during the 'various meetings consisting only of the two chairs, Mr. Holwell and the Secretary'.[23] The suspicion of Holwell was now joined to the unease he felt over the rotation of chairmen issue.

'Governor and Council' versus 'rotation of four', arguments continued, broken by news of the revolution in Bengal, and of Clive remaining in Bengal. Payne's 'majority' urged a continuance of the rotation after Clive had gone; the Sulivan led 'minority' thought it was no longer needed.[24] Payne then gained his objectives by trickery; placing his proposal that 'the rotation of four take place in his (Clive's) absence as before appointed', into the already agreed motion that Clive should be appointed Governor of Bengal.[25] Sulivan, of course, stressed that these questions were separate in character. In the vote Payne's 'majority' won decisively.

Soliciting a big turnout, Sulivan notified Proprietors through the papers of 'matters of the utmost importance' to be considered at the quarterly General Court in two days time.[26] It was only part of a bigger, well thought out campaign. An article he wrote was also timed to appear, accompanied by a canvas of the Proprietors, excellently organised by him. It played upon latent opposition to the rotation system.

At this General Court, on 15 March 1758, he appealed against the 'majority' decision that the rotation would be continued after Clive had gone. This too was novel; until then, if a General Court was called for other than routine affairs then 'special business' was signified. His action took the 'majority' by surprise. The Proprietors would not adjourn, and there and then voted the end of the rotation system for Bengal and a return to the single Governor and Council structure.

The Chairman and his friends went ahead, however, and elected Holwell to the Governor post, by their full number. Although Holwell turned this down, Payne's 'majority' then voted that while Manningham should succeed Clive, Holwell would follow him. Amid great acrimony, Payne's decision was tested at the election of Directors on 5th April.[27] The two lists of prospective Directors were intimated in the *Public Advertiser* of 23 March, and then advertised on 31 March. Unaccountably Payne's 'House' list had Sulivan's name. He voiced his indignation at being double-listed.

The 1758 election was fought entirely within the Company and was unlike those that were to follow. Sulivan won with his list, and had command of 14 of the 24 candidates voted for. He was made Chairman; Roger Drake, uncle of the Governor of Bengal and Payne's friend, became Deputy Chair.

Holwell admitted later that the 'majority' did not pay enough attention to electioneering. Sulivan, on the other hand, had perfected his system of canvassing referred to later by other enemies: 'Sulivan prints lists of Proprietors in small pocket-books with broad margins for use of his canvassers...we have followed his example in this pursuit and commodious books they are for the purpose.'[28] The election result also signified another important change: The traditional type of Director was out. Groups such as the 'Bombay Squad' would now dispute power in the Company.

It was immediately obvious who was in power. By holding back the sailing dates of the *Warren* and the *London,* both of which had on board the decisions made by the previous 'majority', and by changing the command in Bengal, he indicated a personal and absolute control. Holwell verified that the composition of the new Bengal Council was all his work.

The events of 1756 to 1757 in Bengal, and the reaction they produced in England in 1757 and 1758, together with the 1758 contest, ensured that the Company and its management would never be the same again. Holwell, although writing with all the vitriol and partiality of a disgruntled loser, pointed out many of the features that would cause more trouble: patronage issues would separate those involved in the Company; public figures would be drawn in; merchants and bankers would be affected by the disruption to trade. He also correctly spotted that factional fighting within the Company could only follow now that the General Court had been seen to overrule the Court of Directors.

Sulivan would remain in control of the Company's executive for the next six years. He would never pacify those whose control of the Company he had usurped, but, temporarily at least, they were powerless. He had succeeded because he was better organised than his opponents; because the times were right for him; and because he was hungry for power. His knowledge, work rate and insight proved keener than most. From 1757 he had asserted himself and shown his mettle. British success at Plassey made the prize of being ruler of the Company appear even greater; but it would have been no less rewarding, in Sulivan's eyes, to be in charge of the organisation as it existed prior to Clive's victory in 1757.

4

With all the work, worry and vituperation involved, it seems difficult at first sight to understand why Sulivan was so keen to be leader of the East India Company, not just in 1758 but during all the years to come. Yet, the desire to be seen and known to be sovereign over this organisation was everything. He appeared to be satisfying a deep emotional need. As the undisputed leader of a great institution he was respected as such, not just in London, but in Britain, Europe, and the East Indies.

Analysing why this organisation should be his first choice and chosen milieu is quite revealing. Apart from the monarch, the first minister and a handful of men (such as the King's favourites and the greatest of the landowners, and some Church leaders) Sulivan was on the next rung of the most powerful.

As Chairman he 'exercised political and financial powers that were second only to the Crown itself'.[29] His well nigh personal control of the Company and its extensive patronage assured this; as did being in touch with those occupying prominent public positions, who needed him. For a man with no lineage that counted in Britain, unsuited by birth and breeding and bereft of patronage, he had reached the top flight, joining those with power and influence in British life. In no other way could he have attained such heights.

Sulivan was a businessman, efficient and shrewd. An out-and-out capitalist, he relished his life in the 'City'. He was excellent at management; and paid attention to detail. Although he often said he was a dreamer, in every day affairs he always started with the possible, with what he knew. He was forever making plans. The drafts of countless manuscripts and letters in his handwriting are evidence of how much he was doing.

The Company served as a platform; it gave scope for his intellect, and for particular skills that were so useful in political and commercial fields. Because of the organisation's importance nationally, he was also given an exceptionally elevated profile. In size and extent the Company was unequalled by anything else in the private domain – a real power base.

Unfortunately, the total control he came to exert was so great that it stirred severe criticism. He was abused right from the start for the power he could bring to bear; and accused of being dictatorial and intolerant of any rival. It is true he harboured the authority granted through the Company, extended it where and when he could, and fought any attempt to belittle or negate it. He strained to lay his hands on and operate the levers of power, to make things happen.

A superb Committee man, adept and astute, analytical and informed, he used his political expertise. He knew how to organise a faction or interest in order to get his way. At first sight, these committees in India House seem anything but exciting. Composed mainly of merchants and shippers, they appear to spell out dullness. Yet blazing, exciting struggles that took the public by storm flared in Courts and Committee rooms.

Knowledge and advance information were everything to Sulivan, and his intelligence network was unmatched. Secrets came to him whether in or out of the Direction. Many were supplied by the Company's Secretariat – Secretary, clerks, solicitors and notaries. Data came from those officials allotted to the various Committees, from the mailroom, the warehouses and elsewhere. He had spies and informers everywhere, many of them within the shipping interest. Even before the ships were docked their commanders had carried the all-important packets of mail to him. Messages flowed to him from inside and outside Leadenhall. This ensured that he had the vital relevant facts fast; he could test the information for accuracy and was normally more up-to-date and far ahead of his adversaries.

He accepted spying as integral to life, indispensable; it was all around him. He understood that an excellent spy network was the best and the quickest way for him to get to the highest tables where decisions were taken. There is little doubt either that through nature and necessity he would continue to play espionage games all his life. His career attests to the paranoia, selfishness and intransigence of one who would have power. What is more, having served his time getting to the top, he believed that others must do the same before they be allowed to 'play the game'. To him, authority only came with knowledge and experience. Even when outside the Direction his powers were operative.

Understanding him comes from appreciation of these features. They underpin scrutiny of this part of his career, which he considered to be his most glorious. At this stage in his life he still saw himself as seeking for truth, while achieving fulfilment. He must have appeared very much a man of mystery. In the mere twinkling of an eye he was commander of the vessel that was the East India Company. His wish to achieve something, to be somebody, was realised. Henceforth he would be utterly devoted to the organisation that had proved to be the means of his reaching high dominion. He was the authority on Indian affairs.

4

Priorities
1757-65

1

Even before he became Chairman, Sulivan might have shuddered at the enormity of the tasks that awaited solution. The immediate problems were bad enough, but it was only as he spent time analysing and sifting that the deep-seated nature of what was going wrong fell into place. Yet even as he explored, more troubles washed up and over the old ones.

The easygoing Direction of former years was transformed into an extremely busy forum. The work was endless, the responsibility enormous. He was at the centre of everything and all problems and disputes ended up at his door: Company elections, the strife in India, patronage issues and the ghastly state of the Company's finances. Yet a dividend had to be conjured up, the Company run well, and plans made for a better future.

Not to be daunted, he attacked everything vigorously; so much so that he succeeded in stamping his mark on the Company to the extent that his imprint lasted for the rest of its existence. These years were to be among the fullest he ever experienced. It was a unique and sustained era, in which one man enjoyed control of the East India Company and its destiny. It was never to be duplicated.

Throughout most of this period he was impervious to attack, commanding support everywhere: in the Company, in Parliament and in the City. His grasp of all aspects of Company business, and the protection afforded by supporters and backers (who were carefully cultivated) left him supreme. Nor can it be doubted that he was impassioned by his complete command. As he said, 'from 1757 to 1763 at the India House my power was absolute'.[1] He was indeed the leader 'a man of real weight'.[2]

Sulivan eclipsed everyone else in every way. He derived tremendous enjoyment from being able to preside over every aspect of Company business. His word was law at Leadenhall. The appearance given was that everything was his work; but it soon becomes obvious that many others were involved, a colony of people: spies, clerks, lawyers, advisers, readers and researchers. He can never be regarded as functioning alone; many were involved in his schemes.

Nor would it be proper to regard him as the only capable executive. There were able men who grasped a great deal. He was never faced with utterly feeble and subservient colleagues. Some had a wide and general comprehension of how things stood, home and abroad. A few had genuine depth of understanding in one or two spheres. Others were involved in the cut and thrust of politics and were good at it. Many were appreciative of the finer points of patronage, of finance, legal matters, shipping and freight.

What made him different was that he knew it all; and this width and depth of knowledge, experience, plus a willingness to work, made him rather unique. He possessed something else: the ruthlessness needed in applying his many skills to the seizure and application of power. The annual political exercise necessary to retain executive control received his total and undivided attention; and in this he demonstrated great political skill. He was really a workaholic; the Company was his life, his sole interest. He was as much married to it as to his wife.

It is in the sense of being the prime mover in all that transpired that Sulivan was doing things single-handedly from 1757, and certainly from 1758, despite all the help he commanded. He was one of only twenty or thirty individuals at any one time capable of taking any sort of lead within the Courts and Committees; but his was the hand on the tiller. Few were interested in contributing continuously, although perhaps some were knowledgeable enough; and they looked towards him and a few others for proper direction.

Like a composer who hits a peak of creativity, or a statesman whose time has come, so must Sulivan's work, plans and achievements be viewed during the years that stretched from 1757 almost to 1765. These were heady days. He was working at full capacity and under tremendous pressure. His portfolio ranged across governmental, territorial and commercial concerns; measures that spelt out war or peace with European powers and Indian potentates; the finance and operation of a large and complex business empire stretching around the world.

The many items dealt with and decisions reached regarding affairs in the Presidencies were dealt with in General Letters. This was done in the name of the Court of Directors and signed by them – some even contributing; but most of the time they were vehicles for Sulivan. The official directives and advice promulgated there would be backed up in his private correspondence, much of it confirming the single-handed nature of his government. It did not matter the area under discussion or what was involved; whether mere instructions, guidance, dealing with corruption, insolence or evidence of double-dealing, he provided the answers. Again, the voluminous manuscripts in his hand verify this.

This evaluation – that most of what was achieved at Leadenhall was almost all due to Sulivan's endeavours and that in essence it was the work of one man – is an important question. It is also one that might be disputed. Should he be considered in isolation, separate from his colleagues, fellow Directors, Proprietors, and from those who made up his party? Can Sulivan really be singled out when he was only one among many operating within a series of Courts and Committees governing the Company? Shouldn't he be envisaged simply in the sense of leading a faction inside the Company; or (later) of being at the head of a Parliamentary group?

Allowing for the obvious in such views – that yes, he was all of these things – the indications are that for most of the time he was working alone (if espionage agents and secretarial help are disregarded). Once more the enormous morass of papers covered with his scrawl is evidence of his diligence and will to keep informed, and of his alone; there are no discernable depositions of any sort by other Directors during these years.

Single-handedly he could bring about the appointment of any person he wanted. He created bodies of men; set them together to work as teams, and gave them leaders. Home and abroad, he was the one who directed all and sundry towards solving problems and abuses. The fact that these orders were not always followed is a separate issue.

Some fellow Directors and Proprietors came to resent such domination; but most were more than happy to let him get on with it, as long as the dividend was good. Resentment of his supremacy and sole direction of affairs continually revisited him, however. Printed broadsides, newspaper articles and verbal attacks make it obvious that almost anything of importance originated with him, because only he is constantly attacked. Such prominence is underlined by the fact that within the Company it was Sulivan who always led a faction, he was never a follower. There was even a Sulivan party operating within the Company's Courts when he was out of office; and such a group only ceased to exist with his death.

The degree to which he stamped his personality on management tells of great strength of mind. Time after time his colleagues proved that they were lost without his guidance and vigour. As leader he was forced to deal on a number of fronts, usually simultaneously. Yet, no matter the question or problem, whatever the complexity or obscurity, he had to display qualities of command and find answers.

The position of Chairman gave him all the rewards of power, patronage and rank; and he enjoyed these to the full, cutting an ostentatious figure in society at large. He experienced great satisfaction when presented to the King on Saturday 9 May 1761; and kissed his hand on 5 August 1761.[3]

At some point during these six years, the imposing power and responsibility he wielded also brought about a subtle change. He did not lose any of the fundamental qualities that helped place him in high office, but with success and prominence a different attitude was noticeable. This is easy to comprehend, although not to admire. Negative features, a form of arrogance, and an increasingly autocratic manner, reflected in his authoritarian language, began to appear. He became 'a powerful figure…domineering and dictatorial', symptoms that were encouraged by pressures now constantly in attendance.[4]

He was forced to use this stentorian voice to try and bring order and discipline to errant servants in India, and this probably pushed him further along the path of autocracy. It was distasteful to members of this committee-based organisation. Several of those he chose to disparage were able men and only opposed to some of his views. In their eyes and those of others, he came to exert an overweening power; and eventually he came to be actively disliked by many.

The clearest picture of what Sulivan was really like, his character and how much it changed during these years is to be derived from what he did then. It is best drawn from the way in which the many problems and crises at home and abroad were handled; and from his entry into Parliament and the English Establishment. His days were full, both in public and private. This was the reality of his world, a time when he was fully alive.

He was a powerful and controversial figure, regarded as one of London's leading citizens: a town gentleman, 'City' businessman, as well as leader of the East India Company. He went about the process of consolidating his position in social life, entwining his public, business and private affairs as he became established. At the same time, with the outbreak of war in 1756, the work for which he should ever be remembered, without disparaging the colossal contribution of later years, had begun.

2

Sulivan was the focal point of all interaction. What went on in India and in Britain came to roost with him. It was no paltry task confronting him in 1757 when he was virtually left in charge through Payne's indisposition; and things had become much worse by the time he took the Chair in 1758. In fact, the situation was deteriorating so quickly it might even be said from the outset that without his presence and the effort he expended, it is conceivable that the Company would indeed have sunk under the cumulative weight of the troubles it was experiencing.

In his list of priorities the survival of the Country and with it the Company came first. Accordingly, his most immediate mission was the task of fighting the Seven Years War. In India this took place principally in the Carnatic, mainly against France. But he was involved in the pursuit of war in all of the East Indies, against all enemies; and had responsibility for continued successful advances in the territories most contested in the sub-continent.

Sulivan's theatre, therefore, embraced every settlement as far as China, all of which had to be armed and defended. His planning had to guarantee the continued provision of men and materials; he had to provide an adequate strategy for survival; and he must ensure the defeat of any Indian allies of the French, as well as the hostile Dutch. He was in constant fear that the

Company would succumb in the face of never-ending warfare and the financial drain imposed on it.

The main outlines of the Seven Years War within the Indian theatre are well known – and only how events relate to Sulivan are they of direct interest. The war ended with complete British victory. In fact, as early as 1757 the Bengal, Bombay ramifications of the struggle had been resolved, as had the first skirmishes in the Carnatic and at Hyderabad. The fight with the French in South India was to re-commence in earnest in April 1758, the very month that Sulivan came into his own as Chairman. Combat was almost totally confined to a pattern of sieges in the Carnatic area.

From September 1757 the English Company was defenceless in the south; and when the French under Lally landed there in February 1758, they enjoyed an overwhelming superiority. Fortunately Admiral Pocock's defeat of his equivalent, Admiral D'Ache (twice) was to prove decisive. Despite marauding across the Carnatic Lally gained nothing. At Madras a war cabinet was created following a directive from Sulivan that all power should be placed in a committee of the Governor and the four principal military officers; and Fort St. George held out. Nevertheless, from October 1758 only Madras remained in British hands. The French siege only ended with the appearance of the British naval squadron in February 1759.

Further British successes in the Northern Circars and against the French were rounded off when Salabat Jang, Nizam of Hyderabad, who had been in alliance with the French, was defeated; as were the Dutch forces hostile to the Company. The end of the Madras siege in 1759 and a British victory at Masulipatam marked a watershed.

From that point onwards the initiative was with the British. On 10 September Admiral Pocock found D'Ache again and forced him to retire to Pondicherry, from which he departed for good on 1 October, leaving the British fleet to continue the blockade. From his arrival in October 1759, until April 1760, Sir Eyre Coote was victorious everywhere, especially so at Wandewash on 22 January 1760. Both Coote and General Monson then conspired to achieve the fall of Pondicherry. It surrendered on 16 January 1761. The fall of the other French posts at Jinji and at Mahé on the West Coast, soon followed.

The outcome of the war hinged upon certain factors. Probably the most important was British command of the sea roads, which ensured the safe conduct of vital munitions, bullion and of reinforcements. Superior finance also contributed, as did the support that came from Bengal, and the weakness of Lally's character. The stultifying control exercised by the French Administration could also be mentioned; the quality of the military commanders Lally faced, particularly Coote and Forde; the constancy of the Nawab of Arcot to the English Company; and the supplies in money and recruits at vital moments from the British Government.

Nevertheless, these do not adequately explain the triumph of the English Company. Behind the scenes, but central to everything that happened, was Sulivan. He was in command, supported by the most able of his fellow

Directors. He directed, planned and assumed responsibility for everything –
other than for what actually happened in the field of conflict. Most
significantly, he collaborated with Chatham in that Minister's overall strategy
– at a time when the Company was an independent body, free of any
Government control.

It is true that he was far away from the scene of action, and given the time-
lapse before the arrival of his instructions, there existed a never-ending
discrepancy. Vital weeks passed before he received information; and there
were critical passages when speedy action had to be taken without referral to
Leadenhall. It might seem, therefore, that what he had to say was academic.
Not so. Sulivan was only too aware that he could not interfere with field
operations. What he did know was that he could give a directing and
controlling influence from India House.

He knew the importance of liaison with the ministry upon overall military
and naval strategy. He was well aware that the provision of men, money and
materials was essential for success and that it was up to him to provide them.
He could and did inspire confidence at home and abroad among those
actually fighting or involved in the conflicts.

It was particularly important that the Company had the right military and
naval leaders on the spot with an almost free rein. This too was his job,
within the constraints of committees and sub-committees of the East India
Company. To meet the aim of speedy execution he had created almost a war
cabinet with the very strong Secret Committee, over which he presided.

Sometimes he chose the wrong man, sometimes he interfered where he
ought not to, such as when Coote was superseded by Monson in 1760; but
generally his strategy was sound. There are countless indications that Sulivan
masterminded the war effort in India, as he did everything else at this time
that remotely involved the Company. The General Letters to Madras are full
of detailed instructions; and his concern and intimate knowledge can be seen
from his plans and history of events. Even Clive's letters admit that Sulivan
was indispensable: 'Sulivan will continue at the head of the Direction and in
all probability will remain so long as the war lasts.'[5]

He raised the establishment of European officers and soldiers in India
from 2,600 in 1755 to 6,900 in 1765. This was achieved despite the failure to
secure a well-organised military recruiting programme – blocked by the army
and its spokesmen in Parliament. In this era troops were raised through an
intermediary in possession of a 'contract'. Taken as a whole, however, the
number of fighting men involved abroad swelled to some 26,000 by 1763.

The Company's immediate financial troubles in 1758 determined that
numbers were slow in building up. This meant that during some crucial
periods the organisation was dependent upon the Government for help.
Nevertheless, by April 1760 Sulivan had despatched 2,020 Company soldiers
and conveyed them and 1,035 royal troops abroad in EastIndiamen. In 1763
and 1764, the statistics show that 2,757 officers and 2,118 non-commissioned
men were shipped out.[6]

He demanded to know the details surrounding every event, such as those concerning the loss of Fort St. David in 1758. He dealt with the divisions in the Madras Council over military authority, especially those arising in August 1759 regarding the right of the Council to place a Company officer, Caillaud, over royal troops. It was with extreme difficulty that men could be recruited for the service in Madras. Sulivan attended to this. He advised upon the arrival of reinforcements, such as how and when Eyre Coote and his battalion would arrive. He laid down precise military regulations; decided the payment of troops; and advised on recruitment procedures in India. He also handled unreasonable demands, such as those put forward by the Swiss mercenaries.

Nor was he foolish enough to ignore the strength and wisdom of his finest commanders and ablest men in India who alone could deal with the situation on the spot. He applauded Clive's plan that the armies of all the Presidencies should help one another as the situation demanded. He thought the despatch of a force to Masulipatam, under Col. Forde, 'sensible and judicious'; and so it proved.

It was Sulivan who picked the men who would bring success in the Carnatic. He ordered that Caillaud was to follow Polier as Major at Madras. Colonel Coote was to be Commander-in-Chief of the Company's forces under the orders of the Governor in Council in Madras.[7] Robert Palk (after being created Governor of Madras by Sulivan) was used to help General Lawrence consolidate alliances with neighbouring states and tribesmen, such as those of Mysore and Tanjore, and with the Marathas.

He was also the one man who could resolve head-on collisions between the Madras Governor and his Council on the one hand and the Commander-in-Chief, Coote, on the other. He had to do so, often. Direction of military affairs was to continue long after the war with the French had ceased. Before he fell from office in 1765, he had ensured that those he felt to be efficient, such as John Caillaud and Major Sir Robert Barker, were duly promoted.

The same degree of expertise and firmness was exercised in directing naval affairs. He issued orders regarding the deployment of all ships belonging to the Company, synchronising their movements with ships-of-the-line. He appointed squadron commanders, such as Admiral Cornish in March 1759; and tried to make life as smooth as possible: 'On Cornish's arrival at Madras he is to be supplied with all useful information and treated in a friendly and obliging manner.'[8]

As well as transporting all troops (King's and Company's), Company shipping was used to convey stores, munitions and other supplies for war. While doing so, some semblance of commercial freight had to be maintained. Much of his other work in this field involved sending details of shipping movements and intelligence of the whereabouts and strength of the French navy to Government. For example, he gave details of French ships off Brazil in January 1759; referred to a squadron at Mauritius in November 1759; and gave news of those in Ceylon in March 1763. He also sent important

Government advices abroad, showing, for instance the true state of the Dutch armaments at Ceylon in 1763.

Among the shifting sands of native alliances, he more than once expressed himself happy with the unfaltering friendship of the Nawab of Arcot, Walajah Muhammad 'Ali. He seems a rather empty-handed ally, with enormous debts, but to Sulivan he was 'The Company's most faithful grateful and generous friend, and heaven is my witness that in this confidence he has had my invariable support.'[9] He maintained there could be no reliance placed on others, such as the Marathas; Nizam Ali; Salabat Jang; Mahfuz Khan; or later, Yusuf Khan.

Throughout the national emergency, a most important feature was to be Sulivan's excellent working relationship with Chatham and his successor, the Earl of Bute. This was particularly the case with Chatham. There was a fine understanding between them; so much so it would not be too much to say that the war in India was concluded so successfully primarily because of their good liaison and common goals.

As Chairman of the Company, Sulivan had paramount responsibility for conducting the British war effort against the French in the east. Chatham was more than happy that this should be so. Strategy and financial considerations decided for him that the Company, with its own army and navy, bases, supplies and, above all, money, should go it alone. He needed only to strengthen the Company's existing war machine, when and where required, with additional troops and Government funds. A man of Sulivan's calibre and powers of leadership was tailor-made, as far as Chatham was concerned.

A biography of Chatham by M. Peters puts it in perspective: 'For India the issue was not one of planning and implementing expeditions, but of responding to requests for help from the East India Company, which came through the Southern Secretary.'[10] Ships and troops (sent at first by Holderness) were continued by Chatham, who initiated contacts with the Company's Secret Committee headed by Sulivan.

The 'Great Commoner' could not only pick the right men for the field of action, he could recognise and accept the talents of a strong man like Sulivan. Besides, it would seem only right to many that such a formidable Company figure should command affairs relative to the Indies. Sulivan's replies (in his own handwriting) to the separate heads of the Bengal General Letter of 5 March 1759, illustrates this liaison well. He referred to the national emergency, stressing that stores of naval articles would be in strict supply to the Company, but even then, only after the royal forces had been furnished.

The Prime Minister also made use of the Company's administrative, naval and military apparatus. It was very advantageous to be able to graft the royal forces and the best-suited commanders on to this structure. At vital moments reinforcements and funds from the national exchequer were provided without hesitation, no matter how hard Chatham had to fight for them in the Commons. In January 1759 two ships-of-the-line and two gunships were despatched; so was Col. Coote with 1,200 soldiers. In 1760 large numbers of recruits were again sent out. In turn, Sulivan ensured easy relations at Madras by putting Coote's royal battalion on the same footing as Col. Draper's.

In April 1759, at Sulivan's prompting, Chatham proposed to the House that an annual subsidy of £20,000 be made to the Company to assist it during the rest of the war. Sulivan answered for the Direction, and 'gratefully confessed the Ministry's care of the Company'.[11] His rejoicing was every bit as great as Chatham's, when, as Chairman he informed the Court of Directors of the defeat of the French; and that the Pondicherry colours had been captured and sent by Coote to England. It was fully deserved that he, the leader at India House, should then present these to the King, together with a loyal address.

Following Chatham's resignation, Sulivan was to honour the man he considered a great statesman and the nation's saviour. In 1762 he declared that the Company 'not only owed their present glorious situation, but their very existence to his (Chatham's) generous protection'.[12]

Chatham's own fame owes an immense debt to the contribution made by Sulivan and his control of the Company at that time. The words acclaiming Chatham were just as deserved by Sulivan. He said as much to his son, later in life:

> Bengal (June 1757) and Fort St. Davids taken (May 1758) Madras
> Besieged (February 1759)...I boldly attempted and successfully
> prevailed upon that glorious Minister Mr. Chatham to send out
> instantaneously Fleet and troops to India which saved the
> Company, saved the Nabob of Arcot, and from desperation laid
> the ground for the prosperity of both.[13]

The first minister created a strong impression on Sulivan. Chatham was able to concentrate exclusively on foreign affairs and the direction of the war, planning expeditions and raising war loans (£16 million in 1760). His skill in raising such amounts was something Sulivan appreciated. Their discussions were fruitful and a great deal of planning took place. One document, evidently from the Company to Chatham, demonstrated Sulivan's thinking. Appended were his sentiments regarding military expenses; and three separate plans on how to achieve peace with the French.

The national leader also gave him freedom of action, such as deciding the fate of Pondicherry after its fall. The Chairman determined that the fortifications should be razed to the ground; adding that he thought the French had 'been the authors of their own ruin'.[14] Looking to the future, Sulivan showed his line of thought by saying that his ideas would 'be confined to our mercantile interest, we ought not, we cannot, look further, Government may.'[15] He meant only that it was not the role of a commercial organisation to deal with the war in its global framework.

It becomes apparent too that Sulivan was encouraged to converse freely with the Minister. Each piece of India news was immediately carried to Administration, such as acquainting them of the surrender of Mahé. He would also give his view of the situation in India whether asked or not; and was quick to put forward his plans. For example, he held to the view that the Company should retain all its possessions to the total exclusion of the French. Any concessions he was willing to make were of a limited nature.

Chatham's direct intervention also saved him from the repercussions of events in India, such as happened after His Majesty's officers Coote and Cornish took Pondicherry, claiming and possessing it for the Crown. This action was dictated by a history of bickering over booty between the King's land and sea officers and those of the Company. Governor Pigot, obeying Sulivan's explicit instructions, had declared that, 'if the King's officers did not surrender Pondicherry to the Company he would stop every advance for pay and support of the King's troops'.[16] Although the royal troops evacuated the place, a furious protest was sent to England. Sulivan expressed approval of Pigot's 'judicious behaviour'. He was then saved from the 'menaces of great men', such as the Chancellor Lord Camden, because Chatham shielded him.[17]

Sulivan's clear vision was again evident in several expeditions, especially in military counter-actions against the Dutch, and in opposing the Spanish in the Philippines. The scale and ramifications of these operations were to lose him much valuable time consumed in negotiations; and it was the same after the event, because he was extremely useful to ministers when Dutch and Spanish recriminations landed in London.

After hostilities with the Dutch began in 1757, Sulivan refuted their protests that British troops had been used illegally against the Nawab of Bengal. Then in 1758, after Clive ensured that Mir Jafar would be Nawab, they failed in attempts to supplant English influence with the new prince. Sulivan answered fire with fire in his haughty replies to their protests.[18]

Late in 1761 he was again confronted with Dutch complaints, but this time these were sent first to the British Government. It was an astute move since it tied the Company's hands at home. Bute asked the Directors their 'opinion in regard to procedure'; and Sulivan was expected to reply to the Dutch Memorial personally.[19] He was faced with the task of soothing the King's desire to end all disputes with the Dutch, yet had to maintain the Company's position in Bengal. He told Bute that in the treaty the English were only involved as guarantor. He then wrote to Clive for supporting materials.[20]

These negotiations involved the King, Bute and Jenkinson; and for the Company, Sulivan, Clive, Hastings and Sykes. Sulivan called upon the legal expertise of John Dunning, who drew up a document on behalf of the Directors, using information from his friend.[21] To decide what would be their joint action on the Commission that was then set-up, Jenkinson collaborated with Sulivan and Rous. It was agreed that the Dutch should have some support. Sulivan was given approval to explain this stand to those at Calcutta; and also to the Proprietors, who wanted no truck with the Dutch. He, Rous and Dorrien then became the 'commissaries to treat with the Dutch gentlemen,' and eventually agreement was reached.[22]

Projected moves against the French-controlled base at Mauritius in 1761 and 1762 were likewise based upon his detailed recommendations. Like

Chatham, he always felt that the conquest of Mauritius would 'lay the axe to the root' of French aspirations in India.[23] In a letter to the minister's agent, Robert Wood, in February 1761, he showed that a definite plan to take Mauritius had been drawn-up. He advised on how to breach defensive fortifications there and supplied information on stores. He even offered to buy the plunder; and supplied the name and address of a deserter who could give inside information. Yet even he was left in the dark as to why the Royal Squadron failed to press home the planned attack. Nevertheless, it was 1784 before the islands once more become useful to the French, only to be taken by Britain in the years 1810 to 1814.

Excellent documentation of the British conquest of Manila, 1762-63, is provided by the Royal Historical Society. General Draper and Admiral Cornish headed an expedition that set off from Madras in June 1762, supported and enabled to reach Manila by the East India Company's marine. All was complemented by Company supplies, arms, and general organisation. The surprise attack against a settlement neither aware of a declaration of war, nor prepared in any way for defence, led to victory in October. The loss of life was considered small; and the conquerors were offered bills on Madrid for one million pounds sterling, in lieu of pillage.

Sulivan's role was important. He was consulted even before preparations were begun: 'The Chairman (Laurence Sulivan) informed the Court that Lord Anson, First Lord of the Admiralty, had given indication of an attack to be made on Manila and that he requested the Company's help'.[24] This was readily given when the monarch indicated the Company would possess Manila and all other places conquered. Sulivan pinpointed the advantages this offered in his paper, *Reasons and Considerations upon the Enterprise against the Philippine Islands*, which was passed to the Committee of Secrecy.[25]

The new Manila government was to be the concern of the Madras Council. Instructions from the Secret Committee envisaged the despatch of 2,000 troops from there; and the Council would care for revenue, trade and native affairs. It was hoped to have no repeat of previous troubles between royal commanders and the Company's governing personnel. Instructions regarding the division of booty and plunder were made clear; and there was to be full reimbursement of all expenses incurred.

The success of the operation was wholly dependent upon the Company providing troops, ships and stores, and appointing a provisional Deputy Governor and Council for Manila. While aware of a risk to Madras, when so many troops and supplies were drawn off, he believed the expedition would expedite the despatch of silver from there to settlements in China. He also endeavoured to gain a station on the island of Mindano using Royal troops.

Unfortunately, security problems arose in the Carnatic; and financial strain was placed on Madras. Great ill-feeling developed between His Majesty's troops and Company officials; so much so that the backwash from General Draper's complaints disturbed Sulivan's relationship with ministers. Disputes arose over captured cannon and military stores, although Sulivan had gone to great pains to have it understood that the plunder taken should be halved.

General Draper and Admiral Cornish clashed with Governor Pigot at Madras. He referred to Sulivan's directions, insisting on the half share. Captain Thomas Backhouse, in command of the royal regiment, was furious: 'From such another Governor and Council good Lord deliver all honest men.'[26] The acrimony remained until the British departed from Manila in April 1764; and the ramifications in London paralleled the growth of party conflict.

In the end the Company received only one third of three separate distributions of booty; and the Spanish Court refused to recognise either the Treaty signed at Manila or the ransom that was demanded. However, Sulivan kept an exact account of all disbursements, and these were eventually deposited in the Government's lap.

These successes were of significance for the Company's future, and for State-Company liaison. His performance as a war-leader was outstanding.[27] Yet his concentration on the war arena forms only a portion of what he attended to during those years. There seems to have been only one question in his mind: could he help save Britain from her enemies, while preserving the Company and its personnel? He remained true and steadfast to these objectives.

He did not seek praise for what he did; commendation was not sought, although he accepted the thanks of his fellow Directors on occasion. As far as can be deduced, he looked upon his travails as part and parcel of his duty. It is amazing, therefore, that no credit has been given to him for his contribution at such a critical point in Britain's struggle. The usual recitation that success was due to the Chatham Administration on the one hand and the quality of the military and naval forces on the other is not enough. This view was even paraded at the time (deliberately and vindictively) by political enemies, such as Luke Scrafton.[28] The truth is that Sulivan guaranteed that 'superior organisation, military, political and financial, not sheer fire power, which explains British victories in eighteenth century India.'[29]

3

It is no exaggeration to say that the momentous changes being wrought in India were rivalled by what was happening in London. A veritable flood of problems and emergencies engulfed Sulivan and he struggled with some alarming developments. All of this was just as important to the future of the Company (and to him) as the changes being wrought abroad. Many of the difficulties stemmed from bad news from overseas; or bad tidings would inflame what was already taking place at home. Other troubles stemmed from complications originating in the capital. Some of these instances required a deliberate plan to solve; others were dealt with as they cropped up.

Sulivan's leading part in rooting out why things had come to such a pass and seeking remedies was partly due to his position at the head of the Company's administration. Yet, as seen in his handling of the war, in or out of the Chair he provided leadership and solutions. The common cry was that

Sulivan would deal with them; and although these taxed him to the limit, he tackled all and every new calamity with energy.

Nevertheless, as early as 1758 he was forced to increase his pace of work to breaking point, such was the volume of business, responsibility and agitation. The effort now needed was probably more than one man could give; something that he might have realised, but would not admit. Even he could not keep a tight grip so far removed from problems that required immediate solutions.

An ever-increasing threat to stability accompanied the impact of these Indian troubles on the Company's management. From the emergence of political faction inside India House arose the spectre of internal collapse. Company headquarters was to become the scene of furious infighting. Consequently, while Sulivan dedicated an amazing amount of time and enormous effort to the Company's well-being, an equal amount of energy was needed for political survival. The make-up of the Company dictated this was how it would be.

Abroad, loss of control in the face of greedy servants and an increasing sense of autonomy and separateness had to be faced. Carefully laid plans for the future administration of the settlements were thrown into disarray in the face of a different reality from the one envisaged at home. Clive's pre-eminence and views upon the way forward in the sub-continent would create further trouble.

News of the success at Plassey reached the ears of the public in February 1758 and Indian affairs rocketed to prominence. It was the first British success in the midst of the gloom and bad tidings that shrouded war with France. However, it was not received with carefree abandon in all quarters, because a few discerning individuals – such as Sulivan – were pre-occupied with other trials. The stark reality was that the Company was in great danger from a fast deterioration in its finances.

A hiatus was reached, set against the backdrop of war. Additional costs, especially military ones, were testing already overstretched funds. Although signs of a slide were there before the outbreak of hostilities, the deterioration led to a chain of threatened crises that called upon all Sulivan's skill to circumvent. Some measure of all this might be gauged from a later calculation that in the seven years between 1753 and 1760, the Company managed to 'lose' £2.5 million.

For the knowledgeable Irishman in charge, tenure of office rapidly came to mean a never-ending effort to keep the Company afloat. Overriding anxiety stemmed from this seemingly endless threat of insolvency, escalating military costs, and multitudes of accumulating expenses, particularly in Bengal. Avoiding financial collapse and the catastrophe that would follow demanded the utmost in stamina and perseverance.

It began for him with his very entry to high office. Between 1757 and 1758 he discovered that the financially fraught Company faced a liquidity emergency. The whole mighty East India organisation was on the verge of bankruptcy. The crisis that threatened in 1758 was due to several factors, but the immediate, urgent situation arose from 'unexpectedly large demands in the form of bills transmitted from India to London – which embarrassed the Company'.[30]

It is ironic that Sulivan faced an impending disaster which, unintentionally, he had helped create. In exchange for cash paid into the treasury in Fort William, with which to make the Investment in Bengal, he had offered bills redeemable in London. The acceptance of so many bills of exchange boomeranged with a vengeance. His good intention, to benefit the Company and private individuals alike, was abused. Too many bills began arriving. The drafts drawn by the servants in Bengal increased enormously and were falling due for payment before the money from sales could be realized.[31]

Sulivan severely curtailed his own remittance activities upon realising how far wrong things were in Bengal. But it was too late. By November 1758 he was at his wit's end, and even thought of refusing to accept any more drafts. Only the risk to the Company's credit from this course of action made him stop. Nevertheless, he then took a firm stand: 'No persons shall be suffered to pay more into the Company's cash beyond what the Company's occasions absolutely require.'[32]

His peremptory orders to Company servants abroad to stop remitting their fortunes proved impossible for them to accept meekly. Combined with his measures to curb customs-free privileges, they felt that it was too much to bear. Clive and other senior servants in Bengal thought he was too deeply implicated by his own private activities. His change of face, for so it appeared to them, was not acceptable. They simply did not appreciate the seriousness of the position, despite Sulivan's best efforts.

The Company's trade was suffering: 'Because it was forced to buy from its own employees at prices which they themselves fixed in their capacity as agents of the Company.'[33] In this way the Bengal servants, in particular, took away the very wherewithal to pay their bills when offered for payment in London. Sulivan's advices became frantic and his tone increasingly severe. In November 1758 he listed the criticisms levelled against Bengal. Instead of requiring no supplies that Presidency had 'drawn upon us for £167,000 and bills for a larger amount are thought to be on the way.'[34] He was furious:

> The very being of the Company depends upon the practice of the utmost frugality...the unaccountable conduct of Fort William and Bombay, who have drawn heavily without sending adequate cargoes has involved the Company in great difficulties. Even if they had sent cargoes it would have been impossible in time of war to raise the necessary sums within 3 months.[35]

November 1758 was one of the blackest periods in the Company's history. It was a real crisis, brought on by the accumulation of events following Plassey and complicated by war and the weaknesses abroad that made India ripe for exploitation. But above all, the Company was being crippled in November by these excessive numbers of bills, payable at a shorter date than expected.

There was extravagance in the terms offered by the Bengal servants, the same people putting up the money. However, it was the timing of when the demands fell due that was of most concern; and with the drain of funds in England, 'Sulivan's admiration for what he had called, the Company's "old and most capable servants" began to wane.'[36] The Company was almost insolvent.[37] On top of the bills fiasco, the drain upon commerce from war costs was unbearable, with convoy expenses, increases in shipping hire and losses of ships to privateers. Things reached their lowest point just a few months after he became Chairman, and he found the Company foundering under him. Roughly from May 1758 to March 1759 he faced, as he said, 'the Company bankrupt at home in credits, not even £5,100 could be borrowed on their name from man or men'.[38]

But he was equal to the occasion. Many years later he described the drama and his rescue of 'an ungrateful Company':

> In this dreadful hour my fame and fortune (perhaps my personal safety) were hazarded to save them. I concealed their danger, comforted the Proprietors, lent them the last shilling (£40,000) by which I lost £10,200 by selling out of the funds, pawned myself for near as much more, and...secured its tottering internal state.[39]

This would mean that he had personally raised some £80,000, and had placed himself in an impossible position if his gamble did not succeed. If his figures are to be accepted his fortune was certainly insufficient to cover the bills due. The Company ledgers show a record of cash paid back to him in the period 1759 to 1761 that totals only £3,500. But it is more than probable that the remainder of the money loaned to the Company was included in the sums of £105,300 and £52,000, entered under the headings: 'paid several', dated 28 February and 31 July 1759, respectively.[40]

He must have borrowed much more than admitted later in life; and it would seem that he used every ounce of persuasion upon connections in the London money market. These are undoubtedly the people included, anonymously, under the headings 'paid several'. On 24 March 1758 £100,000 in cash was received from the Governor of the Bank of England. Another £50,000 from that source came on 31 May 1759. £70,000 was repaid to the *Royal Assurance Company* on 20 March 1759; and various individuals were paid back in 1759 and 1760, including Henry Savage, Sulivan's Bombay colleague, who was repaid £4,000. By these exertions, it appears he rescued the Company from financial disaster in the winter of 1758-9. From these figures alone the Company borrowed just under £400,000; sufficient to cover requirements and allow the danger to pass.

Meanwhile, he reaped benefits. His position was consolidated; and the policy he must pursue in Bengal became very clear: 'Territorial acquisitions (were)...a course of unjustifiable expense.'[41] The Company was back on its feet; and at the Court of Directors of 10 January 1759 this feat was applauded. He had justification, therefore, in feeling aggrieved beyond words by the infamous Bengal General Letter of 29 December 1759, when it arrived, signed by Clive, Holwell and other Bengal Councillors.

He had been reproached, just after straining every sinew to rescue the Company. What is more, he had saved it from havoc wrought, in the main, by those very same Bengal servants. The reply, drafted in his own handwriting, showed his feelings in no uncertain manner. He castigated their 'cruel' censures, and looked back 'with wonder' at the difficulties surmounted, seemingly impossible 'with our contracted capital'. He thanked the Proprietors for 'generously and without a murmur consenting to reduce their dividend'.[42]

4

As well as solving the immediate crisis of 1758-9, as Chairman he had to tackle the long-term problem of constructing a solid financial basis for commercial operations. He approached the problem in two ways. In order to relax pressures and controls on the Company at home, caused by having to acquire bullion to export to the Presidencies, he inaugurated a policy of cutting back specie, encouraging the settlements to find their own, and promoting the export of merchandise. Secondly, he commenced cutting costs and expenses in the civil and military establishments, backed up by severe and stern censure. Wherever possible he urged Governors and Councils to throw costs upon the shoulders of the Indian powers.

In the first of these approaches he was totally successful, in the latter he brought down enemies upon his own head. Whether or not he foresaw the possibility of a contest in the future, Sulivan gave no sign; and the deadly tone of some of his letters suggests that the critical importance of stopping the drain on funds was all that mattered to him.

From various tallies made in 1766-7, directly related to the Government's new interest in India and the affairs of the Company, a fairly accurate appraisal of how things functioned, and the changes in finances between 1754 and 1766 can be put together. Also, Charles Townshend, Chancellor of the Exchequer in Chatham's administration of 1766-8, had the Company draw up lists giving a truer reflection of its business prior to and during these troubled years. Included are accounts of all the bullion and merchandise sent to India, the total ships at sea and tonnage.[43]

The lists also give the full war expenses in India from 1753 to 1766 and the Company's exports for these years, which approximated to 1,000 tons annually, exclusive of men and baggage. Included as well are conflicting statements regarding the Bengal accounts drawn up by Clive and Sulivan. Much of what was stated can be added to and checked from other sources.[44]

They show that from a steady export of bullion in 1754-55, worth £668,893, there was a drop in 1756 to £620,378. This can be explained by the outbreak of the European war, by subsequent demands upon the Bank of England, and by the risks of capture at sea. There was also a shortage of specie from the New World via Portugal and Spain. The surge of bullion exports in 1757 to £795,007, far exceeding the 1754-5 figures, can be explained by the desperate demands made by the Presidencies. The onslaught of war cut across all other priorities. Troops had to be paid, stores, bullocks and other supplies purchased.

From this high point, bullion exports dropped in a dramatic manner. In the two years, 1757 to 1759, they fell to £172,000 (this was a massive drop of £623,000); then lower still to a mere trickle of £27,089 in 1764. Between times, in 1763, there was a slight rise to £46,876, caused by the threat of war with Mir Qasim. There was another, fairly steep rise throughout 1764 and 1765, reaching a total of £366,526, before slumping again.[45] Undoubtedly this spurt was in response to Clive's return to India and to the troubles expected there. By 1766 bullion exports had levelled off and then fell slightly to £315,161 by 1766. This followed the end of immediate and severe military troubles in India; bolstered by Clive's claim that that enough specie would be raised in India.

This limitation of bullion exports to India during Sulivan's period of power was developed by him as a deliberate policy. It was done upon the understanding that there was sufficient gold and silver in India; at a time when there was a general European shortage of bullion. The policy was also due to the Company's credit being on very shaky foundations, particularly with regard to securing funds from the Bank of England. Regrettably, the severe crises in India and the political struggle for control of the Company that paralleled these events combined to create a volatile picture and the image of mismanagement.

On the other hand, the Company started to show a marked improvement in the export of merchandise throughout the whole period. This fact also influenced Sulivan's decision to deliberately reduce bullion exports while raising exports of every kind. Such a complete turnabout achieved in the relative exports of specie compared to merchandise marks a watershed in the development of the Company's commercial policy.

The figures for exports of merchandise improve dramatically, proceeding in an unbroken climb from £259,602 in the years 1754-5 to £497,395 in 1766. To some extent this can be explained by more markets, by the added territories in India, and by a natural addition to the volume of trade that might be expected over a decade. The increase also reflects the rapid strides taking place in the industrialisation of Britain. Yet Sulivan's vision was vital. His dogged pursuit of merchandising is underlined in the figures. By 1766 the Company was dependent upon each Presidency for most of its bullion for the Investments and for other activities requiring capital. The Directors were then placing full emphasis on the export of goods.

In truth, without the increase between 1758 and 1762 of approximately £200,000 worth of merchandise from England, the total Company commerce in the period 1758 to 1766 would have been disastrously unbalanced. The damage done might have been insurmountable. To some extent the increase in goods from Britain had balanced the £324,000 cutback in bullion exports from there, and which were not made up in India.[46]

The Company's straitened circumstances can be realised from the following figures. The total value of all exports to India from 1754 to 1766 amounted to £8,212,009. This sum was expected to realise enough wealth to keep the Company solvent and pay dividends. To this can be added £5,940,987, the amount the Select Committee of the House of Commons calculated (in 1773) that the Government had injected, mainly through investment. The total was some £14 million, all the money at the Company's disposal throughout the years 1757 to 1766; and it was supposed to pay all costs, some of them enormous. It was quite insufficient.

There was a little more money that would be raised in India stemming from the Company's changed situation there – and from the new territories it now controlled. However, because of the unreliable and varying calculations elicited, it became necessary to put this to one side, temporarily. Military expenses alone were calculated to have been £8,510,360 for the period 1753 to 1766, with Bengal claiming over half of the total. The cost of the Company's military and naval charges could scarcely be borne even before Siraj-ud-Daula's aggression of 1756. The mounting costs of the struggles in Bengal and Madras created intolerable strains.

From the council chamber in Calcutta, even Vansittart ranted to Palk in Madras about the massive military charges and costs. Sulivan told Coote, campaigning in Madras, 'Our military expenses are amazingly large, even beyond what we can possibly support for any time. Pray manifest your regard to the Company by cutting off every necessary charge.'[47] He was also against the Company lending large sums to the royal army or navy; or of taking on the cost of demolishing hostile fortifications. No ill-will was meant, just that it would be impossible to recover the money spent so quickly, if at all.[48]

The General Letters to the Bengal Council continually reflect Sulivan's concern, such as that of 3 March 1758, where he remarked, scathingly, that Bengal appeared only useful for the saltpetre it produced; while its territorial acquisitions were again adjudged the cause of unjustifiable expense.[49] Nor could he recoup war costs. Although the Government helped with these, it expected the Company to withstand the worst of the French challenge in India on its own. Worse still, Sulivan could not afford to divulge the seriousness of the Company's position because of the disastrous lack of confidence this would create, particularly during a national emergency.

On the 8 March 1758, even after hearing of Clive's success, he urged 'our servants (to)...set down carefully and diligently to the Company's as well as their own affairs in the usual <u>mercantile tracts</u>...carrying on the business at all the subordinates without parade, military forces and <u>at the most moderate expense.</u>'[50]

From the very beginning he urged and pleaded for frugality. He referred continually to the immense expenses swallowed by Madras and to its scanty returns.[51] He also said at one stage that while the charges of Bengal were great, those of Bombay went beyond all bounds. Each Governor and Council was called upon to justify heavy expenses drawn; and special reference was made to inordinate lavishness when entertaining the Indian princes.

He urged reduction in field allowances and standardized these for all the Presidencies; and berated the fact that allowances for military officers and others were being 'concealed in the Commissaries books by the entry of large sums under general heads'.[52] In 1762 it was determined that the end of the war with the French, should be fully utilized to procure a good Investment. Madras was called upon to retrieve 'the circumstances of the Company, harassed and almost exhausted by continual and immense expenses'.[53]

He desperately explored trading possibilities and commercial measures that would ease the grinding costs. He sent no treasure to India in the season 1758-9, believing, erroneously, that Bengal would have sufficient bullion following Plassey; and that Madras would support herself from the 'quick stock', that is, cash readily available from local trade and remittance money. Other requirements, he believed, could be met by bills drawn upon Bombay. He also developed trade between China and Sumatra. Profits were being made by the sale of pepper in the Canton market and in the carrying of opium to China. He depended too upon Madras sending 10 chests of bullion (worth £1,000 each) further east. In England he had been able to lade only 10 chests on to each China ship; he wanted Madras to increase this to 30 chests per ship.[54]

Meanwhile, the Company had become the centre of attention in City business circles. Excessive speculation in Company stock was taking place, both in London and in Europe. The credit boom only collapsed in 1763 with the end of the Seven Years War. The financial dislocation started in Amsterdam and affected London. Thus, even after the critical situation of 1758/1759, the Company still seemed to be set on the road to financial ruin; and this appeared even more the case as India House became wracked with political infighting. The confusion this struggle created exacerbated the already unstable financial situation, preventing constructive policies from enjoying success.

The growing issue, therefore, of whether the monopoly should continue as a commercial or a territorial body was worked out against an alarming background. It all contrasted with the visions of immediate wealth that whetted the appetites of ignorant shareholders and feckless, uninformed Directors, provoking enormous pressures. The cost of such fruits could only be the loss of the Company's future independence, as Sulivan saw all too clearly.

Probably the events in India of 1760 and 1763 shocked people in Britain the most. For Sulivan, the 1760 revolution in Bengal (followed by the disaster of 1763) painfully corrected the impression he had gained from Clive that it would be the El Dorado he had been praying for. It was also made clear to him and his fellow Directors that working for the Company's future benefit was of secondary importance to many people in India. If all else had been well this might not have mattered just as much; but there was an insatiable thirst for money. What is more, despite the Nawab of Bengal not being able to fulfil his financial agreements, the Government still expected the Company to defray the cost of the military establishment while the war continued.

The uncertainty surrounding the actual state of the Company's financial circumstances during these fateful years is illustrated by separate and divergent calculations made in 1766 by Clive and Sulivan. Both men were in the best position to know the true state of affairs in Bengal at the end of the 1757-65 period, yet there was no agreement between them.

Bengal was by far the wealthiest and most important Presidency in India, and Clive's calculations showed it to have produced a surplus of £607,000 by 1766. Sulivan, on the other hand, reckoned that it had made a loss of £708,000. Multiplications of these differences appeared in the Company's ranks, by men with less knowledge and competence; and there was wide confusion and uncertainty.

To his consternation, Sulivan had never been able to fathom the true state of Bengal's resources. He had been forced, by circumstances, to rely on Clive and his successors for what he took to be the real condition of the Bengal treasury; and he was similarly reliant on the Governors and Councils in the other Presidencies.

He looked in vain, for example, for payment of the £1 million recompense from the Nawab of Bengal following the 1757 treaty, but 'nothing has gone in and to the Company's returns'.[55] Clive had later promised £2 million per annum, which never materialized. The Nawab of Arcot's worsening debts throughout the period in question only made everything more confused: 'The immense sum owed by the Nawab is a weight too heavy for the Company to support much longer.'[56] The calculations Sulivan made, which were meant for the Company's future and long-term solvency and based on Clive's information, were almost useless:

> I grounded my opinion upon the veracity of his [Clive's] statement of the revenues....Soon after the Battle of Plassey, Luke Scrafton by Lord Clive's order, copied from the King's books, the nett revenues of the three provinces, which Mr. Walsh brought home, and by Clive's order, delivered to me <u>privately</u>.[57]

The gap between what the Company expected and what was actually realised was incredibly large and completely unpredicted by those in London. Exact figures were impossible to obtain.

It was a state of affairs that perplexed Sulivan for a long, long time. In the 1770s he was still making computations and including them in his correspondence to Warren Hastings when Governor General. He said that Hastings might easily see the most glaring absurdities: 'Many arise from incorrectness in our materials, or ignorance in the persons who collected them. The persons were Lord Clive and our auditor...the materials were public papers, laid before Parliament by the Company.' He added, 'No man has taken more pains (I think none so much) as myself, and yet it is impossible for me to form a statement that will in any degree accord with our present circumstances in Bengal...I cannot make out a corrected account.'[58]

What happened, therefore, as the years progressed was that while outwardly the Company appeared to become rich very quickly, it was really shouldering massive debts which would have to be reckoned with. Eventually other criteria ensured there would be further crises. From 1757 to April 1764 Sulivan was at the centre of it all. Faced with war commitments, uncertainty about how things would develop in India, muddled figures and a mushrooming of evils produced by such a sad state of affairs, his grasp of what was going on was affected. The distorted view he was given led to erroneous calculations, virtually impossible to correct.

Some evidence of his efforts to redeem things does emerge, however. In 1758 and again in 1761, he pointed out that the Company's capital was too small for the role that it was now asked to play. In a letter to Clive he said, 'we only want our capital doubled to reap those advantages which other ways we cannot grasp'; and of course, he had changed the balance of specie and manufactured exports.[59] Be that as it may, sporadically he was still forced back upon the Government for help, although wary of the difficulties this could land the Company in relative to its future independence.

Smooth control of finances proved impossible throughout the period, and stupendous effort was needed to maintain credibility. In truth, Sulivan's input really was crucial; this was so in his eyes and in those of his contemporaries. Mid 1758 to mid 1759 was the critical period, and the fact that during this crisis Sulivan gave all the money that he had and could raise to keep the Company solvent was indeed the vital factor.

Even during his fight to become Chairman of the Company he had been aware of approaching financial emergency. When it happened, it was something that had to be handled alone; by the very nature of the trouble public disclosure was impossible. Publicity would have speedily brought about the very state of affairs that he wished to avoid – a disastrous lack of confidence. In the end, he failed to plug the drain on the Company's cash, though not for the want of trying. Yet in the reversal of roles, whereby the export of manufactures replaced that of bullion, he was triumphant in the long-term. This established long-term viability since exports would continue to rise and flood ready-made markets in India; and East Indiamen carried these goods from rising British industry to these markets. This produced further stability within the organisation and led to better standing in City circles. That this was not entirely the case, however, was to be reflected in the financial crises of 1766-7 and then 1772; although additional influences were present at these emergencies. What must be said, though, is that without Sulivan's presence throughout the 1757 to 1764 years the Company might have ceased to exist; or would have been poorer and less prepared for the strenuous years to come.

5

India
Developments and Plans
1757-65

1

Winning the war and securing the Company's finances were Sulivan's priorities, but he had problems without number to face, particularly in India. The Mughal Empire was in meltdown; trade stagnant, there was administrative turmoil and breakdown. Abuse of trust and mismanagement was rampant in each of the main provinces, but especially so in Bengal, which now preoccupied his mind. What went on there affected everything else. Disturbing administrative and financial developments were bad enough in themselves, but there was hostile reaction to his orders, to his ideas and to Leadenhall control. The activities of Company servants and free merchants grew as they strove to get rich quick.[1]

The Company's matchless military machine caused enormous problems as well. Native weakness was highlighted by its power; and although to begin with officers and Company servants had no systematic scheme for using such might, they were able to employ it to increase profits for themselves and for private traders, and to wring concessions that resulted in territorial gains. The example given by Clive and his use of the army did not help; nor did the increasing need to pay and feed troops.

Upkeep of the Company's armies became the biggest incentive to extract grants of revenue, and led to control of territory. Eventually the Company was providing the troops, and they were paid for by the Nawab out of revenue; a policy Sulivan deliberately pursued. This resulted in British forces taking over the duties of administering and collecting the taxes from those territories allocated for their payment. In this way, 'the whole revenue of Bengal was taken over'.[2] Thus began 'the gradual process by which the whole raison d'etre of the Company shifted from trade to tax collection'.[3]

After Plassey the Company was de facto a territorial power; and supervision was by men on the spot. A potential, if not actual, state of empire was achieved, not solely by military success, but by the respect accorded the

Company by the native populace. The English changed from being in Bengal on sufferance to one of fawning reverence. By 1765 the Company had moved from being an ally of self-reliant Nawabs, to exercising a military protectorate, reducing the native overlord to a nonentity.

Following Plassey, there was a noticeable change in attitude among Company officials in Bengal. Latent imperial designs developed, stimulated by territorial and administrative duties that now accompanied commercial ones. Ominously a lack of deference and loyalty towards the Direction also appeared. Clive again has responsibility for fostering these feelings of separation, as well as encouraging conquest. He calculated that 2,000 Europeans could conquer all the territory the Company might require; with the Mogul Emperor paying for it.[4] His pre-eminence was another problem; he was held in equal status to the Directors themselves. This was consolidated by what was interpreted as a deferential attitude by the Company executives towards him.

Later, in his 'History' of Bengal, Vansittart vouchsafed that the Company had become a military and territorial power. Calcutta fortifying itself extensively was proof enough, he maintained; and all was put into effect, with or without blessings from Leadenhall. Sulivan, although raging against money being spent building walls, had given Clive *carte blanche*. He also had a wrong conception of what constituted reality. Before corrective action could begin, loss of control had commenced.

He tried, nevertheless, to minimise the growing sense of separateness in India; he rode events, harnessed and channelled them, disciplined and legislated wherever and whenever possible. As he became aware that Company servants were embroiled in endless intrigues, he also began to suspect they were not fit for, and in some cases not remotely attentive to, their duties.

From his first day in office as Chairman, the scenario in Bengal riveted his attention. The terms of the Treaty with Mir Jafar and the manner in which it came about displayed machination, greed and corruption. Clive had made an agreement with the prince before Plassey, and had entered into the plot against the incumbent Siraj-ud-daula. While Mir Jafar was made *Subadar** of Bengal, Bihar and Orissa, *Zamindari** rights and twenty-four *Parganas** of land were confirmed as the Company's; 40 *begahs** of land were added. The *Dastak** was confirmed and ample compensation paid.

Clive received the equivalent of £234,000, then later, his *jagir,* worth around £27,000 per annum; presents, trading rights, gifts, perquisites, bribes and contracts were all handed out or exchanged.[5] Henceforth the English Company compelled obedience; while the roles of arbiter and judge were also pushed upon its officials. 'Successive Nawabs were exposed to a series of demands which destroyed their authority within ten years'.[6]

Soon afterwards, an invasion of Bihar by the *Shahzada,* the eldest son of the Mughal Emperor, led (through retaliation) to Company forces thrusting up the Ganges valley and into Oudh. Sulivan heard about this, of course, but long after it had taken place.[7] Clive's return to England in 1760 left Mir Jafar with an empty treasury; and there was fear in Calcutta of a period of 'intestine war' and barbarism.[8]

It was October 1760 before Sulivan heard of the deposition of Mir Jafar and the substitution of Mir Qasim by Vansittart and Holwell. After Clive's departure, all had foundered on the basic supposition that there was enough treasure in the Nawab's exchequer. Vansittart stated he was left a bankrupt state of affairs, and that 'it was Colonel Clive's good fortune to leave India before the Company's treasure was totally exhausted.'[9]

Yet the most important and far-reaching point Clive had made was that Bengal would need no money for three years. Sulivan had believed this. It was an error with immense consequences. Based on Clive's estimates, he had believed there would be a massive infusion of capital, easing Investment problems and war costs. This optimism faded with successive advices.

Both Holwell, (in charge until Governor Vansittart arrived from Madras) and his new master saw the substitution of Nawabs as a means of solving financial straits. They felt no obligation to continue with someone who had proved so disastrous.[10] Another round of 'presents' then commenced; too much for an already empty Bengal purse.

On hearing of Mir Jafar's deposition, Sulivan (mistakenly) informed Chatham via Robert Wood, 'of a revolution in Bengal...wherein Pres. Vansittart has shown masterly abilities'.[11] Unwittingly, by deposing Mir Jafar, Vansittart also created trouble for himself with his patrons. Whereas Sulivan applauded his actions, Clive did not; and influenced by the growing struggle with Sulivan, came down hard against him.

Vansittart insisted that the price of Mir Qasim's appointment was to be a grant of lands to the Company, not to mention private emoluments. Thus the Company acquired Burdwan, Chittagong and Midnapore worth £625,000 per annum. Because Vansittart was his man and the Company's financial needs were pressing, Sulivan had to support the substitution of Nawabs. At the same time, the two *lakhs* of rupees sent to Madras for the siege of Pondicherry pleased him. But if Vansittart hoped for peaceful co-existence, he was badly mistaken. Mir Qasim aimed to become independent.

The history of Bengal, between the revolution of 1760 and the next upheaval of 1763, makes disastrous reading. The Governor's indecisive nature perfectly suited grasping Company servants, free traders and most of all Mir Qasim. He was unable to withstand the Nawab's never-ending arguments. Mir Qasim was ruthless, efficient and irritated by the greed he saw at every level of European society. He wished to restore native powers to what they were before Plassey, but misread the situation. The desire at India House to incur no expense in the administration of territory created an utterly wrong impression. He also seriously underestimated the force the Company could quickly put into the field, and its superiority in arms.

Sulivan sent Sir Eyre Coote to Bengal in 1761, where he upset everyone then faced up to Emperor Shah Alam.[12] The defeat of the Mogul ruler that followed (and of his French allies) allowed Mir Qasim freedom of action. He murdered Ram Narrain, Governor of Bihar, and attacked European trading abuses. He criticised misuse of the *Dastak*; and set up Customs of his own, even stopping Company ships.

Vansittart was aware of Europeans unlawfully commandeering the salt and tobacco trades and sympathised with the Nawab over these and other abuses. Although supported by Hastings, he found himself in a minority in Council when it came to sanctioning these actions. The upshot was that he set the military and civil branches of the Company against himself, and created a wrong impression in Mir Qasim's mind.

He was accused of irresponsibility and of supporting the Nawab. He could expect no disinterested opinion, there was too much to lose. His compatriots could not contemplate either a powerful Nawab or erosion of wealth. Vansittart had appeared to abdicate the powers won at Plassey and afterwards. The English servants and traders in Bengal could not allow this and refused to agree. The Governor was hated because he appeared to have turned against his fellow countrymen.

Mir Qasim then allowed all his subjects to trade from March 1763 without payment of duty, thus destroying the value of the *Dastak*. To most Europeans this meant war; the Council was split even further. Vansittart complained to India House; and although it took time, Sulivan dismissed all his opponents on the Board.

To add to the troubles, a serious rift had opened in 1761 between Sulivan and Vansittart that did not end until 1763. Sulivan had confided a passing exasperation to Clive's ears, which his Lordship and Holwell used against them both.[13] Sulivan, who could make no more claim upon this man's loyalty than could Clive, sent a letter on the subject to the Governor, which was received with hurt and alarm. Despite all Vansittart's efforts Sulivan remained sceptical of his integrity.

The rift deepened and the tone of Sulivan's text was resented, 'a vein of ill-humour running throughout the whole which is displeasing and also discouraging'.[14] Relations were only restored when Sulivan understood this misunderstanding was just what their enemies aimed for. The renewed friendship was also due to the efforts of Robert Palk.[15]

The attempts by Mir Qasim to revive the privileges that would have been his under the Mughal regime resulted in war, and yet another revolution. He seized the Seth bankers who might have financed a rising against him. Hay and Amyatt, the two Company representatives sent to remonstrate with him in May 1763, were refused all their demands. With the Nawab's confiscation of a consignment of arms and then the beheading of Amyatt in July hostilities were inevitable. On 4 July he declared war.

Company forces under Major Adams retook Monghyr, but Mir Qasim had already set out for Patna. On the way there he murdered the Seths, and then brutally massacred the Company garrison and civilian population of Patna. It was October before Major Adams retook the city, though the Nawab had fled. Mir Jafar was reinstated on 8 July, and all was restored to what it had been like following Plassey, with regard to the native administration and the

Company. Unfortunately, once more Company servants alone were exempt from taxes.[16]

What then happened in Bengal from 1763 to 1765 was only further demonstration of all that was going wrong in the sub-continent. Mir Jafar's restoration cost a donation of £375,000 to the Company's army and navy, £300,000 to the Company for costs; a total sum almost equalled by the £530,000 doled out for individual losses. Free inland trading rights were re-imposed.

Continued military operations in 1764 against the deposed Mir Qasim continued. Carnac was replaced by Major Hector Munro who arrived on the *Sulivan* with 100 Highlanders; and on 24 October 1764 he defeated the Imperial forces at Baksar.[17] It was a decisive victory. Mir Qasim escaped, but by February 1765 Munro had taken Allahbad. The ex-Nawab, in an alliance with the Marathas, was defeated in May 1765; Oudh was cleared, and some stability (at least in English eyes) was regained.

From 1763 to 1765, however, Company interests and those of the Nawab were neglected; personal objectives came before all others. Mir Jafar complained of the loss to Asians of the inland trade, the very grievance that proved the catalyst of revolt for his predecessor. Numerous opportunities for Europeans in salt and opium dealings brought enormous wealth.[18] George Dempster, a leading director, summed it up: 'Few fortunes acquired in the East will bear a very minute investigation.'[19]

In November 1765 Vansittart resigned the Presidency and was replaced by another friend of Sulivan's, John Spencer.[20] This brought no change of policy, and no improved control; although Spencer expressed his (usually negative) opinion on everything. Fortunes continued to be made.[21]

2

Although Bengal demanded much of Sulivan's time, he by no means neglected the factories in Madras, Bombay, Sumatra and China during these years. Events in Madras would determine the future of the Company in India just as much as those in Bengal. The bulk of the fighting was conducted along the Coromandel Coast; although by 1764 the threat from a combination of French forces and other support from Mysore had been stilled at Baksar. This victory prevented the very real possibility of a collapse in the Carnatic.

The strong military presence in Madras caused problems, especially disagreements between the armed forces of the Company and the Crown. Sulivan was forced to clarify the position: 'His Majesty's officers should never interfere in the promotion of our officers or meddle in any way with the management of our affairs. The Legislature alone can control the rights derived from our Charter.'[22] Yet they still clashed; and he feared their combined might was being used to further private ends; and that military commanders were manifesting imperialist tendencies.

The main task confronting Governor and Council was to restrain the Nawab's aggression towards his smaller neighbours. Maintaining peace with rival princes at Madura, Tanjore and Tulja-ji was at the heart of this. They also formulated relations with Salabat Jang, master of the Deccan, and his brother, the Nizam Ali Khan. Their other major duties were to keep both the Company and its army in funds; and supply men and materials for expeditions.

Heavy expense was involved in such an expedition to Golcanda; and in keeping the French out of Kandy. Dutch jealousy determined that delicate negotiations with its King were also required. Sulivan decided, however, that trade should be secured in those parts of Ceylon not subject to Dutch rule; and in February 1763 sent out John Dunning's opinion that the Company had a lawful right to form settlements.[23]

As always, the main concern was that provision was made for the Investment, and maintaining sufficient bullion in the Company's coffers. Each Presidency was to help the other: thus 'flowing cash' from Bengal was expected to supply Madras and China.[24] It did not always happen. Nevertheless, the Governor (Pigot followed by Palk) was to maintain contact with Spencer in Bombay, and Vansittart in Bengal, forming the third portion of the ring of command that Sulivan had worked for.

Distance and separate growth had led to a sense of independence and of indifference. Sulivan's attempts to change such attitudes brought its own backlash. His orders were increasingly regarded as peremptory and aroused barely concealed hostility.[25] Repeated attempts made to reduce the price of copper in order to break the dealers' ring; and regulating officers' 'privilege of trade' came to nothing. His demand of absolute obedience was, of course, ignored.[26] Some of his decisions stimulated trouble. Robert Orme, who was to succeed Pigot as Governor, was superseded by Palk.[27]

Initially, Sulivan's favoured policy was to maintain the traditional commerce of the Carnatic; but by 1761 a change had taken place, one not at all in line with his approach to Bengal or the Company's settlements elsewhere. This new outlook was summed up in a letter to Chatham:

> The reduction of Pondicherry has given us entire Possession of the Choromandel coast. In a commercial light the advantages can never be extensive, there are but few manufactures and no ports. The great benefit then must arise from possession of countries either by cession or usurpation, whose revenues must maintain armies and draw riches to Europe.[28]

This outlook explains the expeditions sent out among the country powers. It hearkened to the Dupleix-Clive view, yet in the same letter to Chatham he could maintain 'my ideas Sir, will be confined to our Mercantile interests.'[29]

Sulivan relied quite a lot upon personal ties to connect India House with the Madras Presidency. When he nominated Palk in November 1763 he placed a close friend in charge, one who would be attentive to his bidding.

Palk colourfully expressed the debt he owed to him: 'God almighty bless you, Mrs. Sulivan and <u>the Irish Register</u>.' The appointment can be seen as a reward. He had been angling for a seat at Ashburton, and for this had been dependent upon Palk.[30] Palk was to play a large part in Sulivan's public and private life.

Privately he amassed a large fortune and was helped in this by Sulivan, who received in return the odd cask of Madeira wine, and newspapers. He was able to maintain some form of control through this pliable lieutenant, even though executive orders were being largely ignored elsewhere.[31]

The 1756-61 war left Muhammad Ali Khan of Arcot undisputed Nawab of that territory. The 11th article in the Definitive Treaty, composed by Sulivan, confirmed this; but at times he had to remind the Nawab of where his allegiance lay.[32] The biggest problem, however, was the matter of his debts. He had become heavily indebted to the Company because of its assistance during the war and for personal expenses. Territory had been ceded and assignments granted on his revenue to many individuals, and especially to Madras Councillors. Yet he was forced to continue borrowing to pay the original debts.

At first, Sulivan was one of only a few who grasped the need to do something urgently. The liabilities worried him; as did the complications they created.[33] He was scathing about his fellow Directors - that they never read the Madras books and knew nothing of the issue.

The Nawab was made to pay, however, since it was his interests that were being defended. Thus a *jagir* (Tuinally, situated near Madras) was obtained for the Company's use, as part-payment of his dues.[34] No progress in reducing the sums was possible, however, because too many individuals had a pecuniary interest in the debts remaining unpaid. Also, since no comprehensive and reliable estimate of the Nawab's obligations existed, a solution was not possible. Sulivan could only pass the problem on.

3

It was natural that he should treat Bombay with special regard after so many years of service there; and so many of his friends, like Hough and Spencer still in the Presidency was a spur to his interest. Charles Crommelin, Governor from 1761, was not particularly attached to him, but a coldness grew only as Sulivan's ties with Spencer developed.[35]

Sulivan had done a great deal to ensure good government and sound commercial organisation at Bombay. Although considered a backwater, the settlement demanded a great deal in military provisions from the other Presidencies for war costs, disruption to trade and Maratha raids. Also, its defence had to be maintained because the security of all the Company settlements in India depended ultimately upon control of the Malabar Coast.

He demanded, nevertheless, that Company servants cut back and stop squandering precious financial resources. Smuggling was to be investigated; better-ordered accounts kept; costs and wages cut – especially Crommelin's.

The accusation that he had Bombay 'in his pocket', is probably justified; but he deserved one oasis of seeming normality. Bombay spoke of custom and tradition, of barter and of control from Leadenhall Street. He asked for little else.[36]

4

His responsibilities also encompassed interests in the East Indies archipelago and in China. The settlements included Fort Marlborough, Bencoolen and Gombroon, all on the island of Sumatra; and Canton on the Chinese mainland. He kept a keen eye on the China trade, stipulating that it had to be 'plentifully supplied' by both Madras and Bengal.[37] This concern is best illustrated in an address to the *Tsen tou* (or Viceroy) of Canton, who was in charge of Chinese territory around and including Canton. He was a principal Governor, and the Chinese Emperor's representative for Kwantung and Kiangsi.

Sulivan feared the loss of a hundred year old privilege to trade; and of the Company being superseded by the French or Dutch. The Chinese overlord (or *Hsan-fu*) was displeased at the level of misbehaviour among Company merchants. In reply to a charge of fraud, Sulivan maintained in defence that the Company's representatives only desired redress against severe trade restrictions. He suggested a variety of expedients to settle the dispute. In view of the continuance of trade, he was evidently successful.

In Sumatra the need, as always, was to maintain, a brisk trade. The Company was involved in buying and selling opium, silver, timber and pepper. Sumatra also dealt extensively in slaves. Sulivan's personal views regarding this unforgivable trade in human lives does not appear in any of his correspondence. His orders and decisions can only be regarded, therefore, in a purely business-related sense, and in accord with the morality of his age.

East Indiamen were directed to Madagascar and the Guinea Coast to purchase slaves for delivery at Fort Marlborough. Instructions were precise. The slave owners received £15 for each human being. Two thirds of those seized were to be males aged 15 to 40; one third females aged 15 to 25. Boys and girls aged 10 to 15 were to be reckoned on the basis that two of them were the equivalent of one male.

The Captain and Chief Mate of each ship received 20 shillings for each slave taken on board; and a further 20 shillings was paid to each of them (and the surgeon) on safe delivery at Fort Marlborough. The Company's ship the *Royal George* (400 tons), its Captain a Nicholas Skottowe, was used for this type of traffic. In 1764 she was, 'despatched to the Guinea Coast to procure slaves for the Sumatra settlements'.[38]

In May 1762 Sulivan intimated that he 'intended to move the Court to take off the dependency of the Company's important Settlement in the West Coast of Sumatra from the Presidency of Fort St. George'.[39] He proceeded to use examples of what he had created elsewhere, especially in Bombay, as blueprints for the new Presidency at Fort Marlborough; and laid down the settlement's complete organisation. Rules, regulations and the numbers of employees required were all settled.[40]

Despite Dutch opposition, he was determined to make the Indonesian settlements a success. He refused an application from Shelburne, for a change of position for his friend, Alexander Hall, who wanted away from the unhealthy Bencoolen climate. Sulivan stressed his reliance on someone of Hall's ability, who knew the people and their manners, 'to raise these settlements to the height I hope to see them'.[41]

The Sumatra settlements desperately needed defence against overwhelming Dutch power. Holland had assisted French destruction of Bencoolen, Gombroon and Fort Marlborough in 1760. The French had then given the factories to the Dutch, who promptly destroyed all fortifications. In 1763 Sulivan expressed satisfaction at their resettlement. The Dutch were also to be compelled to hand back the two factories at Natal and Tapanuli.

The Dutch and French continued to stir trouble, such as among the Chinese inhabitants; so he sought assistance from Government, asking for men-of-war and troops. He received none.[42] When two French ships cruised off Sumatra in the 1761-2 period, he had to appoint Admiral Stevens to guard the area. In February 1762 he sent a letter to Bute asking whether it would be wise to send off the Bencoolen ships considering the state of war and the paucity of English forces, and appealed for Royal Navy protection. Yet again no action was taken.

Nevertheless, in the 1762-3 period, penetration of the archipelago continued, and was marked, in particular, by the expeditions of Alexander Dalrymple to the north coast of Borneo. In 1762 he made a treaty with the Sultan of the island of Sulu.[43] Dalrymple was then criticised by Sulivan for being too independent in negotiating with the Sultan. The Dutch, already bristling at the strong British presence in Sumatra, took exception to the Sulu expedition, and sent out a force to 'dislodge whoever might be there'.[44] Sulivan informed Palk that he wanted the Sumatra settlements protected.

Like its predecessors, the Grenville Ministry ignored the request made in 1763 by the Company's Secret Committee (comprising Dorrien, Sulivan, and Amyand) for protection against Dutch and French attacks. Then in February 1764, a second application by this committee was also rejected. Gaining intelligence of Dutch designs against the new settlement at Sulu; and of their plans to disrupt the new passage found round the Philippines to China, once more two ships-of-the-line were requested. Again this was refused, despite continued French and Dutch threats. This level of fear and uncertainty was to remain, despite such efforts; and following Sulivan's exit from the executive in 1765, the archipelago was almost totally neglected.

5

Apart from dealing with troubles from abroad as they arrived on his doorstep, Sulivan was responsible for fashioning the road ahead. His prime commission, as Chairman or leading Director, was always to increase efficiency, bringing a greater volume of trade and thus larger profits. Nothing was to interfere with this design. In the Presidencies, ensuring the Investment for the next ships took precedence over all other things; just as every ship hired in England was of the utmost importance. Financial considerations always guided his course of action.

Securing his objectives, however, depended upon dominance at India House, upon those he chose to fill the leading positions overseas, and his methods. His aims also had to be attainable. His normal course of action was to send a full exposition of requirements to the settlement concerned. This was the thinking behind his '*Observations on the Bengal Establishment…,*' inserted into the General Letters despatched to every Presidency. Detailed statements were included in his private correspondence, supplementing the directions given in the General Letters.[45]

His predicament was that although circumstances might have changed, with no precedent he must pursue the traditional mercantilist route both inherited and favoured. Also, after 1757 and the revolutionary transfer of power, agreement had also to be reached with any Indian prince who had power over the Company's material goods, because it had become a feudal vassal with territories. He thought it possible to provide adequate supervision and control because in theory he was able to see the whole picture. His vision was to bring into existence a perfectly run organisation, one that would last throughout his life and beyond; and he set out by attempting to define the role of the Company following Plassey.

Every plan for India was centred on Bengal; and he spent immense time and effort in planning more efficient forms of government for it. The other settlements were only peripheral. His policy for Bengal was: 'The security of their present possessions and privileges, the preservation of peace, maintenance of the Nawab and prevention of border raids.'[46] However, from the start, despite a fundamental need to plan ahead he encountered antagonism, in both India House and the Presidencies.

The Company being in India solely to barter and carry goods to and from England was guaranteed by Charter, which also maintained its independence. The question being asked was whether power over so big an area, and one that involved territorial possessions, could be left to an assembly of shareholders.[47] He reflected upon this in 1761, four years after Plassey:

> It is extremely easy to parcel out upon paper, kingdoms that are infinitely larger than Great Britain, but to carry such schemes into execution might prove an arduous task, even to government; surely then too bold and imprudent for a trading Company.[48]

In other words, he still adhered to the commerce-only policy that dated from 1757. He rested satisfied with this, plus the limited territories ceded in Bengal, and informed Chatham, 'my ideas Sir, will be confined to our Mercantile interests.'[49]

Sulivan had enunciated his resolve not to endanger the commercial foundation of the Company when in 1759 he restrained it from entering into a territorial role by rejecting the offer of the *Diwani*. He kept to this aim: the Company was to function as a trading organisation.[50] Even after the events of 1757, 1760 and 1763, when it was obvious the English no longer relied on the native government and that they themselves compelled obedience, he would not change. He maintained the policy of not accepting the *Diwani*, and Vansittart was warned against this in 1764.

Over the years, however, he had to use ever more forceful directives to have his orders fulfilled. He was particularly angered at continued defiance and neglect of his orders to concentrate on trade, cut military costs and not interfere in internal struggles. Even though he came to see that his former rigid views had to be loosened, and indeed were by 1763, he still could not contemplate full-blooded territorial aggrandisement in every theatre. The danger to the Charter was too acute.

In 1761 he planned to regain the initiative abroad, particularly in Bengal. The 'General Letter to the Governor for the Time being of Fort William', dated 6 May 1761, demonstrates as much, with strict instructions on naval and judicial matters. He placed a priority on the Investment and upon efficient management. Customs dues were to be paid; with an improved conduct and bearing among officers. Better relations were needed among the Presidencies. These enjoyed only limited success; although Bengal purchases grew from £350,000 per annum in the early 1760s to £1 million in 1770, and to more than that in the 1770s.

That same year, he sensibly used Palk to change direction in the Madras Presidency, from a purely commercial strategy to one that embraced limited territorial ambitions. It was a course partly dictated by hostile native powers, by French intrigue, and by the rather limited trading opportunities available.

Between 1760 and 1763, the direction in which events turned in Bengal and the Carnatic; and the changed circumstances flowing from war and protection of sea routes forced him into new channels of thought. Only Bombay could be treated in the old familiar 'trade not conquest' way; but even there, strategic requirements began to superimpose upon traditional commercial policy. In Bengal, however, he merely wanted to trade as before; and to draw the territorial revenues and customs dues from the new limited area granted around Bengal, but no more. Such demarcation required strict regulation and it became increasingly impossible to curb ambition, acquisitive tendencies and autonomous inclinations, despite severe condemnation.[51]

Sulivan had no wish for conquest. He neither wanted, nor thought it proper to create subject peoples and then legislate for them, but could not be rid of this problem. Whether western concepts of government should be introduced in India was something he could not decide upon. The initiative for subjugation, in this period, always came from those abroad; although, apart from Clive, there was little idea at first of a systematic design for acquiring territory. Most Company servants agreed that this was not in its best interests. But neither was there any effective restraint upon them from superiors abroad. Directives and censures from India House were circumvented or ignored with shattering effect.

Until 1761 and decreasingly up to 1765, Sulivan still denied Dupleix's doctrine that only revenues derived from possession of territory would 'maintain armies and draw riches to Europe.' He said in 1761, 'if I could not clearly confute his reasoning...that no trading company can support itself unless they adopt similar methods...I should wish our trade to India at an end'.[52]

His view was a reflection of a mercantilist frame of mind under pressure from *laissez-faire* ideas, and endangered by the accretion of territory. He was certain the Company generated sufficient impetus to satisfy the needs of India's internal commerce; that it could create surplus wealth for growth, reinvestment and dividend, over and above costs. Such beliefs were an echo of the seventeenth century belief that: 'Profit not grandeur is our end in trading.'[53] The opposite view, espoused by Clive then and later, was summed up in a quote by Gerald Aungier: 'The times now require you to manage your general commerce with your sword in your hands', that is, sword first, commerce afterwards.[54] Sulivan struggled in vain to keep the sword as the handmaiden of commerce.

In the sub-continent he was utterly reliant on the Governor and Council in each Presidency to promulgate his wishes. The Governors were particularly important. Yet events took a line of their own despite a constant stream of directions promulgated by handpicked men, like Vansittart followed by John Spencer in Bengal; Pigot and Palk in Madras. Sumatra and China were ancillary to his overall design, but of importance in that they served as windows upon the Dutch; and gave finger-holds in potentially lucrative markets.

These Governors and some Councillors, like Hastings, tried to comply with his policy of a limited interference in country matters and minimum involvement in Indian politics. Nevertheless, even they began to listen less and less to what their employers had to say. The reality of life forced a different approach from that wished for at Leadenhall. Governors continued to be involved in illegitimate trade and in the receipt of presents. The temptation of accruing great wealth affected everyone, in every Council.

Sulivan tried to take temptation out of the way of the Governors through larger emoluments, but to little effect. In complaining that the 24,000 rupees commission he received from trade was not enough, Spencer illustrates the extent of the problem. He also echoed the feelings of his predecessor.[55] Such concern for their pockets by employees at the very summit of their careers portrayed the change in attitude wrought, and the need for adequate official remuneration. However, the attraction of easily acquired riches would maintain its allurement well into the future.

As all this became clear to Sulivan, the leading servants were deemed to lack personal clean-handedness. He went too far in his expectations, given the morality of the times and the personal needs driving the men involved. Nevertheless, Vansittart (then Spencer) made some effort to follow his dictate where possible; activities were confined to commerce and the administration of the territories granted to the Company in 1757 and then by the various revolutions. In Madras, Governors Pigot and Palk likewise deviated little from what Sulivan required him to do; and Crommelin in Bombay, felt it was in his best interests to do so too.

Unfortunately for them, the Governors were hemmed in too much. Sulivan was extremely rigorous with instructions and detailed in his answers to each clause in the Despatches. There was little room left to manoeuvre if orders were obeyed to the letter. The enormous bulk of material sifted through, and answered by him, reflects the restrictions placed upon his acolytes, and the limited role he expected them to fill when faced with his direct observations. Bombay really had to increase revenue from the farms; Bengal was advised to base the proposed Presidency at Scindy (Ceylon) on the Bombay model. Madras was warned that too much 'private' cotton was being sent to China; and so it went on.[56]

Yet even although each settlement was swamped with orders and advice, he demanded strict control by strong men over unruly servants harbouring a predilection for independent action. The Governors were also expected to counter moves by hostile country powers. It is a pity these men were asked to do the unpalatable and impossible: be servile to him while being all powerful in each Presidency. All in charge found it impossible to stick to a policy of non-intervention. Yet a new, more dynamic role was needed between the Directors in London and the Governors and Councils.

In Bengal, the appointment of Vansittart had seemed at first to guarantee Sulivan continued control, and Clive's backing for his successor had helped.[57] Friends were sent out to be of assistance, while enemies like Sumner, Maguire and Carling Smith were on their way to England. Regrettably the new men would also succumb to the temptation of easy pickings.

In Vansittart he also made a mistake. He held a high, yet unsubstantiated, opinion of him: 'From his character he is high in my esteem and from his virtues and abilities I expect that lawless settlement of Calcutta will be reformed to decency and order.'[58] In fact, Vansittart proved rather weak; and Sulivan was not entirely happy about the deposition of Mir Jafar, or his friend's moneymaking schemes.

The trouble was Sulivan did not feel comfortable giving more authority to his Governors, always afraid of signs of irresponsibility and self-government. He did not trust anyone; and was uncertain of what had developed. In April and again in September 1762 Vansittart sought more authority. A third request was sent in the form of a reminder in October. But in December the Governor still awaited explicit directions. He called in vain, because Sulivan and his fellows could not give him what they could not envisage, and were fearful of even making a stab at.

Spencer echoed Vansittart's plea, while commenting that extraordinary powers could create a dangerous precedent. Eventually, however, both became certain that the policies they were trying to implement went against forces that were too powerful to dam. The Company had to govern or abstain completely from involvement in Indian affairs. The latter path they considered impractical; and were stuck, therefore, in the position of judging, in an arbitrary manner, how far their own jurisdiction stretched.

In the end there was a loss of control. But in Bengal, blame cannot be laid solely at Vansittart's feet. He had only one vote, and all decisions were made by the Governor in Council. Most men under him were quite irresponsible, and gave no loyalty or cooperation. They were eager to exploit the freedom of action allowed by the new situation. In Madras, most Councillors were intent on becoming the Nawab's creditors.

Sulivan and others in the executive were not helped by having no clear picture of ongoing events. It was impossible to work out in advance what might happen. Deposition of Mir Jafar in 1760, and then of Mir Qasim in 1763 brought additional money and territory, but this camouflaged the true state of affairs. Ostensible gains in Bengal soothed rank and file Proprietors, creating a false rosy picture, just when the economic reality was being recognized by Company leaders as desperate.

It was not surprising that a sense of independence and indifference to India House grew. Company officials were civil administrators, not trained government officials; and low salaries drew them further into clandestine activities, and away from the Company and authority. There was little wish to be regulated from London. This feeling and outlook is reflected in the boom in private trade; and more 'country' ships being engaged in the coastal trade.

Although limited amounts of trading privileges were considered right and proper, to top up the miserable Company pay, it had all gone too far. Indian traders now wooed the lower ranks of Writers and Factors as well as Senior Merchants and Council members. Evasion of customs dues, and misuse of the *Dastak* continued; adventurers were illicitly involved in the internal trade in salt, grain, bullocks, betel-nut and tobacco. Secret partnerships existed with native merchants; money was loaned to rulers and to the Company.

Sulivan pursued those he considered personal opponents and hostile to his Governors and the Company. His aim was to demonstrate support, and show that the Direction was still all powerful. Carnac, Johnstone, Hay, Batson and Watts, for example, all senior Councillors at Calcutta, were dismissed. The authority of the Directors was being minimised, however, because many dismissals were overturned later. John Johnstone secured his reinstatement by a vote of the Court of Proprietors. In this way, command continued to slip away; private interest took over from public concern. Thereafter, the studied indifference paid to instructions and the contempt shown accredited representatives was all too apparent.

When Sulivan left the Direction in 1765 the objective of re-establishing control over all the Presidencies, and in particular Bengal, was not achieved. He had discerned, however, that he must cancel out the lure of easily made money. He strained to provide 'noble and exclusive emoluments for the Company's senior servants'; particularly for the man at the top, and tried hard to put the Governor beyond pecuniary interest.[59] Vansittart was granted two and a half per cent commission on all money coming into the Company's accounts in Bengal.[60]

His policy of non-interference, however, ran into trouble. In Spencer's view the Direction would have to take over eventually, because in 1764 governing requirements and the Company's involvement were already nearly blended. Also, to continue with a mercantile policy limiting Governor and Council duties to trade, and the preservation of existing territory was well nigh unworkable. Sulivan's view, however, was that he supervised a Company with a limited fiscal capacity, and he had to check expansion. He also believed that finding a solution to the Bengal troubles would put the whole organisation back on an even keel. All plans, therefore, were subordinated to this; but with the inaccurate data supplied by Clive it had no hope of success.

In the end, it was not possible to keep Company servants in check; deal with latent independence symptoms or head off the cash crises that had led to the revolutions of 1760 and 1763 – all to the accompaniment of general and local wars. His directives emphasising avoidance were just too idealistic in the aftermath of conquest. Unhappily for him, the reluctance to go forward was unable to withstand 'the many forces that sought constantly to draw the Company in deeper and deeper'.[61]

6

Feuds and
Peace Treaties
1757-1763

1

It is absorbing to think that parallel with everything else that had to be cared for during these years, Sulivan was forced to fight for his political life. The struggle that developed with Clive for control of the Company was to have a remarkable impact on the future course of events. It was one of the most engrossing contests on record; the colour and furore that surrounded the protagonists has lent the whole a sense of spectacle. It is almost the only portion of Sulivan's long life that is generally known; and even that has been severely distorted. The aim here is to give a more balanced view of what happened.

It was a bitter clash, and coloured their lives to a degree that neither man could have anticipated; and would dog their steps until death. India House was the main, but not the only arena in which the fight for primacy was played out. Members of Parliament and ministerial figures would be involved as well. The followers of both maintained a ferocious hostility that can be felt echoing through the Impeachment of Warren Hastings.

It ensnared and cut-across everything else: business, politics and patronage; and in its first phase coloured the negotiations ending the Seven Years War. The extreme denunciations that issued from either camp, expressed in the press and in pamphlets, underlined the extent to which the Company was divided. As well as intensifying faction inside India House and Parliament, the rivalry deepened discord and confusion in India, sucking in everyone who had an interest in Indian affairs. Sides were chosen, and numerous changes of alliance continued throughout the struggle.

The Company was such an integral part of the London money market and of the public credit system that the feud even made its mark upon the nation's finances. In many ways it helped create the circumstances that led to the Company being swallowed by the State. A connection can he made from these events through to the Parliamentary enquiry of 1766-7; and from thence to North's Regulating Act of 1773.

Their opinions upon how the Company should develop in the future might be incompatible; but the outcome of their struggle would shape the way ahead in India until 1773. The 'Dual System' used by Clive after accepting the *Diwani* in 1765 was in may ways like a compromise between trade (Sulivan) and conquest (Clive).

As the quarrel advanced, it became increasingly difficult to separate wilfulness from principle. They were easy bedfellows. Perhaps the curious fact that both were disposed to quoting Alexander Pope tells something of their natures; and (continuing the literary parallels) they seem almost 'star-crossed' in the manner in which their destinies entwined. Each was at the pinnacle of his career when they clashed, which in both cases was set firmly within the East India Company. Both were ambitious and self-made, with dominating personalities. One was sovereign in Bengal; the other monarch over all the Company's operations. Each saw himself as superior to any other in the organisation; and was willing to fight to retain the prestige associated with being the leading force.

However, even when flushed with conquest, Clive was still a Company servant, and as such had to report to the Court of Directors, then under Sulivan's control. That they would collide seems certain, since Clive could not bear to be thwarted in his purpose; and viewed opinions opposite to his own with great suspicion. Sulivan was equally stubborn, though able to listen to others.

Yet strangely, whereas the name of Clive has lived, indeed, has been dwelt upon, time has not been so kind to Sulivan. It took the two of them to make a quarrel, yet he seems to have become invisible. Mervyn-Davies put forward probably the first positive statement emphasising his significance: 'He (Sulivan) was, during the most critical years in its history the uncrowned king of the East India Company.'[1]

The general approach among Clive's many biographers has been to portray Sulivan as jealous of the great man's success and aimed to bring about his downfall. Dodwell's depiction of him as 'a man without an idea in advance of the low level of his time' is both a false and demeaning estimation. His personal qualities and the policies he proposed have been completely ignored, if recognized in the first place.[2] Sulivan's influence was as important as Clive's, and in the eyes of most contemporaries with knowledge of Company, City, and political affairs, much greater.

The struggle really sprang from Sulivan's domination of the Company. He was regarded with a mixture of respect and jealousy. The jealousy persisted, the more so because of his very success. The autocratic tenor he developed helped stir feelings of resentment. The tone of the General Letters cut deep; and there were many eager to stir trouble. At first Sulivan felt impervious to all this. He was fortunate in being able to add to his impressive armoury an unequalled grasp of Company politics. He knew his way around the labyrinth of tangled interests and felt no fear.

A new development accompanied his appearance as Company leader, old and new-found money was used to buy Company stock, not just for its gilt-edged intrinsic worth, but because of its accompanying votes. Large amounts were split into £500 blocks for this purpose. Many who bought stock did so only to oppose Sulivan. They had no interest or understanding of Indian affairs, of how to reform the administration in India or of furthering the Company's business interests. India Stock came to be regarded as a 'stake' in the scramble for wealth. Riches could come via the stock market; through prime jobs abroad, or contracts at home. It was bought to manipulate proceedings at India House and to further personal interests. Attention was paid to financial circles where large sums of money necessary for its purchase for use at elections could be found.

Following Plassey, the insolence and insubordination employed by a clutch of Bengal servants, most of them censured or sacked by Sulivan, began transferring to London. These returned servants joined opponents of his dating from the 1758 election, and everything with which he was concerned was criticised: leadership, management of the important Committees, and the patronage he controlled. They congregated in the General Court of Proprietors. This was the supreme political body; and until changed in 1784, could override any decision of the Directors. The very number of special General Courts now held outside the regular quarterly meetings (which had to be called by a quorum of nine Proprietors) signified the growing antagonism and division.

Sulivan and his supporters, known as the 'Sulivanites' or 'Bombay Squad', had filled the Court of Proprietors from around 1755. Now, with the influx of disgruntled, rich senior servants, who came to be known as 'The Bengal Squad', the 'Indian' interest was split. Soon, dissension was also heard in the Court of Directors as well as the Proprietors Court. These new voices acted as the catalyst for much that was to follow; and set the acrimonious tone.

Jealousy and commitment led to parties becoming entrenched. The Courts and committees became noisy, ill-tempered political arenas where disagreements were aired. The annual April election became a showdown, and only then was it possible to know anyone's true interest. It was also from here that the shrewd politicians in the Company, like Sulivan, built their plans of campaign for the following year.

Collectively these Courts and Committees (such as that of treasury, shipping and correspondence) were where the major interests now tested each other. The Committee of Correspondence became a political arena; while the Committee of Treasury gave ammunition and the means by which executives could get at the truth, if properly understood. However, only a small group of Directors knew the reality about anything. Needless to say, Sulivan was one of them.

The attack on him targeted the Secret Committee, the strongest executive instrument. Its formal existence as a piece of administrative machinery had been developed by him because of the call for confidentiality during the war, and the need to re-establish firm control over the settlements in India. Used increasingly from 1757 onwards, it became a vehicle for application of the Company's full weight and authority. By means of this committee, it was easier for three or four men at India House to handle all the essentially secret business in a time of national and Company danger.[3]

It attended to delicate matters as they arose; many were military, others were political in nature. Members would wait upon ministry regarding items such as naval protection; or were engrossed in negotiations, such as in the peace terms concluding the Seven Years War. The Committee almost always incorporated the two 'Chairs.' Invariably, Sulivan was to be found there. Unfortunately, a greater personal attack than he could have foretold accompanied its use. His enemies accused him of exercising exorbitant power through this channel; alleging that it had become a cabinet council where everything was prepared for the Directors to sign rather than approve.

The factions fought for power, prestige and the right to dispense patronage, the only secure road to continued success. Loyalties became strained, cynicism and distrust reigned supreme. Just as in 1758, he was blamed for showing partiality in return for the promise of votes at annual elections. Newspapers, broadsides and pamphlets were full of scurrilous attacks. He was the one to approach, it was alleged, because he could corruptly 'influence how votes would be swung'.[4]

As the dispute grew, a section of the general public was awakened to eastern matters. There was a feeling that India should be the nation's affair, not that of a private company. Among a few there was acknowledgment of her separate identity and concern over her despoliation. There was genuine resentment too, at the sordid and petty pursuit of gain at the Company's expense; and annoyance with the mushrooming political interests at India House. Company servants, home and abroad, were portrayed as despoilers and parasites. Unfortunately, lust for wealth from the Indies affected even more of the public, many of them now deliberately associating with the Company and its affairs. Greed and the prospect of untold riches, created a bad public image. This was the background to the feud proper.

2

Their separate views appeared immediately after Plassey, grew rapidly after Clive's return in 1760, reaching a decisive point on 17 February 1763. Yet, it all began so well. On 20 February 1758 Sulivan wrote to Clive offering his congratulations following the success at Plassey. He urged him to stay and consolidate the government of Bengal and put the 'noble colony beyond the reach of danger'. It was a warm letter, full of praise.[5] A few weeks later he became Chairman. Clive expressed his personal satisfaction at Sulivan filling the Chair in his reply on 30 December 1758. He also directed his family and agents to support him at future elections; even to the extent of employing his funds.[6] He expected great things from Sulivan.[7]

This letter of 30 December from Clive was very rare; nothing like it was ever repeated to Sulivan. He seemed to think the Chairman's view of things would be exactly the same as his own; and the display of his nature and stance throughout the manuscript was most revealing. It indicated how he envisaged the future in India; and the extent to which the despised the indigenous population.

In fact, if Clive had deliberately sought a breach with Sulivan he could not have written a letter better calculated to cause one. Racialist overtones were predominant, advocacy of even more military plundering, with an army of occupation and government by the sword. The fear and distrust that had accompanied the Company's first voyagers to India lay behind this attitude. It was to be answered by creation of the same fear and distrust in native minds.[8]

Sulivan replied to this communication in a cool, rather detached way.[9] Yet, his humanitarian, as well as commercial, instincts must have been shocked at the language of conquest and expansion. He was never reconciled then, or ever to a policy based on blatant force and favoured persuasion and bureaucratic control; might was to be kept ready in the background. He comprehended a growing desire for some sort of justice for the peoples of India – to be called forth later by Edmund Burke at the Bar of the House of Commons. This was never equalled by Clive.

Clive mirrored another feeling spreading among Britons, the need to expand, to seize territory and riches; that if they did not do so they were weak or fools, or both; that another state would certainly do so. Like Dupleix, Clive wanted to exploit at once what he had gained by conquest. He maintained that 'Force only can preserve and prevent acquisitions in the face of the Mussulman's lack of gratitude, narrow conception and method based on everything by treachery rather than force.' He foresaw further conquest when the 'luxurious, ignorant and cowardly' nature of the 'Moors and Gentoos' was considered.[10]

It was his opinion that only a strong and commanding military power could give continued stability: 'Peace…must be made sword in hand in this country if we mean to preserve our possessions.'[11] In many ways he was merely furthering principles laid down earlier by Sir Thomas Roe, that peaceful co-existence was impossible. The development from factory to fort, he argued, was a defensive necessity, backed-up by the power of maritime traders to enforce their demands at sea. Relationships with locals built on fear could only continue on the basis of fear.

Clive also perceived the importance of placing control in India, especially military authority, in the hands of one man. He did not yet know that this was, and remained, one of Sulivan's objectives; albeit that the man chosen would still come under the control of the Direction, and of himself.

By 1760 Clive knew that he and Sulivan held divergent views. He thought Sulivan's policy of non-involvement and concentration on commerce impracticable, but nevertheless promised to comply.[12] At this stage, he only paid lip-service to what came from London. Later it was common knowledge how much their policies differed.[13]

Clive's letter of 30 December helped determine Sulivan's future attitude and approach to the hero of Plassey. Clearly, the great man did not really know his titular employer; but more revealing was his lack of prudence in expressing views without knowing how they would be accepted. It did not seem to occur to him that Sulivan might not want territorial acquisitions. He must have thought it inconceivable that the Chairman could refuse such a rich prize. Sulivan, on the other hand, revealed that he was cautious; that he wanted no involvement and envisaged a mutual regard between Briton and Indian at the point of commercial contact. He would agree to change only after extensive tests; and usually only after unavoidable dictates demanded these be made.

3

For some time after Clive's return to England in 1760 Sulivan did not conceive of him as a serious rival for that power over affairs that he relished so much. While Clive remained in India he had regarded him as inferior to himself, but first in command on the spot. Clive had still to answer to him, and only in times of dire emergency, such as war, was he to be answerable to nobody. Clive could never really accept such a role; but it was only in the run-up to the hero's return that Sulivan realised master–servant restraints no longer applied.

Clive's eulogisers viewed Sulivan as being fearful and envious of their hero. This was not the case. Even a minimum understanding of his power and prestige reveals that the Company's chief executive had no need to feel jealous of a soldier who had just won a battle; indeed he was very happy about it. To Sulivan it would have been inconceivable that his position was at risk with Clive's return. He was too deeply involved in London politics to be susceptible to any danger. He had more pressing problems.

Unfortunately, Clive's letter of 30 December 1758 was written a bare two months after the Company's General Letter to Bengal, dated 1 November 1758, which expressed critical views that were very definitely Sulivan's. The letters crossed each other. The severity of the criticism, which appeared to include Clive, and cutting tone of the despatch was dictated by concern over mounting costs.

The crossing of these letters meant Clive became aware of Sulivan's sentiments just after he had bared his soul. Sulivan's confidence too was shaken by what he regarded as betrayal by the servants he had trusted. The scenario in Bengal was quite unlike the one envisaged from the figures Clive had given him. To make matters worse, even before the arrival of Clive's letter, full of camaraderie, Sulivan had despatched yet another General Letter, on 23 March 1759, which was also acid and bitter. Thus, Clive received two severe jolts, when he had sent only friendship. It was a crossing of letters so contrasting that neither would have written in the manner he did if each had received the other's letter first.

The second letter condemned everyone in Council, including Clive, although Sulivan later tried to maintain this had not been intended. He faced the spectre of a credit crisis towards which there was indifference in India; Clive alone had drawn bills upon the Company amounting to approximately £40,000. Moreover, Sulivan was involved, having participated on the understanding that Bengal had wealth enough. In a sense, he had been made a party to things. The dam burst and he poured out his frustration and indignation. Accusations of extravagance and disregard for the Company piled one upon the other, as the ending indicates:

> In short…you seem to have acted like men divested of your understanding…If contrary…to our expectations, your conduct should not be entirely reformed we must then be under indispensable necessity of doing ourselves justice.[14]

In a letter to Chatham on 7 January 1759 (eight days after the one to Sulivan) Clive developed the views that were so wounding to the Company. He urged the annexation of all that had been gained in India, and advocated that the nation should declare its sovereignty over the new territories. British rule in Bengal should be extended as opportunities offered: 'So large a sovereignty may possibly be an object too extensive for a mercantile company; and it is to be feared they are not themselves able, without their nation's assistance, to maintain so wide a dominion.'[15] He would also have remembered that the offer of the *Diwani* from Shah Alam had been rejected by the Sulivan-dominated Direction.

He was aware that this letter would eventually reach his employers, yet seemed able to bypass the Company's need to exist as a commercial organisation. He appeared to expect no obstacles to the Company handing everything over to the state; and did not seem to realize that they could not be so disinterested as to surrender a possible income of some £2 million per annum; and all because of their alleged inability to run things properly – even if that might be true.

It must have been even more galling that the proposal came from a covenanted servant. Clive was certainly not empowered to suggest or make a present of anything that belonged to the Company. To Sulivan it must have appeared that he was contemptuous of their executive prowess; and ready to betray every effort to guard chartered rights from encroachment by the crown.[16] Cost and inadequate knowledge, among other factors, made Chatham turned down Clive's suggestion.

Sulivan, meanwhile, was resisting ministerial pressure to pay back a large part of Company borrowings. He also harboured suspicions of self-seeking servants, Clive included. He was dismayed at military expenses. Clive's predicament was different, he had been publicly 'spanked' by the two General Letters, and seen to be chastised. He had lost face.[17]

These two men, who followed vastly different approaches to the future development of the Company in India, had found each other out. To Clive's mind, a conqueror could never relinquish his gains. Also, his touchstone was the England he knew. Sulivan opposed Clive's way forward; was alarmed at the way he had gone about things; and was shocked that he was oblivious of the hurt and resentment engendered. The Chairman begrudged such blind disregard and was concerned at Clive's lack of tact. He had to ask himself what the man was doing in other spheres if this was his approach.

The struggle was much deeper, therefore, than just expressing ideas of territorial acquisition versus commercial enterprise. Clive was suspected of not merely holding a contrary view, but was actually scheming against the Company – his employer; and advocating surrender of its possessions. He was also displaying an independence of mind that signified trouble in the future.

While to Clive there was a world to be won, practical reasons dictated to Sulivan that additional territories had to be rejected. So long as the Company did not become a major territorial power it was safe for a while behind the shield of its charter. In the 1758-1765 period the State, as Chatham confirmed, did not want to shoulder the costs. The Company, as Sulivan never tired of maintaining, could not afford to voyage upon a course that in his opinion was the wrong one.

Both men were greatly annoyed at the letters they received – Sulivan's worst fears being confirmed when he got wind of Clive's letter to Chatham. The Directors' savage despatch of 23 March 1759 and its precursor thoroughly traumatized Clive and his colleagues. The great man was knocked out of his stride and the communication drew an immediate response, contained in the 'infamous' General Letter to the Court of Directors of 29 December 1759. The signatories proceeded to write in a fashion that aped in tone the despatches that had so incensed them: 'Permit us to say, that the diction of your letter is most unworthy of yourselves and us, in whatever relation considered, either as masters to servants, or gentlemen to gentlemen.'[18]

It was a grossly insulting letter for the Board in Calcutta to send to the Directors of the Company that employed them. Sulivan was incensed. Similar phrases to servants had been used on numerous occasions. Never had such language been received in return. It signified a challenge that could not go unanswered. At the head of that challenge stood Clive.

Clive's eulogisers maintain that the General Letter was specifically aimed at Sulivan who they all knew to be in charge at India House. Perhaps the Council members were justified in feeling offended at the severity of the allegations, but it was a different thing to reply in like kind. Besides, by mid-1759 Clive was aware of the Company's difficulties, being kept informed by Walsh. It is possible that he made a mistake in what he did, and only the smart from Sulivan's bitter recriminations made him do it. He was perhaps too hasty in putting his name to something at least partly concocted by Holwell, a man he knew disliked Sulivan, and who understood exactly how to get under the Chairman's skin.

It is still not certain who wrote this reply; yet Clive had made a fortune and a reputation and he was quitting India anyway. To all intents and purposes, he had 'wearied of his employers and of Bengal', and was 'determined to throw up the service'. This, and alleged ill-treatment by the Directors, was the substance of his address to the European inhabitants of Calcutta before his departure.[19]

This 'infamous' letter was the last despatch to the Company before he left for England in 1760. It reached London the day before the regular quarterly meeting of the Court of Proprietors, at which, as fate would have it, he, together with Vice-Admiral Pocock and Colonel Stringer Lawrence, were to receive the thanks of the Company for their services. Consequently, it was January 1761 before all who signed the despatch were dismissed; with the exception of Clive.

Sulivan was then criticised for the removal of these men. It was certainly his work, even though he was out of the Direction by rotation. He had made a major blunder, however, in turning a blind eye to Clive's participation. The flimsy excuse that not one of the charges was intended for him, and were in response to negligence prior to his being connected with Bengal affairs, simply does not stand up. The truth was that Sulivan felt he was too powerful to treat in the same manner as his fellow signatories; and wished to avoid the storm such a criticism would evoke with the hero of the hour present and being lauded in London. It was probably his biggest mistake.

The hurt felt from these letters and despatches marked a decisive shift in attitudes. Clive's sentiments are expressed in a letter written later to Vansittart: 'Sulivan…could never forgive the Bengal letter.'[20] But it was probably Clive's lack of care for the Company that provoked Sulivan the most. The other (dismissed) signatories eventually transferred themselves to England. Others Sulivan had either sent home or exposed returned with real or pretended reason to dislike him, such as John Johnstone. More were to be added.

The 'Bengal Squad' they joined was now dedicated solely to bringing the Irishman down. The group attacked his integrity as well as his leadership. Most had been followers of Clive in Bengal; they continued this allegiance. The Court of Proprietors reverberated with incessant, virulent harassment. That Sulivan was both roused and wounded is reflected in a comment to Sir Eyre Coote: 'The ungrateful wretches, late of Bengal have hurt my temper.'[21]

Even before Clive's return to Britain, the attack by the 'Bengal Squad' had led to a sharp change in fortune for Sulivan; and to a strained atmosphere at Leadenhall. Clive's homecoming would not have been very comfortable either, because it marked a complete reversal in stature. From virtually master of all he surveyed, he became an ordinary mortal. Perhaps this return to earth shook him, and might even have ensured that eventually a contest for supremacy would come about, for emotionally he required a substitute prestige for the one enjoyed in India. Sulivan, entrenched like a spider in his lair at India House, would have appeared a challenge.

Yet, despite the coaxing of erstwhile Bengal friends, he did not join in their opposition, although identifying with them. He had good reasons to be restrained: he had been absolved of all blame for the chaos in Bengal; and his signing of the 'infamous' letter of 29 December 1759 had been skipped over. He was also concerned about the safety of his *jagir*, the basis for much of his future wealth; and he was not certain of the political strength at Sulivan's disposal.

Nevertheless, in the coming years Clive was to preside at the infamous Bengal Club, a centre for returned 'Nabobs'. There, he gave the appearance that he would join them against Sulivan at a time he chose. He was also decidedly unhappy at receiving only an Irish peerage; and this added to his general disgruntlement. He held himself in check, however, secure in the knowledge that the 'Bengal Squad' was at his beck and call, and would respond whenever he saw fit to make a move.

4

Sulivan had already faced several serious crises at Leadenhall, and was in the midst of an increasing tangle of problems associated with events in Bengal and in India at large. He was an extremely busy, preoccupied man, who quite naturally would not relish adding to his trials; and for two years at least, had no fear of Clive. The fact that the great man had been excluded from all criticisms and had 'every honour and compliment paid to his great abilities and extraordinary services', vouches for his being cared for. Even his baggage was delivered free of charge, and he was given a present of plate worth £2,500.[22]

He now knew that Clive's views were unlike his own, but would have seen no need to box him out of things. The returned hero was hardly inclined to indulge himself in Company business, altogether too boring. He was more inclined, Sulivan thought, towards a Parliamentary career. He was annoyed, however, by the activities of the 'Bengal Squad'. Their accusations lies and half-truths built up. From the Chair, he expressed his awareness of the personal attack being mounted against him by 'many persons without doors'; and in open Court he spelled out the extent of the temptations offered to him, such as £28,000 'for Governments alone'.[23]

He upheld his honour, principles and honesty emphasising that he had never taken a bribe or allowed others to take one for him; and had never received a present 'to the value of £20'. He would take no inducement from anyone. The Directors accorded him a vote of thanks 'for great services rendered'.[24] By late 1761, however, things had deteriorated; control over the Court of Proprietors was slipping. This was serious because the authority of the Directors' Court was vital for the proper conduct of affairs.

In November 1761 he protested to Clive at 'the falsity of those assertions that have been thrown out against me'. He was referring to the accusations of the 'Bengal Squad', whose influence on his rival had been steadily growing.[25] At this stage, Sulivan still placed a great deal of confidence in Clive's candour.

It was misplaced. Clive used a letter of Vansittart's, placed in his hands by Sulivan, to try and break the Sulivan-Vansittart bond. A bare four months later, in February 1762, he informed the Governor of Bengal how hostile he now was to Sulivan, although this was still veiled from his adversary. He also showed Vansittart another letter of Sulivan's to Eyre Coote, no friend to either Clive or Vansittart, which was portrayed as full of 'treachery' against them both.

Clive's own 'treachery' was symptomatic of views hardening on either side. Between November 1761 and February 1762 severe irritation entered into things. Sulivan became apprehensive of a united front composed of the 'Bengal Squad', Clive and the envious Director, Thomas Rous. It now became apparent he could also be faced with the opposition of the Governor of Bengal. The quarrel with Vansittart was patched up. The challenge to his power grew stronger in 1762; and with this, the Court of Directors and General Court experienced essential changes in function. They became venues where control of the Company, via the annual election of Directors, took precedence over all else.

Meanwhile, Clive's frustration grew. He informed his friend Pybus: 'Sulivan...follows the same plan of keeping everyone out of the Direction who is endowed with more knowledge or would be likely to have more weight and influence than himself.'[26] The 'Bengal Squad', quite willing to harass their great enemy in any way, backed this view.

Yet in February 1762 there still seemed no intent on either side to give harm.[27] Nonetheless, setting them at odds continued to be the goal of the returned Bengal servants. In July 1762 Sulivan was hitting back. By making enquiries into the so-called losses claimed by the European sufferers in Calcutta in 1756, he threatened many.[28]

In the spring of 1762 Clive, in attempting a Parliamentary career, linked with Grenville. The courtier held no brief for Sulivan because he had tied himself and the Company with the Bute Administration. Clive now openly espoused the opinion that since affairs in India had assumed proportions greater than those of a mere trading enterprise, the whole had become a matter for gentlemen; that Parliament understood better than merchants the arts of war, politics and diplomacy. He had associated himself with the natural enemy of the commercial interests of London, offering its traditional adversaries the very gains won in India. Sulivan believed his mistrust justified.

As Clive's Parliamentary hopes faded, Sulivan suspected that he would settle on his second choice, the Company; and focus on penetrating the executive, using his great wealth to fill it with his own nominees. He feared that implementation of his ideas regarding India would follow, and the Company would be swallowed up by the State.

There was too much for them to differ over; and Sulivan was as stubborn as Clive, wily and with a mind of his own. He would not give way to anyone's wishes with regard to policy, patronage or anything else. They began to fight over the distribution of favours. Frustration turned to anger; and eventually, serious quarrels over patronage broke out; and especially over military promotions, where each thought that he should have the last word.

Clive was annoyed that Sulivan had not followed his recommendation and promoted Colonel Forde to the Bengal command. Sulivan had not denied Forde's merit, but he did not like his 'over-lucrative views'.[29] He was also determining a point: denying anyone the right to absorb patronage that rested in the hands of the Directors alone. In September 1761 a friend, 'Sir Rowland's son', could not be placed, because Clive's own relation, Judge Clive, had Sulivan's last nomination.[30] Sulivan answered: 'Whenever it was in my power last year to offer you a good voyage for any friend you might name, I did it with pleasure. But could I be influenced by any other motive than my regard for Col. Clive? And if so, why do you ask me if the same reason subsists?'[31] Clive ignored this pointed remark, and went on to press the claims of his favourites: Carnac, Knox, Forde and Caillaud.

They continued to disagree over military policy and personnel. Squabbles developed over the merits of Carnac and Knox; and they remained at loggerheads over Forde and Coote.[32] Sulivan's appointment of Coote at the expense of Forde was a main irritant. Clive hated him for many reasons. Nevertheless, the Irish General's honesty had been marked by Chatham as well as Sulivan; and in Coote's version of Plassey, Clive was not such an heroic figure. It might also be significant that Coote patronised Sulivan's nephew-in-law, Colonel John Wood. Clive was alarmed at a Coote-Sulivan alignment. When he heard of his grand reception from the Directors he seemed to think that a man who had been a thorn in his side had stolen some of his glory.

Sulivan's public cancellation of Forde's appointment was done on purpose, as a reprimand for Clive. He also publicised that in his opinion the hero of Plassey came second to General Lawrence, 'the greatest military officer that ever was in Asia.'[33] He also praised Coote to an embarrassing degree, his intention not so much to discredit Clive, as make the point that he was not unique. Others had done as much for the Company, though not with such flair for self-publicity.

For some time he had entertained the suspicion that Clive wanted to exert indirect control in India through Vansittart, Forde and Caillaud. Before leaving for home in 1760, Clive had laid down what he proposed to do in London: fix Vansittart in government, and place Forde and Caillaud at the head of the armed forces, with Major-General Commissions for Governors of the Bengal and Madras Presidencies. Upon arrival in England he urged Sulivan and his fellow Directors to implement these proposals. Sulivan was opposed; he believed Clive was trying to put into practice what was paraded in the letter to Chatham of 7 January 1759.

Sulivan's promotion of Coote to be temporarily in charge in Bengal was probably done to foil Clive. With Coote's temperament it was impossible for him to exert military control in India through him. Clive was certainly incensed enough at Forde being passed over to justify such an interpretation. In a letter of commiseration he promised to rectify things. He failed.[34] One of Clive's eulogisers, Gleig, thought that he had gone too far in his disparagement of Coote, but this is to miss how crucial the appointment was to his strategy.

Yet this did not mean Clive would quit Company affairs; he now set about removing the obstacles to successful accomplishment of his plans. Sulivan had to be crushed. He now decided an effort to discredit him had been made with promotion of a favourite, Forde, being brushed aside, something he felt involved his honour. This only came to the fore after his overall plan had been foiled. Throughout 1762 he was prepared to argue every point. Military patronage flared again, and only Sulivan's withdrawal from the Direction saved a possible confrontation. He probably sensed that an altercation had to be avoided at that point.

5

Adding to their growing dissatisfaction were disagreements over aspects of both the Preliminary and Definitive Peace Treaties with France of 1762-63. In both agreements, Sulivan was deeply involved, formulating those clauses dealing with the Indian theatre of war. He also played a principal part in the discussions with the French, stretching from 1761 to the Peace of Paris of 1763.

He was immensely proud of the outcome because the wording of that part of the final Definitive Treaty dealing with India was wholly drafted by him and accepted by Government. The views portrayed in the document reflected his thinking developed as early as 1760. The closing settlement determined for the foreseeable future the course the Company would take regarding the Carnatic. That he saw the clause he drew up enacted in the shape in which he had framed it was (in his own eyes) one of the major achievements of his life:

> My power tho' on the wane existed in 1762, and the Company's terms in the Treaty of Paris settled entirely in my own words, not with the inclination of the then Directors, but from their inability they were drove to ask and adopt my ideas...The plan for peace which was adopted is every line my own.[35]

He was quite correct regarding the significant role he played in those events. Despite mounting hostility within the Company and the complications of ministerial involvement, he stuck to his views religiously.

Of just as much consequence, however, as regards his public life, was what transpired in other spheres because of involvement in these treaties. As well as figuring in his deteriorating relationship with Clive, they reckon in his Parliamentary dealings; and had much to do with what happened in Company politics in the lead up to the 1763 Company election.

Although initial talks with the French broke down in 1761, Sulivan's connection with members of the Parliamentary front bench was to continue.

A letter in his handwriting, which from internal evidence is dated 1760, and addressed to Chatham and Egremont, shows that even at that early date he had been studying what was required to bring about an acceptable peace.[36] Another Sulivan letter to Chatham, of 27 January 1761, formed his 'Private sentiments of a plan that may best secure...solid and permanent advantages...to...our Company.'[37] In this early communication, he pleaded with the first minister not to injure the Nawab of Arcot; a plea emphasised throughout the subsequent transactions and honoured in the final treaty.[38]

After the fall of Chatham, he conveyed the same thoughts to the new government. Charles Jenkinson wrote to him in January 1762 that Bute had perused his memorial on the proposed peace terms and that it had given him great pleasure. Jenkinson added, 'It is certainly well drawn and will be of much service to the Company. Alterations, if any, will be very few.' He desired him, therefore, to 'expedite the French translation'.[39] Before going out of the Direction in April 1762 it is the case, therefore, that Sulivan was involved in propagating the same plans that he had kept in mind for at least two years. The evidence shows the reliance placed upon him by ministries, despite internal wrangling at India House.

In the end, the peace settlement secured the original aims of the war and satisfied most people in its final form. However, during the course of events, the India clauses of the preliminary settlement, signed on 3 November 1762, and then those of the Definitive Treaty of 10 February 1763, aroused criticism within and without the Company. A general hatred of Bute lay behind much of this, fuelled by a never-ending prejudice against Scots. The dislike was abetted by his position as a royal favourite. Nevertheless, real controversy existed over the provisions for the settlement in the East Indies.

The Bute government assumed the attitude that it was conferring a favour on the Company by involving it in the talks. However, through his friend and fellow Irishman, Robert Wood, under-Secretary to Lord Egremont, then Secretary of State, Sulivan maintained communications with the ministry. In June 1762 he, together with the Chairman, Thomas Rous and his Deputy, John Dorrien (Sulivan's friend), were involved in consultations using this channel.

Following renewal of negotiations with the French, Company claims were based on Sulivan's letter to Chatham of 27 July 1761; its contents were used as a basis for 'systematic consideration'.[40] This was then followed by an outline of the Secret Committee's plan, delivered to Robert Wood for consideration in September 1762. He passed this on to Egremont.[41] The Government remained unhappy with the proposals, and only a modified version of the claims was to be pursued by the Duke of Bedford in Paris. The negotiators left out French recognition of Muhammad Ali Khan as Nawab of the Carnatic, and English agreement to Salabat Jang as Subahdar of the Deccan.

This caused disquiet within the Company and in the Secret Committee. Government's proposed conditions regarding the Preliminary Treaty were to be placed before Parliament in November 1762. This sparked a furious reaction in Leadenhall. Sulivan, who was still out of the Direction, favoured agreement with the ministry, wishing to retain confidence in himself. He had an eye on a better long-term solution; and (privately) seems to have been promised inclusion of clauses regarding the Nawab in the final settlement.

The Government then used force. The first step in the peace settlement was to be concluded before the end of the Parliamentary session. Egremont wanted agreement or India House would be left out of all negotiations. He hinted at future compromise by Government should the Company concur; and gave it two days to produce suitable proposals. After some moderate changes, the Directors accepted this dictat. The Government left the impression that other points would be sorted out in the final treaty.

Thus the Preliminary Treaty of 3 November 1762 included clauses relating to a French presence in Bengal for commerce only; and the restoration of French possessions held before the start of hostilities in 1749, as against 1745. In exchange, the Company would receive the return of the *comptoirs** in French possession before that date. Dissatisfaction in the Company over the preliminaries continued, however, and it was also denounced by Chatham in the Commons. Nevertheless, Sulivan continued to back the ministry. This was vouchsafed in a letter to Shelburne on 12 October 1762. He proceeded to give the minister advice on how to win acceptance for the Preliminary Treaty in the Commons.[42] Shelburne recognised his 'zeal for the Public interest'. As it turned out, the ministry won a vote of confidence convincingly.[43]

Talks upon the Definitive Treaty followed, and the ministry's hint of some better terms took on some substance. There were only slight variations in the two treaties in general terms, but there was, 'Greater precision'. It was conceded within the Company that overall the terms were more advantageous than the preliminaries.[44] Instead of the French handing over those factories held 'at the start of hostilities in 1749', they had to restore what they held 'at the beginning of the year 1749'.[45] Most important, however, as far as Sulivan was concerned (and to most in Parliament and in the Company too) the final treaty reintroduced the clause concerning Salabat Jang, and Muhammad Ali Khan.

In 1762, although out of the Direction, Sulivan's power in India House had been little affected. His follower, John Dorrien, was Deputy Chairman and a member of the Secret Committee used in planning the Company's approach to the peace settlement. Sulivan remained friendly with Government through Shelburne; and earlier he had given Bute a copy of his sentiments regarding peace terms with France, with regard to the Indies.

The degree of ignorance inside the Company, as well as the dependence of the new ministry upon the few knowledgeable men, such as himself, decreed that little difference was made whether he was in or out of office. He had continued to play a part midway between the Directors and the Government, acting as a mediator and conciliator, bringing them together to accept what in many ways were his own plans.

Within the Company, however, things were not going well. In many ways Sulivan's view of himself as chief executive, whether in or out of the formal Court of Directors, was to blame. It was particularly irritating to the growing ranks of discontented returned servants; and especially so when flaunted before Clive.

The Company's Secret Committee made a point of consulting both great men throughout all proceedings relating to the Definitive treaty. Their combined wisdom and experience contrasted starkly with the ignorance of others.[46] Unlike his rival, however, Clive had played no part in the initial talks; and was now aware that Sulivan, whose views were being pushed in the Secret Committee through his friend Dorrien, was upstaging him. What is more, he appeared to be forging ever stronger bonds with the Bute ministry. Sulivan was assuming the type of position that Clive had probably seen himself occupying.

Fox and Bute were trying to link up the City in defence of their peace policy, which made it sensible come closer to Sulivan so that the Company and the prevailing ministry could remain closely bonded. Nor were Clive's ties with the previous Chatham-Newcastle administration easily forgotten. The closeness of Sulivan with Dorrien, and with the Bute ministry was common knowledge. Newcastle was satisfied they were both 'Creatures of Lord Bute.'[47]

Clive disliked the final article, but not principally because Sulivan's memorial upon India affairs found more favour with Bute than his own. Clive saw the threat to English possessions as being very real; that territory, not just commerce was the magnet that would attract unwelcome attention from other powers. In his *Memorial as to the East Indies,* he again followed Dupleix's argument that commerce in India was already too regulated and not nearly enough to make a continued European presence in India feasible. A policy of military conquest was needed, from which territorial revenues would stem.

Of course, in the end, apart from the clauses concerning the Princes, Clive's reasoning led to the very same thing Sulivan wished for, the entire exclusion of the French from Bengal; only it had very different motivation. Sulivan's view (the antithesis of Clive's) was that the French had failed because they had not remained a mercantile body. Only with regard to the Carnatic alone, did he modify his 'seventeenth century ideas'.[48] He still did not want conquest, but embraced limited territorial revenues.

The one absolutely discordant note that existed over the peace to be agreed upon with France was the inclusion of the native Princes in the treaty. The fact that it was a clause from Sulivan did not at first enter into consideration. Apart from everything else, Clive also felt the French should be given no role for fear of giving them a future pretext to interfere in Mughal politics. Sulivan managed to have the clause reintroduced into the Definitive Treaty; but he had to fight hard for it. He referred to these events later in life:

In the article that included the Nabob of Arcot I was opposed by
Lord Clive as an unnecessary clog which the French would resist
and in his opinion useless for another reason, to wit, 'that gratitude
would never be found in an Asiatic'.[49]

He mentioned this issue again in the 'Letterbook': 'The late Lord Clive, who
was consulted, opposed the 11th article as of no importance and the Duke de
Choissieul the then French Minister, contended strongly to expunge it.' He
continued: 'The honour of the Company was pledged to secure this faithful
ally; that the eyes of Asia were upon us.' The strength of his resolve over this
clause is further indicated when he said: 'I kept firm and my friends in
Government succeeded.'[50] In yet another letter he commented: 'The Minister
gave it in my favour.'[51] Sulivan hinted in this correspondence that events, as
they transpired, vindicated his earnestness over the matter.[52] The Clive party
in Leadenhall after 1765 was unable to efface the terms of the treaty or those
clauses dealing with the position of the Nawab of Arcot.

In 1763 Clive voted with the minority in the Company against the peace
treaty; this was done mainly on party grounds. In a pamphlet to the
Proprietors he was sure that they would all benefit; but was fearful that
guaranteeing the Indian Princes might be the cause of later disputes between
the Companies. Nevertheless, the Definitive Treaty was accepted, probably
because the views held by all sides could be read into the document.[53]

Clive's admirers generally take the line that although Bute followed the
suggestions made by Sulivan and the Secret Committee, he had displayed
much the same ideas. Yet this is not really the case. At the time (and not as
written up after the event) his views regarding the native princes were
immovable.[54] The withdrawal of the clause regarding the Indian princes in
the preliminaries is also depicted as a triumph for him. This is a false picture,
conjured up by the heavily charged atmosphere that came to exist in the
Company. In fact he had chosen not to speak up on the issue before the first
stage began.[55]

Sulivan's pursuit of harmony with government at every stage of
negotiations had dismayed Chairman Thomas Rous and his friends. They
were against compromise and resented his interference. The scene was set for
major trouble within India House. The course of the final treaty stirred these
factional disputes; and by his opposition to re-inserting the Nawab of the
Carnatic and Salabat Jang clauses, Clive was viewed as again crossing swords
with Sulivan.[56]

Rous charged Sulivan with being to blame (through his purported
ignorance) for initial errors made in the proposed terms of the earlier
Preliminary Treaty. He was also held responsible, together with Wood, of
deliberate deception in getting Egremont to agree to them in the first place.
The whole issue was too good an opportunity for the 'Bengal Squad' to miss,
and they helped stir up Rous and his associates. Yet Sulivan also exacerbated
the situation by totally ignoring all their views, such was his contempt.

Ostensibly, the argument was over the qualifying date for the *comptoirs* to be agreed upon with the French. It was only during the run-up to the signing of the Definitive Treaty that it was realised Dupleix had gained more territory before the war began. Rous was blamed for this slip, although the phrase was subsequently corrected, with Government help, to read in the final treaty, 'at the beginning of the year 1749'. Both Sulivan and Clive claimed the credit for spotting and correcting the *comptoirs* error, but there is no doubt that Sulivan deserves the recognition. His letter to Pitt of 27 July 1761 also shows that he had wanted the date of the *comptoirs* reckoned even earlier.

Among the many dramatic scenes to be played out, the one in the General Court before the election, that of 22 December 1762 proved most difficult for Sulivan. His enemies put forward a hostile motion that he should explain his reasons for keeping so close to the Bute ministry throughout the negotiations. According to an open letter to the papers, this enquiry was only suspended, 'because of the importance of affairs'.[56] Sulivan was certainly angry and fired up by then, he was not the kind of man to endure censures by the likes of Rous; or accept Clive's moves to have his views quashed.

In many ways the whole issue of inserting or keeping out clauses on the Indian Princes constituted a trial of strength. The measure of Sulivan's fight back is seen in their eventual inclusion the Definitive Treaty. In so doing he got the better of Clive. It was also a struggle between the ministry and Clive. While Sulivan's advice had been asked for from the beginning, Clive had been ignored, and he had to force his attentions upon ministers. Then, despite making a point of having the clauses removed, Bute had them incorporated in the final treaty. What was worse, Sulivan's own words were used. It was difficult for Clive to forgive the ministry. He probably did not recognize that Sulivan had, at the very least, an equal right to have his words and views enshrined in the document closing that chapter of history.[58]

The omission in most histories, of Sulivan's prominent role in the peace negotiations of 1761 to 1763 is regrettable. He was clearly the major inspiration as well as drafter of the Indian clauses in the treaty. Even Clive, who certainly knew enough about events in India, could not comprehend the whole picture like Sulivan. In addition, the Irishman was really the only man able to supply the crucial liaison required between the ministry and the Company. Bute, and seemingly Chatham before him, realised this and were themselves dependent on his knowledge. He alone in the Company seemed to appreciate that Government had to be given as much help as possible in negotiations that dealt with the Indian theatre. Finally, it was surely right that the man who had done more than any other to wage successful war against the French in India should be called upon to provide the concluding words.

6

Sulivan and Clive had moved from friendship, to coolness, to collision over fundamentals and were heading for estrangement; but Sulivan was not yet prepared for confrontation. Ever the politician, he was aware that he was not adequately prepared. He would not duck a fight, but merely chose his own time and weapons.

His absence from the Direction in 1762 was at his request; he pleaded illness and neglect of his own affairs. To Chatham he complained of poor health; and had been absent from India House a good deal. The volume of work and weight of responsibility were taking their toll. Yet, the move was also a rather diplomatic one, in view of the disputes with Clive and the disturbed state of the Direction. The reality, however, was that he remained firmly entrenched, virtually invincible. His close friends formed a constant majority in the executive.

What caused Clive most disquiet was the question mark that hung over the *jagir* he had enjoyed since 1759, because the Company had still to be convinced of its legality. According to Clive, the Secret Committee was willing to meet him halfway in some amicable agreement. He was then too sick for discussions. It was an opportune time to be unwell. Clive knew he was expected to surrender the *jagir* after a few years, so he continued to be too ill for any meeting. Nothing was accomplished; and the issue remained unresolved.

In February 1762 his stance changed; friends in India were urged to get the gift confirmed. Amyatt was to have it corroborated by the Mogul Emperor. Vansittart was pestered and asked to go to impossible lengths; serious enough to endanger his friendship with Sulivan. In November he was still pressing the Governor hard, but failed to have the *jagir* ratified.[59] It was a bitter pill to swallow. It showed once more Sulivan's mastery; his control over the Governor; and (as Clive saw) an extended governance over Bengal. His own arrogance could scarce endure this.

Clive's possession of the *jagir* had created an unprecedented situation, and it had a curious legal position; so much so, his claims were never formally accepted and were eventually challenged. Sulivan was perplexed and seemed to think it better to let sleeping dogs lie. It continued to confound him and his advisors. Clive was also too popular for harsh treatment. The last thing Sulivan wanted was a public outcry over enormous riches going to a 'Nabob'.

Clive considered the *jagir* a life-rent. He also came to see that through the grant he and the Company were firmly linked, that it gave him a vested interest in the organisation's continuance. The apparent loss of such an amount every year was a tremendous irritant to Sulivan. He thought that by 1762 the Company could have been enriched by around £100,000. He knew too that Clive was wealthy enough; and felt the *jagir* money was due to the Company, not to Clive alone. Yet he was stuck with the fact that it had been presented to him by Mir Jafar.

The customary view has been of a vindictive Sulivan threatening Clive's *jagir* to keep the national hero from involvement in Company affairs. Sulivan did indeed warn him of a general threat to his prize, leaving the implications deliberately unsaid. It was not difficult for his Lordship to see that he wanted them to live in peace. He was also cautioning Clive against serious collaboration with the 'Bengal Squad'. Nor is there any doubt that he wanted to paralyse Clive in terms of Company politics.

The unspoken pact was in force from 1760, the Leader blocking any efforts by others to enquire into it. Writing to Vansittart in 1763, Sulivan said that stopping the grant 'would have taken place years ago' but for his personal intercession.[60] The *jagir* appeared as an issue only when Clive was thwarted; and it was only after his Lordship ran against him at the April 1763 election that Sulivan made any move against the prized possession. Until then, the instrument fashioned for his own enrichment had been used as a muzzle, and as security for his good behaviour.

The *jagir*, however, had become a financial necessity, not a luxury, as Clive spent furiously in an effort to establish himself in Parliament and as a country gentleman. He had made himself a 'hostage' to the Company, and this dictated a great deal of his future actions. He seemed to feel a threat to it in February 1762, but was reluctant to make a move.[61] On the same day he talked to Pybus of keeping Sulivan in awe of him by threatening to join the 'Bengal Squad'. He added, 'Though I do not mean to hurt him, I can do such a thing if he attempts to hurt me...My future power my future grandeur all depend upon receipt of the jaghire money.'[62]

Still, it would be wrong to pick out the *jagir* as the factor that drove Clive into open opposition. The truth was that he had been thwarted in his plan for control of India through Vansittart and Forde. Nor was his word law in India House – that belonged to Sulivan. He was frustrated and envious. He had been stalemated over the *jagir*; his military appointments bypassed; and his advice looked upon as secondary by the Bute ministry. Nor was it clear that the Company's future course would be to his liking. He had to be content, on the other hand, to witness Sulivan's excellent handling of the aftermath of war and the deliberations upon it; and observe his rival's political artistry within the Company.

In addition, high hopes of a dazzling career in national politics were dashed. He had thought his political future lay with Newcastle and Chatham and using his great wealth had built up a Parliamentary interest. It all fell through when Bute came to power in 1761. As 1762 advanced he found difficulty in remitting money to England; he no longer had Sulivan as an agent. He faced closed doors both in the Company and with the ministry; and could not bear the thought of losing his *jagir*. His temperament and the insistence of the 'Bengal Squad' made things worse. It became increasingly impossible to withstand these urgings.

Throughout 1762 their positions had become entrenched. There was also a decline in any sense of unity and responsibility within the Company; and it was with difficulty that Sulivan focussed on Indian affairs. During the last months of 1762 and the first quarter of 1763, while the final enactment of the Definitive Peace Treaty was taking place, a series of quarrels split the Direction.

The Company also reverberated with the first salvoes of the approaching election, and Rous attempted to shift the blame for the earlier mistake over *comptoirs* made in negotiations with the ministry. Clearing his name took pride of place. Yet in spite of the mud-slinging, Rous had been slipshod in his scrutiny of the proposed Definitive Treaty. It had taken Sulivan's perception to make the final draft watertight. This was again referred to in the *Public Advertiser* some time later.[63] Sulivan was also openly contemptuous of Rous, made worse by knowledge that the 'Bengal Squad' cultivated and abetted him.

Rous promoted the view that Sulivan was too much under governmental influence for the good of the Company. Clive felt much the same. In November 1762 the Chairman and his followers publicly joined with the 'Bengal Squad'; and news of the continuing confrontation within India House spread in Parliamentary circles.

As the election grew nearer, Sulivan was accused of high-handed action over the Definitive Treaty, and that he had forwarded answers before they were called for through formal channels. Rous alleged only a show of consulting the Directors was going on and that Sulivan was using the negotiations to have himself 'considered at the West End of the Town as the Dictator to the East'.[64]

More than anyone, Rous brought the invective against Sulivan down to gutter level. The personal and vindictive tone of the attack was astonishing, even in an age of very free expression: 'Truth and justice did not exist' in his 'little soul'. He was also charged, perhaps more accurately, of indulging in Machiavellian politics.[65]

In an effort to implicate Sulivan and exonerate Rous, the terms of the preliminaries were raised yet again in the Court of Directors and in the General Court. Rous claimed that he wanted to give the Directors a full account of the transactions, but was only prepared to do so at a later date, that is, after the Company election. In an open letter to the press Sulivan's 'crime' was enlarged upon. He had not informed the Company's Secret Committee of his action over the *comptoirs*.

At last Sulivan's enemies tasted success among the Proprietors. Rous was absolved of blame for the miscalculation over the *comptoirs*, and this was interpreted as a censure on Sulivan. It was a real setback that his supporters were unable to stem; and executive cohesion immediately disappeared. Clive's sense of opportunism told him the moment was right to make his move, and on 17 February he published his junction with Rous.

Later Clive stated that his 'opposition originally arose from the defects in the preliminary articles'.[66] He probably pin-pointed the moment when he had finally made up his mind to go against Sulivan; and then waited for the best opportunity to do so. It arrived in February 1763. He also said later that his involvement 'arose from a conviction of his (Rous') integrity'.[67] This is hardly satisfactory when the build up of ill-will towards Sulivan is considered.

When their rivalry was made public in February 1763, it served to focus all the opposition that had built up to Sulivan's command. However, he did not intend to see his predominant position changed; or his network of connections and ties in Parliament, in the City or elsewhere destroyed. Clive was correct, however, in thinking the right opportunity had presented itself. Sulivan's alarm was real. He wrote to Bute seeking his help 'against those nobles now rallying to his enemy'. The united front that he had been so afraid of was poised to deal with him. Concern is obvious in his letter to Shelburne on the 24th:

> Those I depend upon were frightened and kindly took upon themselves to seek Mr. Rous and picture to him his situation, sent him to break these connections (with Clive and the 'Bengal Squad') promising if he did, their endeavours with me; that I would suffer him to continue in the Direction.[68]

Inside Parliament, however, nothing was very clear, but Bute's suspicion of Clive turned to distrust when in February 1763 he voted with the minority in the House that condemned the peace. It was believed the minister determined to crush him from that point; but in his letter to Shelburne, of 24 February, Sulivan demonstrates that this was not so.

Clive claimed later that 'Sulivan might have attached me to his interest if he had pleased'; but it is doubtful if such a union could have taken place.[69] The armed camps were lined up: Sulivan and his friends, together with the Bute ministry; versus Clive, the 'Bengal Squad', the Rous party, and the Parliamentary Opposition.

Sulivan might have asked himself what had really fired Clive to fight. He perhaps thought of the crossed letters in 1758; and the vexed General Letters. Clive's failure to secure patronage for his acolytes, underpinning his grand plan for control was another sharp blow. Or perhaps Sulivan knew too much about his financial affairs.

From Sulivan's point of view all was quite clear: obedience to the governing body had been flaunted; the day of the over-mighty servant had arrived. He took exception, and applied himself to the task of elimination, as he would any threat. Unbelievable determination had got him where he was; Clive's equal sense of worth meant a fight to the death.

The major difference between the two men was the manner in which they esteemed the Company. Sulivan could not stomach it being viewed as an instrument for the plunder and sack of India; or that it might be given over to the State, abandoned. He cherished everything about it. Where Clive would destroy, Sulivan would protect. The next Company election would provide the setting for their first public battle and might provide an answer to whose views would prevail.

7

Activities Public and Private
1757-63

1

During these tumultuous years, Sulivan was no less busy regarding his personal affairs. By strengthening his interest in the City, purchasing an imposing estate in the country and a grand mansion in the town, he was buying himself into the establishment of the day. He adroitly used the years of power to scramble up the social ladder; consolidating his position within the upper echelons, entwining his public, business and private lives. His superior position in society was then employed to bolster even further an ongoing Company career, while laying down roots for his son and others connected with him.

Apparently, it was all made possible by private trade through Bombay; remittance activities; profits from the 'Marine Society' (the trading triangle involving himself, Captain Samuel Hough, John Spencer and others); and through savings. The latter, by his account, amounted to at least £40,000. From 1761 his prosperity was markedly apparent; and that year saw a significant change in style and manner of living.

He joined the ranks of the well-to-do merchants 'whose country houses ringed London...near enough to town for their owners to ride easily into the City in summer.'[1] In doing so, he aped his fellows who had returned enriched from India, of whom Clive was probably the grandest. Nevertheless, he was also investing capital in the securest manner possible, in land; while providing a good foundation for future prosperity.

Ponsborne Manor, the estate he purchased in 1761 (some 900 acres), was in Hertfordshire and lay within four miles of the county town and about seventeen miles from London. He bought it for £13,590 from a William Strode. The necessary Private Bill had already been passed in Parliament in 1760, whereby the land was vested in trustees for the purpose of sale. It was an extensive and respectable property. The South Isle of the Chancel of Hatfield Church was acquired as well. The estate was to remain in the Sulivan family until his son Stephen sold it in 1811 to a William Busk, MP for Barnstaple.[2].

It was also situated near that of his greatest friend, Stephen Law, who had already moved from Queen Square to Broxbourne Manor, in the vicinity of Ware. Ponsborne was only a short ride across the fields. The friends shared adjoining pews in Hatfield Church. Nearness to Stephen Law, therefore, would seem to explain Sulivan's purchase of an estate in that particular part of the English countryside.

A great deal of information exists concerning his purchase of Ponsborne, all of which indicates he did not do much to the property. Yet despite this neglect, because his attention was nearly always focussed in the 'City', the estate managed to do well; and land prices continued to soar. With the amount of work his eminent position demanded, he could not have spent very much time there. His heart and soul were to remain always in the commercial world of London.

There is reason to think that his purchase reflected more a desire to be seen as a man of property and substance than anything else.[3] Being buried in the countryside was not something Sulivan really wanted. Prestige and social position lay at its core. He was certainly not typical of the 'Nabobs' beginning to figure within British society by mid-century and richly parodied in verse and play.

Ponsborne was in sound order with good woodland breaking up the meadowland, pasture, enclosed arable, gardens and orchards. Curiously, although the Sulivans sold part of the estate in Bishops Hatfield to a Christopher Hooke, the records state that in 1811, Sulivan's son, Stephen, who inherited the estate, still had 900 acres. There might have been some undisclosed enclosure of common ground going on. The estate was rich in history, which Sulivan might have appreciated; and it traced its existence to the thirteenth century when it formed part of the Bishopric of Ely.

The old manor house was described as, 'Very stately and large...will cost a considerable sum annually to keep...it was built of red brick having two wings with the entrance door in the centre.'[4] Nonetheless, he elected to pay £1,300 to knock it down and have the bits and pieces carried away. It cost him a further £450 to have Hill House demolished and the materials removed, and he did not rebuild this mansion. He built his new manor on a higher site, in the centre of the estate. The style and appearance was not changed too much It was surrounded by seven acres of walks and lanes.

Some of the more unusual items belonging to the old house were purchased; such as the circular windows and glass, the stone ball, large fireball, the brass hearths with their brass wings, and the marble chimneys. The old stables had held a turret bell and clock; and among the outhouses once stood a Brew house and offices. To complement all this, he bought a coach house, pavilions, greenhouses and dove houses.[5]

Sulivan had quite a few tenants: twelve held their land freehold, three copyhold. Land held freehold amounted to more than 389 acres; copyhold totalled over 451, spread over the lands at Ponsborne, Berkhampstead and Bedwell Louth. There were six farmhouses and six cottages, some with gardens, orchards and meadows. Altogether some fifteen families lived on the estate.

It could have been a time-consuming occupation, but Sulivan, aged forty-eight when he became 'Lord of the Manor', clearly spent little time there. His name is infrequently mentioned in the county records. This might suggest that he was humane in the treatment of his leaseholders, but all the signs are that he was a rigorous, though paternalistic master. Although he had a sense of the obligations that came with power, he would never allow liberties to be taken.

The entries in the County records suggest a strict, but also protective, attitude. There is a reference to a James Clapham of Bayford, yeoman, being indicted (though found not guilty) of stealing '2 boards worth 10d' from him. There are also indications that he provided employment. Under the heading 'Entries of Gamekeepers' he hired a John Barraclough from 1761 to 1771; a Joseph Clapham from 1771 to 1777; a Jonas Pratt from 1777 to 1785; and a James Ellis in 1785.[6]

When in the country he would have led the life of a country squire. His family would have enjoyed all the trappings of their position and hunted over the pastures and meadows. He might have been seen, occasionally, calling on his tenants and checking stock on the home farm. On the Sabbath the Sulivans would attend church at Hatfield, sitting in their own pews on the south side of the chancel beside the Law family. Obviously, a very close bond existed. The friendship formed in Bombay was renewed in London in 1753; it was consolidated in the depths of rural England.

2

Although 1761 was a very busy year for Sulivan, in the midst of everything else he made a first attempt to enter Parliament by contesting the seat for Ashburton, in Devon. As in everything, his shift into national politics was linked more with business in Leadenhall and with what was taking place in India than with anything else. He also wished to impress, and this would be an indication of his climb up the social scale. Westminster was the best club in town. But there was more to it than that. Deference to Parliament defined what it was to be British: King, Lords and Commons stood for 'sovereignty'. In this he believed, and was no different from his fellow travellers. It made sense to publicly proclaim as much.

The impact of India on British life was being felt at Westminster. MPs were becoming embroiled in its affairs; and the Commons would serve as another arena where contests for supremacy in the Company would be fought out. Sulivan would soon face the dominant Parliamentary force of the landed gentry.

Returned enriched servants or 'Nabobs', represented the new wealth from India. They came to be envied and derided in equal measure as they bought their way into land and into Parliament. At one and the same time they were found attractive and repugnant, scorned and admired. There was some revulsion at ostentation built on the back of poverty and exploitation in India; but in both Houses covetousness overwhelmed embryo humanitarian sympathies. Landowners sought the wealth and patronage the East Indies promised, to the extent that gentlemen from the 'West End of Town' jockeyed increasingly with their fellows 'East of Temple Bar'. Members and leading political figures became increasingly interested in the parties within India House, and were willing to use Parliament to help achieve their ends.

A mounting number of East India Proprietors and Directors became MPs. In 1764 Clive calculated that 66 were so involved; with 181 between 1764 and 1774. Many others held India stock for political, financial and speculative reasons. MPs, who were also Company Directors, included: George Amyand, Crabb Boulton and Robert Jones. Proprietors like George Colebrooke, Peregrine Cust, George Dempster, George Johnstone and John Stephens (who were to become Directors) would also be elected to Parliament. Two others joined Sulivan at this time, both former Governors of Madras: Robert Palk, and George Pigot.

Men of high rank and influence operating through Parliament had always enjoyed weight in the Court of Directors and among the Proprietors. For generations there had also been harmony with ministries. This too began to alter. Ministers increasingly came to believe they could exert more influence in the 'City' through direct contact with the Directors, so their entry into Parliament made everything so much easier.

Groups and factions within Westminster took sides in the struggles that erupted at Leadenhall. They did so according to interests and personalities, but also with the ever-growing desire of gaining some of the Company's vast patronage and revenue. Parliamentary figures began fishing for friends at India House. Through private channels they sought to influence decisions there. The interests of MPs and individuals within the monopoly became hopelessly entwined; and the fate of the Company and what would happen in India came to depend just as much upon groups and conflicts in Parliament, as upon their counterparts at India House.

Parliament then lacked political organisation and on the whole was unaffected by public opinion. It worked through a 'fragile balance between public and private interests expressed in the system of political connection and political management'.[7] This did not make it any easier for the government to handle, because the Company defended its Charter well. War, the accession of a new monarch in 1760 and a succession of ministries combined to give it an astonishing amount of independence. The first intrusion appears during the contested election of 1763.

It was natural during Sulivan's years of absolute power that he should develop strong ties with Westminster; good connections were needed there. This was so, independent of a wish to be an MP or to further a Parliamentary career. Nevertheless, becoming a member of the House made sense. It helped maintain his government of the Company, and might benefit the organisation too.

Association with well-known public figures was important; and it might be thought his candidature for the borough of Ashburton in 1761 would indicate who these were, and show which Parliamentary interest he lined up with. Yet until 1761 his progress was most marked for the lack of attention to him by ministry. This was partly due to the coolness of Newcastle who had supported the old Directors led by Payne, ousted in 1758.

A positive relationship developed, however, with Chatham during the war against France. The extremely amicable way in which they integrated led the first minister to view Sulivan in a favourable light. Relations with Newcastle, nevertheless, remained cool, and Sulivan was never invited to the 'cockpit'. Yet the continued need to renew the Company's Charter dictated (as far as Sulivan was concerned) that the Directors and Administration must always be in close contact. That is why he clung doggedly to the Chatham-Newcastle ministry, ignoring Newcastle's snubs.

With King George III upon the throne in 1760 the political situation was about to change. Chatham's anti-Hanover speech meant he would be on his way out of office as soon as the exigencies of war allowed. The revolution in politics that took place under the new monarch was thus delayed. It was to be the end of political stability for a number of years. Fluctuating ministries and uneasy factions were to mark nearly all Sulivan's years in Parliament. It was a situation that had its parallel at the India House.

On 5 October 1761 Chatham and Temple resigned. Bute took control of the ministry, although Newcastle remained its nominal head until May 1762. Sulivan was faced, therefore, with the awkward task of creating and cementing ties with the royal favourite, the Earl of Bute, while keeping in touch with Chatham. His own eventual entry into Parliament was to ease this transfer of allegiance to Bute; and the way it was achieved led to a personal and Company interest with members of the new Government.

Nevertheless, upon hearing of Chatham's resignation, Sulivan was immediately in touch. He was of the opinion that the Company had been, 'Tardy in its respectful acknowledgements to Mr. Pitt'; and followed this tribute by sending Lady Hester Pitt a 'Lury' bird from the Spice Islands.[8] These can be seen as moves to retain Chatham's friendship. He wanted a seat in Parliament and it suited his purposes to have an influential man like Chatham on his side as he intrigued to gain favour inside the Westminster. Even after he had acquired his seat he would not relinquish this acquaintance. In June 1762 he wrote, 'I beg you'll always honour me with your commands, be assured Sir the East India Company retains very grateful sense of their obligations to Mr. Pitt.'[9]

These harmonious relations with Chatham were retained through the good offices of a fellow Irishman, Robert Wood. He was Under-Secretary of State in 1756 and became Chatham's right hand man. He remained in office after his chief's resignation, and aided Sulivan in transferring his own, and the Company's allegiance to the new ministry.

Wood continued to act as a linkman, keeping his old leader in touch with Sulivan and with the City interests, as well as remaining a source of information for all that was going on. It was useful to Sulivan that Wood had already done good work as Lord Egremont's secretary; and Egremont was very close to Bute. It was with some justification, therefore, that later in life Sulivan could refer to this man as his very good friend. He had handled all confidential communications; and taken charge of the patronage Chatham disbursed, emanating from Sulivan. It was he who made the arrangements when the King formally received him as Chairman of the East India Company.

As a go-between, Wood was central to everything Sulivan attempted at this time remotely involving Westminster. It was through him that he was able to count on the Parliamentary support of Charles Townshend. This courtier made an appointment to see him on 2 January 1762. This early contact was to bear fruit later, in 1766-67, during the Parliamentary enquiry into the Company's affairs. It is also possible that Townshend's visit was a direct consequence of Colonel Isaac Barré's attack upon Chatham in the Commons in mid-December 1761; and that he was checking on Sulivan's political stance. Was he a Chathamite still? Barré was a friend of Sulivan's through the Earl of Shelburne.[10] This might also partly explain Sulivan's protestations of friendship sent to Chatham in June 1762, as he tried to retain the tie.

Sulivan's connection with Shelburne and Bute had been forged by late 1761. For this he owed a great debt to John Dunning (afterwards Lord Ashburton) and to Henry Fox (later Lord Holland). Sulivan's friendship with Dunning was attendant upon the connection he had already made with Robert Palk. Both men were natives of Ashburton. Shelburne, Sulivan, Dunning and Barré were in close association. In the 1760-61 period, Sulivan met with them often, and was introduced to more of the Earl's followers.[11] After Chatham's downfall he tied himself closer.

It wasn't until the advent of Bute, therefore, and Sulivan's personal association with Shelburne, that the close links with Government he desired could come about (outside the exigencies of war). Only then were the bonds created in any way similar to those enjoyed by his predecessors in the Company's executive.

It is rather likely that at first Sulivan did not trust Bute. This would have been in line with the anti-Scots feelings the Earl engendered. In the beginning Shelburne was to be the bridge between them; and Sulivan's connections were to be very heavily weighted towards the Earl. Possibly shared interest in areas of Counties Cork and Kerry strengthened the relationship. He was accused, however, of insinuating himself with the minister, and there is evidence to justify this allegation. Even while sending

Chatham's wife the unusual 'Lury' bird, he was introducing to Bute a Mr. Hyde, Governor of the *London Insurance Company.*.

Sulivan was keen to immerse Bute in City of London interests, and desired to bind together himself, the Company and the new ministry. He vouched for Hyde's respectability in the City, and took the opportunity to present him once more, at Bute's levee. The wily Chairman was interested in the financial implications as well as the political features of such a connection. He told Bute that he would wait upon him to 'further explain' himself.[12] By October 1762 he was acknowledging his high opinion of the minister in a most sycophantic manner. Charles Jenkinson assumed the position with Bute that Robert Wood had filled for Chatham. Information on India business was channelled to and fro in this way. Two-way patronage was initiated.

What Sulivan had managed to do was get close to Bute through Shelburne while maintaining a connection with Chatham. It was a not inconsiderable feat given the instability of ministries and faction within Parliament and the Company. Nevertheless, his great respect for Chatham and gratitude for all the help he had given also influenced him. Once the great man stood aside, however, the Company was once more allied with the King's Government.

The election for Ashburton, a little woollen town in Devon, was held in 1761. There is nothing mysterious about why he should choose this particular borough. Although their joint interest was not overwhelming, Lady Orford and Sulivan's friend, Robert Palk, controlled it. Palk's influence dictated his candidature. However, it was the Devon man's lack of complete control of the borough that in the end was responsible for a contested election, which Sulivan lost, much to his mortification and cost. He took some time to recover from the shock. It was the first defeat in public since his emergence as Deputy Chairman of the Company in 1757; and it came at a point in his career when the influence he could exert was at its maximum.

The Ashburton contest reveals, and typifies the springs of action behind elections for the unreformed Parliament; the amount of bribery required and attendant costs. What it also demonstrates is the intimacy of contact with borough-mongers and the degree of influence exerted from Westminster, especially at ministerial level.

Briefly what happened was that in 1760 Nathaniel Newnham, an East Indian Director and London merchant started an interest there. This was abandoned upon the discovery that he would have opposed the Duke of Newcastle. He suggested that Sulivan should use this commercial interest. He could promise, in return, the export of Ashburton long ells (lengths of woollen cloth).

Four people fought for the two seats. Thomas Walpole, a cousin by marriage to Lady Orford was assured of one. A John Harris had held a seat in 1754, and stood again upon the strength of these fourteen years of representation. He had the friendship of Chatham and the neutrality of Palk. Sulivan faced Chatham's pleading that he must not hurt Harris; and Palk also urged him not to clash with the man. John Duke was the other candidate and like Sulivan was an outsider.

Sulivan seemed to have a very good chance of success. He could not hope to compete with Thomas Walpole, but certainly carried the highest expectations for the other seat. In London he enjoyed the influence of Shelburne, Henry Fox, and thus the Earl of Bute, and appeared to have the neutrality of Chatham. He was also an important man in his own right. He had money, influence, and could place orders with the local cloth industry.

His first canvas was made in December 1760. Robert Palk went with him. It cost over £171 in expenses for treating 'ringers and wool combers' at public houses. But by January 1761 Palk was already having doubts about the outcome. It all went wrong, despite well-meaning help from Palk and the activity of Dunning. He was enraged at the result and determined to petition against it. This in itself, while revealing for posterity, is indicative of the embarrassment felt and the degree to which he felt betrayed. His entry to Parliament was considered very important at this particular stage of his career. The uncertainties of Parliamentary affairs, as well as the attendant political patronage, were better understood by him from that moment.[13]

Sulivan claimed to have polled a greater number of votes than either Harris or Walpole; and had overcome wholesale bribery and 'every species of wickedness' including control over the returning officers. He added that his opponents had created 'false and base' votes, pronounced good by 'the wretch that had sold himself', namely, the Portrive (the returning officer).[14] He was also bitter at the enormous cost of the enterprise. 'So much my estate suffers by this contested election.'[15] At this stage his expenses totalled over £1,994. Palk's requested that Sulivan deliver them to him.

His counter to being outmanoeuvred by Walpole and Harris was immediate and so characteristic. Although in April his opponents were formally returned for Ashburton, fifteen days earlier he had intimated to Chatham his determination to petition Parliament. He solicited his support, while complaining bitterly at the treatment he had suffered.[16]

The determination to pursue what he considered a fraudulent election was to prove lengthy; but the blow to his pride, although severe, was probably timely. He carried his cause forward for a year; and again it cost him. He paid out a further £775. This heavy financial drain was obviously not borne foolhardily. Eventually, his petition, plus that of the Freeholders of Ashburton, was forwarded in January 1762 and heard at the Bar of the House of Commons on 9 February. The truth was that Sulivan did not really see any chance of reversing the election result. Rather, he was playing a game of political blackmail with those leading figures whose support he had relied upon. If they wanted continued access to the patronage he commanded, something would have to happen.

It appeared he stood on very strong ground, a supposition strengthened by the efforts made to prevent his petition from coming forward; and by the strenuous pressures put upon him to desist. There was furious activity at Westminster and Whitehall. He said that he faced Newcastle and the power and influence of 'the greatest familys in England'.[17]

He contacted a host of eminent politicians, among them Chatham, Henry Fox and Shelburne. The latter interested Bute enough to give help. He even got in touch with Clive: 'I am heartily glad that the Honours are settled (a reference to Clive's peerage) but in a selfish light I must wish they may not take place until <u>my contest</u> is ended.'[18] He canvassed well and had real support. In his daily occurrence book, he gives the best account of what subsequently happened:

> The Friends I had obtained amazd and terrifyd corruption (Harris, Newcastle and their friends, including the Walpoles) and as a defeat which they foresaw would have been distruction to their famous power – the D. of Newcastle wrote me a letter promising to take care of me if I wd withdraw my petition, the offer I rejected contemptuously.[19]

He also discarded Lord Hertford's overtures; while to Newcastle he haughtily declared, 'I never made a proposition to your Grace, the Duke of Devonshire, Lord Anson, or any other person concerning my election for Ashburton.'[20]

Finally he heard what he wanted to hear, that a seat would be made available. Bute put pressure upon him in February to give up the election, to which he agreed, and then changed his mind. He had not yet heard what he wanted: the guaranteed promise of a place. He didn't have long to wait:

> The whole Phalanx (Newcastle and Harris' supporters) then applyd to Majesty, and Ld Bute by a card desird to see me. He told me things were going into such a flame that at this juncture might do infinite mischief, to avoid which the King wd take it kind (wd my Honr. permit me) if I withdrew my petition, and in return I shd come into the first vacant Borough...as a good Subject I instantly submitted.[21]

He had won, even although Henry Fox avoided making the presentation until forced to do so.

Sulivan's petition appeared to have been enough to threaten disruption to whatever harmony still existed within the ministry in 1761-2, and excited many national figures. It did help that it was a time when new permutations were forming, stimulated by pressure from the new King and his favourite.[22] He was prepared to upset the calm required in the corridors of power at that crucial time. This was not forgotten.

Hurt pride drove him on to this end. However, the seriousness of his intent clearly belies something deeper. He felt that he had every right to expect a sure seat from ministry in return for the firm support given by him throughout these years of war. Moreover, he still enjoyed unprecedented control over India House. He was disgruntled that Chatham had not ensured his success at the election. His sense of grievance is seen in the determination to push forward the petition, and in a further swing away from Chatham and Newcastle to Bute. Besides, the more the Great Commoner's friendship with Clive increased, the more disenchanted with him Sulivan became anyway.

Other reasons underlay his desire to enter Parliament. The gathering uncertainty and heightened interest relative to India affairs, and their intrusion into national affairs, meant he would concern himself even more with events there. A place in the Chamber to keep track of what went on was needed; as was the maintenance of political connection. In this period, his allegiances within Parliament were determined by those who backed his plans for the Company; and who wished to maintain its independence. National politics were regarded by him as an adjunct to Company politics.

The imminent conclusion of hostilities with France added to the pressure to enter Parliament. The Company (and his own reputation) would be helped if he was present during the deliberations over the terms of peace in the Parliamentary sphere as well as at India House. He must not be absent from any discussions that related to India. Increasing rivalry with Clive also dictated it was prudent to be there.

Already Clive had a Parliamentary interest, which was later to be in opposition to Sulivan. He too wanted entry to Parliament, because it would reflect the level in society he had attained. He was rooting himself and his family into English life. He was a City of London man, the head of probably the most powerful, instantly recognised, independent institution in Britain. Parliament was the perfect vehicle for promoting himself, and where he identified with the great Whig families he seemed to favour. He wanted to be seen as one of the well-to-do; an image that would have been strengthened with his purchase of Ponsborne Manor, bought in the year he had expected to enter Parliament.

Bute, through Shelburne, arranged that he be elected MP for Taunton in March 1762. It was an open borough but subject to the influence of Government, and especially of Egremont. Yet Sulivan was left to feel that he was 'under no Tyes or Clogs whatever, just as free as I shd have been at Ashburton, and without a Shilling Expenses'.[23] He finished this note to himself in the same self-congratulating manner:

> So extraordinary a Triumph with so much honour to myself I deem an ample recompense for my infinite Trouble and great expense...to his honr. (Shelburne) and thro' the goodness of a gracious Prince I very soon recd a message from Ld. Egremont

acquainting me that there was a vacancy at Taunton…and the King had recommended Mr. Sulivan and for this place I was chose.[24]

He also thought that he owed his success to having no opponent. Whether his constituents thought along similar lines is another matter. Although not unusual, there is no evidence that he brought any benefits to them whatsoever.

Sulivan was certainly given the Taunton seat to silence him. He used blackmail or leverage to bring this about. In his eyes the tactics were sound because they achieved their ends. He was a tough and resilient man. In his world, there was the quick and the dead; he could not afford a conscience, nor was it expected of him. He had undergone yet another baptism of fire in the effort to enter this new arena.

He remained MP for Taunton until his transfer to Ashburton in March 1768, through an arrangement with Palk. The ex Governor of Madras had vowed his friend would return there on the first vacancy; and so it came to pass. Dunning supervised the whole business, and Shelburne was once more active on his behalf. With Orford's agreement, Sulivan and a Charles Boone filled the two seats on offer, and received the combined support of Palk and Orford. It was a compromise which lasted until 1774, his last year in Parliament.

Sulivan did not attempt both a Parliamentary and a Company career only to risk falling between two stools. Nor did he endeavour great reforms in the administrative system of India using ministerial influence in the manner Clive entertained. Edmund Burke was correct when he stated that India House was always more important to him. It is hardly coincidental, however, that 1761 marks the date of Clive's entry into Parliament and his own attempt to do so. He had to monitor what was happening; and if the occasion so required, thwart Clive's designs using a Parliamentary base.

He made no pretence of brilliance as a Parliamentarian, although a competent speaker, making some thirty-three speeches, invariably upon, or referring to India business. He was inclined to use a well-known orator, such as Barré. Outside of anything connected with East India affairs he was non-committal. There is no mention of any participation by him on national issues; or on the two boroughs he represented between 1762 and 1774.

At root he was a proponent of English Constitutional government; a Whig. He was never too committed to one party or the other, always leaving his options open, willing to change allegiance as and when it suited him, seeking after privilege with a number of leading Ministers.

In doing so he laid himself open to the charge of capriciousness, and worse, especially in the eyes of Edmund Burke; but this did not bother him much. It might be that the confrontations he found in Parliament excited him. In this theatre, where he lacked the levers of power he had at

Leadenhall, he might have felt panic; but as usual he would have kept this well hidden. In one instance, however, he was to know real fear, when as he left the Commons he was mistaken by a mob for the Speaker, Onslow. He only narrowly avoided injury.[25]

3

Soon after he took the reins of power at India House, Sulivan had set about a wholesale internal reform of its secretariat. Good management was perennially difficult and routine clerical and administrative work, added to the fine accountancy detail required, took its toll. Innumerable copies of nearly everything were sent by different ships, such was the loss en route. In addition, the Company's diverse, sprawling nature, and its dependence on sea links, made it very difficult to govern. On top of this, there was an incredible increase in the amount of work to do in the years after 1757 with the rapid expansion in terms of territory, manpower and commerce.

He set about reorganising India House in a manner that reflected his own efficiency. It came to be regarded as a model administrative structure. It was done in cooperation with the Company Secretary, Robert James, to whom he paid high tribute, and with whom he formed a good relationship.

As Chairman, Sulivan was first to receive intimation of a request, a complaint, or whatever. In his absence the Deputy Chair claimed this right. Depending upon confidentiality, the matter would then go to the Secretary and from him to the Committee concerned. Invariably, Sulivan would pass to James any subject not requiring his own touch or supervision. This is seen in a letter to Mrs. Watson, the wife of Admiral Watson, in 1760: 'Our Secretary Mr. James will…receive your commands, who is entirely master of the subject, and whose province it is to have the immediate inspection of these matters.'[26] That Secretary James had to work hard is reflected in a reward of £500 for 'his good works' in March 1761.[27]

This revamp stood Sulivan in good stead. Sooner or later it would have been required to reorganise the ramshackle way in which things were run; but given the increase in pressures brought about by war and by what was happening in the sub-continent, it became imperative that this be done quickly. It had become a much more formidable task to collate material and make estimates, with the volume, complexity and variety of occurrences. Unnecessary lumber and outmoded practices had to be abolished. He overhauled the establishment at India House; and ended the taking of fees and perquisites by the clerks of the Secretary's office.[28]

Unbroken communications played a vital part in keeping him informed; and links were to become even more important as difficulties abroad accelerated. At each Presidency, Secret or Select Committees were set up, modelled by him upon the one in Leadenhall Street. Like the one in India House, they functioned as an inner Cabinet. Sulivan depended upon these. Equally vital was the private correspondence with Vansittart, Palk, Spencer and others. Vansittart passed on all inside information that came his way, giving him time to plan ahead.[29] The ties among these protégés were consolidated by their friendship and correspondence with each other; a state of affairs he welcomed and actively cultivated.[30]

Apart from routine business, there were some unusual matters to attend to. One concerned six Russian officers sent to Madras, in order to 'Perfect themselves in the science and business of navigation.'[31] Then in 1761 he and Secretary James had to organise the presentation of gifts from the Nawabs of Bengal and the Carnatic to the Royal family and to the British Museum.

In October 1760 a request was received from the Royal Society for the Company's help in making observations of the transit of Venus. Charles Morton, Assistant Observer at the Royal Observatory of Greenwich, thanked Sulivan in advance for all the help he could give.[32] The King had agreed to pay all the expenses of the expedition and provided a ship-of-war to carry the observers. Sulivan gave orders for their proper accommodation if they should land at Madras, en route to Bencoolen; to be paid for by the Company. He wanted to send observers as well; and Governor Pigot confirmed they had people in Madras qualified to make the observations. There was just one snag: there was 'No good time-keeper with instruments, etc. for adjusting its (the sun's) motions by apparent time.'[33]

Organising this expedition was a light-hearted affair compared with the problems posed by smuggling; an activity that gave great worry and cost the Company dear. It involved all kinds of goods and all classes of personnel. It was on board ship that the greatest mischief took place, such as that going on aboard the *Delawar*. In mid-February 1759 he once more brought up the subject, where it was discussed at length. There was no satisfactory outcome, however, and customs evasion become more serious.

Throughout 1760 and 1761 there were many further instances: Copper was being unlawfully shipped aboard the *London* and the *Egremont* bound for India; large quantities of unlicensed goods were being laded upon the *Neptune* and the *York*. Orders to stop this illegal trade had little impact. He produced evidence of more smuggling. Diamonds were being brought home from Madras in the Company's small packet ships without being registered. Sulivan instructed that public notice was to be given that all those unregistered would be deemed illicit trade. However, he found it almost impossible to control. In January 1764 the Company Secretary informed Governor Palk in Madras, that 100 boxes of hats, scarlet cloth, coral and other materials had been clandestinely laded on the *Caernarvon*. She was to be searched upon her arrival, and cargo not covered by the manifest was to be confiscated and sold on the Company's account.

4

The events of 1763 were to have a seminal impact upon Sulivan's career. He faced the greatest danger from his political enemies. In the weeks leading up to the April election, Company politics built to fever pitch. It helped being out of the Direction, and he kept his head down, and only with Clive's entry into the fray did his passion show. It clearly astounded him, as his terse words to Shelburne indicate:

> It is too true...Thursday (17 February 1763) he published his junction with Mr. Rous – Friday and Saturday (18 and 19 February) he canvassed the City in person and made qualifications by dozens – and yesterday (23 February) ...suffered his friends, as I am told, to declare that he had altered his instructions at standing for Director. Lord Clive stands.[34]

Clive's move was a clear signal to others, and all that was needed to rouse Sulivan's opponents. Their feud had been made public.

Sulivan's obvious apprehension underlined the fact that the situation was serious. He had been confident of handling Rous and the Bengal malcontents. Now, it was indeed a 'civil war', as Namier called it. Clive was fairly confident of success or he would not have entered into such a struggle against a foe he did not underestimate. He could count upon his own support, sure of their tenacious backing, but did not really understand the depth and spread of Sulivan's connections, or his stubbornness.

It was also an election fought at great expense; and drove the contestants to unprecedented lengths. The importance (and value) placed upon winning meant massive propaganda campaigns. Courts and Committee rooms, ante-rooms at Westminster, coffee and chop shops all over the city were full of gossip – and the press echoed with propaganda. There was an edge to the contest, because a public confrontation between figures of such substance was not too common. Also, a pyramid of public and private interests relied upon the outcome.

From his letter to Shelburne of 24 February, Sulivan was taken aback to think of Clive standing for the Direction. His Lordship was rather embarrassed himself, as he remarked to Vansittart: 'I have no thought of ever accepting the Chair; I have neither application, knowledge, nor time to undertake so laborious an employ.'[35] In many ways this was an unconscious compliment to Sulivan. His decision had also been taken out of pique; and he admitted his opponent was, 'better versed in such business' than himself.' He never put himself forward at Leadenhall, and worked through intermediaries, especially through his follower, John Walsh.[36]

He also maintained it was the resolve of Sulivan and his friends to keep him out that determined him to seek in. This does not excuse him from censure, for instead of the public spiritedness that he claimed was the motive for engaging with Sulivan, he was willing to sacrifice the Company's structure and stability by admitted ignorance, to further his own interests and satisfy his ego.

The scene was set for a stirring contest, and generated tremendous interest. The election was better prepared, harder fought, and more wide-reaching in its repercussions than the 1758 one. Its specific features consisted of the personal dislike Clive and Sulivan had for each other; the introduction of Asiatic wealth into the political arena; and machinery for the creation of voting qualification by the splitting of Company stock into £500 blocks.

The attack launched was made in a manner calculated to appeal to as many as possible who nursed some grievance. Clive's personal feelings and involvement were camouflaged. Much was made of Sulivan's support for the unpopular Bute ministry. On 17 February the factions began to solicit support in earnest: contact was made with bankers and other types of financiers; and people in Parliament, especially in the Opposition were sounded out. A bewildering network of ties came into being as the factions struggled to influence those that they could, and to qualify others through the requisite £500 of India stock.

Probably the most striking feature of the election was the role of the Proprietors Court: its assumption of real power and the weight it brought to bear on the Direction. The anti-Sulivan forces within this body also used rights that were seldom exercised. Sulivan's own accession to power in 1758 had witnessed the last stirring example of this. The powers of the Court were vast. The executive could be questioned on all aspects of policy, their salaries cut, or be dismissed. The Board was accountable to those who had entrusted it with their money, the share holders. These assemblies, as Lord Macaulay said, were now large, riotous and stormy, full of trickery and corruption, 'the debates indecently virulent'.[37]

Sulivan enjoyed support from various quarters. The 'Bengal Squad' aside, he remained popular with many who had seen service of some kind in India, and especially ex-Bombay colleagues Stephen Law and John Browne. There was assistance from Madras servants such as Timothy Tullie; and from Bengal, William Barwell, who was no friend of Clive or his fellows from Bengal.[38] Sir Eyre Coote backed him, and because of Coote, John Purling too, just as he had done from 1758 to 1761. Robert Palk in Madras, because he was also a friend of Clive, kept a middle road in relations with both contestants.

All the Irishman's many connections within the shipping interest were used. He virtually monopolised this body, an area in which Clive had little or no presence. His friends included assorted mercantile, insurance and seagoing people, like Charles Gough, George Stevens, the Godfrey brothers, Samuel Hough and Thomas Lane. He also drew on those who represented the old merchant banker type of Proprietor; and upon great numbers of small shareholders in the City. Friends in business rallied, such as George Amyand and Frederick Pigou. They were sure of their man and knew his capability for serving the commercial side of the Company. He enjoyed the continued loyalty of most employees at Leadenhall.

Most important, he was able to draw upon the influence of the Bute ministry, and used Government funds to create faggot votes. He pooled the King's influence (and that of courtiers and leading ministers) using the weight of the monarch's friends in the Commons and the House of Lords. He was able to call upon Government officers, members of the Secretariat and Post Office and innumerable dependants.

Bute and Sulivan had been in league for some time; they had collaborated as early as November 1761 in settling the peace with France. India patronage (through Sulivan) had also been funnelled to the scions of powerful families north of Berwick with the purpose of securing political backing at elections in Scotland. Many Company posts were being granted to Scots according to Government wishes.[39]

Sulivan had been alarmed because at first he could not count upon Government intervention in the coming clash. His consternation at Bute's lack of action was shown as early as October 1762 and then again in a letter to Shelburne four months later:

> Do not blame me if I feel neglect in a juncture so nearly affecting my honour and the interests of a great Company. A line from Lord Bute (and I have seen his letters to those I look down upon) would have been esteemed by me to have the extent of my expectations…could I know what dependence I may have upon the Ministry.[40]

With ministerial funds in mind, Shelburne suggested Sulivan keep in touch with Fox, who controlled the Pay Office. This he did, all through the months from October 1762 to March 1763. Shelburne also suggested he call upon Fox personally – which he did.

Bute's hesitancy is explained by Clive's formidable interest in Parliament, which the minister did not wish to rouse. He kept in touch with Clive through the Proprietor Joseph Salvador for as long as he could; or at least until it was certain his independent position was shading towards the Opposition. Only then were Sulivan and the 'House' list fully supported. It was never the minister's intention to bring Clive to heel using Sulivan. Soon the continual prodding paid off. In March Henry Fox took out voting qualifications and was followed by Shelburne, which enabled Government supporters, who knew nothing about Company business, to know which way to turn. The Secretariat used its influence; and the enormous resources of the Pay Office were put to use.

It is futile to blame Sulivan for the disasters that befell the Company through deliberately bringing Government influence to bear in Company elections. Clive's great wealth, combined with that of the 'Bengal Squad', meant he had to seek funds and take whatever he could find. He might also have felt justified in seeking help from the ministry against a threat to monetary confidence. It was imperative that Government, the Bank of England, the great monied Companies and the City as a whole worked closely with one another. That Government support was required for a struggle within the Company might have seemed justified in his eyes.

Clive threw his massive resources into splitting stock, which were then transferred to friends to vote with. His endeavours were gargantuan, and he created large-scale machinery for the purpose, such was his determination to destroy his opponent. Sulivan commented at the time, 'I confess myself a novice in the business.'[41] He could only have referred to the scale of the operation. He soon emulated his enemy. Nor does his observation to Shelburne that 'Clive and a select band of Eastern plunderers first taught the creation of nominal votes', stand up.[42]

Splitting machines were remarkable organisations; and the men who managed them and organised the campaigns were closest to the main adversaries. They were usually bankers or prominent in the City. These managers paid great attention to those with large holdings of India stock. They also worked hand-in-hand with 'stockjobbers', using stock that otherwise would have been permanently immobilised, placing these holdings in the hands of one controller or the other. Smaller jobbers and brokers split their own stock, or split the blocks of stock entrusted to them by trustees. There were also those who 'split' their holdings among friends and relations. Clive used the firm of *Cliffe, Walpole and Clarke,* and that of *Francis and Robert Gosling.*

Sulivan really ran his own campaign in 1763, although Thomas Lane acted for him a great deal. Much was expected of Shelburne: 'If your Lordship or friends have interest with the bankers they are the men that can do us infinite service.' He added, tongue in cheek: 'Messrs. Fox and Calcraft Bankers may do great things.' Calcraft was Fox's man and in charge of the Pay Office. Sulivan was convinced that this support could: 'Make a number sufficient to overturn all opposition.'[43]

There is evidence of some success from this quarter: Lord Eglinton used his weight with associates; the financier Aaron Franks helped through a Mr. Talbot, after clearance from Bute; Shelburne influenced a Colonel Scott and Lady Betty Germain, and made public his support for Sulivan's list. There were limits to Government influence, however, Sir Mathew Featherstonehaugh still split for Clive.

Bute's involvement was a signal to his compatriots, and many became involved. London-Scottish bankers, such as: *Drummonds; Grant; Fordyce;* and *Coutt*s, and the Dutch *Hope* firm, (with Scottish origins) lent money to both sides engaged in splitting. With support and help from the ministry Sulivan was convinced that he would have sufficient to win the day. In the end, of the votes created for him at the election, 100 were directly due to Government influence and money.[44]

Although optimistic, the crafty campaigner was well aware of the hostility he now faced, even in the City. He was also rather apprehensive of the antagonism roused against him because of the Scottish minister: 'The supposed regard Lord Bute bears Mr. Sulivan has lost me my influence at this end of the town.'[45]

The other camp, controlled by Clive as if he conducted a military campaign, was extremely busy. It comprised a rich, amoral group of men. Especially vicious were those most recently returned from Bengal, and the Rous faction in the Direction. This was the hard core of opposition to Sulivan. *Goslings* Bank backed his Lordship; and the Newcastle-led Parliamentary Opposition drew towards him - the Duke working through his friend in the Company, James West.[46] Clive's entrance provided the landed gentry with the excuse to search for more footholds in the Company. Sulivan referred to this development, 'A noble Duke – the race of Walpole and Clive opposing me.' The nobility and gentry still looked upon the Indian scene with distaste – but with greedy eyes.[47]

Clive's stake was enormous. The total stock amounted to £3,200,000 and it was not easy to obtain. Yet he bought up £100,000 of this through the firm of *Cliffe, Walpole and Clarke*, creating 200 votes. His ally, Rous, split his stock and that of his friends. He also lied that he had struck an understanding with Bute, implying that Sulivan had little hope of support from that quarter. Sulivan was 'thunderstruck' at his 'effrontery'.[48]

The notoriously clannish Johnstone group also joined Clive. The brothers George, John and William (Pultney) Johnstone, sons of Sir James Johnstone of Westerhall, led this formidable party. Since 1761 they had been buying stock for splitting activities, and working against Sulivan in the General Court. They used a variety of funds, including those accumulated in Bengal by John Johnstone. The Proprietor, Andrew Stuart, of Craigthorn and Torrance, a relation of theirs, made loans to them all.[49] The Johnstones were infuriated at Sulivan's dismissal of John Johnstone after the Patna massacre.[50]

For the campaign, Clive followed Sulivan in the use of small canvassing books, ideal for drumming up support. There was to be a preliminary trial of strength at the General Court of 15 March, followed by the ballot proper. The exoneration of Rous from any blame during the preliminaries to the Peace of Paris was again to be the issue. The real aim, however, was to stir up resentment by heaping blame on Sulivan and the Government. Enormous heat was engendered; controversial issues were picked out and used as targets. Anonymous letters in the papers spread lies and propaganda. One in the *Gazetteer*, which Clive was sure had been written by Sulivan, accused him of abusing his Bengal office.

Both factions realized the importance of this General Court, held in *Merchant Taylors Hall*. They rallied their respective supporters the night before. Clive's followers and the Rous group went to the *Queens Arms* Tavern, St. Paul's Churchyards. The Sulivan party gathered at the *Kings Arms*, Cornhill. There was a very large attendance of 800 Proprietors at this Court: 657 voted in the ballot, and it cleared Rous. A show of hands beforehand also seemed to indicate that Clive would have a comfortable majority of the Proprietors on his side at the forthcoming election. Clive thought his party would become even stronger, but tempered his enthusiasm, noting that Sulivan and the ministry were active, canvassing and persuading all they had a call upon.

Sulivan's hectic electoral activity meant that his 'House' list was ready before Clive's. He gave a copy to Shelburne. Clive presented his 'Proprietors' list for Newcastle to peruse, much later. The Duke expressed his pleasure at his promising calculations. On 9 April the two lists appeared in the press. Of the twenty-four names shown on Sulivan's list, fourteen appeared on that of his rivals, that is, they were double-listed.

At 7 p.m. on 14 April, and following a preliminary skirmish over the use of the prestigious 'House' list title - where precedent won, the ballot was held. It showed that Sulivan had scored a handsome victory. Greater numbers had turned out than either Clive or Newcastle expected. It was also represented as a triumph for the Government over its enemies. The 'highest in Lord Clive's list was 81 below the lowest in Sulivans.'[51] The entire 'House' list was voted for, and the new Directors thanked the Proprietors for their success, 'After so warm and extensive a contest as never to have been equalled since the Company has existed.'[52]

The backing for Sulivan and the impact of the ministry's influence and cash had been badly under-estimated. As James West remarked, acidly, to Newcastle, 'Lord Clive must have been strangely misled in his calculations.'[53] Thomas Walpole sneered, 'We have been cheated out of the election by the clerks of India House.'[54]

The moment of victory was one for Sulivan to savour. He had shown his worth as a Company politician and had fought back against his detractors with a vigour that inspired further confidence. Clive had sustained his first defeat, and this in a contest he was sure he would win. But the nature of the struggle indicated that this joust would be only the first of many. As Holwell had prophesised in 1758, the factions in the Company were now at loggerheads. The annual elections meant that each April there would be a challenge; success or failure would depend on who enjoyed Government support.

5

In 1763 Sulivan moved from his villa at Mile End Green, to number 46 Great Ormonde Street Bloomsbury, a very fine, dignified mansion on the north side of the Street, which ran into Queen Square. He was the second largest householder, and immediate neighbour of the Venetian Ambassador. Aesthetic appreciation of what the street had to offer might have figured in his mind, ostentation certainly did. It was in his nature, and such a residence was expected of a man in his position.[55]

He had spent at least thirteen or fourteen years in a very unhealthy Indian climate; and there was always the danger this would cause difficulties in later life. But his general health (and that of his family) remained good, though he was ill in 1761 and suffered breakdowns.[56] Many small gifts, tokens of respect, flowed into London, not just from those who owed their careers to him. They are indications of the high regard in which he and his family were held. Vansittart sent muslin, via a Captain Jamieson. Then he despatched 'attar of roses' and Dacca muslins, through a Captain Richardson.[57]

In June 1763 his son Stephen, aged twenty, was admitted to the Middle Temple. Many assorted Sulivan, Owen and Irwin relations were also reaching young adulthood. They looked towards him for help, and he responded. John Sulivan, second son of Benjamin of Cork, was sent to the 'Academy of Greenwich', before being found a position as a Writer upon the Madras

establishment. He continued to care for his nieces, Anne (Nancy) and
Elizabeth (Betsy) Owen. The girls were now of marriageable age. This
created some discomfiture while they remained in England. But soon the
problems were set at some distance when in 1761 both sisters proceeded to
Madras on the *Fox*, travelling with Mrs. Palk. In Madras they joined the Palk
household.[58]

Within a year of their arrival and before they were both twenty, the two
sisters were married. Darvall, Nancy's husband, later became an agent for
him in India. Betsy was married, in July 1762, to Captain (later Colonel) John
Wood of the Company's army. Sulivan and his wife were kept informed of
their well-being by Palk, who acted as patron and mentor. During his
lifetime, Sulivan remained sole executor of their trust. According to Palk,
there was some disagreement between the sisters. 'Betsy' Wood complained
that her uncle was only allowing her £150 while her husband was away
fighting in Manila.

There are many indications that from 1760 onwards he begun to get
wealthier. He had at least £40,000 in 1758 which was certainly larger by 1761.
He enjoyed the proceeds from the sale of his house at Mile End Green; and
the capital he had invested would have brought a return. This would have
been much reduced by the purchase of the Ponsborne Estate and his town
house in Great Ormonde Street, but overall his portfolio was much
enhanced.

He remitted nearly £32,000 from Bengal in the 1757 to 1759 period,
working mostly alone. Around 10 per cent of this, would have remained in
his hands.[59] Separate accounts with Captain Hough showed a distinctly sound
balance of around £4,000 credit in 1762; and with him he had shares in the
freight of various East Indiamen, and a stake in the country trade. In 1763
the scale of these operations became even bigger.

His main activity, however, was the 'Marine Society'. This was a syndicate
in operation from Bombay days, consisting of himself, Henry Vansittart,
Robert Palk, Charles Crommelin, John Spencer, Peter Amyatt and Captain
Samuel Hough. Distribution of shares in the *Winchelsea* for the twelve months
from April 1763 to March 1764 exemplifies how it operated. Vansittart,
Spencer and Crommelin took three sixteenths each; Palk and Amyatt took
one sixteenth each; Captain Samuel Hough (who was ship's husband) took
eight sixteenths. Sulivan shared with Hough, Spencer and Vansittart. For
political reasons, his name did not appear on the records. It paid handsomely.
His duty was to ensure that everything would be to advantage when it came
to the sale of freight. Nor did the news that this ship had been run aground,
cause much concern. Vansittart ordered his attorneys to take two sixteenths
freight of the new vessel.[60]

The 'Marine Society' continued to prosper, growing ever more profitable;
and a list of subscribers was built up. Vansittart took out a second
'subscription' in March 1764. A safe channel was found in Captain Tinker,
but remittances were be forwarded through other channels.[61] Sulivan also left
some money in India for general investment in the country trade.

Most of his fortune, however, was almost certainly placed with the *London Assurance Company*. It would have been managed for him by Thomas Lane, his close confidant and a Director of that company. He had many other connections there: with Governor, John Hyde; the shipper Thomas Godfrey was a Director; and with Crommelin Pigou, the brother of Frederick Pigou (another East India Company Director) who was the assurance company's Accountant. Around 1760 Thomas Lane 'bought' a total of £7,500 East India stock from Sulivan. In all likelihood this too was transferred to the *London Assurance Company* on his behalf. It was politically expedient for him to keep such transactions out of sight.

Between October 1759 and January 1760 he accumulated £8,500 India stock; but had 'sold' £7,500 in dribs and drabs to Thomas Lane by April 1761. He then bought £1,000 stock needed to qualify as a Director. Much of this money Lane would have invested with the *London Assurance Company*.[62]

In 1765 his fortune would have amounted to between £40,000 and £50,000, and outright ownership of Ponsborne estate and his London town house. Possibly there was more. In September 1763 Robert Palk congratulated him on, 'The subject of the letters from the Lords Commissioners of Trade and Plantations.'[63] In August 1765 Palk alluded to another transaction, saying, rather cryptically, 'I congratulate you on the credit you must be in of purchasing in Ireland or Scotland.'[64]

On a personal level it was a very rewarding period. Launching into Parliament, becoming a country squire, life at Great Ormonde Street, all opened new fields of experience. His family and relations coming of age added new elements to everyday life. They became part of his growing network when they penetrated to India. His affairs were in a prosperous way; and he had not yet succumbed to any foolish gamble that might throw all at risk.

8

Challenge: Defeat:
And Reflection
1757-65

1

Sulivan faced a constant stream of hostility in newspaper and pamphlet form as the April 1764 election approached. The major features in the papers were about how obnoxious the Nabobs were, and the party divisions appearing in the Company and Parliament. Unavoidably, the ongoing struggle with Clive acted as a focus for everything and he found himself in the eye of the storm. He was also controversial because he was so central to the turn of events in National, City and Company politics; so much so it was scarcely possible to find an impartial appraisal of his contribution. Men feared him because he was in a position to help or hurt them.

The broadsheets reflected envy of his ability and meteoric rise to power. His ruthless cold-blooded approach to executive decisions and ready criticism had earned him enemies. Yet he was not being innovative in applying this level of censure, the 1754 Direction had railed against licentiousness in Bengal. His censures echoed the even earlier ones of Sir Josiah Child in the 1680s.

Perhaps the best pro-Sulivan statement is that which appeared in the *Public Advertiser* on 9 April 1768. Referring to these earlier years, it maintained that he had been at the head of affairs 'in the most dangerous and perilous hours that the Company ever experienced.' He had conducted himself with 'unquestioned ability and an unsullied character', at all times 'distinguishing himself for an honest and disinterested attachment to the Company. Nor was he the man to swerve in his devotion to the Company in its days of prosperity when he had more than once saved it in adversity'. Sulivan made much the same claim himself in 1778: 'My fame and fortune (perhaps my personal safety) were hazarded to save them.'[1] These views, however, are more than balanced by the opposite interpretation his enemies gave.

Two collections of real hate stand out. One was written by Thomas Rous, no name was appended to the other.[2] It was a much more formidable document; in pinpointing Sulivan's thoughts and actions during these years and in strength of attack it outshines Rous' work. In the eyes of both, every evil that beset the Company had its origins with him. He was portrayed as the 'arch-villain'. The author of the more formidable piece accused him of creating all the 'violent dissentions at home'; of 'aspirations to a despotic sway in the India Direction, symptomatic of an overbearing spirit that could brook no control'. The catalogue of alleged misdemeanours was endless.[3]

Readers were solemnly assured that Sulivan had created the struggle with the 'good-natured Clive' with his 'shining qualities'.[4] It was denied that he extricated the Company from the danger and distress it had laboured under in 1758 and 1759. This refutation is in itself significant, showing it was a commonly held view. Saying that it took the efforts of Dudley and Rous to put things right, must have appeared absurd to contemporaries who knew even a little of these men or of Company affairs. It was an endless tirade, but at least one truth was admitted, doubtless distasteful to them: Sulivan's diligence.[5]

Parts of the stream of disinformation and character assassination were very wounding, especially the assertion that his plans and instructions had nothing to do with success in India. This honour was awarded to the soldiers and servants of the King and of the Company alone. Such efforts to exclude his name beget the truth. The reality and the commonly held view was that Sulivan's input at this critical time was absolutely vital.[6]

Diatribes like this must be read in the context of cabalistic journalism. Yet, what his enemies said dampens any tendency to admire him uncritically, or to dwell on his many attributes without adverse comment. It is sobering to come across denial of features that he was praised for elsewhere.

A truthful picture, however, would be that he was honest; that he had the gift of instilling confidence in others; and reacted to critical situations without flapping. He was well-informed and knowledgeable of the ways of the world. His frustration can be readily imagined, faced with enforced ignorance of recent events abroad and confronted by baying enemies at home. Most of these were entirely unmindful of anything other than dividends and driving him out of office.

2

Of course, apart from policy-making, administrative duties, personnel problems, tumultuous events in India and remorseless attacks in the public newspapers, there was the little matter of resolving the struggle for mastery with Clive. The first round had gone his way in 1763, but before the contest was resumed, as it was certain to be at the next election, Clive was to be made to pay the price of defeat. Sulivan launched an attack on the *jagir*.

In April 1763, almost immediately following the election, Vansittart received orders to pay the *jagir* money accruing for the current year into the Company's treasury at Fort William. Sulivan had held misgivings about the *jagir* from the time it was granted, but had turned a blind eye. Following his challenge at the election, Clive could scarcely expect preferential treatment to continue.

The day after the instructions to Bengal had been signed the great man received word of it. He was indignant, and wrote immediately to Vansittart, Amyatt and Carnac in Bengal urging that they delay the implementation of the Court's resolution. Vansittart was to, 'act like an honest man and a man of honour' over the issue.[7] Incredibly, he then went on to warn Vansittart and the Bengal Council not to comply with the orders they had received from their superiors; and Amyatt and Carnac were to bring an action against them if they obeyed their instructions.

Meantime, in England he looked for a loophole to prevent the Company's instructions being complied with. The Directors refused to give him a copy of its proceedings relating to the fate of the grant, so he filed a Bill in Chancery and placed the case in the hands of his friend Lord Hardwicke. Three separate writs of subpoena were served: upon the Company, the Chairman, and Deputy Chair. The machinery of the law then took over and its ponderous slowness suited Sulivan.

To Clive the Company was only the collecting agency, and the annual *jagir* payment, though drawn from the Bengal treasury in essence did not belong to it. The lawsuit stifled his wish to be a Director, however, and he fumed 'of making the aggressors pay dear'.[8] Meanwhile, the executive wanted to know the real state of affairs regarding the *jagir*.[9] Vansittart and his Council were to discover how Clive obtained the grant; and it was to be examined for any imposture. The Secret Committee did not think there was any valid patent or title to it; and did not want to become 'tributary as it were to its own servants'.[10] Clive was depicted as having failed in his duty by procuring the *jagir* for himself rather than for the Company's benefit; and the committee did not want this to set a precedent. Additionally, since Mir Jafar was deposed in 1760, any original grant must be obsolete.

Revenge seems to have been uppermost in Sulivan mind in the summer of 1763. Nothing had happened regarding this matter until Clive's public opposition. Yet the move against the *jagir* was not altogether petty; a very real struggle for supremacy was going on where Clive's money was hugely important. Also, the sorry state of the Bengal treasury suggested that such a sustained drain on it would have a devastating effect.

Sulivan's enemies considered his action spiteful as well as illegal.[11] It was certainly his decision because he masterminded nearly everything. Yet in letters to Vansittart, he stated that Clive had forced his hand. John Dunning ably answered Clive's legal argument. Clive had charged that Sulivan's resentment of his wealth led to his (supposed) ill will; and that he had also approved the *jagir* arrangements from the start. Dunning pointed out that Sulivan had since given his reason for suspending payment, and this satisfied most Proprietors. Even if their friendship had ended, there was still the position of the Proprietors to be taken into consideration. Sulivan no longer stood in the way of the *jagir* payments being stopped. As Dunning put it, Sulivan had not actively pursued an end to the payments; he need only agree with the body of opinion in the Company. Dunning also thought it was only natural that Clive's personal enmity and opposition would mean Sulivan could have no further confidence in his Lordship.[12]

In stopping the *jagir* Sulivan was only doing what everyone expected. To most contemporaries it was well deserved. What has made his action seem so sinister was the swiftness of it all. Yet the reason was quite simple. A positive move had to be made before the April 1764 election, which could change the whole complexion of the Court of Directors.

Clive now sought the influence of his Parliamentary friends: Chatham, Lords Hardwicke and Powis, the Dukes of Newcastle and Devonshire. They were all unable to help. He then promised his support and Parliamentary interest to the new Grenville Administration, to no avail.[13] The Company was approached and offered a deal: that he keep the *jagir* for twelve or at the least ten years more, in return for abandoning his East Indian interests. The terms were unanimously rejected.

However, with Bute's replacement by Grenville in April, Sulivan lost his principal Parliamentary ally. He was then approached by Lord Sandwich, on behalf of the ministry. The Company was an integral part of the City where the new Government sought backing. This was also why Grenville and Sandwich tried to stop the Sulivan-Clive feud. Grenville had discussions with Sulivan and John Dorrien on 12 December. Clive thought the minister 'too sanguine' in his hope of success.[14] He was right. In September Sulivan had already written to Shelburne on hearing of his resignation from the Bute party and vowed his continued support.

It was at this juncture that news arrived of the revolution in Bengal, and all Sulivan's feelings of safety were cast to the winds. He was caught off guard, mainly because of the on-going struggle at home. The later official despatches were panic-stricken. Bengal had 'become a scene of bloodshed and confusion'.[15] Nothing else was talked about at Leadenhall.

It was utterly incongruous, however, that he, who for years had grappled with the emergencies erupting in India, might be struck down because of one of these crises. It was even more derisive that Clive, in this period at least anything but a public-spirited servant, should find his fortunes retrieved by the same sequence of events.

Reaction to the bad news soon appeared. The Proprietors were alarmed. It was feared dividends would suffer; India stock plunged; and news that Vansittart had dismissed some of his Council sent its price even lower. Differences with Clive were forgotten, and it was urged that his return to India was the solution. It was a heavenly opportunity for him, and the disconcerting news breaking so near the April 1764 election, made the moment even more opportune.

All his Lordship's forces from the 1763 election were still there to be called upon; and the newly dismissed Bengal Councillors swelled the numbers. The attack was launched when nine Proprietors, supporters of Clive, demanded a General Court to consider the situation in Bengal. It was fixed for 27 February 1764. Sulivan was charged with being responsible for the dismal state of affairs in Bengal. Aware that his attackers might suggest a vote of no confidence, he agreed with a resolution that Clive be asked to return to Bengal. He managed to make his followers do the same. Clive would give no reply there and then. However, the Proprietors were made aware that his going out at all depended on his rival being ousted and the *jagir* question settled.

Clive and his friends were also lobbying in Parliament, where Charles Jenkinson and the Treasury promised their support. By intervening on the 'rebel' side, however, the Grenville ministry did not act in the public's best interest. In choosing to reject the incumbent Directors (Administration's normal allies) the move challenged the traditional alignment; as did rejecting it because of good terms enjoyed with the ministry's predecessors.

On 1 March Sulivan and his group narrowly won the ballot on whether the executive was responsible for what had happened in Bengal. Yet another General Court was fixed for the 12th March. It was boisterous and clamorous. The Clivites again proposed that their leader should go out; and it was agreed that he should be made Governor and Commander-in-Chief in Bengal. He would supersede General Lawrence. Four others were to be nominated to form with him a Select Committee, empowered to act without reference to the Bengal Council. Sulivan could see very well the need for a strong man exercising vast powers; but Clive was not the man he thought best suited for this work.[16]

An attempt to force a ballot on whether his Lordship would accept these positions there and then was unsuccessful. He would only go if the Directors (meaning Sulivan) were as well-disposed to him as the General Court. A resolution was also passed that all proceedings against the *jagir* be dropped so that on that account he could make no objection to taking ship for India. Again Clive deferred giving any decisions. It suited his purposes to leave everything hanging fire just before the April election. Just as equally, it was to Sulivan's benefit to have him fixed in position.

The next thrust in this deadly 'game' came from Sulivan on 16 March. Pleading the seriousness of affairs in Bengal, Clive was urged to embark immediately, all being prepared. Clive, of course, had to stay for the election, as Sulivan would have figured. But at least he was given a new line to pursue – that the 'saviour' was dragging his feet. Whether he was the right man for the job must be looked at anew.

A showdown was expected at the quarterly General Court on 21 March. Again Clive declined to accept the posts until after the Company election. Sulivan and his followers seized upon this as a refusal and tried to annul the offer. They pointed out that on four separate occasions the great man had declined to give a firm acceptance of the posts offered to him.

Sulivan's move failed, however, because most Proprietors were persuaded they wanted him out to India at any price. If he would not go until after the election, they were not prepared to argue further. His Lordship was again asked if he accepted the offices and once more declined. Then, in the middle of heated exchanges, he rose and stated blankly that before he would undertake the management of the Company's affairs in Bengal, Sulivan had to be removed from office and from power.

Pandemonium ensued, everyone was on their feet, and nobody could be heard. Sulivan only just managed to maintain his composure. The Proprietors were forced, against their will, to choose between them. When the hubbub had died down Clive continued, stating how much he differed from Sulivan in policies and plans for the future; and that he did not consider him a right and proper leader. He said he could do nothing while Sulivan continued in power, because his enemy would simply cancel out all he attempted; adding that in his opinion Sulivan was ignorant of the real nature of East Indian affairs.

Once more there was uproar. This last assertion was staggering, such was the overwhelming evidence of Sulivan's adroitness and unimpeachable knowledge of India matters. The next accusation that Sulivan was his personal and inveterate enemy was an attempt to imply that all rancour stemmed from his opponent.

Clive's outburst was not liked. Sulivan contrived to be heard above the din. Cleverly using the current of sympathy, due to the predicament his enemy had placed him in, he painted Clive with his own words of hostility. By restating his wish for friendship, appreciation of his talents and a desire to cooperate, he made him appear boorish and placed his adversary on the back foot. The Proprietors pushed for some sort of amicable agreement. Clive was asked upon what terms he would engage in the Company's service. He requested a few days to consult his friends before giving his reply. Seven days later the letter sent to the Directors was published simultaneously in the newspapers. He would not accept the position if Sulivan continued in control. The Proprietors must choose between them.

As the election approached Clive appeared to have all the advantages: prestige; a majority support among the Proprietors; and some backing in the Direction. The 'Bengal Squad' was ready; he had his dazzling wealth; and the splitting machinery used in 1763. Most important of all, he had the support of the Grenville ministry.

Shelburne had left Bute and gone over to Chatham, so Sulivan drifted back there too – although still managing to keep some links with Bute. He also wanted to reach Grenville, but by November 1763 Clive had made the strongest connection with the minister through Jenkinson. Thereafter, Grenville would permit no approaches from him.

Within the Company Clive again worked with Thomas Rous and John Payne. The same old spurious arguments appeared and repeated *ad nauseum* in the press. However, the attack on Vansittart eased because he was making the Governor's followers hostile. His Lordship was also making converts.

Sulivan, however, faced the opposite. He lost the support of Henry Crabb Boulton and Henry Savage. The Johnstones were actively engaged, as they put it, in 'making a great push to turn out one O Sulivan, a Damned Irish Scoundrel who is chairman of the Directors'.[17] They entered the lists, desperate to have their brother John reinstated after being dismissed by Sulivan for receiving presents. Jenkinson, meanwhile, touted among the ministry's supporters; and was busy among officers of the Customs and Excise and clerks of the Post Office. Joseph Salvador, canvassed the 'Proprietors' list. Defeat, it seemed, was out of the question; Clive had the kind of backing that Sulivan enjoyed in 1763.

Nevertheless, the outcome was not at all clear until the very end. Once more Sulivan brought into play all the entrenched support he had enjoyed in 1763, minus ministerial backing. He verified later that this was decisive, but claimed that the desertion of someone like Amyand proved just as fatal. He also said the 'SCOTCH' were against him, referring to the Johnstones and their connections.[18] In Parliament only Shelburne, Barré and Calcraft of the Opposition stirred themselves on his behalf.

Yet 'the real natural strength of the Company' was still with him.[19] Colleagues from his service days in India gave unreserved backing. The bankers, brokers and underwriters were called into action once more. He summoned friends among the Proprietors: the Barwells, James and Lane; and from the Direction: Boyd and Thornton. Streams of connections were canvassed, such as the families of friends in India like Palk, Vansittart, and Spencer. The results were impressive.

Altogether both sides produced well over two hundred votes. Clive had between ten or twenty more. Thus through his 'natural interest' Sulivan had neutralized the Indian wealth of Clive and his allies, and almost that of the Government. Twelve candidates were 'double-listed', leaving the twelve remaining places to be contested. The Clive party gained six, Sulivan the other six, giving a dead heat. Sulivan, however, was only just returned; and it was reported in the *Gentleman's Magazine*, that 'Mr. Sullivan's being elected into the Direction depended upon a very nice question, whether Mrs. Drummond, Lady to the Archbishop of York, could be considered as a stockholder in her own right.'[20] It was decided that she could not, and this left Sulivan with a majority of one vote over his nearest challenger.

He also had an edge over his rival in the early stages of the election. First indications suggested he would have twelve selected, while Clive could be sure of only ten. Then additional Clive money and the waywardness of relationships in this cauldron of interests took over, and John Harrison appeared in Clive's list.[21]

Precedent had long established that the Deputy Chair automatically became Chairman the next year, but Sulivan's desire to be placed in the Chair without a ballot was denied, despite a majority for him in a show of hands. The reason given for a ballot was that the 'draw' in the election of Directors had been without example. The denial was crucial, however, and marked the watershed of Sulivan's control in these years.

Yet it was a close-run thing. An alarmed Clive-Rous camp had thought of coming to terms. The ballot result saved them: the number for and against was equal, which Sulivan interpreted as a personal insult. More importantly, he knew that he had lost the confidence of most Proprietors. He and some friends withdrew from the Court in what was described as a very strained atmosphere. Sulivan said afterwards that he would not vote for himself or he would have had the Chair. The humiliation was made complete with the immediate election of Rous and Boulton. It was reported that it was with some difficulty he was persuaded not to sell out his stock; and that five of his close friends, including those who had walked out of the General Court with him, also meant to sell out. That none of them did meant that the struggle for outright supremacy continued for at least another year.

3

Sulivan's withdrawal from the Court and not voting for himself appeared foolish then and seems so even now; he still commanded half the Direction. His withdrawal was interpreted, correctly, as a win for Clive in a trial of strength. Meanwhile, Company stock rose with the abatement of bad news from India, the cessation (it seemed) of the political contest, and Clive's imminent return to Bengal. His Lordship had three things to do, however, before he could safely go abroad. He had to secure the *jagir* money; obtain the favourable terms he had demanded for his government of Bengal; and make certain that Sulivan would no longer offer a political challenge.

For Sulivan the initiative was largely lost. He could only reply as best he could in the Courts and Committees, and prepare for the 1765 election. He would use his latent support to prevent Clive from achieving overwhelming supremacy at home and abroad. Without such action, the ground lost would be irrecoverable.

The struggle recommenced on 19 April 1764 when Clive expressed his views on the state of the Company's affairs and how far these diverged from Vansittart's (and thus by implication, from Sulivan's). He seized the reins of Company patronage, but had little to work with. Before the next Court assembled, however, the Direction was made aware of what he expected: the *jagir* issue resolved; John Spencer returned to Bombay; and the end of the Nawab's independence.

Ten Directors, Sulivan included, had already voted against or abstained regarding these terms, repeating their objections on 27 April. Sulivan strove to stop Clive from stamping his will on Bengal. To his relief, the enemy (who had just received the Order of the Bath) did moderate his demands, fearing he might endanger renewal of the *jagir* by alienating the Proprietors. He was only sworn in as Governor and Commander-in-Chief of Fort William. Spencer, however, was returned to Bombay. The *jagir* issue, and other terms that would give him special powers were left unresolved.

The rest of the Company only heard about all this at the General Court on 2 May, recorded as one of the stormiest ever held. It witnessed the struggle to see whether Clive would return on the Company's terms or his own. Sulivan launched an attack upon the *jagir* hoping to further weaken Clive's hand. Limiting his Lordship's Bengal's powers was as important to him as the *jagir* money was to Clive. This was of such importance to the great man it dazzled him; and symbolised the personal vendetta with Sulivan.

His terms were just as asked for in December 1763 – that he should enjoy the money for ten years more. The Proprietors, while they wanted him in India, had no wish to give him this money. It was an angry debate. Twenty Proprietors, all Sulivan's friends, voted against the *jagir* motion. Sulivan also pressed for a regulation that would shackle Clive and the other servants in India from accepting presents. A vote was called for.

Luckily for the Clivites, Grenville, Jenkinson and Joseph Salvador were busy, and when the ballot was held on 6 May Clive won, and the *jagir* was safe for ten more years. On the other hand, the powers he wanted were still not granted. Finally, on 17 May it was resolved that he and a committee of four would be given full authority in Bengal until the restoration of peace there. Even then, eleven Directors, including Sulivan, voted against these 'extraordinary powers', on the grounds that they were both 'unnecessary and dangerous'.[22]

Sulivan had every reason to be disturbed, Clive was almost unassailable. His Lordship was now President and Governor, Commander-in-Chief, and Chairman of the Select Committee of four, all of them hand-picked by him (Sumner, Carnac, Verelst and Sykes). When all powerful, he had planned similar powers for Vansittart, with the important difference that he would govern him from India House. There was no shackle on Clive. Sulivan was also aware that this further defeat over the *jagir* issue, plus the powers Clive had been given, were signs of failure to stop his foe; and his support drained away. In this sense, the *jagir* issue certainly merited its widespread infamy.

Although almost down and out, there was no mistaking his opposition until all was lost. A letter to his fellow Directors, on 1 June expressed 'Objections to signing the General Letter to Bengal with the certain powers contained therein to Lord Clive and a part of the Council there'.[23] Yet, although his enmity is understandable, the new Governor needed more authority to remedy things in Bengal. Sulivan was refusing to give Clive what he was prepared to give Vansittart. Suspicion and belief that some sort of control from India House had to be maintained governed him.

Clive sailed on 4 June 1764. His *jagir* was secure; he had a majority in the Court of Directors and had powers sufficient for his purposes in Bengal. He envisaged the final collapse of Sulivan in April and control of the Company shifting with him to India. Sulivan remained embittered. Even while Clive (as reported by Walsh) was intimating that he did not intend to 'enrich himself one farthing by any pay or emoluments he might receive', he remained convinced his enemy's return to India was for pecuniary advantage.[24]

Despite Clive's absence, strong forces were at work on his behalf during the build-up to the election. John Walsh wrote that Grenville would give every assistance against Sulivan, of whom 'the Court have a personal resentment…to the point of shutting him entirely out of the Direction'.[25] Within the Company the Clivites strengthened their grip. They knew Sulivan was capable of taking advantage of their splits and disagreements, and this held them together.

By February 1765 Clive's supporters were encouraging friends to split stock; and £4,300 of Clive's, and £20,000 in Walsh's name, was divided. The 'Bengal Squad' gave their usual backing; and before the election proper they were sure of fourteen of the twenty-four Directors. Yet the group's instability remained; that it did not break up was owed almost entirely to Walsh.

Backing for Sulivan was uncertain, both in the Company and in Parliament. Bute influenced some great Whigs, such as the Duke of Northumberland.[26] Luke Scrafton put it down to 'petticoat influence'.[27] To cajole support, Sulivan declared publicly, at *The Feathers* tavern, that he had no designs against Clive. Bute and Colonel Barré echoed these sentiments in Parliament. Walsh, not unnaturally, thought Sulivan was lying. Now in a minority in the Direction, he would not succeed, as Orme put it, 'until the Shelbournes Calcrafts and Barrys succeed in the Administration'.[28]

However, at first he had some success. Walsh wrote of the 'greatest alarms' Rous and Boulton were under, because he 'opposes all their measures and perplexes them much'. These two could scarcely get thirteen Directors to sign a letter merely advising the arrival of a ship.[29] His campaign really commenced in November 1764, when Walsh said he was 'very active and preparing for another tussle…He relies, I conclude, upon his orators.' He referred to Barré and Dunning. He also spoke, warily, of his great support among the shippers and ships' husbands.[30]

In the interim Clive lost the backing of the Johnstones and their Scottish allies. They disliked his effort to take John Johnstone's wealth from him in the Court of Chancery. It brought them over to Sulivan's side. He, meanwhile, had been building his own Scottish support, adding the powerful Proprietor John Stewart and Charles Boddam and all his relations. He also secured the backing of George Dempster, a firm friend of Bute; and inept electioneering by Rous won him the support of Sir James Cockburn, his relation John Stewart of Buckingham Street, and Sir Gregory Page. By February, though, he was hard put to find other backers. Captain Hough's death was a heart-felt blow. His plan seemed to be to set his own name singly against Crabb Boulton.

At the election he used the dexterity perfected in almost a decade of Company politics, employing the hand lists purposely developed. Again Walsh referred to them: 'Sullivan certainly means to make a push this year…printing off lists of Proprietors.'[31] The steady stream of desertions grew, nevertheless, as he shouldered the unpopularity from opposing the supposed saviour. The support of Luke Scrafton was lost. Walsh said he had opened his eyes to what he was really like.[32]

The loss of the financier Aaron Franks and the bankers *Devon and Child* was catastrophic.[33] Pigou, Chambers, and even Barwell followed. Walsh also hinted that Shelburne was half-hearted, and that Sulivan's friends, Lord

Howe and Robert Wood, would make peace with the ministry. He believed the Irishman was finished 'unless our friends (Rous and Boulton) prove themselves as impracticable in business to the ministry as they have done to me'.[34]

The Clivites and their Parliamentary associates also blocked Sulivan's effort to stop the creation of fictitious votes through the splitting of stock. They believed, probably correctly, that Sulivan tried to trick them when he split his own stock at Christmas, then tried to stop them from doing so. The Company (really Sulivan) had presented a petition to Parliament, followed by a Bill, to this effect. He threw all his weight behind both petition and Bill, as he saw them as a last chance to turn the tables. The Bill was defeated on a technicality.

It was the first effort to stop an iniquitous system; and a typical Sulivan mixture of public and private interest. Although of help to him, it might also have secured the Company's welfare. He probably over-emphasised its importance to his cause, however, because it is doubtful whether the prevention of about 200 votes for the Clivites would have changed the final result.

The passage of the Bill is interesting. It was thrown out at the second reading, according to Walsh, for: 'Not being drawn up conformably to the Company's Petition…it arose from accident not design.'[35] Walsh's analysis does not tell the truth, however. Sulivan had made it impossible to go against it on principle; but Grenville was under no illusions that it had to be stopped. The 'technicality' excuse was too coincidental.[36]

Again, as the election approached, the tirades in broadsides, and comments in daily papers increased. Scrafton, having renounced Sulivan, informed Clive that he would be 'turning pamphleteer' against the 'crafty insinuating little dog's application to the Proprietors'.[37] Only Mr. Cave's *Gentleman's Magazine* tried to give the truth, and in a remarkably fair assessment, Sulivan was both condemned and praised. He was chastised for his hostility to the Rous-led Direction and to Clive; had signed no General Letters to Bengal; and had shown too much favour to Vansittart. Nor had he paid a big enough dividend. Here the writer was quite wrong, there was no spare money.

He was then praised for his ability, his honesty and the fact that he was against the splitting system. He was needed 'to save the Company from ambitious and greedy servants', not to mention 'blundering and biased Directors'. His presence was essential to 'prevent another tenth of their whole capital from being granted away to the next officer who…shall demand £300,000 payable in England for a frivolous claim extracted by violence in India'.[38]

Newspaper harangue gave way to the election itself, which resulted in a sweeping victory for the Clivites. Scrafton's thought that out of despair 'the wretch (Sulivan) would now sink into oblivion'. He could not have been more mistaken.[39] His defeat was total, however, and every Clive supporter displayed relief. Boulton was elected Chairman and Dudley was made Deputy

Chair.[40] In Bengal, Clive rejoiced at his rival's overthrow, and now portrayed him, unbelievably, as a dangerous enemy to the Company. His continued fear of him as 'a very great rival', is revealed, however, in a letter to Joseph Fowke.[41]

Nervousness among Clive's disciples that their adversary might stage a revival continued until December 1765; and Sulivan might have been prepared to end all connections with the Company at that point. In Parliament his associates, headed by Sir James Hodges, tried to revive the Bill stopping splitting; and at Leadenhall attempts were made to rekindle interest in his fortunes.[42] All this was ignored. It was only in February 1766 that Clivite fears were finally put to rest. Scrafton wrote: 'Sulivan is making application for single votes for himself but I don't hear anything of a list.' He was still politically alive, but only just.[43] His defiance remained, however; and for his enemies a continued attention to Company affairs was ominous.

4

By 1765 the English had reached the point where they would never voluntarily relinquish the position that military prowess had won in India. The territories ceded and the degree of individual exploitation revolutionised everything. Control transferred to the Company; and with it went the burden of responsibility. Much of the native country trade was added to existing commerce, bringing economic ascendancy. Sulivan failed to stop any of this, because neither his agents (the Governors) nor indeed any serving Nawab was heeded. An army resolved the situation; and all was finalised at Baksar in October 1764, 'Squashing any nonsense' of native independence, and determining the English hold on a lucrative commerce.[44]

Sulivan had attempted to place the right men in India, with proper systems to work with. However, the men and systems had to be chosen by him, and the men had to take his guidance. Through Clive, Vansittart and Spencer he attempted in vain to have his policies implemented in Bengal; it was the same with Pigot and Palk in Madras, and Crommelin in Bombay. But no man would have been equal to the task. All the forceful directives, forward planning, instructions and attention to detail only worked to some extent in reversing the trend towards independent action in India.

He abhorred the abuse of *Dastucks*; and warned servants to keep their hands clean.[45] He tried to 'build a spirit of trade, industry and mercantile engagements'; but could not curtail private enterprise and corruption. Clive's non-compliance and his own failure to maintain obedience were fatal. It was all in vain; and to most Asians the English appeared, 'vile, worthless, without honour and gratitude.'[46]

He was on the right lines, however, in attempting adequate payment for the Governors. His uncertainty over the correct course of action, especially slowness in empowering Vansittart, did not help either; and the same doubt explains some tardiness in implementing regulations. He was not prepared to go as far as was required; hesitating to give Governors powers to quell insubordination and disobedience without referral to London. Those given to Vansittart and his Council in 1764 could be considered a late move, a grudging acceptance that the feeling in India of separateness from India House should be acknowledged.

The expected opposition to such a development appeared at Leadenhall, expressed in a memorial from Governor George Johnstone and George Dempster. They referred to the 'extraordinary powers entrusted with Mr. Vansittart'.[47] Nevertheless, an irreversible shift in the position of the Company and its servants in Bengal had taken place.

Some praise is due however. In this era, only his activity and stentorian voice prevented even more serious loss of control from London. He managed to put some kind of check on the move to autonomy because he dominated for so long, and was able to implement one-man control. As a consequence, executive control from India House, although diminished, was not doused. Later the Governor-General concept would embrace the development of semi-independence, beginning with Sulivan's nominee, Warren Hastings.

As far as his long-term blueprint for India is concerned, it was successful in the methods laid down, and in the direction given. The idea of limited sovereignty and maximum trade was tried and failed; but the transformation from trading post to empire that followed was established on his pragmatic approach to difficulties and realisable solutions. Contemporary ideas could wither and die while underlying arrangements served as guidelines for future developments.

He had preserved order when faced with chaos; and in clinging to the sanctity of the Company's Charter mapped the way ahead in State-Company relations. His cautious approach also saved his precious Company from bankruptcy, disintegration and collapse. On a personal note, the degree to which he enjoyed these struggles should be noted. He thrived on them. He did not want to be anywhere else; only India House could give him what his heart desired.

5

The dispute with Clive was not all about pride and vanity. They both had clear visions of what they wanted – reflected in their contrasting futures for the Company. However, there were very obvious differences in temperament, not just those reflected in their occupations of soldier and businessman. Generally, Sulivan reacted to how he was treated or accepted. Clive found it easy to have a love-hate relationship with people. Sulivan was startlingly honest throughout his public career.

From the start Sulivan was a conservative force, opting for slow change. Keeping the Company solvent was his prime objective; buying time to make adjustments, correct abuses, curtail military expenditure and put the Company on a sound commercial basis in India. Swamped by traumatic events he tried in vain to find a settling down period.

Company independence was maintained, and Parliamentary intrusion kept at bay until the day Clive fully committed the Company to a territorial role by acquiring the *Diwani*. The fact that developments then took a different path was outside his control; and led to State intervention. The wealth his rival brought to bear was a problem, and to match it he was not too fussy where the money came from. This allowed infiltration by undesirable elements. Yet it was never his intention to undermine the Company by this, or permit the Parliamentary control Clive wanted.

As far as he was concerned, Clive was a traitor; a servant bent on the Company's liquidation. And to him it was scandalous that he had to counter someone working against its best interests from within its own body. He also found it astounding that he, the acclaimed leader of the Company, presiding over everyone, was forced to combat an employee who insisted upon placing himself before anything or anyone else. He, on the other hand, knew his duty: 'The Company's interest must ever with me supersede all other considerations.'[48]

Clive respected his rival, but did not really understand him. This gave Sulivan an advantage, because he had come to know the military-Governor type of mentality. He had spent fourteen years close to successive Governors: Horne, Law, Wake and Bourchier. In fact, Clive's two secretaries, Walsh and Strachey, probably understood Sulivan better than their master.

6

As long as Sulivan had power, everything was kept strictly within the framework of how well the Company's best interests were served. Its monopoly, independence and chartered rights, wrung from successive Governments, were untouchable. What he did was of tremendous benefit to the British nation, not just the Company. He had been a very effective war leader and organiser of victory in the East; planning and executing expeditions and campaigns against the French, Dutch and hostile Asian powers, most of which were successful.

His aim of reforming the administration of India was only partly achieved; but increasingly he came to see this as his life's work; and his labours helped shape what the Company would become. The next twenty years of his life would complement this. He looked to the future and carefully plotted long-term measures for the better government of the Company's possessions in India. Towards this end he introduced sound organisational bases and efficient methods that would stand the test of time; improvements that were recognised, long after his demise:

> The East India Company's three presidencies of Calcutta, Madras and Bombay stood out like oases of order and comparative plenty. The inevitable happened. Efficient organisms swallowed inefficiencies...the old trading Company...graduated into one centralised all-powerful bureaucracy.[49]

He has been unjustly traduced over the part he played during these years. This wise man was more than equal to the responsibility placed upon him during a period of dire emergency.[50] No charge of mismanagement of Company's affairs can be laid at his door. On the contrary, he maintained and perfected its traditional policies. He wished to avoid the complications that accompanied imperial design; wanted no involvement in Indian politics; and had no wish to bear the brunt of the legalities and expenses that would arise. Nor had he any wish to be caught up in the moral and material problems arising when one culture becomes involved with another. He hated what might be termed racial imperialism that he sensed developing with Clive.

An exceptional clear-sightedness was combined with determination to see a thing through to its conclusion. In this period of great stress, he provided drive, grit and guidance. His diplomacy is reflected in the way he deferred to Chatham during the war, while carrying inordinate responsibility himself. Colleagues praised him for numerous rescues. His discernment and grasp were recognised and remarked upon despairingly by enemies. From 1757 until April 1764 he enjoyed complete control over all facets of Company business never before enjoyed by any man, and never enjoyed by him or any other again.

As far as he was concerned the East India Company had to pay its way, and produce profits. This would also stop the State from threatening its independence. Strict bookkeeping kept the whole rambling structure within practical bounds. Hard-headed men of business, like himself, ran the Company and put their money into it. They might have spent early careers elsewhere, as traders, insurers and bankers, or they might be from the landed gentry; but when they became Directors and Proprietors of the East India Company, all was different.

The vast quantities of money invested dictated that each situation had to be looked at principally from a business point of view: the value of the stock and the soundness of the commercial organisation. Then as time went on this came to mean something else – although always kept secondary to making a profit. Any other manner of control would have meant bankruptcy.

This balance-sheet-conscious man helped lay down the foundations for a host of future developments. His groundwork during such a troubled era, later both amended and defended by himself and others, was to last as long as the Company existed. He was certainly the central figure in all that happened, just as he would be later. He would fight to regain the power within the East India Company that he valued above all other things; and for the Company's independence from Governmental control, which he associated with British liberty.

The high regard he was held in was reflected in a number of ways. A street in Madras was named 'Sulivan's Gardens' in his honour. Two East Indiamen, the *Sulivan* and *Ponsborne,* echoed the popularity he enjoyed among ship owners. This mixture of approval and awe is reflected in the words commonly used to describe him: 'Leader of the Company'; and even more evocative: 'Uncrowned King of Leadenhall'.

7

With his exclusion from the Direction and with Clive in India, the feud was removed from the forefront of Company and national news. The struggle for dominance had been long and painful, but Clive's success could only be temporary. The confrontations would only flare again as Sulivan strove to regain the position in the Company that his ability warranted and his enemies denied. Nevertheless, their first clash had been very severe. The personal nature of the quarrel led to further feuding that continued for a quarter of a century.[51]

He kept himself abreast of events after 1765 through place-men within India House and correspondents in India. He was too good a politician and too revengeful to be permanently exiled from power. With so many nonentities in control, it was always possible that his exclusion might be of short duration. John Walsh summed up the qualities of his allies:

> As to our friends, the Chairman and Deputy, they go on as might be expected of them. It is certainly the greatest joke upon all government to see such people jostled into the management of affairs of such extent and of so much consequence to this Kingdom.[52]

That he did not return quickly, however, was partly due to the fatigue felt by many, and their relief to have an end to the seemingly never ending struggle. It was also partly because Sulivan needed longer than a year to fuse into a party the disparate interests and numerous adventurers who now jockeyed for position among the Proprietors.

The tight control exerted by Clive's able deputies, John Walsh and Luke Scrafton, also kept him at bay. These same lieutenants sifted through papers at India House, but could find nothing incriminating, and Clive was forced to admit Sulivan's honesty. His Lordship had also transferred his support to Rockingham when the Grenville ministry fell in mid-1765; and was helped in that no major East Indies questions had to be faced; there were no issues demanding Sulivan's kind of expertise.

In Bengal, Spencer was indignant at the speed with which he was torn from office. He eventually left Bengal for Bombay on 25 October 1765, his bitterness deepened by the death of his wife from the 'dropsy'.[53] On arrival, Clive found that Mir Jafar was dead and Spencer had made the prince's second son, Najim-ud-Daula, Nawab. The Prince was totally unsuited to govern, but had no power to remove his leading ministers, now appointed by the Company. Clive had only to complete the alliance desired by the Mughal Emperor. The Vizier of Oudh, Shuja-ud-Daula, desired reconciliation as well, following Baksar; and ceded lands at Benares and Ghazipur.[54]

Clive's activities in Bengal kept proprietary influence inclined towards his continued direct rule in India and indirect control at India House, especially with his acceptance of the *Diwani*. The Company received the entire revenues of Bengal, Bihar and Orissa. In return, it was responsible for paying the army; had the accountability and expense of government; collection of revenues; and administration of justice. The Nawab, now a mere cipher, received 50 *lakhs* annually.

The new Governor used the Bengal Select Committee to great effect. He ignored criticism of it expressed by Sulivan, the Johnstones and George Dempster in the General Court. They were especially fearful of its secrecy and the threat it offered to the civil authority. He also fixed an income for himself and friends in salt, involving the sum of £30,000. Warren Hastings was refused a part of this because he was Vansittart's friend.[55]

Implementation of the 'Dual system' of government enabled him to further his plan of bringing the new territories under the nation's control at the expense of the Company. He was lucky that the Company Proprietors, apart from the likes of Sulivan, did not see this and that the Company did not fold. Fortunately, the Irishman's earlier overhaul of the organisation's commercial basis enabled the system to function. His Lordship lost no time, however, in blackening his rival's name. John Spencer's information was that:

> His discourse in common talk respecting you is most improper, nay, even to me he can scarce contain his contempt...You honestly express yourself as having no Personalities as to Lord Clive, that is not his case respecting you. You are so frequently the subject of his discourse and that in so indecent a degree...I cannot subject you to the insult and wrong.[56]

Spencer thought they could never reach an accommodation. Astonishingly, and true to Spencer's report, no words of blazing anger or expressions of everlasting enmity towards Clive can be found anywhere in Sulivan's correspondence.

9

Fresh Start and New Game
1765-67

1

Sulivan quickly picked up the thread of his public life and concerned himself with what was required to return to power. He was not yet prepared to sink into obscurity, to be remembered as a once powerful man who had been swept to defeat and ignominy. Not a year was to pass in which he was not preparing to contest an April election. He clutched tightly to Shelburne and his circle, especially to John Dunning and Colonel Isaac Barré. With their support, inside and outside of the Company, he would begin his climb back to power.

Even after his defeat, he remained a figure to fear. He carried with him a permanent support within the Company, his so-called 'natural strength'. What is more, his artistry in bringing together individuals and parties made him dangerous. John Spencer had alerted him to the fact that the Johnstones had abandoned Clive, and they came over to the Sulivan–Vansittart alliance, even though John Johnstone and the Vansittarts had always been at variance. Henceforth, Sulivan set out to be receptive to this Scots phalanx, regardless of like or dislike. The addition of Henry Vansittart (family and connections too) was very welcome. It followed Clive's ill-advised criticism of Vansittart's governorship.

A veritable maelstrom of public sentiments now affected Leadenhall. The general feeling was that shackles on trade should be loosened. The attack centred on entrenched monopoly and chartered rights; that force was still being used to back up so-called 'open barter' in India. Within the Company the feeling spread that accretion of military and naval power in India was uncontrolled. Pockets were still being lined; military costs continued to rise, shattering any real expansion in trade. The Company's financial structure was too limited to allow it to ease over these hurdles.

There were new interests in the General Court; groups whose numbers were continually added to. Sulivan had to develop his talents in fresh directions to deal with these intruders. They were also threatening the Clivites; and grappled with the old commercial interest. The most menacing was the ministerial grouping. In return for promoting within India House the initiatives of their Parliamentary friends, many, such as George Wombwell, and Robert Jones, received contracts and Government business. Courtiers like Lord Sandwich began to gain more influence. Luckily Sulivan had kept his connection with the Godfreys and other prominent ships' husbands, because the shipping interest became even stronger.

He wooed many people, aiming at bringing diverse individuals and factions together, merging their desires with his own to create a new political force. His mantra was that all their wishes would be accomplished if a party, led by him, predominated at India House. They formed a motley collection: ministerial friends; former associates from the Court of Proprietors; his confidants within the Company's shipping interest; contacts from the City's commercial world; and 'Indians' who were, in the main, contemporaries of earlier years.

The new people merged with the supporters he still had within the Company. Their one common denominator was opposition to Clive or to anyone he influenced. He added Leycester, Gray, Burdett and Senior, all disgusted with Clive's 'reforms' in Bengal. He aimed at pitting the wealth of these returned Company servants against that of Clive and his colleagues. Gradually he began having more success, and ever more strenuous efforts were needed to keep him out of office.

His exclusion from the executive had led to a serious lowering of standards. Neither of the 'Chairs' had his kind of expertise; and they remained highly suspicious of him.[1] Their general level of incompetence and the fact that his Lordship backed such men gave Sulivan every incentive to harass them. Clive's absence until 1767 was also a great help, because a growing unease at his untoward control enabled him to work up a dislike of over-rich Nabobs. He also fanned into life his anti-splitting Bill to counter the influence of rich men like Clive.

What developed in Bengal during Clive's last sojourn there was to have a bearing on the Company's development and Sulivan's manoeuvres. The Battle of Baksar in 1764 had removed the main threat to stability in the Bengal region. That, and the defeat of the exasperated Mir Qasim, who died in 1765, led to relative tranquillity. But Clive's return put a stop to plans Sulivan had already launched for a proper system of joint-government, centred in Bengal, which was in operation before his arrival.[2] With Clive's implementation of the 'Dual System' (following assumption of the *Diwani* in 1765) Sulivan's administrative system, better suited to trading concepts, was pressed into other uses, and employed in ways never intended.

Under the 'Dual System', each position had its European and Indian counterpart. It turned into a disaster, creating a burgeoning bureaucracy, and led to corruption, brutality and inefficiency. Neither redress of grievance or accountability became possible. It created intolerable strains. The dispensation of justice, policing and keeping of law and order generally was a nightmare.

Yet at first Clive reinforced order in the military and civil establishments. He quashed a threatened mutiny; and struck at illegal private trade. This created new and dangerous enemies who, on return were welcomed by Sulivan who was blind to real worth in some of his adversary's early attempts at reform. Seen through his eyes, Clive could not be allowed more laurels, which would have made a return to the Direction even more difficult. Besides, his Lordship supported all attempts to exclude him; and in Bengal was flushing out his men and replacing them with his own.

In Britain, sovereignty over such large areas of the sub-continent sparked off an attack on three levels. First, Edmund Burke voiced a growing belief that the Company should not be allowed to hold the, 'Delegation of the whole power and sovereignty of this kingdom sent into the East.'[3] Secondly, it was proposed that the situation could only be corrected by Parliament, a perfect opportunity for MPs to interfere in Company business

The third consequence was a massive new interest in Company affairs among many with money to spare. It centred on India stock, and Leadenhall became a magnet for speculators. Sulivan was in a difficult position; political ambitions dictated he did nothing to dispel speculation, although uncomfortable with it. However, he was driven to using 'jobbers'. His need for rich, allies was desperate. He took refuge in the figures Clive sent home, which gave the impression of great wealth in Bengal; and envisaged money flowing into the trading network, propping up all commercial activity abroad without recourse to bullion from Britain. Trade to the Far East would also be encouraged.

By Clive's estimates, the *Diwani* would bring a surplus of £2 million per annum. He had instructed relations that his money was to be invested in India stock; and with this the great boom began in March 1766; intense speculation broke out in the London, Amsterdam and Paris. Also, the character of the stock altered, until then it was regarded as a Security; from that point it was to become ever more fluctuating until the world credit crash of 1772-3. Speculators, many now allied with Sulivan, saw a way of making money through using the Company's vote-making machinery. Any man or measure promoting a boom in the price, which in turn made possible an increase in the Company's dividend, was to be helped, encouraged and voted for.

He had persuaded himself his return to the executive would be beneficial all round, and found working with these gamblers useful and effective to this end. They provided money for splitting campaigns; while he brought immense knowledge and political skill. He integrated the speculators aims with his own, and applied himself to increasing the price of Company stock. The higher dividend paid could bring success at Company elections. His own anti-splitting desires were temporarily forgotten. Also, in pursuit of high dividends he now wished to retain revenues from the new territories, but was prepared to allow a payment to the State.

At times, however, it was difficult to reconcile efforts on behalf of his stock jobbing connections, such as promoting the end of the ban on dividends in 1766, with plans for the Company's benefit. He had placed himself in a weak position through alliance with those 'dealing in the alley'. Throughout the summer of 1766 the Directors blocked every attempt to raise the value of stock. In August the speculators turned to political measures, and became set on gaining a majority in the General Court. This brought them into even closer contact with Sulivan. The stock jobbers then organised a press campaign, mainly using the *East India Examiner*. The *East India Observer*, produced by the Directors, replied.

In September a great splitting campaign began. Sulivan was involved, but did not use his own agents. The upshot was a victory for those 'bulling' the stock, and the dividend was raised to ten per cent. Sulivan was prepared to ally himself with the stock jobbers because of the need for votes. He would have been in two minds, however, over damage created by allowing the speculators full rein; but it is doubtful if he could have stopped them anyway.

After his defeat in April 1765, the general belief was that he would not contest the 1766 election. However, he managed to blend several important men to his cause, such as the influential Henry Fletcher, and his friend in the Direction, William Webber. They joined Vansittart and the Johnstones. Although none of this was a secret to Clive, Sulivan's list, in opposition to the 'House' list, was still something of a surprise. He was easily defeated, however, Lord Rockingham throwing his weight alongside that of the Clivites.

The 1767 election was fought against the backdrop of yet another of the Company's temporary financial crises, and the Parliamentary inquiry that attended it. The need to work out a new agreement between Company and State gave Sulivan the sort of electoral opportunities he needed. Thus, suggestions for solving this crisis always served the double purpose of furthering possible success at the election. Despite the hostility of the Clivites, he felt hopeful. He was encouraged by some real growth in his party. He also pinned great hopes on Westminster now that Chatham was back in power; and this ministry included his friend Shelburne.

It was in the lead up to the 1767 election that he began his association with the Ulsterman, Lauchlin Macleane, who in 1766 was under-secretary to Shelburne. Macleane (who was also a Doctor of Medicine) was a man of startling personality and hypnotic presence. He could press friendship on the one hand, and prise information on the other. He was a rogue and trickster of the highest order; the most important of the speculators and adventurers that Sulivan thought he could use. However, it was to be Macleane who used him.

Working with Macleane and a John Motteux, Sulivan held a form of joint-leadership over the jobbers, many operating from within the monopoly. He was also involved with the Scottish group: George Dempster, Lord Elibank and his nephews the Johnstones. His own holding of India stock does not reflect his real involvement because he made use of intermediaries.

Macleane was Sulivan's strongest link with this motley crowd; and such was the Ulsterman's mesmerising clutch, he seems to have come completely under his spell. Macleane set about uniting Sulivan with the *Hope* banking firm of Amsterdam; with *Goslings, Coutts, Grant* and *Fordyce* banks; and brought introductions to the influential Wedderburn and Leycester. For elections, he was forever forming interests and alliances (of a very dubious nature). However, through him Sulivan remained on good terms with General Conway, the other Secretary of State, as well as with Shelburne.

Several other ties strengthened at this time were with old colleagues William Barwell and Henry Savage; and with Sir George Colebrooke and George Dudley. In September 1766, Lord Verney, together with William, Richard (the younger) and Edmund Burke (though the latter was acting secretly) also joined the group, via Macleane. They were all under Verney's umbrella. Macleane and Edmund Burke had been at Trinity College Dublin together and had renewed their acquaintance by December 1765.[4]

The Clive camp feared this group would bring Sulivan back to power. In the period February to March 1767, while acting on behalf of Lord Holland, John Powell of the Pay Office split £43,000 for Sulivan and other Government-backed candidates. Although forbidden to do so, Macleane would also employ Holland's hundred votes in favour of Sulivan and Vansittart at the election. A surprising number of votes, from a variety of sources, were in fact created for them.

They were not enough. Despite hoping for some agreement with Clive, by not opposing the renewal of his *jagir*, he lost the election; and his humiliation was complete when Clive's prize was renewed for another ten years. The hero of Plassey was unremitting: 'Mr. Sulivan still entertains hopes of being a Director, to which ambitious view I shall give every opposition in my power.'[5] His Lordship's support in the Company was still too entrenched to be moved. Rockingham's backing for the existing Directors also helped determine the result; as did that of Charles Townshend and Sir George Colebrooke, the latter entering the Direction as a Clivite.

2

The Parliamentary Inquiry of 1766-67, which threatened the Company's independence, is best explained by the late Dame Lucy Sutherland in her *East India Company in Eighteenth Century Politics*. However, Sulivan's participation in what happened was so deep, extensive and relevant, it needs to be made explicit. He understood precisely how important this inquiry was for the future of the monopoly. Also, the emergency that gripped the Company ran concurrently with his effort to re-enter the Direction in April 1767, and had a bearing on what transpired.

All began with yet another financial crisis in the Company's affairs, one that became public in 1766. Even as the dividend was being raised from ten to twelve and a half per cent, through the efforts of the stockjobbers, bad tidings from India arrived. The Inquiry followed – the Government's first direct intrusion into Company business.

When Chatham seized the excuse to interfere he had no grandiose scheme in mind; nor did he wish for expansion of empire; he merely wanted a portion of the income the Company was drawing from its new territories. He envisaged an additional £1 million going into the Treasury. In exchange the Company would receive an extension to its charter and all the privileges this conferred. His claim was based upon the sovereign right of Great Britain to all territories acquired by conquest. Personally, Chatham believed the nation deserved a reward for helping the Company attain what was believed to be great riches. Royal naval protection had been essential to success.

The first warning of impending intrusion came in August 1766, when the right to enjoy sole profits from territorial gains was challenged by Alderman William Beckford, who did not disguise his dislike of the concern. The direction of the Government's attack was soon made clear: the Company's Charter was to be threatened.

Realising the enormous threat to the organisation's independence, Sulivan gave the matter his unswerving attention. Although out of the Direction he was to fill a liaison role that made him central to all that transpired. His seat in Parliament also meant he had opportunities and channels at hand for discussions with ministers and other parties concerned. As a Proprietor operating within the General Court and knowing the competing factions there, indeed he headed one of them, he was fully implicated.

He welcomed the role because it called upon his knowledge, abilities and interest in the Company's welfare. His major objective at all times was to safeguard the monopoly's autonomy. Paradoxically, the alliances he had made with so many mushrooming interests within the Company placed him in the forefront during early discussions on the monetary crisis. He was one of the first to treat with Administration, contacted because of his knowledge, skill and availability.

His Parliamentary connections were of even greater significance, and his drawing room was the first port of call. He had unfettered communication with both Chatham and Shelburne. The ties with the latter had been renewed and greatly strengthened, primarily because of the machinations of Macleane. By then, of course, the Ulsterman was deeply involved with him in more clandestine activities.

Members of the Macleane-led group also had connections with the Rockingham Opposition that could be utilised. George Dempster, Lord Verney and William and Edmund Burke provided the links. Grenville, though he found him useful, never liked Sulivan. Perhaps this was because, as Charles Townshend's, *Estimate of the Strength of Parties in the House of Commons 1766/7* suggests, he was regarded as a Chathamite at this time.

Sulivan played a bigger part, therefore, than his exclusion from the Direction might suggest; and in fact, the plans he put forward were probably more readily accepted because of this. He was regarded as the best channel for the receipt and dispersal of information; was to be essential for Company dialogue with the ministry; and was used in the same way by those parties who both supported him and had an interest in what would happen. However, there was no attempt by any group to control the Company through him; he was too able and too respected to be used in such a manner. Nor was he ever a ministerial Trojan horse inside India House for any Parliamentary party or minister.

He was not slow in recognising the weaknesses within the Administration, although the only real disagreement within the ministry was over how the assault on the Company should be made. He exploited the divergent opinions ministers voiced on how to handle the whole business, with the aim of ensuring the Company's best interests and continued survival.

The ministry split into two distinct factions: Chatham, Grafton and Shelburne on the one hand, with their Parliamentary followers, such as Shelburne's John Dunning and Isaac Barré; on the other side stood Charles Townshend and Conway. The divergent views soon became apparent. The Chatham group wanted, 'A direct attack on the Company for challenging in Parliament their right to derive any revenue from Bengal.'[6] The Government would simply deny the Company possession of the territories, allowing the revenues to accrue to the State.

Townshend and Conway wanted the State to have a share of the gains already made by the Company and a portion of the wealth from all its future acquisitions as well. This was to be achieved through negotiation with the Directors – holding the threat of an inquiry menacingly in the background. They believed it impossible to push the view that the Company had no legal basis for its territories. At Westminster, Parliamentary Opposition, through the voice of Edmund Burke, condemned the Government's proposals as an attack on the sanctity of property.

Shareholder wishes could be summed up as a desire for a portion of the territorial revenues; preservation of chartered rights; and a defence of private property. Many Proprietors agreed, however, that the State did deserve some payment in return for help in the acquisition of the territories. It was also thought by many (in and out of the Company) that some sort of investigation was required anyway. There was a need to sort out the confusion created by speculation, by uncertainty over the true state of the Company's finances, and why there was persistently bad government in India.

Unfortunately, this was not the Administration to carry out such an inquiry; and Chatham's withdrawal from public life meant there was to be no leadership. As the first minister faded into the background, Shelburne assumed control over their joint supporters. He guided the group away from an attack in Parliament and towards negotiation with the Company's Directors, the view shared by the Townshend-Conway set.

In August 1766 Charles Townshend, informed the Company that he was preparing a Bill, 'For carrying into execution the several resolutions of the House of Commons...and he desired to hear whatever the Chairman and Deputy might have to suggest in relation to the subject as soon as was convenient to them.'[7] The General Court (with Sulivan to the fore) was the first to respond to this.

Taking the initiative in ascertaining the facts, the Proprietors discovered that between 16 September 1766 and 24 June 1767 there would be a deficiency of £628,000 in the Company's trading account. Various ideas on how to resolve the crisis were discussed, such as those of Joseph Salvador.[8] All of these Sulivan repeated to Shelburne. He then headed a group of Proprietors that called upon the Directors to ask Parliament for an extension of 37 years to the Charter, in exchange for the revenues from territories that had been acquired after 1757. After the Company getting £480,000 per annum for ten years (as a yearly dividend of fifteen per cent), Government would enjoy the rest of the money.

More plans appeared, such as that by Solomon da Costa and one by Mr. Stewart of Buckingham Street; but out of all the proposals, those of the Directors were accepted and went forward to the ministry. In point of fact, the views put forward by the executive were moderate enough and allowed Townshend to avoid the threat of a Parliamentary division.[9] But he now acted a part by temporarily refusing to receive the Directors on the issue.

Having failed to see his own efforts accepted, and instead witnessed the Directors' proposals being forwarded, Sulivan reverted to Parliamentary circles and was busy among his fellow MPs. In December he met the Chatham ministry at Conway's house to help consider the policy needed. He did not say much there, but during the debate in the Commons a few days afterwards was complimented by Administration upon his great knowledge of Company business. This suggests he had really been airing the ministry's views in the proposals made to the General Court on 14 November (with which he concurred), and was working hand in hand with the ministers.

In January 1767 Chatham reaffirmed that Parliament had the right to intervene in the Company's affairs if it so wished; and that the Inquiry was meant to establish this fact. However, all was postponed until the final terms offered by the Company were known; and in a sense, this marked the end of the first phase of the Inquiry.

Sometime in January, Sulivan gave Shelburne a paper, the substance of which was to be communicated to Chatham. He appeared to promise that the Proprietors (whom he admitted, all too knowingly, were the source of much mischief) might be brought around to agree with the ministry if their own terms were used as a starting point, and not those of the Direction. His main aims were to preserve the initiative gained by the Proprietors' Court; and to ensure that neither Government nor Direction should be precipitate in their actions. He was still tenaciously pursuing the ideas he put forward on 14 November 1766: of gaining an extended Company Charter in return for territorial revenues.

By February, however, his positive attitude had begun to wane. This was mainly due to bad publicity – but he still urged a Government initiative along the outlines he had proposed. Chatham would not budge. He thought Sulivan's paper very good: 'It contains, as whatever comes from that gentleman always does, very considerable lights', but thought the lack of restriction upon the Company's use of the territorial revenues dangerous.[10]

The suggestions presented by the Directors in November 1766 were eventually forwarded to the Cabinet on 14 February 1767. They were immediately referred back for further explanation, only to return as quickly, replete with additional comment, on 20 February. By then Chatham had retired from public affairs and would give no further guidance. Grafton fought the Townshend minority for the right to reject the Directors' terms and won. This split the Cabinet, and an open breach was only narrowly avoided.

Alderman Beckford moved for the printing of all the accumulated India papers that he had first demanded on 10 December 1766, including the proposals made by the Directors. Townshend opposed this as being premature. Parliamentary Opposition took these differences within the ministry as the opportune moment to interfere. Grenville's supporters agreed with Rockingham's group to organise a petition (ostensibly from the Company) against the printing of the papers. This was effective. On 9 March the Government was thoroughly outfaced. Beckford's motion was dropped; and with it went Chatham's attempt to force the Company to give money to the Treasury from the new territorial revenues.

The next phase of the Inquiry really opened in February 1767. Parliamentary interest had now faded because it was no longer an open issue between the ministry and Opposition. Sulivan again played a pivotal role as it all unfolded. The main reason for this was that he had maintained his contacts with Shelburne and with the majority within the split Cabinet.

By February the ministry's original plans had been wrecked upon the rocks of Company obstinacy and disquiet; by the opportunism of the Parliamentary Opposition; and because of a divided and leaderless ministry. However, there still existed the chance of an accommodation with the Company through Sulivan. Although Chatham had rebuffed his plan, neither he nor Shelburne (increasingly left to make do) were willing to give up; and Sulivan was ready to re-introduce it into the Proprietors' Court.

His accord with ministers is not difficult to understand. If successful through them he would be received within the Company as the one who solved the crisis in Government-Company relations. He would be sure of Shelburne's support and that of others within the Chatham ministry at the April 1767 election.

In the meantime, on 12 March the Directors sent back to the House the suggestions Government had already rejected. Sulivan criticised the fact that there was no separation of trade and revenue, which he considered were 'distinct considerations and stood on different ground'.[11] When it was alleged that these could not be separated, he set out to prove otherwise.

He sent two plans to Shelburne as advance notification, indicating which one he proposed to offer for consideration. Shelburne thought his points too detailed; however, a high regard for his friend prevented harsh censure, so he gave his support. The plans were really continuations of those they had discussed and promoted in November 1766, and had continued to work on since that date.[12] They were now very close in other ways; and Shelburne was heavily involved in finding the votes that might return Sulivan to the Direction. This is reflected in the amount of stock splitting that now commenced in earnest as the election date loomed.[13]

Sulivan's proposals were read in the General Court on 16 March. His idea of dividing the territorial revenue from that of trade pleased Government; and he proposed a fourteen per cent dividend, thus satisfying his followers in the Company. In mitigation of the charge against him of purely electoral motives, the scheme did display his general policy, clear from 1757, of pursuing commercial revenues at the expense of territorial ones.

His proposals also had the effect of giving the initiative in Company affairs back to him. It would appear too that these suggestions impressed Rockingham and his followers. Woodhouse told Newcastle that the plan he had put up was greatly commended by the majority of the Proprietors. No objections to it were raised, even with over six hundred people in the room.

A determined attempt by a totally hostile Direction to destroy the plan was launched, and despite the efforts of Dempster and William Burke, the General Court voted to send it to the Court of Directors for consideration. It was a death knell. On 24 March, and as expected, his proposals were found to be unsuitable. Meanwhile, the Direction prepared the way for its views by agreeing to an understanding with Parliament.[14]

In the General Court agitation continued; and a total of twelve proposals were heard and discussed between 3 and 6 April. Sulivan's was the first to be read again. Most of the others were modelled upon his, including the one from the Directors. The only disparity was that in that of the executive's there was no separation of territorial and trading revenues, and no fixed annual sum to the State. It was then put to the ballot on 8 April whose plan should be forwarded as the basis for agreement with ministry. This was the day before the annual election of Directors, and how the result would influence the election next day was widely understood. Sulivan lost by 199 votes.

The struggle of Chartered Rights versus Parliamentary control continued. At first, however, Government refused to accept the Directors' proposals; it had been allowed time to temporarily patch up internal differences with no loss of face. The Parliamentary Inquiry proper then commenced, only to be adjourned the same month (April) and the Directors' plan was left in abeyance until May.

Simultaneously a storm erupted in the Company. A promised increase in the dividend had been abandoned in the ministerial discussions, much to the annoyance of many Proprietors, and especially the Sulivan-aligned speculators. A stock-splitting campaign followed, with the aim of forcing a rise in the dividend anyway. There is a suggestion that a revolt against Sulivan was also contemplated by these jobbers. In other words, he was expected to play ball or be sacrificed.

The ministry signalled that they would consider any increase in the dividend at that particular point as a deliberate breach of faith. This was interpreted as direct interference in Company business and aroused immediate hostility. Speculators, who included Verney, Dempster and William Burke, pushed harder for an increase. Moderate proposals by the Directors were lost, and the dividend was raised to twelve and a half per cent. Ministers and Commons were infuriated, and the triumph of those in the 'Alley' was immediately checked by a Bill in Parliament on 8 May, which prevented the Company from raising its dividend within the next year without Westminster's consent.

In reply to further violent Company opposition, yet another Bill was introduced that put a stop to the splitting of stock. Although he had asked for this a year before, a thoroughly concerned Sulivan now joined in petitioning against it, because in his eyes Parliament could not be allowed to take the initiative and create legislation for internal matters without being asked.

A wish to smooth ruffled feathers in the ministry, and a sense of opportunity led him to propose again (on 8 May) that the ministry be offered £400,000 a year instead of a share in the profits. In return, Parliament was to cancel legislation controlling the dividends. The Directors refused to listen and Sulivan and eight of his followers then called a General Court for 18 May.

His next moves, squeezed in before this next Court convened, suggest a degree of desperation. He mustered all his strength in the Company, temporarily abandoned Shelburne, and contacted Townshend and Conway. They met him, together with the leaders of the Parliamentary Opposition, at the *St. Alban's* tavern. Townshend pledged opposition to the Dividend Bill in return for improvements in the Company's terms.

Sulivan was prepared to use Parliamentary Opposition leverage to force the Directors into offering better terms; but at the General Court of 18 May he still did not get his way, and obtain what he had already proposed. Anger got the better of him and he accused Rous and his friends of giving the Government its opportunity of intruding into Company affairs via the 1767 dividend; of reducing the dividend to ten per cent when it was really worth seventeen per cent; of issuing more bonds than the laws of the Company allowed; and of losing the Company its chartered rights. In the midst of turbulent scenes, the proposal to give £400,000 to Government was passed; but no mention was made of the dividend – apart from a petition against the Dividend Bill.

By this date the committee investigating the Company had found that the money Clive had spoken of was just not there. Fruitless General Courts protested against the imminent Dividend Bill: one on 19 May, another on 27 May. A motion to limit the dividend to twelve and a half per cent was even agreed upon on 3 June. It was all to no avail, and to Sulivan's regret, the Dividend Bill, giving a limit of ten per cent per annum, was passed.

In return, the Company had its territorial possessions and rights to the revenues confirmed. The Bill became law on 29 June, binding both for two years. It was renewed in 1768. Thus Sulivan's main objective of retaining autonomy during this last stage of negotiations was lost; and the precedent was set for a later, more serious intrusion into Company affairs.

A body in the General Court, headed by Sulivan continued the futile struggle, holding General Courts on 'special affairs' on 15 July, and on 23 December. At these he fought in vain for a list of qualified voters for Company elections. Finally it all fizzled out. The Company bound itself to pay £400,000 per annum for two years, a sum of money it could not afford. This was later extended to 1772 and was to prove disastrous to the Company in the long term.[15]

In the end, nothing much was really done to alter the constitution, method of government or calibre of the servants in India. All the old privileges were retained and no examination of the state of the settlements or redress of abuses was made. The State offered no help to the Company in adapting to its enlarged responsibilities. The need for a permanent agreement between the Company and the Government remained; as did the State's 'right' to revenues from the new territories.

The Bill checking the splitting of stock was helpful, though inadequate. The right to vote now had to be held for six months, thereby pushing forward the whole splitting process by half a year. The temporary statutory limitation on the dividend did restrain speculative influence, but only for a short time. Taken together, however, these features mark the start of a limited degree of State responsibility; and the whole Inquiry, by linking Company interests to Parliamentary ones, took the involvement of the House in its affairs to yet another stage. What the Inquiry had really done was enhance the sense of anticipation in the public mind that something really ought to be done about Indian affairs.

Sulivan was only willing to pay the blackmail demanded by ministry, because in return the Company had the right to retain its lands and revenues in India. Most MPs did not like it either. They had witnessed an attack by the State on the civil liberties of citizens and private companies. Sovereign rights and proprietary rights remained powerful issues.

On the other hand, the Inquiry had helped immeasurably in his never-ending efforts to return to power. At its conclusion he was again considered a force to be reckoned with. The attack by Parliament had fused together ambition and defence of the Company's independence. He was certain that he was needed to stem the assault; it suited him to think so anyway. The whole Inquiry had put him on red alert; and the 'great game' imagery, usually scattered throughout his text, is not so evident. Nor were his proposals any worse than others; and were based on the confusion over the true state of the Company's financial affairs. Founded on estimates from Clive, his calculations convinced him of a more hopeful picture than was in fact the case.

He had become engrossed in this struggle because it mattered to be at the core of anything that affected his East India Company. It was not for money, but for involvement and influence. Percival Spear flawlessly captured what was his heart's desire: 'And of course there was Sulivan, to whom the air of the Court of Directors was like oxygen to a heart-sick patient.'[16]

10

Great Designs and Personal Struggles
1768-72

1

Anticipating success in April 1768, Sulivan looked forward to a place in the Direction for himself, office in India for Vansittart and money for the stockjobbers. Many supporters acting on his behalf in 1766 and 1767 were to be relied upon again; and he added others. Shelburne brought in Sir Gilbert Elliot; and a letter from Lord North indicated that he might give assistance. Splitting of stock intensified, regardless of the new Act.[1]

He did not delay pressing into use the resources of his friend Robert Palk, who had just returned from Madras; and with this help almost made the breakthrough. Strange as it seems, he very nearly forged an alliance with Clive too. What made this possible was the unstable situation within the Direction; and Clive's uneasiness following his return from Bengal. Palk, who was friendly with both, was to be the channel of communication. This explains why on 13 September 1767 Sulivan was itemising his terms for entering into a 'solid sincere and hearty coalition' with Lord Clive.[2] He agreed to all Clive's demands. In return he asked that the coalition would be made public; and that Vansittart be returned to Bengal as Governor. He was willing to submit all points and the whole agreement to 'their common friend' Palk, who would be sole guarantor.[3]

But Clive would not budge. He would only support Vansittart for Governorship of Madras. In early 1768 his spite at his ex-friend spilled out in a letter to Verelst: 'I am fully convinced V--- is the greatest Hypocrite the greatest Jesuit and the meanest, dirtiest Rascal that ever exited...and I must request you that you must fix his guilt before you leave, beyond all measure.'[4]

Within the Company, John Manship's recommendation that Sulivan be placed on the House list created a storm of opposition, kindled and timed to erupt at the General Court of 8 April. Manship and Sulivan attended a meeting at the *King's Arms* Tavern, Cornhill, to place Sulivan on this register, but this was refused. An effort to appear on the Proprietors' list was given short shrift as well; and when scratched out, his hopes of being a Director were gone. The only positive thing from all this was that he was assured of Manship's future support. For the first time in nine years he had been left off the House list.

2

From the summer of 1768 it was common knowledge that Sulivan would launch yet another attempt to enter the Direction. He saw a real opportunity for success because of its disunity, largely created by Sir George Colebrooke who could not be relied upon. His aims remained constant: to recover power in the Company and return Vansittart to Bengal, preferably as Governor. According to Palk, Sulivan 'would not be dissuaded from trying his luck once more'.[5] He would be appearing upon the Proprietors' list, and Palk thought he would fail; but at least this might 'put an end to all contest'; presumably something he would have been grateful for.[6]

It was a fierce competition, with an unprecedented number of votes created before the lists closed in October 1768. A 'Directors' list fund was administered in the names of Clive, Colebrooke, Crabb Boulton, and Lord Sandwich's man, Robert Jones. Clive's opposition was pitiless; and by February 1769 he was certain in his own mind of preventing Sulivan's return. This was the only issue that induced him to get involved in General Courts again.

The efforts made by Sulivan and his friends were truly prodigious. A tripartite executive arrangement was set up. Sulivan was the linchpin holding together Vansittart and Lauchlin Macleane. He and Macleane had grown very close. It was also useful to Sulivan to have Shelburne's right-hand man alongside; and he remained on good terms with the minister.

Macleane connived at being the confidant of both Sulivan and Vansittart; and became the chief organiser, taking charge of money borrowed by the triumvirate for splitting purposes. He brought into being a particularly large fund consisting of £100,000 stock, subscribed to by at least twenty-three persons, the cash coming mostly from *John Hope,* of Holland, and involving other Dutch investors. The terms agreed upon were favourable to the lenders: the stock was to be returned to them after the election at a fixed high price regardless of the going rate at the rescounter.

The 'Great Scheme', as it was called, seems to have been initiated in response to Clive's exertions. Eventually about 200 votes were created. Lord Verney and the Burkes were involved. Macleane brought in Shelburne and his connections. Sulivan and Vansittart underwrote most of it. Stock had never before risen to the high price they agreed to; and it was foolhardy of them, to say the least, to guarantee this.

He and Vansittart had the backing of those Bengal servants who were Clive's enemies. They could also now rely on the Palk household. Sulivan had support among City connections and ex-Bombay colleagues. As ever, the shipping interest was with him: the Raymonds, William George Freeman, Charles Foulis and John Boyd split £150,000. He was helped in that the expansion in shipping had caused harm to many ships' husbands, and led to friction with the Direction. Robert Gregory was a strong ally; and the wealth of the Johnstones was worth pursuing. This clique remained wary, however, of Macleane and his speculator friends. To them, he was 'one of those Knots of Knaves.'[7]

Other Scots were involved; £100,000 of Sir Lawrence Dundas' money was split by Sulivan for stock purchase.[8] Any real hope of success, however, was pinned on Sulivan himself; he had the experience and promise of patronage that still pulled men to his side. Thomas Lane, handled most of the business. Through him and Elias de la Fontaine he was able to raise further sums while remaining anonymous.

He made many promises of patronage in exchange for support. The appointment and entry of Sir Gilbert Elliot's second son Alexander into the Company as a Writer readily reflects the way in which this worked. It transpired that in 1769 Sir Gilbert was dealing in Company stock through *Coutts,* the London-Scottish bankers. Via an agent, Andrew Douglas, £2,888 was introduced.

Shelburne placed funds in Macleane's hands to purchase votes, but was enmeshed by his assistant a great deal more than he realised. Meanwhile, Sulivan had won some support from Government by promising to back the extension of the 1767 agreement concluding the Parliamentary Inquiry.[9] This offer was indicative of the degree to which his influence was again being felt in the field of Company business.

Although it was only a temporary occurrence, he was also supported by Rockingham. The Marquess desired the impossible, reconciliation between Clive and Sulivan. He certainly knew nothing of the earlier attempt by Palk and others to bring the two together. He thought that jointly they had the strength to resist Government interference.

Again, a never-ending tirade of abuse filled the newspapers; and a survey of the *Public Advertiser,* from February to April 1769, reveals all too familiar accusations: his so-called overbearing manner and tendency to despotic control. These were answered in like manner, the worst rebutted on each point. The press reflected the bitter undercurrents affecting everything. The *Public Advertiser* carried a particularly mocking piece of anti-Sulivan election propaganda:

> East India intelligence extraordinary – A figure in bronze is now preparing of Laurence O'Sly-One, with his right-hand upon his heart disclaiming party resentment, and his left under his coat, aiming a pocket pistol at the Chairman. This figure is taken from the life.[10]

The *Gentleman's Magazine* finally gave the world the names of the new Directors, 'After the greatest contest that has been known.'[11] Sulivan was made a Director, and became a member of the Committees of Secrecy, Shipping, Accounts and Buying. In many ways it was a tremendous victory, and for the most part unexpected. It was due to a change of heart by the Johnstones and their Scottish allies. £13,000 was split on his behalf at the last moment. The timing of the move was crucial; what probably dictated it was the belief that stock would be boosted by his return to power.

Sulivan's return was a major talking point. To many it was looked upon as a blessing because of his talent and indifference to Court influence. His feared abilities were reflected in the very finger-pointing of his enemies; as were the use of words like 'single-minded' and 'determined' to describe him. The success was like a heady wine. He, his supporters, and their fellows abroad bubbled with joy. The immediate concern was to consolidate his position; the next was to return Vansittart to India. Reform had to be introduced; and abuses stopped before the Company (and he) succumbed, or further ministerial encroachment came about.

His close attendance once more at the Royal Society of Arts during these months is significant. The Society still served as a sort of club where friendships among groups of Company shareholders, speculators and others were cultivated or consolidated. A competition developed in 1769 for the post of Secretary, between John Stewart of Hampstead and William (Pultney) Johnstone. Wisely, Sulivan abstained from voting. He wanted to keep in touch with both sides. John Stewart, who had proposed Edmund Burke for election to the Society, was also acting as a secret agent for Shelburne, a fact Sulivan would have known. Stewart was also Macleane's confidant. He kept close to Sulivan in the years to come.

That something unusual was going on is suggested by the sheer numbers put forward for membership. Macleane and his brother Henry proposed eleven; Sulivan sixteen. Included in his list were Richard Burke Senior and Theobald Burke, Joseph Hickey and Stephen Lushington. He was also careful to keep in touch with the Johnstones and other Scots. This can be deduced from the fact that he nominated all twelve of their group for re-election.[12]

Then, in the midst of all his plans and great expectations, disaster struck. It was unexpected and of colossal magnitude. His position was at once reversed, though he managed for a time to camouflage this serious turn for the worse. The losses incurred also dictated an immediate change in priorities. Vansittart must return to Bengal as planned, but now his principal task was to retrieve their fortunes. Temporarily at least, that came before anything else.

The terrible tide that engulfed Sulivan resulted from the many tortuous engagements he had freely entered upon to ensure a return to the Direction. A great number of these are lost, others are hard to follow, they were so shrouded in secrecy. The unscrambling is made more difficult since he was working through an agent when secretly jobbing in Indian stock for his allies, with their electoral support in mind.

His nightmare opened in May, with the spread of alarming rumours from India, followed by official reports of great unrest, particularly in Bengal. It put an end to the boom in Indian stock, affecting many contributors from overseas.[13] Reports said Haider Ali was on the rampage and that French troops were massing. Although these rumours were found to be false, the damage had been done and the slide could not be checked.

The price of stock, which stood at 274 on 1 May (meaning that at one stage it cost £274,000 to buy £100,000 of India stock), was at 270 eight days later. When the exchange shut on 20 June for the midsummer rescounters, it stood at 241. On 18 July (the day of settlement for the Sulivan group) its value had dropped to 232. By October it was 217; and finally on 28 November it reached its lowest point, 214.

Sulivan and his associates had not only purchased stock at 268 (already a high price) they had promised to pay for it at the rescounters on 18 July at the astonishing one of 280. The stock falling so drastically in price caught everyone 'before it was convenient to sell'.[14] The *Hope* family had insisted that Sulivan and Vansittart stand security for this money; and later Sulivan said that he and Vansittart became security for £200,000 capital India stock. What this meant was that they were guarantors for £100,000 worth of stock on top of the £100,000 pledged to the *Hope* bank by underwriting the 'Great Scheme'.

The £100,000 of stock purchased by those in the 'Great Scheme' now cost £280,000, but would only raise £232,000 when sold (232 being the price of stock on the day of settlement). The net loss was £48,000 for the group. Split among the twenty-three members of the consortium this totalled £2,100 each, which would have been borne easily. The panic sprang from the ways in which money had been raised by members of the consortium for purchase of stock via the 'Great Scheme'.

Ultimately, only six members of the 'Great Scheme' were unable to meet their liabilities, costing the other seventeen participants roughly an additional £3,000 each. For Sulivan, however, who acted as joint guarantor, the 'Great Scheme' alone cost him £15,000 through the inability of many involved to pay even £3,000.

He was certainly the victim of unfortunate circumstances. On the other hand, he was taking risks – and in this particular case had entered upon what was a calculated gamble fraught with danger. Perhaps the high stakes forced his hand; but for re-entry to the Direction he paid a hefty price. Just how hefty, only became clear when he knew the full extent of his partners' difficulties, within and without the consortium. These events would colour the rest of his life.

He found himself in the deepest trouble when he discovered how few were the real assets of his so-called friends. Being guarantor (along with Henry Vansittart) of the 'Great Scheme', he had to repay the £15,000 now owed because of the default of others. He was enmeshed in a complicated financial web. There were separate ties with Vansittart; and others with Lauchlin Macleane. He was also part of a Vansittart-Palk combination; and caught up in a Macleane-Shelburne one too. In many of these separate transactions he was forced to pay back the money raised, because he and Vansittart had underwritten them as well.

Quite apart from these, and the 'Great Scheme', he was indebted (through Macleane and Vansittart) in a second instance to *Hope* of Amsterdam. He had joined a combination that consisted of Vansittart, John Boyd, John Motteux and Edmund Boehm the elder. At the same time he had entered yet another partnership with Macleane and Colebrooke. Besides these, he had financial engagements with Lord Verney and the Burkes.

In his correspondence of later years Sulivan played down his own position in all that transpired. He had nothing to be proud of, and was largely responsible for his own plight, despite claims that he was treated shabbily by his former associates and duped by Macleane. Sulivan understood perfectly well that in such times it was every man for himself.

He admitted as much to his son, saying that what happened came from his own weakness; and through acting as a moneylender and being a guarantor. 'I fell a victim', he said, ' to a (then unknown to me) set of desperate gamblers with outside characters, Earl Verney at their head and a greater rascal is not in this country.'[15] This is anything but an objective summary of these transactions.

His fellow collaborators shared his fate. Verney lost nearly all his fortune; the Burkes were set on the road to bankruptcy. Shelburne lost heavily; and was fearful that Macleane would expose his part in the whole business. Sulivan's affairs were seriously entwined with those of this dangerous manipulator, who hourly involved him deeper by his manoeuvres, without either his knowledge or consent.

Sulivan's account book tells part of these complicated arrangements with Macleane. Most entries referred to money for creating votes. An interim account in June 1772 of the money due, came to £8,968–15/-. Later, Macleane admitted to debts of £90,000, and the secrecy cloaking so many of Sulivan's dealings with him would indicate that more was owed than was shown in his ledger. As Palk said, he and Macleane were behind 'all the split votes the Dutch could furnish'.[16]

The depth of Sulivan and Vansittart's indebtedness is reflected in that as late as 1770 the *Hope* bank still would not 'renew their loans without a large additional deposit'.[17] Later Sulivan related to Hastings the 'melancholy and confidential' subject of the financial disaster. He also gave the sources of more borrowed money, which totalled around £55,000.[18]

Yet more was borrowed from the Johnstones. These loans, raised by them from the *Hope* bank, were to be paid back later, with interest. They were guaranteed by Sulivan and Vansittart before being issued. Colebrooke later maintained that Sir William (Pultney) Johnstone was involved separately with Sir Laurence Dundas and Duncan Clerk in yet another loan to Sulivan and Vansittart. The Director John Motteux gave at least £5,000. The banker, De la Fontaine and Sulivan's friend, Isaac Panchaud, would appear to have been the most likely sources for the rest of the money.

It was only after Vansittart set out for India in the autumn of 1769 that Sulivan realized they had not set out on equal terms. Whereas he had enjoyed financial independence, his ally's affairs were in a dismal state. As part of a begging letter to Palk, Sulivan gave details of their joint transactions and of sums mutually pledged. Although £12,000 had been paid back, Vansittart had only contributed £3,000 before sailing. He left £20,000 'of French Bills'; £2,000 India stock; his Company salary; and license for Sulivan to draw upon him for up to £10,000 through his attorney John Motteux. This left Sulivan in a 'dreadful situation'. It was made worse because Vansittart's agent, Edmund Boehm, would neither part with Vansittart's meagre resources directly to Sulivan, nor release them following Motteux's directions.

Throughout the spring of 1770 Sulivan was 'almost distracted' with the fall in India stock, leaving 'scarce enough to cover his and Vansittart's joint stock and only sufficient to support it against another fall in value'. He was sure that a deliberate plan, to start a panic ('complicated villainy') was afoot to lower it by rumour mongering.[19] His intelligence network indicated that Clive was behind things, and he was satisfied that 'the noble lord would go to any lengths' to reach himself and Vansittart.[20]

Edmund Boehm continued on his course of signing no agreements, even endangering a contract that involved John Boyd. Vansittart had pledged to repay Boyd at least £9,000 whenever it was demanded. Boehm would release nothing, and after Sulivan's own security was refused, he appealed to Palk to get the man to do as instructed. He was puzzled by it all, and thought if his friend had not given his agent the power to transfer money and assets to him, then he was both deceived and ruined. Vansittart could not escape the consequences either.

Palk immediately loaned Boehm £5,000 with which to serve Vansittart; and Motteux scraped together £1,500. Nonetheless, by May 1770 their joint affairs were in a state of desperation. Raymond, *Martin & Co.* and the *Hope* bank required payment or additional security. John Boyd, he said, 'has nearly distracted himself and me'.[21] The only resource he had left was Vansittart's French bills. At last, Boehm consented to the sale of these, and he was able to pay Boyd £12,000 in part-payment. This saved them from the 'total ruin' prophesied, by removing the threat of immediate legal action.

He was working for time, hoping that if he could hold on until August stock would rise in value, and they might survive. Yet it remained at the low price of 225 to 221 despite excellent news from India and elsewhere. By the summer of 1770 he realised all his other high hopes from good Investments, and profits from raw silk were to no avail. The serious state of their joint affairs made him vow to Vansittart that 'bad usage by those from whom more had been expected' now made him 'determined to give up forever' all connections with the Company, 'upon the single term of fixing you Governor of Bengal. And if necessary I shall be bound in writing.'[22]

In 1773 Sulivan cast more light on what he many times referred to as this 'melancholy subject'. 'The whole burthen,' he said, 'has fallen upon his (Vansittart's) estate and me in a sum not less than £60,000.'[23] But this figure of £30,000 each was not the final figure. Sulivan told his son that the 'misfortune closed with a loss to himself and Vansittart...of £80,000, each a moiety.'[24] He just did not have any resources left. No full list of his debtors exists, but of those known, Macleane owed £9,000 from his part in the 'Great Scheme'. William Burke was in debt to them for £6,000. A consortium of Macleane, Shelburne (whose share was £4,000), Verney and a Mrs. Forrest, owed £9,070 – a total of £24,070.

His personal fortune had only ever amounted to some £40,000 to £50,000, plus Ponsborne estate and his town house. Since he had loaned just short of £25,000 that is known about, had spent the £12,000 held in reserve, and also his £3,500 stock, £40,500 in total, his fortune was all used up.

Resources in hand during the midsummer of 1770 were Ponsborne Manor and his town house. The Manor would have to go on the market or be mortgaged. Fortunately the latter course was taken, and his friend, John Dunning took it on. After (presumably) the sale of the house in Great Ormonde Street, he leased the Queen Square house he would occupy from 1774. All his capital and everything he possessed disappeared between May 1769 and October 1773.

The consequences were truly enormous. His fortune and ease of mind were gone; and with them a change in life style, from one of independence and security, to uncertainty. His son's career prospects were ruined. Sulivan had purchased for him a 'reputable post in Ireland of £1200 to £1400 a year'. Stephen was forced to sell this. This blow to his son's prospects had a profound effect. As late as 1778 he was still asserting that his son had 'always lived in a liberal manner' and 'had a right' to do so.[25]

The great tragedies of Sulivan's life were the death of two of his children in Bombay; the struggle with Clive; the loss of his fortune in 1769; and the death of his wife in 1782. Even the fitful periods of exclusion from the Direction he endured were nothing compared to these calamities. The loss of his fortune, however, seems an unbelievable piece of folly, destroying his family's independence, so hard fought for, and affecting so many people.

From mid-1768 to May 1769 he was seized by a madness, which in more serene years, amazed him and caused renewed distress. The losses were a result of his willingness to gamble to regain authority and influence. Sheer bad luck was an ingredient, but he was prepared to take a chance. Of course, in many respects his behaviour was also determined by the situation he faced. He was persuaded that the only certain support for him was that of speculators and finance houses, and this led him onwards.

3

His re-entry to the Direction in 1769 was marked by strenuous activity on both public and private fronts. One of these pursuits would culminate in the shattering certainty of his penury; the other in the long-dreaded Parliamentary intrusion into Company affairs, followed by the crushing blow of the 1773 Regulating Act.

As usual, he wanted to be the source of everything from within the Court of Directors; yet now had to balance serious personal needs against what was termed the 'public' good. The goal of regaining influence turned into dire necessity with the further collapse of his fortune; because only from a base of authority within the organisation could he hope to recover anything.

This is not to say that private aims blotted out the wish to enrich his beloved Company. Its business always came first. Only on rare occasions did personal distress threaten to tip the balance he held between public and private interest. Efforts to retrieve his fortune meant he came to be influenced still more by the same speculators partly responsible for his situation. He was ensnared by adventurers who had penetrated the Company, and dogged by dangerous men.

Apart from 1770, Sulivan was to enjoy a stay in the Direction that lasted from 1769 to 1773. He concentrated his efforts in two ways. The first was to build a strong position within the Proprietors' Court. He had to add to his supporters there and use their momentum to dominate the Direction by flooding it with his followers. All long-term hopes depended upon this course of action. His second task was to forestall further Parliamentary intervention by correcting things from within the Company. Right away he got down to the task of drafting resolutions for the better management of affairs. Fortunately, his powers of application, and appetite for hard work had not receded.

Leadenhall was witnessing many changes, and the years from 1769 to 1772 gave rise to an assortment of groups. The Clivites, Sulivanites and shipping interest remained. The banking-cum-mercantile insurance group also held firm, and came to be identified with Colebrooke. The newer ones forming would represent first the desires of the Grafton ministry, then that of Lord North (from 1770). Directors and Proprietors would also echo the wishes of the Parliamentary Opposition: the followers of Chatham, Rockingham, and various courtiers or Parliamentarians.

The Company's patronage and wealth had also become objects of desire in themselves. A new breed of administrators with experience and knowledge of Indian affairs was also appearing, men such as John Robinson and Charles Jenkinson – the latter having served his time in the maelstrom of 1764-65. With their grasp of detail, and given the opportunity, they would soon be able to facilitate ministerial designs.

As far as the Company rulers could fathom, ministerial goals remained the same. Government, especially in the person of Lord Sandwich, working through Robert Jones, still seemed intent upon destroying its independence. It often seemed debatable whether Government was really pursuing the oft-professed objective of achieving a peaceful relationship. With increased ministerial knowledge of India business, and rivalry inside India House rife, opportunities for interference abounded.

These new forces were to pose difficulties for Sulivan. He became entangled with leading figures among those politicians jockeying for control, as well as with the speculators and adventurers he had consorted with from 1766. His return to office also brought to life all the old antagonisms. Hostility was voiced in the newspapers and in pamphlets. One entitled: *A Letter to Laurence Sulivan* from 'An Old Proprietor', was typical. Everything was raked up.

He based the prospect of his own future well-being and that of the Company upon the success of a Supervisory Commission he initiated in 1769. This was a serious attempt to deal with the growing number of grave problems in India. The need for a thorough, impartial investigation had been recognised by late 1768. So bad was the cash situation in Bengal the revenues collected from the *Diwani* territories were being used to pay for purchases of Indian goods and of tea and silk from China.

The position was to be made worse by the 1769-70 famine in south west Bengal. A great proportion of the revenues were irredeemably lost; and the disaster was eventually to contribute to the credit crisis of 1773. Of course, commercial factors pale into insignificance beside the immensity of this tragedy in human terms. There was great suffering and countless lives were lost. Neither Sulivan nor anyone else was aware of this calamity early in 1769.

The Carnatic did not offer much in the way of relief. With the continuing war in Mysore, and Haider Ali's depredations revenues were drying up. Regrettably too, it was November 1768 before details of the private debts due to the Madras servants began to appear in the public records, and their lack of good faith unmasked. Henceforth, debts owing to the Company were supposed to be recognised before those of a private nature.

Sulivan was employed in everything to do with the Supervision. He led the nine Proprietors who, at the General Court of 6 July 1769, called for a meeting with the ministry. After a ballot that defeated opposition in the Company, the Commission, consisting of three members was established. Those appointed were Henry Vansittart, Luke Scrafton and Colonel Francis Forde. Vansittart's inclusion was unquestionably a direct result of Sulivan's election success. He was placed at its head, with a large salary.

That agreement over the choice of Commissioners had been reached was miraculous; and explained by enough interested parties being willing to encourage the coalition. The state of affairs in India was also serious enough to override factional strife; and since Vansittart's appointment held out the hope of financial salvation, it made Sulivan and Vansittart agreeable to compromise, even though Scrafton and Forde were Clivites.

The main disagreement was over the appointment of the third Supervisor. Clive put forward Col. Forde, to join Scrafton, because Vansittart had been appointed leader. Desperate for financial salvation through Vansittart, and confident in the benefit to be conferred upon Bengal, Sulivan agreed. Sir John Lindsay, a protégé of Lord Mansfield, was to command the naval forces that had been requested. The Government only succeeded, however, in securing plenipotentiary powers for Lindsay.

Much was also due to the Rockingham Whigs, with Edmund Burke at the leader's elbow as they attempted to gain influence. Rockingham worked through Jenkinson's brother-in-law Charles Cornwall to bring together Colebrooke, Sulivan and Clive. His aim remained that of creating a united front within the Company against ministerial influence. Their hope was that the Commission, together with the coalition would create a formidable opposition to the Administration's control.

Clive agreed to the Commission because he thought he was preventing Vansittart from becoming Governor of Bengal; and that he was forcing a compromise from both. Cornwall (with Charles Raymond as intermediary) was used to secure the agreement. Sulivan was uneasy that the pact was only to be concluded verbally, and it awoke all his deeply-held suspicions. However, acting upon Clive's instructions, Colebrooke was able to fob off his request for documents and signatures. Sulivan was only satisfied after a public airing of the proposed share of offices; but a struggle developed over the instructions the Supervisors were to follow. It was only after pressure from Westminster that this was settled.

Finally, the Supervisors sailed in the frigate *Aurora* in October 1769, only to be lost at sea in December after leaving the Cape of Good Hope. Apart from the dreadful loss of human life, Sulivan's hopes for financial salvation disappeared with his friend. Even the portion that was due to Vansittart's estate from this enterprise was too little and too late for his immediate needs.

Sulivan certainly wished to influence the work of the Commission through Vansittart. He intended to employ his collaborator in the same way he had used him throughout 1760-65. They would form an all-powerful London-Bengal link. The Commission was meant to implement the plans thrashed out in intimate discussion. His shrewd eye had picked out the areas to be examined; and Vansittart was urged to gain the confidence of both Haider Ali and the Nawab of Arcot. Weight was placed upon the beneficial effect of this on both Company stability and stock. Treasure was to be sent home as quickly as possible; the remittance of half a million pounds in gold as well as raw silk, within the year, would consolidate the Company's position.

In October 1769 the features that had led to the Clive-Sulivan-Colebrooke coalition began to disappear. Sulivan, in his need for political support from some source went over to the Grafton ministry in return for backing at the April 1770 election. His move, or defection, as it was regarded, created a stir. Nevertheless, as Edmund Burke noted, he could not be blamed. His position had become untenable. Reduced circumstances and the absolute necessity of being returned to the Direction dictated the switch. It meant the end of allegiance to his long term ally Shelburne. Both were less enchanted with each other anyway. Because of Macleane, Shelburne still owed Sulivan money; while the Earl was unhappy that he had not found Macleane a place on the 1769 Supervisory Commission.

Sulivan was well aware of the acrimony he would bring upon his head by the move; but ever a realist, he chose his own route through the political quicksand. However, from harmony with the Opposition groups, his relationship changed, to the point where he earned the undying hatred of the Rockinghamites, and especially of Edmund Burke. From that point onwards he was also increasingly distrusted by others across the parliamentary spectrum; but particularly by Burke, who had financial losses, many of which he could conveniently blame on Sulivan.

He lost much support in the Company as well. This was more than just unfortunate, because his switch coincided with the growth of influence there of various ministries, starting with that of Lord North. From 1770 he was *persona non grata* to so many more people.

Although at first Charles Cornwall believed he had broken off the treaty because of pressure from his anti-Clive friends, the truth was that Sulivan was convinced in October 1769 that his position was desperate. He had put no trust in the coalition with Colebrooke and Clive. He embraced the ministry of the day to insure himself against his so-called partners turning against him. Clive's correspondence with Colebrooke illustrates how right he was. In November he met Sandwich's man, Robert Jones, at the *Half-Moon* tavern to form a list for the 1770 election. His schemes were dashed, however, with Grafton going out of office in January 1770 and North's entry.

Quite a struggle ensued in the run up to the 1770 election where again he had to face Clive's hostility. By December 1769 their respective forces were once more facing up to one another. This lingering hatred and fixation with his rival is glimpsed when Clive grumbled to Verelst about the admission of Sulivan into the Direction in April 1769. He even listed this as one of the reasons for the low standing of India stock; talking of anarchy and confusion, while pretending, feebly, to be exempt from it all. In March Palk said that both sides, Clivites and Sulivanites, were confident of success. He added, more in hope than anything else, that this might be the last great contest.

Sulivan lost, and did so for several reasons. By his connections with Grafton and Sandwich's man Robert Jones, he damaged his prospects of help from the North Government; and he was deserted by the Johnstones. He vowed (wrongly it was to prove) that he would never talk to them again.[26]

Although out of the direction, Sulivan was bubbling with enthusiasm in May for what he thought was a flourishing state of affairs. He told Vansittart (unaware of his death at sea) of an expected surplus of £510,000 for the period August 1769 to August 1770. It was proof, he proclaimed, of the Company's ability to pay dividends and satisfy the ministry. The Directors would be able to provide a million pounds indemnity on tea; cover the cost of loading the freight of 31 ships, and still have a handsome surplus of between £4-500,000 per annum. In the light of future events, it is a pity he was so mistaken; yet he can hardly be censured for making calculations based on the only information he had.

Because of the additional financial distress he faced, Sulivan played no significant part in public life from April 1770 until his re-entry into the Direction in April 1771. His selection for office was safeguarded, principally because of Lord North's desire to achieve some sort of peace within the Company. This, the minister knew, could only come about by re-admitting

Sulivan; and to this end, he backed and encouraged a coalition between him and Colebrooke. Again, Charles Cornwall was the go-between.

For this election Sulivan had a higher estimation of his bargaining power than was really the case. Not knowing of Vansittart's demise, he blustered that he could 'raise a storm that may shake them'.[27] The truth was that he tried to cajole North into giving him one of the Chairs, with two or three of his friends allowed into the Direction. He thought he had sacrificed North's sustained support by his connection with Grafton. But the minister, although he was not prepared to back Sulivan against his old rivals, would not back them either. Before the election, therefore, the Irishman knew that North would bring him into the Direction singly.

He knew the game was up; but had to return to the Direction on any terms. In December 1770 Robert Palk described his friend as being given the '*amende honorable*' with his re-admittance; adding shrewdly that it was 'clearly necessary that there should be somebody there a little acquainted with India matters'.[28] In April 1771 Sulivan, 'humbled but in no way daunted', returned to the Direction.[29]

Palk was amazed by Sulivan. After all that had passed, the state of the times, and all his friend's bad luck in 'so unprofitable an employ' as Indian business, he found it incredible that to his mentor it was still the '*summum bonum*'. Palk might also have asked himself where else could his friend possibly find financial salvation.[30]

Sulivan was made a member of the Secret Committee; and by December 1771 Leycester was informing Hastings, 'If he remains united as at present with Sir George (Colebrooke) he will...very shortly lead the India House.'[31] In fact, it was Sulivan who took charge within this marriage of convenience and was left virtually in charge of the Company. This was due to his greater ability and experience; and because Colebrooke's stock jobbing activities took his interest elsewhere.

He had no fear of failure, therefore, when the 1772 election came round. The support of Colebrooke's friends was assured; and they joined with his followers. The Barwells: William, Richard, Roger and Mary brought 30 votes.[32] He was assured too of substantial backing from the shipping interest. The policy followed from 1769 of using fewer ships continued when Sulivan became Deputy Chairman. Thus fears of an increased share-out, and a diminution in returns because of would-be interlopers, was avoided.

Nevertheless, he almost lost the post of Deputy Chairman. In April 1772, he said, 'Colebrooke and I had the game in our hands, but by an indecision habitual, almost natural to him, we lost that ground which we never could recover; and in place of bringing in firm friends I carried the Deputy Chair by my own vote.'[33]

However, the happy scene he had depicted in his letter to Vansittart didn't exist. Troubles that the lost Supervisory Commission might have rectified had become more acute. Yet he had to maintain a façade of confidence. He made efforts to preserve the credit-worthiness of Company shares; and continued to do so in the face of events which, in the ordinary run of things must depress their value. It led to accusations of bulling for personal reasons. If he did indulge, there is no record of this because he would have used an agent; but it would also have to be with borrowed money, he had none.

Apart from financial troubles, Sulivan and his fellow Directors faced other difficulties. Much of the worry abroad sprang from Clive's earlier assumption of the *Diwani* in Bengal; and the inadequate administration that accompanied the dual-system of government experiment. At home, he had to accept as irreversible two developments against which he had fought tooth and nail: the growing influence of Government upon the direction of Company affairs; and the principle of the Company being a territorial as well as mercantile power. His dependence upon ministerial support since 1769, and the naked power exhibited within the Company's Courts by Parliamentary groups, hammered home the first of these developments.

Nevertheless, the continuance of commerce as the Company's prime function remained a cardinal point with him. Once again he became familiar with the real state of Bengal: the extent of famine there; and the condition of its administration, trade and revenues. His considerations on these issues, together with those of Clive and the two 'Chairs', were laid before the Committee of Correspondence. He drew up a similar methodical assessment of Carnatic business.

Sulivan was truthful when he said that at this juncture the General Letters (embodying so many innovations) were all drawn up by him, and done in a 'spirit of fairness'. The cumulative effect of his endeavours was that in these years 'the Court of Directors managed to send to Bengal a series of despatches of epoch-making importance'.[34] That the credit for this must go to him is more than backed up by the amount of materials carrying his imprint among the India records.

His energy is attested elsewhere. Efforts were made to establish a settlement at Balambangan, in Sumatra. All the plans came from Sulivan and Gregory. Palk also told of his friend's opposition to the 'oceans of people...gone this year to India' with no provision made for them.[35] Yet, no matter what he did, it was not enough; and soon events affecting the Company, and the course of Sulivan's life, would take an even more serious turn for the worse.

11

Defences Breached
1769-73

1

For the Company's financial crisis of October 1772 Sulivan has received an unwarranted bad press. The emergency would lead to another Parliamentary inquiry, to Lord North's Regulating Act of 1773 and loss of the Company's independence. Because of these enormous consequences and the blame that has attached to him, the record needs to be set straight.

He was still one of a few men who could be relied upon to get to the heart of a problem and try to do something about it. This being the case, it must then be asked (as it was by contemporaries) why he did not, or could not, change the course of the Company's fortunes before the crisis. The major criticism has been that he placed his own needs first; and was deeply involved in activities that were diametrically opposed to the good of the concern, such as in the speculations of Sir George Colebrooke. It is alleged that as the private affairs and executive control of both became ever more linked, so personal circumstances affected their decisions – to the detriment of the monopoly. This is the view that is challenged here.[1]

The major requirement, before even looking at Sulivan's involvement, is to enumerate the many factors that came together to create this crisis. Abroad the situation was appalling. When Sulivan re-entered the Direction in 1769, the Nawab of the Carnatic's debts continued to be the source of corruption; and Clive's 'Dual System' of government for Bengal had been a failure. Extortion and misdemeanours there by Company and native officials alike continued. There was also the threat of a military coup; and corruption plus penetration of local business by army officers continued.

Expensive defensive alliances, large military establishments, and a strong presence in border regions drained funds. The threat of French sea attacks, and Haider Ali's marauding raids into the Carnatic had a severe impact on commerce. There was a growing shortage of silver in India, a state of affairs scarcely realized in Britain, but which was to have severe long-term consequences. This was to be made worse by the Company's acceptance of larger bills of exchange from the Presidencies.

On top of everything else, nature played a vicious stroke, when the famine struck Bengal in 1769. The effects of it were still visible twenty years later. The result, in financial terms, probably accounts for the decline in territorial revenues to the Company of about £400,000; at a time when military costs rose by £160,000.

The Company was also being undermined by loss of revenues from tea. Three and a half million pounds of the commodity had been imported in the 1750s, which turned into an over-supply in the 1760s and early 1770s. Meanwhile, the lack of a distribution network and any control over consumption had resulted in massive smuggling. This threatened to the core the 'legal' traders and led to an appeal for reduced tax duties on the commodity.[2] By February 1772 a mountain of unsold tea had built up, by which Sulivan calculated that the Company had become the losers to the tune of £1 million.

Apart from dismay at the accumulation of bad news from abroad, sensationalism in Britain helped depress the value of Indian stock further. There were ugly stories circulating that referred to the wealth and ostentatious living of Nabobs. The scandal surrounding one such gentleman, William Bolts, was common knowledge. Accusations and counters to them spread like a rash in the newspapers. They were accompanied by various 'histories' from people like Alexander Dow, who wrote a *History of Hindustan*. This, and *Considerations on Indian Affairs* by Bolts, had a determining influence on the public mind. Sulivan's long-running quarrel with Clive was even dredged up as contributing to the disruption.

The monetary crisis fast approaching reached a critical stage with the arrival of an international credit crisis in 1772. By virtue of its financial position the Company could not escape. It was not helped by its dependence on a short-term loan type of financing from 1769.[3] The cumulative effect was to further depress stock, making exports impossible and loans imperative.

Sulivan believed the failure to maintain a cash flow began in March 1772. He was probably correct, because it was understood at the beginning of the year that an injection of £500,000 was required. Yet, where was this sum to be raised? It could not be elicited from the settlements abroad, cash problems were just as serious there; and to meet Investments, Presidencies were increasing their bond debts.

The large number of bills accepted in Britain between March 1771 and March 1772 probably did more than anything else to exacerbate an already impossible situation. Altogether, the Company was liable to meet (during the three years 1772-4) no less than £1,578,000 for bills drawn upon the Presidencies. As early as March 1772 there was nothing with which to meet these obligations, neither from sales nor reserves. Tea had been stockpiled, which tied up funds. Money could not be found in the 'City'. Banks had been weakened by the efforts of the Dutch to become involved in India stock. Finance houses began to fail, caught in the grip of the credit crisis. *Alexander Forsyth's* bank crashed, *Drummond's* only just survived.

The crisis built quickly from March 1772 onwards. The Company needed money to tide it over between the sales of March and September, but could not get this, or was forbidden to raise it. On 22 September the Directors informed the Proprietors that they would not be able to issue the half-yearly dividend. The publication of this state of affairs, and the resultant outcry in the newspapers, then activated the Government. The Directors, with Sulivan at their head, were involved in negotiations with the ministry for a loan, realising that the Bank of England was the single hope of survival. The terms offered were deemed unacceptable; and the Bank of England then refused to enlarge or renew its loan beyond 29 October. The Company had reached breaking point.

As Deputy Chairman, able and interested in all that was going on, Sulivan was in a position, it would seem, where he could have done something to avoid this crisis. Why did he not take the positive action needed at the opportune moment? The answer is that it was outwith his power to do anything; and he was not a member of the executive when restorative action should have been applied. His past record demonstrates that without exception he always put the Company first, no matter if his own situation was desperate. Just as he became aware of how bad things were, events quickly snowballed. He had no opportunity of remedying an emergency that had reached massive proportions long before he re-entered office. He did not return to the Direction until April 1771.

Most accusations concern the period September 1771 until the crisis of October 1772. He and Colebrooke were charged with encouraging the policy of borrowing money from Government and of making no reduction in the dividend. They are depicted as concealing the true state of affairs from their fellows. Sulivan also stands accused of permitting the excessive bills of exchange during these vital months, to the extent that they completely prevented any remedial action being taken. This last allegation can be discounted; it flies in the face of all contemporary evidence, which casts the blame on the disobedience of Company servants in India and upon their avarice.

It is also alleged that even between July and October 1772, when the crisis was upon the executive, the efforts he made were not in the best interests of the Company. This would be difficult to substantiate given that he was one of a committee of thirteen Proprietors formed to consider 'Proper regulations for the Better Management of the Affairs of the East India Company at Home'. He wrote a pamphlet, entitled *Plan for augmenting the Capital and Extinguishing the Debts of the East India Company*. Also, by the end of July his proposal for another Superintending Commission was up and running; and he was a member of the Committee of Treasury which, in July and August, borrowed a total of £100,000 from the Bank of England over a short-loan period of two months. These are not the actions of a man who, can be accused of neglect. His long-held general policy, all his plans and last minute efforts, negate such a view. When his personal dependence upon a thriving and independent Company is considered, it becomes even more absurd.

Bad tidings were aired for the first time at Committee of Treasury meetings held in July 1772; and it was obvious to everyone then that the difficulties to be faced were incapable of being easily solved. To allot the blame to Sulivan it must be shown that despite being out of office from April 1770 to April 1771, and a Director (not one of the Chairs) only from that point until April 1772 that he was instrumental in fermenting the crisis that was only generally recognised in July.

He might have been severely encumbered by difficulties of a personal nature, but early in 1772 he really believed the Company to be performing adequately. His convictions were based on figures provided by Clive, upon whom, in this field – and despite all else, he placed a degree of reliability. In addition, Sulivan felt absolutely certain of continued Government support. He considered that because of the risk offered to national security and stability it would not be allowed to falter.

The first shock in July 1772 was the seriousness of the Company cashier's report, which confirmed the financial miscalculation made in September 1771. The second jolt came when North would not fully come to the rescue. This was even more surprising to him since he was on friendly terms with the minister. He and Colebrooke, as a matter of course, had expectantly notified Lord North on 11 August that the Company needed a further £1 million; the minister merely referred this to Parliament for a decision on 5 October.

Only after April 1772 would Sulivan have had the opportunity to peruse the accounts relating to September and October 1771. In his account of what happened, he firmly placed the 1771 Chairman, John Purling, in the forefront. In September 1771, the Committee of Treasury had brought out a dividend of six and a quarter per cent. John Manship had opposed this, because he had worked out (correctly it proved) that the bills of exchange paid from the funds would mean that the Company would have to borrow all of the money needed to pay the dividend.

Purling and the Company accountant made a projected assessment of expenditure as far as March 1772, and they calculated there would be a small surplus without borrowing. Manship's opposition to Purling's calculation continued, and he called a General Court in October 1771. According to Sulivan, the Proprietors were beaten back by Purling who said the Accountant would vouch for his estimates. Thus, in early March 1772 his figures were accepted as correct, and a dividend of six and a quarter per cent was agreed upon. Even Manship acknowledged that he must have been mistaken. Sulivan had nothing to do with all this; a fact brought up by himself and by 'Honestus' in the *Public Advertiser* for 6 April.

In truth, he had little to do with consultations on the Company's financial position up to this point, because he was so tied in with Colebrooke. They probably had the same friends engaged in 'jobbing'; and he was prepared to accept any figures that appeared favourable. Yet his cool stance must be set against a background of depressed shares. He must have had reservations about Purling's claims, but had to argue for their acceptance, or the Company's credit was gone. The impact that a further fall in India stock would have on his personal circumstances must also have been in his mind.

It would be completely wrong, however, to hold him responsible for what happened before April 1772. It is also extremely doubtful that he had any control over John Purling, he had been in the Clive camp for years. Sulivan's own way when in power, such as in 1758, was to play down danger and conceal it from the public to prevent a loss of confidence.

According to Sulivan, he had been content to accept Purling's figures down to March. In April he was one of the 'Chairs' and privy to information of all kinds, and still was not stirred by a sense of impending catastrophe. In his reminiscences, Colebrooke said that the Bengal bills and the guaranteed payment of tea duties to the ministry created the crisis. He too pinpointed Purling as the culprit and promoted the view that the difficulties could have been overcome even without the help of Parliament. This was always Sulivan's assertion. Colebrooke mentioned one of Sulivan's ideas, which was to raise a loan in Holland through a Mr. Wentworth who would speak to the Dutch banker *Hope*, on the subject. The Company's tea stores, worth £17 million, were to be surety. North axed the scheme.

The impact of interest groups, and peculiarities in the Company's operating methods in London did not help this evidently avoidable liquidity crisis; nor did the Company's bureaucratic strength. It was so good, it allowed business to continue as usual, despite the growing difficulties. The efficient India House clerks and the adaptable system (perfected during Sulivan's period of absolute power) were geared for survival.

It is in the executive arm that most interest and blame for what happened has been attached. To be more precise, it is alleged that by 1772 the oligarchic structure of the Direction ensured that only a few men had real power and influence over Company policy. Central to this was the undue control exerted by the Chairman and Deputy Chairman. This is where the spotlight has been focussed and why Colebrooke and Sulivan who filled these positions stand accused. The fact remains, however, that the emergency, which still had not manifested itself clearly in April 1772, was not their doing. It only became obvious in late June, that something was very wrong.

When the gravity of the situation was realised by North in August, all the Company's accounts were asked for. Stock fell to a new low of 160. At the first indication of distress, the Treasury had indicated that it was willing to help, just as Sulivan thought would be the case. Only the extreme seriousness and depth of the crisis stopped this then happening – or so it was alleged.

Later Sulivan could say to Hastings, 'stock purchases were all remembered, the sufferers were violent in the extreme and it must be acknowledged (though I believe the parties innocent of any sinister views) that appearances were very unfavourable'.[4] His own innocence, suggested by the objectivity in this letter to Hastings, can be substantiated by the fact that both the Palk and Vansittart estates were hurt in the crash, and he would surely have helped there if he could.

The attack upon Sulivan's integrity and the loading of blame upon his shoulders remains unjustified. Indeed, it can be construed as a compliment to his ability and unsullied behaviour that he faced such rancour after the event. He was the one they all depended upon in the end. The losses to so many gave added venom to the later accusations. This measure of blame was doubled with realisation that the Company had fallen into the hands of the ministry.

Yet, here was a leader with a long and proud history of service and responsibility. Accusations of guilt, when challenged, cannot be substantiated. The real question to be asked is why the ministry refused to give succour to the Company in its hour of need? The Government and Bank of England refused to provide the kind of help normally given. That the Bank did not do so was due to circumstances beyond Sulivan's ken – but could guess at.

All he tried to do was keep quiet about the organisation's financial troubles, for the best of reasons, to maintain public confidence. Colebrooke more or less corroborated this, by saying that his colleague was 'never disposed to show the weakness or inability of the Company and always thinking its resources more than sufficient to surmount its greatest difficulties'[5] Rockingham also noted that Sulivan kept his mouth shut and borrowed when in debt rather than lower the dividend. Even after the event, Sulivan maintained that if the Direction had remained united, if Boulton in particular had not betrayed the situation, then the 'storm might have been weathered'.[6] When the crunch came, his involvement at the centre of things made him a convenient scapegoat.

2

It is typical of the man that just as his personal credit was reaching its lowest point through impecuniosity and undeserved blame for the Company crisis, Sulivan was trying to do something about it all. He had already embarked upon what can only be described as outstanding endeavours to eradicate the evils bothering the Honourable Company. These were launched through both Parliamentary and Company channels.

The attempts originating within India House were ongoing and introduced in a variety of ways. Behind all of them lay the aims of correcting abuses and reforming administration within the settlements, and especially Bengal. He also wanted to keep at bay Parliament's growing interest in Company affairs – reflected in the King's speech of January 1771. At home, he and Colebrooke made efforts to reorganise the Company's recruiting service. The measure fell through, partly because the necessary Parliamentary Bill failed. They were also unable to prevent a Bill going through limiting the Company's tonnage, one initiated to save timber for the Navy.

The early months of 1772 found him very busy in Parliament. He had been an MP for ten years and knew his way about. The Judicature Bill he introduced was a step in the right direction. This measure was intended to make the task of creating good government in Bengal a lot easier. In addition, at his insistence, Warren Hastings had been newly appointed to the post of Governor of Bengal. The proposed new legislation was designed to give the Governor more power by extending the authority of the Court of Justice at Fort William. The Bill also contained clauses for preventing unlawful private trading and strengthened the Company's control over its servants.

Messrs. Nuttall (the Company solicitor) and Sayer helped him prepare the clauses. Opposition within the Company was checked because opinion was overwhelmingly in favour of reform. It was also resolved to apply to the Crown for a new 'Charter of Justice' in Bengal as well as the Act to regulate the Company's affairs and servants there. On 30 March Sulivan introduced the Bill into the House personally.

The Bill's objective was to redress the disobedience and malpractices among Company servants in India. The desire for autonomy rampant in the Presidencies was a development that Sulivan had fought against from 1757 to 1765. In Parliament it was mistakenly interpreted that he hearkened back to Clive; and this was reflected in the increasing number of attacks (by others) on his old enemy. There followed an increasingly bitter but knowledgeable debate in the Commons upon the proposed measure.

Clive spoke fully, aware that his whole career was under attack. Believing that Sulivan had deliberately engineered things against him, he openly declared this conviction in the House. By inference it had to be true to some extent, though there is not a scrap of evidence. Sulivan must surely have harboured feelings of animosity; it would have been difficult for him to avoid such sentiments given the continuing open rivalry between the two. Yet he had been fighting corrupt and ungovernable servants in general since 1757. In this instance it was resurrection of the authority of Leadenhall that he sought.

Certainly, Clive's constant enmity would give ample justification for Sulivan's repugnance. Yet, the truth was that he was more interested in sorting out the problems he saw in 1772 than shifting the spotlight onto the past. Regrettably, as far as the course of the Bill was concerned (and for Clive-Sulivan relations) it was impossible to delve into the evils in Bengal without Clive's contribution coming under scrutiny, in turn awakening a sense of the overwhelming authority he had enjoyed there.

In the Commons discourses the great man contrived ineffectually to place the blame for the present situation in Bengal upon Sulivan's shoulders. In turn, he faced an interminable and vicious attack mounted by the Johnstone family. Clive responded and repeatedly managed a few scathing and detrimental remarks against Sulivan, who he believed (wrongly) to be in harness with the Johnstones.

Lord North spoke for the Bill, Townshend and Edmund Burke against it - he thought the Bill a lame one, but later said nothing better appeared. It received its second reading and a motion for going into a committee upon it was passed. Disagreement then broke out over who had the power to nominate the judges to Bengal. The Directors were refused this power, and the passage of the Bill became unstuck. Sulivan's response was, 'If the Attorney-General and his friends meant at this clause to make a stand against the Bill he would sooner give it up than see the Company suffer.'[7]

He had read the situation perfectly. The intention was to kill it off by dragging things out to the end of the session. Wedderburn, who owed his seat in the House to Clive, while annoyed at such delaying tactics, then demeaned himself. He seized upon Sulivan's manner of speaking to the Commons, took him to task, and expressed feigned surprise at his language. Referring to Sulivan as 'The Dictator of Leadenhall' he asked:

> where and to whom does he think he is talking? Is this the House of Commons or the room of the Secret Committee in the India House? I protest I am obliged to look around me to see whether I cannot recognise this to be St. Stephen's chapel...this is not the place to act the monarch.[8]

This tirade marked the end of the Judicature Bill's life. It is, however, possible to hear the honed, viper like recriminations of his old enemies, Clive especially, coming from Wedderburn's mouth.

Thus Sulivan's effort at reform through Parliamentary legislation failed because the hostility of the House towards the Company had been brought to bear. Scandalously, grave problems were dealt with in very brief fashion, due to lack of interest and great ignorance among Members at large. As before, Parliament wanted the riches that India seemed to offer, but had no wish to shoulder the responsibilities entailed.

Again it says much about Sulivan that even before all this had become public knowledge, he had initiated yet another move towards reform through Company channels. In July the desperate monetary situation confronting the Company became all too clear to him, and on the 29th of that month, by means of the Committee of Secrecy, he proposed sending out another Superintending Commission to India to regulate the Company's affairs. By 29 September the Proprietors were resolved to appoint a Commission consisting of nine men. Six of these would be despatched from London. They were to act in conjunction with the Governor of Bengal, with the second in Council there, and with the military commander-in-chief. The whole Commission was modelled upon that of 1769, and Sulivan was author of both.

It was then that his plans went awry. The days from 29 September to 23 October were taken up with the financial crisis itself, and with political scheming among the Proprietors and Directors over who should be appointed to the Supervision. The whole operation became an exercise in patronage. Eventually, by ballot the Directors chose Lt.-General Robert Monckton, Edward Wheler, William Devaynes, Peter Lascelles, Daniel Wier and George Cuming to be the six Supervisors. Sulivan insisted on sufficient remuneration and advised that the Commission should be of three years' duration. In this, the 1769 format was again copied.

He still hoped to stave off Parliamentary interference at this stage; and aimed to relieve his own dismal fortunes by inviting Supervisors of his own choice: 'The Supervision...will end all my difficulties.'[9] His hopes rested with Andrew Stuart, a friend of Maclean. Supporting this 'Scotchman' brought him great ill-will; and he described Stuart as having been 'scoured to a most illiberal degree'.[10]

Unfortunately for him it was not to be. The aversion of North to the whole idea marked its demise in December 1772. Despite contacting Burke through Maclean, he had been unable to convince anybody of stature to take a post, apart from General Monckton. George Dempster had also pushed Burke to accept the position, 'to give the Supervision a good name'.[11] He had even thought of going on the Supervision himself; and Colebrooke later insinuated that he was offered the Governorship of Madras. It would have meant certain death.

Despite an appeal to 'Chartered rights', the Act prohibiting the Supervision was passed. The Company was in disarray, made helpless by its financial collapse. All initiative lay with Government; it alone had the power to remedy affairs. All Sulivan's efforts had been in vain. That he had failed in his efforts to reform the Company from within and via Parliament, can only be described as a calamity. His hopes were now centred upon the man in Bengal. With doors closed to reform via Parliament and through the Company, he turned to Hastings. It became vital that North read letters that contained details of his efforts to crackdown on things in Bengal. The minister was to be aware things were progressing, and how well the new Governor was handling things.

Even though Sulivan thought the Company's independence could endure, he was really not seeing things right. By December 1772 the House had become the arena where the struggles that would define the Company's future would now take place. Such activity was already underway and the shift of power from India House to Parliament was effective from that date.

The worst outcome was that the Judicature Bill, and all that preceded and attended it, led to Burgoyne's motion to set up a Select Committee to investigate the abuses in the Company's government. When this was passed, to widespread acclaim, Sulivan was faced with a threat of the governmental takeover he had always feared. While the Committee was to act as a tool to investigate scandals, it could also serve as a means of settling old scores. It did not solve current problems and only interrupted the good work he and Hastings had planned for the years ahead.

It is quite probable, therefore, that the Deputy Chairman foresaw his own ejection from power in April 1773, a disastrous finale for him to face – set against the high hopes of recent months and his increasingly perilous financial condition. The final ironic twist was that his latest skirmish in the Commons with Clive took place when Parliamentary control of the Company, the course Clive had always favoured, was becoming a reality.

With the end of the Company's credit by late 1772, and failure of the attempted reforms, the North ministry was given the opportunity, through no effort of its own, to evolve an Indian policy; and it had achieved a cherished ambition of direct entry into Indian affairs. The Government's problems were formidable, nevertheless. Not least of these was opposition from within the Company, fortified by Parliamentary Opposition.

Sulivan was prepared to give his strongest support to anyone who would resist measures that further eroded the Company's independence. He would never in any circumstances advocate that the Government should administer Company territory; nor would he ever promote force in the collecting of revenues. This would be the antithesis of everything he stood for. Every attempt at reform he initiated was made to avoid just such eventualities.[12]

From January 1773 onwards India House was virtually lawless, its leaders and the Direction as a body were immobilised because of dependence on Government help. The General Court was in temporary command of sorts; and the great opposition to ministerial interference Sulivan saw there meant he could lead a challenge to threatened chartered rights. He hoped to prevent Government from succeeding in its grimmer demands.

The ministry was split. One side wanted a sweeping extension of responsibility. The other side, which included Lord North, was less inclined. The first minister was inundated with plans from people like Clive. His advisers, however, such as John Robinson, did not think the machinery of Government was strong enough to take over the responsibility of running affairs in Bengal and elsewhere. What remained true, however, was that the Company's future was out of its own hands. Eventually, it would have to succumb to those changes in its organisation and rule suggested by others from outside its body.

North's Government, (notably Charles Jenkinson) carefully prepared a plan of action that was to begin with the speech from the throne. First, however, Parliament was to inform itself of the true state of the Company's affairs. Throughout December and January Sulivan was extremely active, preparing proposals to forestall these ministerial designs. He realised that constructive moves had to be put forward. If not, he could see a situation where the Company would just do as it was told. Chartered rights would become outdated, wither and die.

He wanted reform within the Company, while giving minimum concessions to any outside body. That is why on 3 December 1772 he laid a plan before the Court of Directors that would 'enable the Company to make a dividend on the Company's stock.' In other words, he wanted to show to the world the monopoly's continued viability, and its healthy future.[13]

On 14 January 1773 he met Lord North to go over 'thirteen points' of discussion, pertaining to the reform of Company business, the financial help to be received and Parliament's rewards. These far-sighted 'thirteen points' came from Sulivan, were part of his own initiative and proved to be immensely important. They also served to represent the views of the Direction.

The more important heads of conversation included: renewal of the Charter; and £200,000 to be repaid to the Exchequer in £50,000 instalments – after all debts were reimbursed. Government was to loan a total of £1,500,000 at four per cent interest for four years. The country was to benefit from the Company's territorial revenues; Proprietors would receive a fixed dividend of eight per cent – the remainder to be divided between Government and the Proprietors.

Regulations regarding the administration of justice were to be granted, based upon Sulivan's Judicature Bill of the previous year. Parliament was to be given copies of revenue books, charge books, copies of consultations, and supplied with every help to understand Company affairs. Tea was to be exported duty free; and two ships were to be sent direct to America, annually, with tea and other India goods. They would return to England loaded with American commodities. (It would appear that Sulivan's initial proposal led eventually to the 'Boston Tea Party'.) On 23 January 1773 North let him know that he was ready to consider these measures.

It was February before Colebrooke, Sulivan and Wheler presented a formal petition to Parliament for relief from financial distress. This was based broadly on the 'thirteen points' outlined by Sulivan and shown to North on 14 January. Carefully excluded, however, was any mention of grants of revenue to Government from territorial acquisitions. Sulivan suspected all along that North was grasping at control of the Company, the 'glorious object' as he described it to Hastings. Colebrooke too indicated that he was sure North was after territories, possessions and trade. The Proprietors, however, had no idea of the extent of the minister's claims. As guessed, revenue from commerce and from territorial gains was exactly what was expected.

When these demands were aired through Burgoyne's Select Committee, there was a general revolt in the Company. The challenge to chartered rights and to the Company's territorial acquisitions caused outrage. North was informed there could be no acceptance of the loan unless the Company's views were incorporated in future proposals.

The course of events, and of Sulivan's future, was further complicated by the looming election of April 1773. This was recognised to have immense importance. The make-up of the new Direction would reflect which interest had succeeded at Leadenhall. It was fully understood that the Directors returned would be important to the continuing negotiations with Government, which had reached a delicate stage

Electoral activity had already commenced by October 1772, but Sulivan put no great effort into putting forces into the field. He did not have the wherewithal in terms of patronage and support. His mind was also distracted because Colebrooke, who owed him a great deal, had just crashed. Nevertheless, his confidence in being returned to the Direction was well-founded at this stage.

Inexorably, though, events turned against him. This might have become a little obvious when he found out that he alone of all the Company leaders of

1772 stood for re-election. He did not consider himself constrained in doing so, in the face of public accusations, many of them ministry inspired. He took the minister's approval of Purling's request for and inquiry as an indirect censure upon his own behaviour, and so made it clear to all and sundry that his conscience was untroubled. He made a public statement that he feared no interrogation and, furthermore, declared his intention of standing for re-election. He would do so because not to offer his services would be tantamount to an admission of guilt. Besides, he argued, the pressing state of the Company's affairs demanded the endeavours of its most experienced servants.

Sulivan's speech was much approved of. He depicted himself as the only pillar of strength left in the Direction. He expected the ministry's attacks upon him to be violent, and they were, because with him gone the Company would be completely at North's mercy. He said to Hastings, 'could I be prevailed upon to retire, every art was practiced, to cajole, to intimidate me, but nothing could move me for I had nothing to fear.'[14] So vicious was the censure, he was forced to issue a printed declaration that outlined his position and his interest; and gave a reminder of all that he had done for the Company.[15]

The election proper resolved itself into a struggle between Crabb Boulton, heading the Proprietors' list and supported by Ministry, against Sulivan and the House list, with such support as he could muster. Sadly for Sulivan, apart from Palk and the Barwells, most shareholders backed Boulton; while the crash of his ally Colebrooke threw his erstwhile supporter Rumbold on to the side of Clive, Sykes and Government. Fear of probes by the Select Committee influenced many others; and all was conducted amidst a great deal of public revulsion at Nabobs. The Proprietors' list won convincingly. Boulton was made Chairman, with Edward Wheler his deputy. Lord Sandwich had astutely handled the Government's management of those within the Company holding pro-ministry feelings, and of those fearful of anyone prying into their personal affairs. Sulivan blamed himself for Sandwich's degree of control.

Yet he was still surprised at the result, describing it as 'a revolution ...extraordinary and unexpected'.[16] Most contemporary evidence, on the other hand, pointed to him being crushed, and his friends had predicted it. What he referred to was the defection of his long-time friend, the ship's husband, Charles Raymond, and others in the shipping interest. This 'betrayal', left him utterly crestfallen. This interest had been his constant support, his great strength. He was broken at the result. He said to Warren Hastings: 'Ten days ago all the world thought my power was riveted.'[17]

He was really signalling the loss of his core support, his power base. No wonder he was despondent. From April onwards he had few backers, and faced the hostility of North's ministry. He vented his rage, remarking disparagingly that such an incompetent Direction would scarcely last a year, especially with Crabb Boulton a dying man. But his own resigned attitude is indicated by the admission that 'the power of ministry was not to be resisted...in future they must govern the Company'.[18]

The April 1773 election was the last of its kind. It returned a majority of Directors who would prove amenable to every Government suggestion. Henceforth, Sulivan would only be able to pressurise the ministry and its lackeys in the Direction indirectly, from within the General Court. His departure from Parliament in 1774 did not help either. Far from filling the Chairman's post, which ordinarily would have been the step up from Deputy Chairman, he was not even in the Direction. Yet, although down, he was not out; and symptomatic of his ever-soaring spirit he still hoped to influence the final form of North's Regulating Act

3

The King's speech of 21 January 1773 asserted the State's right to intervene; but that and the April 1773 election, denotes the high point of what was really a remarkably short term of interest by Administration in the affairs of the East India Company. What the ministry really had to do, however, was secure control over Company servants – the same object worked at by Sulivan throughout that fateful year. To this end, as was related to Hastings, 'he very early' conveyed his ideas on reform at home and abroad to Lord North, 'the fountainhead'.

Restoration of credit to the Company came in October 1773. A series of small loans for short periods meant that a repeat of the disaster of October 1772 would be avoided. Eventually, the ministry was armed with the findings of its own Committee of Secrecy. Here the difficulties faced were all spelled out: the Company's 'debts, credits and effects'; the perennial problems of military costs, and reform of abuses abroad – the very difficulties that Sulivan and people like him had fought for years.

Naturally, the greatest opposition to North's terms came from India House; yet the ministry needed the help of Directors and Proprietors in framing the necessary clauses and having them accepted at Leadenhall. Sulivan and Richmond figured prominently. The Duke represented the animosity felt by Parliamentary Opposition. Proprietor stubbornness showed, when a committee of thirteen Proprietors, which included Sulivan, was appointed: 'To draw up proposals for the reform of the Company's organisation in England.'[19]

The Government's own draft ideas were based upon the reports of the Committee of Secrecy; unofficial knowledge of various Company proposals; and, Sulivan reported sarcastically, 'by the advice of many individuals including even Laurence Sulivan'.[20] In dismissive language he referred to the unfair terms accorded Hastings' position; while still willing to forge a constructive policy with Government representatives. Yet so great was his mistrust, before being ousted in April, he had set up a 'committee of twenty-five' to watch over the interests of the Proprietors. By dint of this committee the Directors were forbidden to offer terms to North; so the minister threatened dictated terms.

Reluctantly a general agreement along the lines of the proposals first put forward by Sulivan in his discussion with North on 14 January was settled upon. These 'thirteen points' were forwarded to Parliament by 2 March. They were debated in the House at Committee level and the Bill was drafted there – primarily by Robinson, helped by Jenkinson. It was known later as the 'Loan Bill'.

After the removal of Sulivan in April, the Direction meekly followed ministry's wishes; and by May the minister was ready to state the proposals in the Commons. In the meantime, the persistent lack of negotiation led to protests among the Proprietors. North called their bluff by asking if the Company would rather reject the loan. He had won; but in fact, he could not hold back anyway, the Regulating Bill was complete and the House awaited it.

4

Such are the paradoxes of life, at the very moment of his greatest worry Sulivan had taken under his wing the individual who would come to the rescue of his and the Company's affairs. He was responsible for Warren Hastings being allowed to return to India in 1769. After that, he appointed him to the position of Governor of Bengal; and later, in 1773, ensured he was made Governor-General. The evidence is quite clear on all this. It is even more striking because before Sulivan's advocacy, nothing in the least remarkable career-wise had happened to this Company official.

There had been some earlier links with Sulivan, of course. For instance, the loyalty he had shown Henry Vansittart from 1760 to 1763 was not lost on the Company leader. Even closer ties came about from 1763 onwards because of Clive's coldness to the young man. Again this was due to Hastings' loyalty to Vansittart. Clive had shown hostility to his erstwhile colleague in other ways. In 1767 Hastings had applied to the Directors for re-employment, and was refused. Clive, whose followers dominated the Court, inspired the rejection. The friendship between Hastings and Vansittart explains why.

However, despite this antagonism, he acquitted himself well when giving evidence at the Parliamentary Inquiry, and attracted the attention of North and Mansfield among the ministers; Colebrooke and Purling in the Company. This helped, of course, but what really explains the success of his re-application in April 1768 was that Clive had temporarily dropped his opposition. Why he should do so is explained by efforts made by Sulivan to come to an arrangement with him in September 1767 using their mutual friend Robert Palk as an intermediary. In his letter of 13 September 1767, Sulivan offered an alliance to Clive. In a footnote to this letter, he added that he had omitted to state that he wished Warren Hastings 'to be returned to India, in his standing.'[21] Sulivan got his wish; Hastings was to succeed Josias Du Pré at Madras. He sailed for India in March 1769.

Hastings then attempted to draw into a closer association the friends he and Sulivan held in common, such as Palk, Vansittart and Elijah Impey. He entreated Sulivan to secure Colebrooke's friendship too. This was all stimulated by Sulivan's return to power in 1769. Then from 1771 to 1772, although in alliance with Colebrooke, he was the one who took charge of affairs. Sulivan's aim was to shake up the whole of the Bengal Administration. He wanted it remodelled and the Clivites out.

His power within the Direction in 1771 was made evident when on 10 April a General Letter to Bengal notified the authorities of Hastings' appointment as 2nd in Council. The next General Letter to Calcutta of 25 April dismissed Cartier and his Clivite colleagues Becher, Claude Russell and Charles Floyer. Again this had Sulivan's unmistakable stamp on it.

Before Hastings had even left Madras, yet another official letter followed on 8 August, again advanced and authorised by Sulivan, which instructed him to go on the *Lapwing* to Bengal and take over as Governor. Sulivan required a man accomplished and experienced enough to manage major restructuring, and so turned to the already earmarked Warren Hastings.

It is also true, of course, that others seemed to want Hastings to take charge – his service and talents would warrant this. For example, Francis Sykes, an old confidant certainly canvassed on his behalf. Even Clive, it has been claimed, recommended him; although this softer attitude was short lived. Moreover, it only happened after Vansittart's death in 1770, thus ending Hastings' connection with someone Clive regarded as an enemy.

In Hastings Sulivan had someone who was perfectly suited for what he wanted. Through him he meant to channel his plans and ideas. Basic to everything, however, was the wish to re-impose the authority of the Direction on Company servants abroad. This was supposed to be done through his protégé. What developed, of course, was not exactly what Sulivan had in mind. Hastings seized the opportunities presented to him through being on the spot in India and made his own mark. He doubled his endeavours, developed great will-power and demonstrated ability to handle the complex problems before him. Yet he never ceased to welcome Sulivan's views, entered in both public and private correspondence.

At first, after being made Governor of Bengal, Hastings heaped all the praise for his appointment upon Sykes. It was late January-February 1772 before it dawned upon him that Sulivan had been instrumental in securing his promotion in 1769 and again in 1771. Only the interest that Sulivan commanded in the General Court and in a section of the Direction, especially in alliance with Colebrooke, could have secured these appointments and what followed; not the wishes of Sykes and Palk, however well intentioned.

Hastings was already impressed by Sulivan's abilities however: 'Your superior knowledge and long practise in the Company's affairs…give you that ascendant which you formerly possessed in the administration of them.'[22] Referring to his nomination for Governor of Bengal, he expressed thanks to Sulivan:

for this fresh instance of your benevolence to me. I am as yet unacquainted with the means by which this very unexpected change in my fortune was brought about; but I know that it had all the help that your influence could give it.[23]

Sulivan, he declared, had 'uniformly supported him and had never once lost sight of his honour, his interest and his reputation'.[24]   Later in his career he came to know just how great his obligation to Sulivan really was; and admitted that he owed more to him than any other man in the world.

The task of governing in Bengal was not an easy one, and from the beginning Hastings faced immense problems. He was forced to introduce some energy into the art of government in what was an exceptionally corrupt and lethargic environment. He also faced the consequences of the 1769-70 famine and the decimation of the Company's wealth that followed in its wake.

The Secret Committee at Leadenhall, with Sulivan on board until 1773, helped him in all this, proving formidable in its attack on the powerful Mohammed Reza Khan who had controlled affairs as the Indian half of the dual system. Sulivan had him removed. In Hastings' first year of office the foundations of the future British ruling structure were laid down. As *Diwan*, a proper system was devised, which meant that after long opposition Sulivan had bowed to the inevitable. The upshot was that Clive's system was ended, Bengal was kept alive financially, and Hastings set a course for the future.

From hindsight it can be seen how crucial this appointment was for future developments. It was not altogether fortuitous, however. Sulivan had concentrated on him as the man most needed to take charge. In doing so he showed great discernment. Noting Hastings' mastery of Indian culture, he surmised that he could apply himself in a constructive and reforming way for the future good of the Company and the subcontinent.

This was the thrust of his argument during Company-Government negotiations on appointments to the Supreme Board at Calcutta. He pushed Hastings forward for Governor-General against competition from Rumbold, Pigot and Du Pré; arguing that he was untainted and had already made inroads into the problems in Bengal. He pointed to the vast overhaul of the Company's governing and judicial framework already achieved; and to his general experience and continuity of service. He made sure that his letters recommending Hastings reached the right people – especially Charles Jenkinson, who was impressed. Ministers settled for Sulivan's choice. Lord North praised Hastings in the debates and the post was secured.

Hastings was appointed a reforming Governor-General, and had to divert subverted energies back to Company work. Besides his civil and judicial duties, he was responsible for defence of the Company's possessions and preservation of its gains. He was entrusted with the direction of military action against the French and hostile princedoms alike; but had to return profits sufficient for a dividend.

The exceptional talents he possessed were much appreciated by his mentor, Sulivan, such as his good knowledge of the Urdu and Persian languages; and understanding of native law, customs and politics. British officials had to become judges and ambassadors dealing with local matters. In fact, Hastings (and Sulivan too) would have liked to leave control of Indian affairs in their hands as much as possible.

He had a bureaucratic, authoritarian cast of mind, more so when opposed; but also had vision and statesman-like qualities that placed him beyond the normal. Sulivan endeavoured to keep the Governor-General tied to him. He never faltered in his support and advice; and he was to fight Hastings' corner in the dirty business of Company politics until his return.

This support was crucial; in particular it upheld Hastings 'during the critical first two years of his administration, those years when the foundations were being laid of a decent government in Bengal'.[25] The post of Governor-General that then followed was certainly 'an appointment Lord North would not have made without the sanction of the Company's Chairmen'.[26] Somehow it seems fitting that Sulivan was able to fill this first ever Governor-General position with his own man.

5

Sulivan's telling remarks on the Regulating Act, and on its operation, illustrate a piercing understanding of just what was happening. The main stages in the passage of the Bill and its terms are well-known. In the Parliamentary struggle, ministry faced the argument that the Company still had the right to territorial revenues. Lord Rockingham, with Edmund Burke at his elbow, led the Opposition on this; and the issue was expanded into a general attack upon the Government, claiming that such interference attacked the liberties of the citizen while it increased the power of the Crown.

The Bill was a composite measure, transitory in nature, and was regarded as a means in itself for future reforms. Its primary function was to bridge the gap between the years 1773 and 1780, the end of the Company's current Charter. Balance was its main feature, since it attempted to satisfy the wishes of the Company and those of the State in the choice of members for the new government in Calcutta. Representing the Company's choice were Warren Hastings and Richard Barwell. For the Government was 'The Triumvirate' of Philip Francis, Colonel Monson and General Clavering, who was to be Commander-in-Chief and Hastings' successor if he resigned.

The Supreme Court set up in Bengal was based on Sulivan's Judicature Bill of 1772, but married to the Ministry's desire that the Crown would appoint the Judges. Most of the provisions for checking corruption among Company servants contained in the Bill also owed their existence to Sulivan's Judicature Bill, as did the proposed reform of the Company in London.

The measures included Sulivan's desire to curtail even further the 'splitting' of stock, by ensuring that people owned the shares for longer, before they could count as qualifications at Company elections. The voting requirement itself was increased: from £500 to £1000; and the cumulative vote for large holders of stock was reintroduced. A four-year rotation of Directors was to commence from April 1774; and there were to be no plenipotentiaries in India.

Even as the Bill was being thrashed out in Parliament, Sulivan and his fellow Proprietors were presenting a petition against it, signifying the simmering opposition within Leadenhall. However, the Solicitor-General, Alexander Wedderburn (and Charles Cornwall) succeeded in having this rejected. North was then able to reintroduce the Bill, and it became law on 21 June 1773; but only after hot debates in the Lords.

It would be 1774 before all of this legislation created the desired changes and before the ministry would have direct influence on Company affairs. Even then, it still had to face the anger and hostility of most Proprietors, and was going to have difficulty in making them cooperate in the new arrangements.

From the first, the inefficient operation of the new system reflected it was a compromise. Indirect Governmental control through its agents in the Supreme Council in Bengal, and by John Robinson and the Earl of Sandwich within the Direction, was disastrous. There was no doctrine, and it was clumsy; with the Government dependent upon Company machinery. More difficulties were created than it set out to resolve. Hastings could only ever expect – at the very best – a compromise with North and Robinson. 'The Triumvirate' utterly horrified Sulivan and his friends.

In the end, the Act was to fail in India and was only just kept alive in Britain. It inaugurated another period of 'General Courts', stimulating power struggles among the body of Proprietors. It was a continual struggle for Government to maintain some form of control in the Proprietors' Court as well as the Direction.

Becoming involved in the Company's affairs and learning how its labyrinth machinery worked was now one of the Treasury's most active pursuits. Robinson, Jenkinson and Dundas gained much needed expertise; and with them, although it was negligible at this stage, began the participation of the British Government in the administration of India. Here again, inadvertently, Sulivan had helped in a more mundane way. The organisation within India House (completed earlier by Secretary James and himself) was so sound that the investigating commission, set up in 1773 in preparation for the Regulating Act, felt compelled to congratulate the Company upon the competence of its clerks and the state of its books.

Sulivan's letters abroad, principally to Hastings and Richard Barwell, demonstrate how quickly he grasped Government's real intentions. They reveal how useful he was as a commentator and critic upon events; and provided Hastings with vital knowledge, and insights. By May 1773 he had come to the conclusion that 'the system now adopted must be productive of anarchy and confusion...I deem the men bold who have launched upon such a bottom.'[27]

He saw the looming struggle for control that would develop, and commented, 'Sacred writ says that no man can serve two masters, yet such is the task.'[28] By October he was lamenting that Hastings was 'not empowered to act singly', and that the 'crown had carefully preserved a majority...in the new government of Bengal, with the succession well secured'.[29] At that point Sulivan did not know how firmly Government controlled nominations to the Bengal Council. His own conclusions, however, were that 'in equity and sound sense the scale ought to have preponderated with the Company'. He feared that the prevailing view within the ministry, Parliament and the public would ruin the organisation.[30]

Between October and March 1774 he comprehended the overall design and was horrified. The Act and its consequences would annihilate his beloved Company. To him it dissolved 'a solemn compact, dearly purchased and secured...by so many Acts of Parliament'. Although it restrained the Company for five years only (from 1773), he commented shrewdly, 'add the time before this can reach India and the term extends nearly to the expiration of the Charter itself'.[31]

He was deceived over the Supreme Court articles too. They struck against the Company: 'The first Magistrate reduced to a common J.P.' Sulivan was under the impression that North had agreed with him that there should not be too much interference with local custom and laws. Yet the Supreme Court had been given 'extensive jurisdiction and immense power'. He foresaw that every native would seek legal decisions in 'an English Court of Justice'. It was also wrong, he thought, that the independent powers of the other Presidencies should pass to Bengal. He said to Hastings, 'It will require all your philosophy to bear with temper the Parliamentary system which in a great degree annihilates the Company's powers and privileges, disgraces and degrades the service in India.'[32]

He did not think that Hastings could accept such an arrangement; and feared, all too correctly that he would lose real power and be faced with rivals in the Council. He went on to picture a dismal future in which the power of Parliament was to be dreaded; where Hastings would find it impossible to conduct Company affairs; and the Council would belong to the Crown. The lack of experience and knowledge in the Bengal Council, together with the rejection of Hastings (which he foresaw), would be ruinous. He now bemoaned the four-year Direction and the £1000 stock qualification to vote, which had to be held for a year beforehand. His keen eye saw that the future independence of the Company was lost.

His letters continued, filled with lamentation. The ministry, he said, would have the 'entire management of the Company at home and abroad'; and added, 'love of my country and its happy Constitution warrants me to call this a dreadful hour'.[33] His greatest fear was that the end result would be the surrender of the Company Charter. His only hope lay in, 'A confidential union' between Hastings and Barwell. Above all, he put his hopes in what he termed Hastings' own 'superior abilities'.[34]

In his correspondence Sulivan belittled what his own role in future events might be, saying: 'My affection can suggest no counsel – its beyond the reach of my abilities.'[35] Yet he went on to offer a never-ending stream of plans and advice on every topic. One of his fervent hopes was that 'the arrival of my much loved friend Mr. Impey' would help him.[36] In light of the feud that developed later between them, it is ironic that Sulivan should give the new Chief Justice such an outstanding character reference.[37]

Impey had been Warren Hastings' 'old acquaintance…school fellow and intimate friend'.[38] Sulivan had benefited from his friendship. It enabled him to make connections in the Cabinet, especially with the Attorney-General, Edward Thurlow, from whom he gained considerable information as well as a firm alliance. Impey was also the close confidante of his long-time ally, John Dunning. These joint friendships made the link with Hastings stronger. He also thought, wrongly it proved, that Monson would be a close collaborator.[39] In this way, friend and foe were identified; although it was only late in 1773 that he learned Francis was Clive's friend, through D'Oyly 'whose interest brought him (Francis) into the commission. D'Oyly and Clive are inseparable.'[40]

What is most apparent in these letters of Sulivan's is that he (and through him Hastings) realised that by the Regulating Act, Parliament had all but taken over control of the Company and its possessions. He was to be proved correct in every prognosis; and knew that all the 'lucrative and tempting power' would eventually be in Government's hands.[41] Hastings' situation, with its duties and obligations, he saw would be both delicate and dangerous. Nevertheless, he maintained that it was the duty of both to keep on course: 'They stood on a precipice…but the eyes of Parliament, the Company and the British nation were upon them.'[42]

Sulivan's use of terms like 'Chartered Liberties'; 'Rights of an Englishman'; for the 'public service' and so on were not employed in the sense of looking after the general good, for the benefit of trade or perhaps the alleviation of poverty; nor did they refer to impartiality, parity, justice or of equal reward for equal work. They can best be described as colloquialisms. The language appears to betoken a common attitude held by those who were from his class or strata in society.

The expressions might be taken to represent a Whig view of the times; of a ruling oligarchy against both monarchy and the non-property owning mob.[43] Even as the leader of the East India Company, Sulivan was not required to undergo public examination – limited as this was in eighteenth century Britain. He objected in the strongest terms to Parliament's efforts to enforce just such an inspection (as opposed to regulation) in what was perhaps an early movement towards public accountability. He certainly regarded North's Regulating Act as breaching the walls of hard won and (to him) justified privilege.

The loss of Vansittart and the other Supervisors early in 1770 had been a body blow, although the Supervisory Commission itself had been a good idea. A Parliamentary route, not a Company one, would have sufficed; and the Judicature Bill he introduced, or something similar, if given a chance might have succeeded. His real concern and painstaking work is shown in the details of this proposed Act, and in the plans and ideas willingly given to the Secretary of the Treasury, John Robinson. Now that the ministry had overall control, Sulivan was to express his schemes and proposals privately, to Warren Hastings and to others among his close friends and family in the east; until once more he was asked for his ideas by Robinson, Dundas and Pitt the Younger later in the 1770s.

Through ministerial confidence in himself he had hoped to continue making a personal contribution to the better regulation of Company affairs. This hope, fortified by ministerial use of his 'thirteen points', only lasted until the 1773 election, when it was made clear that the last thing the North Government wanted to face was the continued rivalry between him and the Clivites.

He had known for some time that he must put the right man in charge in India. Abroad, this person would have to work alone, yet act in tandem with him. He must take heed of all that was said, and act on the advice sent by him from Leadenhall. Hastings was just such a mortal; and he tried to give him unlimited power.

In the end he could do nothing about ministerial takeover via the Regulating Act. Nevertheless, in the period 1769 to 1773 (similar to the years prior to 1765) he probably did more than any other person to set up the framework required for the future territorial administration of British India. His work was to be built upon and pursued vigorously by Hastings in his own individual way.

Sulivan's own assessment of his contribution at this time is probably correct. He said that as a member of the April 1769 to April 1770 Direction, in particular, he helped create substantial groundwork for reform in India. He wanted to operate a form of benevolent, but firm rule, giving security, impartial justice and regular administration. In his heart of hearts he would have already given way to Parliament's right to superintend eventually, while still defending the sanctity of chartered rights. The form of government he desired was one that would operate, as far as it could, within Company confines, while preserving laws and customs that had become adapted to the needs of Asians through time.

12

Desperation and Defiance
1774-78

1

From August 1769 Sulivan had made prodigious attempts to escape from the financial trap he was in, and in so doing became further involved with Colebrooke, Vansittart and Macleane. He faced a truly appalling situation; a state of affairs particularly humiliating to him when he was at the helm of the Company from 1771 to the end of 1772, and in the right place, it might be thought, to remedy things. Hastings was told that he and Vansittart were so much in debt 'it forced the children (Owen and Sulivan connections) to India and brought me to the brink of ruin. For though I was independent, not anxious for more, I never was rich.'[1] Vansittart's death made the situation so desperate he was forced to mortgage everything with any value.

By 1772 he owed over £10,000 to Palk and more than £7,000 to Vansittart's estate. Macleane and others owed him more than £9,000. In exchange Sulivan received securities on the estates the Ulsterman had transferred to Vansittart, worth £6,000. These embraced three lots of land on the island of St. John, Newfoundland (later known as Prince Edward Island). He also held Macleane's bond payable to the executors of Henry Vansittart's estate, worth £1,593-15/.

Towards the end of May 1772, the ongoing negative conduct of Edmund Boehm, Vansittart's executor, forced him to turn again to Palk, a trustee of Vansittart's estate. His other hope of succour was through Colebrooke, also in his debt through a move of Macleane. His optimism terminated with the collapse of India stock in 1772 and the failure of Colebrooke's banking firm in 1773.[2] That same year, Colebrooke, Sulivan, Macleane, the Barwell family, the Burkes (William and Edmund) and Lord Verney were participants in a plan which, although the details are lost, involved the redistribution of India stock. It came unstuck.

Colebrooke was declared bankrupt in 1773, and an unsuccessful attempt was made to put his bank in Threadneedle Street into the hands of Sulivan and John Boyd. Sulivan's predicament was so bad in 1774, he was forced once again to seek John Dunning's help. His pride choked him, however, when he found people at his friend's house who smirked at his reduced circumstances. Unable to face the humiliation he turned away.

Although author of his own predicament, he was certainly dogged by bad luck. The country and the Company were in the grip of a credit crisis which he was powerless to do anything about. Nor could he have legislated for the death of Vansittart. It was the lowest point in his fortunes. In late middle age his world had literally come apart. He was out of the Direction and only one step removed from debtors' prison.

2

Great Ormonde Street and neighbourhood would have been very beautiful in the spring of 1774, but the sixty-year-old Sulivan might not have appreciated it too much. He was very much changed from the forty-four-year-old who came to power in 1757. The never ending work and responsibility, Clive's remorseless enmity, and the effort to regain office in 1769 had left their mark. The wreck of his personal finances that followed was accompanied by the loss of his much-loved Company to the State, and with it ministerial control of what had been his to rule over.

His character had changed in countless little ways. He was more cynical, sceptical and suspicious - although still able to enjoy a fight. In 1739 he had been a mysterious figure but in every other way open and above board. Now, though still secretive, life at the white-hot centre of so much of consequence had tempered his views of mankind, and made him play his cards close to his chest.

He still sought fulfilment, but this search had changed subtly from the original one. He had luxuriated in authority, and the trappings of success. This had substantially gone, but he still hungered for the exercise of power. The pride of his early years had turned to conceit when he took the Deputy Chair in 1757. It took the debacle of 1769 and the abject defeat of the years 1773 to 1774 to make this tendency disappear forever. Henceforth he was to be respected (and hated) for his skill, knowledge and ability in relation to Indian affairs.

Yet, there was still one trait he just could not subjugate, one that lay at the root of all his troubles: he could not resist a gamble, a joust with lady luck. This characteristic had been demonstrated time and again. Yet he could never stop. It was part of his nature, blended into his soul. Nothing else mattered other than to be 'in the game'. After 1773, although still possessed of the same compulsion, he could not indulge it because he did not have the wherewithal and lacked opportunity. It was as if a rogue gene forced him to seek authority and use it, and in many respects his conflicts and struggles within the Company were all to do with this. Unquestionably these battles reflect a compulsion to be the master. It was the same with the contests in the press, against ministers, and with powerful servants, home and abroad. He had to be in command.

Sulivan enjoyed the exercise of power; and had aspirations to change so much of the world. This is reflected in plans and proposals, administrative reforms, Parliamentary bills and everything else. These embraced territory and life in the East; and every conceivable sphere of Company business. In his private and Company correspondence, in Parliamentary speeches, press statements, books and pamphlets, the same impulses to control, command, but also to do good, are evident.

He always wanted 'the confidential powers', seeking command, fame, and riches (strictly in that order); and only through and within the East India Company. He regarded riches as necessary only for pursuing, gaining and retaining influence, and for a certain standard of life. He enjoyed the demonstration of power, however, and the accompanying prestige; but his influence was used to push others towards riches and lucrative appointments, not himself. Nevertheless, he always sought to earn this authority and not just be given this because it went with the office. Self-awareness, knowledge of society and the workings of the world lay behind this attitude. His excellence and expertise were the outward manifestations of knowing his inner self.

The wish to exercise power was at the very heart of this intelligent man. Like Machiavelli's Prince he too planned with foresight and clarity; executed ruthlessly; and winning was everything. Fulfilment only came when he alone governed a successfully-run Company. He used the tactics of a professional politician: wheeling and dealing; remaining inscrutable; giving nothing away; and holding his tongue. These ploys become habitual.[3] He maintained a deliberate aura of mystery and ensured that his reputation went before him; enlisting others, such as Thomas Lane, to do much of the work that had to be kept secret. The impression he contrived to impose was that without him there would be chaos.

By the nature of things those superior in social and political standing did not necessarily love him, usually the opposite; they could resent, fear or ignore him. Sulivan knew his position and what he could reasonably achieve. Also, because of his high-powered activities and the dirty politics that enveloped him he would have to be untruthful at times, though without sacrificing honour. Many of his tactics 'like Machiavelli out of Tamany Hall', were surely devious. He studied everyone, continually searching for motivation and traits. There is the impression that apart from his wife, he never trusted anyone completely.

He had the ability to plot and counter-plot, so necessary to get to the very top. Perhaps the stimulus for such driving ambition (and use of Machiavellian tactics) lies too deep to be analysed properly, and is to be found in psychological and genetic features, or even his ancestral background. Nevertheless, it was probably the most striking feature of his personality. There was a down-side to all this, of course. The pursuit and application of great power surely bled him of some feelings and created illusion. Without the warmth his wife could provide and a normal home life, he could have become a hollow shell.

3

In 1774 Sulivan and family moved westwards, only a matter of several hundred yards, from 46 Great Ormonde Street to a less imposing and not so costly house on the south side of Queen Square. He would dwell there until 1782. This square was a special place and the house stood in one of the loveliest backwaters in the heart of London.[4] Doctor Burney and his daughter Fanny (Madame D'Arblay) were his immediate neighbours. Hannah More, one of Dr. Johnson's circle, was a resident.

It was a rather fashionable area, favoured by the intelligentsia and by commercial men. Robert Louis Stevenson later described the Square as, 'Grave and kindly…set apart from the humanities of life and the alleviations of all hard destinies.'[5] The house had many rooms, all of a handsome size and providing enviable living conditions.

In the space immediately south of the Square right in front of Sulivan's house, stood an iron pump. This provided the best water in the neighbourhood. 'It was a sight to see the procession of jug-carrying servants from the great houses and children from the poorer houses making their way to the pump each day.'[6] It was at this time he became a member of the church of St. George the Martyr, Queen Square. John Luxmore, Rector from 1782, was to lay to rest both he and his wife in its burial ground.[7]

Sulivan was engrossed so much in money matters and political skirmishing that his other qualities tend to be squeezed out. Nevertheless, he did appreciate many forms of beauty. This is reflected in his love of Persian and ancient Indian artefacts, and appreciation of portraits. It is also illustrated by his patronage of the artists Tilly Kettle, Richard Crosse and Sir Thomas Lawrence, who all finished portraits of him.

He was not spiritual in a religious sense and was really more of a humanist or atheist. He often described himself as such and said that he abhorred religion, though using Biblical terminology a lot, and attending ritual for his wife's sake. However, he would not offend the protocol of religious life. Encircled by so many devout people, like his wife and Robert Palk, he could do little else. Why he was so irreligious is not obvious – although clearly steeped in scripture. Possibly it was because he had observed so many different beliefs, especially in the East; and had seen enough intolerance in the world.

Even before his move to Queen Square itself, Sulivan was known far and near, as 'The Old Man of Queen Square'. His association with this part of London was to remain rooted for a quarter of a century. Many of his friends and enemies, such as: Clive, Vansittart, and William Barwell had ties with the area or lived close by. The Square was certainly at the centre of affairs, judging by the number of East Indians who lived thereabouts. It was a short carriage ride from India House and the rest of the City, yet near enough, for a merchant and Company man, to the society of the West End. It was convenient for Westminster and Whitehall, for the Court, and his country estate in Hertfordshire – if he should ever repossess it.

4

By acceptance of the new situation created by the Regulating Act, Sulivan again displayed that he was a realist. In order to ensure some form of independence the executive had to forge a fresh relationship with Administration; and although not in the Direction, he worked hard at establishing the ground rules that would accommodate the Company's new masters.

Nor was he was disheartened after defeat in April 1773. Hastings was told, 'I certainly do not give up the game, and my prospects are rather solid.'[8] He referred to renewed ties with the Johnstone group; and with others among the Proprietors opposed to ministerial control of the Company. He was forging links too with members of the Rockingham party, who formed part of the Parliamentary Opposition. By September, Richmond was asking Rockingham to forget the aversion they both entertained, and to vote for him at in April 1774. Richmond wanted Sulivan to be part of the alliance Sandwich had formed with the Johnstone group.

The real political arena now was the General Court, where the struggle for domination developed. The groups had to fight along organised lines, in contrast to earlier times, largely because of the changes introduced by North's Act. One quarter of the 24 man executive would be elected annually for a four-year term. The regulation came into force for the first time in April 1774, giving sharpness to the election. To inaugurate the scheme a quarter of the Directors were to be elected for the full term, a quarter for one year, the same for two years, and again for three years.

Sulivan was the only one of the old leaders still skirmishing, and his adherents started to regroup. He observed that the death of an old enemy, Crabb Boulton, might be to his benefit. He also revealed that he and Charles Raymond of the shipping interest were 'fast friends again'.[9] This was extremely important. It probably came about because he recommended ample provision should be made for commanders of ships deprived of employment due to new regulations reducing Company shipping. They received £200 each. He was troubled, however, by the attitude of Lord North, who he described as pretending to be sorry for his conduct towards him, which he did not believe. This and the confusion at India house left him beginning to feel a little more uncertain of success.

The 1774 election was exceptionally significant, therefore, because the result would be long lasting. However, by Christmas he knew North had decided against him, probably influenced by his dallying with the Rockingham group. He returned this hostility as his own views hardened.

His aims were to support Hastings; restrain or redirect ministerial pressures bearing upon the Company; and preserve its semi-independence for as long as possible. To him this was 'a dreadful era'. He saw the struggle ahead and described Lord North, with no small measure of sarcasm and anger as 'The boldest minister...since the days of Oliver Cromwell.'[10] He thought the forthcoming election would be the last real contest, since he expected that Government would seize hold of Company management by having their own nominees returned.

He described the period December 1773 to January 1774 as full of scenes of confusion. He was also aware that Clive had joined the ministry, but thought this would make no difference. He was wrong. His Lordship had realised the importance of this election and brought all his influence to bear. It was to be his last but effective storm of activity against Sulivan. Walsh and Strachey, in collaboration with John Robinson (who was acting on behalf of the ministry) filled the Direction with their men. Thus a coalition of ministry nominees and Clivites was formed. Sulivan described them as, 'more contemptible, if possible, than when Bolton [Crabb Boulton] presided, broke to pieces among themselves and at this time there are four and twenty chairmen – a melancholy but true picture.'[11]

In early January 1774 he consented to form a coalition with Governor George Johnstone. This was a real turnaround. Apologetically he said to Hastings: 'To you and my friend Macleane nothing could perhaps be more disgusting than such a union and my best friends have a right to an explanation.'[12] It was done because the shipper, Charles Raymond, wanted it. With the North ministry's unfriendliness, Sulivan reflected that he would not 'accept a junction with them but upon very explicit grounds as I have been so often betrayed'.[13] In this way he was sucked further into the Johnstone, Richmond and Rockingham camp.

All involved in this alliance were urged to buy stock for splitting, and Sulivan resorted to a series of publicity campaigns. A comparative state of the Company was published under the name 'An Old Proprietor'. He also had another article ready, which he described as 'A vindication of the Company and its Directors...it marks the minister (North) as the origin of our present misfortunes.'[14]

He harnessed the support of Colebrooke and Sir James Cockburn to that of the Johnstones, George Dempster, Lushington and Yorke. Robert Palk's backing was vouchsafed, together with that of all his connections, and those of the Vansittarts. The Rockingham Opposition supported him. Yet, even with this show of support, neither his son nor Palk thought he had much chance.

Stephen Sulivan was out early in the day 'to do all in my power by soliciting at the door of every Proprietor'. He saw the tide swing against his father in everything, and reckoned he had 'not even a glimmering of chance'.[15] Palk reported the same bad tidings. He thought his friend would be 'entering the lists' for the last time, 'for it does not appear to me that he has the smallest chance of being chosen, but he cannot be prevailed upon to give up the vain pursuit'.[16]

However, two letters from Sulivan to Hastings, one on 28 March before the election, the other on 15 April, just after it, show what his real aims had been. In the first of these, he predicted that a ministerial government would be in Leadenhall, but added, indicatively, 'The 24 (Directors) this year, bad as they are, may be much worse the next.'[17] He too had come to think success was impossible; but it was so important he was determined to make a hard struggle of it. He professed to be 'supporting the interests of the Proprietors against the Administration who had invaded the Company's chartered rights'; and saw himself as having no other choice but to act.[18]

He attempted the manoeuvre of promoting and publishing a House list without Government consent. The ministry refused to even contemplate it. Lord North then published a 'House List Amended', with the fourteen they would support and ten alternatives, who were all Clivites and friends of the ministry. Sulivan was furious that North and Robinson, who were not part of the East India Company, had actually made a list of Directors. He raged about it to Warren Hastings: 'so daring are men grown in subversion of our liberty...in this country there is little honour or gratitude'.[19]

The 'House List Amended' duly appeared on 24 March, reflecting the wishes of Robinson, and Clive's supporters, Walsh and Strachey. By 3 April this group had wind that Charles Raymond would back Sulivan in place of Becher in the category 'class for four years'. Clive's supporters then set about countering Raymond and his friends by 'building for Becher'. In this way, Sulivan was even blocked from entering singly, and his defeat was confirmed. In fact, none of his group survived. Philip Francis sneered, 'Mr. Sullivan made but a poor figure.'[20]

Sulivan disclosed to Hastings that he had gambled everything to create a favourable situation for the next election: 'We played a desperate game...risqued our own prospects for the year to secure a majority of the late Directors who were pledged to bring me and others in next year.'[21] It had been a valiant attempt: 'Such an effort was never made in the memory of man, only 950 votes in the 3 kingdoms, and 890 balloted for.'[22] He was now tired and dejected. North had shown he was resolved that he and his group would not return to power. Strachey crowed to Clive: 'Sulivan and George Johnstone have been thrown out so we may be said to have carried our best point.'[23]

The defeat was indeed a shattering blow, every bit as bad as that of 1765; and again caused by an alliance between Clive and the Government of the day. Robinson now had the opportunity to maintain ministerial power, with a perpetually weak and disorganised Direction, devoid of ability and resolve. He would be able to determine the mould of Company politics for the foreseeable future.

5

That Sulivan should experience such immense suffering in the very year that his great rival Clive died by his own hand was ironic. One of the last confrontations between the two was in Parliament on 3 May 1773 during a debate on North's Regulating Act. To the very end Sulivan had remained Clive's *bête noire*, while the Johnstones continued to be his chief persecutors. Clive believed (incorrectly) that Sulivan provided them with the ammunition they used in their scathing, venomous attacks. Sulivan did not join with the Johnstones; he could not forget that they had deserted him at the April election.

During the debate, Clive's speech centred upon trying to clear himself of wrongdoing in India. At one stage a little humour broke out. He shifted the spotlight upon his rival and had a dig at his near bankruptcy. Sulivan, he said, had searched the India Office records for charges that might be laid against him, and that he was 'so assiduous in my affairs that really, Sir, it appears he has entirely neglected his own'.[24]

The humorous interlude continued as his Lordship illustrated just how low Company officials had sunk in the popular mind. Referring to the fact that the Jacobite heads on Temple Bar had fallen down, he thought they might be replaced, with his own in the middle, Sulivan's on one side and Colebrooke's on the other. He could not resist yet one more entertaining swipe at Sulivan and his fellows. He pictured them gorging on free meals at the Company's expense, 'Devouring the turtle and all kinds of viands out of season and in season, and swilling themselves with whole hogsheads of claret, champagne and burgundy.'[25]

Sulivan would depart Parliament for good in 1774. On the surface this was due to Palk's request that he have the seat returned to him. He claimed he had never gained any satisfaction there and that if he had his fortune back would never go near the place again. He admitted, however, that he or his son had to be, 'in the Senate'; and that he had been 'building castles...not unusual with me' at the possibility of this coming about. In September Palk's kind offer to allow him to continue was declined.[26] He was in an extremely serious financial state.

It is incongruous, however, that at a time when he most needed to be in the Commons, he was forced to retire. What is more, North's determining influence at Leadenhall through the terms of his Regulating Act, coming at the very moment of his exclusion from the House, doubled the effect of his expulsion from the Direction. In this blackest and most desperate of times, with no patronage to offer, he consolidated those ties already made and depended heavily upon the network of friends in every settlement. An outcast from the Direction, he had no other means of gaining accurate intelligence and information.

Public life for Sulivan in the mid 1770s can be summed up as a defence of all that he stood for and defiance of his enemies. He struggled to build the new relationship between the Company and the State. He was rocklike in his support of Hastings, and in rallying others to the Governor-General's cause. This was his role from 1774 onwards.

There were three phases to the Regulating Act's operation. First came a two-year introductory period from 1774 to 1775; followed by two years of dislocation stemming from events in India. From 1777 to 1779 there was a partial run-down, explained by the Government's harassment elsewhere, with war in America, Europe, and then in India too. No business was possible until the new Court of Directors was constituted in 1774. From then on men willing to adapt were required by Government inside the organisation. North worked by using Treasury influence in the Company Courts and committees – ably directed by Robinson and Sandwich. Voting patterns at Leadenhall were strictly orientated towards matching Parliamentary ones.

From within the Proprietors' Court Sulivan had to employ all his impressive energy and intellect to the defence of Hastings against the attacks of the North ministry and its allies in the Company. Ammunition was being supplied to them by Clavering, Francis and Monson. The struggles developing in Calcutta impacted heavily upon politics in India House and in Parliament. This clash over Hastings occupying the post of Governor-General was the major disagreement with ministry; it would run like a thread throughout the rest of Sulivan's public career.

However, his defence of Hastings was not just about ministry, 'Triumvirate', or the strictures created by the Regulating Act. He was convinced during his last spell in the Direction that the Company was almost ungovernable abroad; and servants would not listen to the Board. It was a development he had fought since 1757. Hastings was to be helped as he strove for better administration within all the Presidencies, and engaged in wars to defend the Company's position. He also wished to serve his superiors in India House, a desire rendered almost impossible by the ministerial puppets beside him.

Sulivan had to maintain a constant support in London and sponsor anyone in India who backed his friend in Calcutta or himself. All aspirations were pinned upon the success of this one man. If the ministry was successful in removing Hastings and his ally Richard Barwell, this would really signify an end to any show of independence, and prove the superiority of ministerial influence at Leadenhall. It would illustrate Parliament's ability to get rid of the Company's most powerful official in India; and in the process negate the influence of its most able and knowledgeable enemy, Laurence Sulivan. To all of this, the Irishman made strenuous objection.

Only remarkable endurance (fortified by his desperate financial straits) enabled him to remain a force in the Company. At the head of the pro-Hastings group he fought with almost fanatical zeal to protect his friend from merciless attacks. Hastings' friends in the Commons were to be similarly used in his defence. Although now absent from Parliament, Sulivan shepherded all these forces.

The correspondence between Sulivan and his protégé was like an umbilical cord; and indicates a clear and uncluttered exchange of ideas. The Irishman made a point of transferring his knowledge to his friend. Each came to understand the other. This reassurance served each man in his own private hell: Hastings, faced with the 'Triumvirate'; Sulivan, against a Government-dominated and hostile Direction. They formed an axis around which rotated the most important issues involving the Company. While they remained united it proved impossible to break either man. Lord North and his two leading agents, John Robinson and Charles Jenkinson, realized this only after eleven years of effort.

His other major task was to create a role for himself within the new arrangements brought into play by the Regulating Act; and he was forced to combine with Government if he was to achieve reforms within the Company. A whole range of new rules had to be learned; and his future and that of his dependants rested upon how much he could keep abreast, or ahead, of developments.

The real problem affecting the Regulating Act was the relationship to be struck by Government and Company. It was all about management of the monopoly at Leadenhall. Control was achieved by various alliances, some quite tortuous, although overt patronage was quite common. Efficient management was difficult, however, because people had so many different reasons for being involved in East India affairs.

Any upset in India created havoc in Britain. In Bengal all the faults inherent in the Regulating Act were revealed, creating policy and leadership problems, mostly in the Supreme Council; and the bitterness built up festered and travelled back to London. News of the Pigot scandal (the imprisonment and death of the Governor of Madras); the Nawab of Arcot's debts; the Maratha war; Haider Ali's ravages in the Carnatic; and the threat of a united native front in India against the Company all created uproar at home; yet were overwhelmed in importance by the revolts in the American colonies.

Distinct groups were in competition at Leadenhall: London merchants and bankers; former Company servants, primarily from the civil service; the shipping interest; speculators and financial manipulators; and dotted everywhere, ministerial lackeys. Some factions were a direct result of the controversies overseas, the Hastings and Pigot ones in particular; and although Clive was dead by 1774, his followers continued their antagonism, which now embraced Sulivan's friends and protégés. Sulivan commented emotively, 'The ghost of Clive haunts me.'[27]

There was also some attempt at reform of the Company from within, and as usual Sulivan was all for it; but all had now to go through Government channels. Specialists like Robinson, Jenkinson and Dundas had begun to put their learning to use. There was no doctrine behind it all – and there was no machinery put in place to subsume the Company and its Indian administration. The Regulating Act lurched on, and only the most strenuous efforts kept it going on a year-to-year basis.

13

Fight for Survival
1774-78

1

It might have been felt that after securing Hastings his appointment to the supreme position in India that he was safe. Yet, Sulivan had no peace of mind, knowing better than his protégé did that his own constant presence inside India House was crucial if his friend was to continue in office. Hastings could be certain of this unswerving backing because apart from genuine friendship, both their salvations, and Sulivan's plans for the future of the Company, dictated it be so. He paraded his friend's achievements; bolstering his protégé by telling him of the utter confidence he had in him: 'I can add but three to your own name with whom I would have lodged unlimited authority, and these were Stephen Law, Henry Vansittart and Robert Palk.'[1]

This promotion and defence required liaison with a diverse group of supporters. Forming the nucleus of the faction were friends and allies of earlier years, such as Shelburne, Thurlow, Impey and Dunning, as well as Palk and George Vansittart – and their families. Sulivan's own relatives were part of it. They combined with his followers in the Company. Sulivan's home in Queen Square became a rallying point.

As the Hastings party developed, it came to include ever more supporters at Westminster as well as others from London business life.[2] Although Edmund Burke's dislike of the Company was growing, he and the rest of the Rockingham Opposition still stood behind him, their support based upon 'chartered rights'.

Regrettably, some of the so-called friends were really adventurers who had no hesitation in betraying a trust. The worst were Lauchlin Macleane, John Stewart of Hampstead and John and James Macpherson. They used Sulivan to get close to Hastings, seeming to promise him deliverance from financial difficulties; and for Hastings, riddance of political fears. In Macleane and the Macphersons they were presented with opportunists who acted on a scale of ruthlessness and cunning that left them largely defenceless.[3]

The fact that Hastings was backed by Sulivan created him enemies; and years of political activity and struggle with the Clivites meant that all these adversaries were hostile too. The only exception was Sykes, Hastings' old friend; but even he told him lies about Sulivan. He faced the dislike of the monarch too, who was committed to General Clavering. Cocking a snoot at them all, Sulivan told Hastings, 'no opportunity has been lost to establish you upon the noblest ground.'[4] He made sure that copies of the Governor-General's letters portraying the excellent work he was doing went to North and from thence to the King. Hastings' exertions were made known to the leading figures in the Company. He warned his friend of people, home or abroad, who meant him ill; and protected his reputation.

In the General Court he fought every issue, such as first opposing the appointment of Clavering as Commander-in-Chief of Company forces in India, then neutralising it by having Hastings commissioned Commander-in-Chief of the Fortress and Garrison at Fort William. He carried the fight onwards, through what remained of the North ministry's time, and into the 1780s against the Rockingham, Shelburne and Portland administrations.

Even before Hastings became Governor-General Sulivan tried to give him allies who were supposed to help in his endeavours. With many he made a mistake or was deceived; as with Monson, John Stewart of Hampstead, Lauchlin Macleane and John Macpherson. Others turned out well, like Richard Barwell and Alexander Elliot. Richard Barwell played an important part in what developed. Early in 1772 he had offered his loyalty in exchange for a strong footing in Hastings' entourage. The Irishman realised that Barwell's position was as hazardous as the one Hastings filled. He worked successfully to keep them together, to the extent that Barwell remained the Governor-General's sole supporter during his years of severest trial.[5]

Sulivan's enduring feud with Clive left a legacy. Before his death, the noble Lord had proclaimed that he was 'particularly acquainted with Mr. Francis'. He referred to his contact with Francis through D'Oyly and the Fowke group; and all his dislike of Sulivan and Hastings was transferred to him.[6]

Francis was also close to Edmund Burke, now more antagonistic to Sulivan. This resentment seemed to stem from the loss of financial independence by the Burke family, which was blamed on Sulivan; and the fact that in 1771 Sulivan shifted from (seeming) alliance with Parliamentary Opposition to a union with Lord North. Writing to Henry Strachey in 1775, Francis promised that henceforth he would consider Edmund Burke's friends as his own.[7]

Faced with the 'Triumvirate's' hatred, Sulivan shored up his friend's confidence. He enthused: 'The general voice runs so strongly in your favour I am satisfied all is right.'[8] As they began to understand the importance of the Hastings-Sulivan connection, and the strength the Governor-General gained from Sulivan, these enemies even objected to their correspondence.

By January 1775 Sulivan was beginning to sniff greater hostility, and reported that 'an ill humour was growing' in the Company Courts.[9] He kept Hastings informed of the developing struggles; advising him to be careful and to hold firm. Symptomatic of this need to take care was that Mohammed Reza Khan, who had been deposed by Hastings, had the effrontery (in Sulivan's eyes) to make a personal approach in London, lobbying for restitution of office. Sulivan also marshalled the defence at home, following the attack by the 'Triumvirate' over the Rohilla war.

For twelve years the struggle was unremitting. The numerous investigations into Hastings' conduct made by Clavering and Francis created corresponding disturbances in London. Resistance, on most occasions, was organised by Sulivan, who invariably defused the criticisms. The secret to his success during these tortuous years was his espionage system. It was truly remarkable. He knew exactly who were the enemy and what they were up to. Thus he was well aware of Francis' efforts to drum up a personal support. Many Proprietors he approached were pro-Sulivan; nevertheless, he persisted in sending them beguiling letters. They all reported back to the Irishman.

A massive crisis arrived in 1775-1776 over Hastings' supposed resignation; this shook Sulivan to the core. It all revolved around Lauchlin Macleane who had become very important within the sphere of Sulivan-Hastings relations. At this date it was impossible for Sulivan to know that he only posed as a friend and cared little for Hastings or himself.[10]

In 1773 Sulivan had helped get him to India to retrieve his fortune, and thus repay his debts. A potentially lucrative post as Commissary-General at Bengal, placing him under the Governor-General's protection was secured. The letter of recommendation from Sulivan, which referred to this 'man of substance', was exceptional; Macleane's charm was all that was needed, thereafter, to place him securely in Hastings' confidence. The arrival of the 'Triumvirate' ended his money making activities, however; and in December 1774 he resigned before (at Francis' insistence) he was dismissed. In the meantime, he had secured for himself one of the two available posts of personal agent for Hastings that empowered him to act for the Governor-General in London.

Unknown to Sulivan and Hastings, Macleane also held an Agency from the Nawab of Arcot. In 1775 he arrived home accompanied by John Graham, Hastings' other agent. Both were armed with materials and legal instruments to defend the Governor-General against further grievous attacks in London. Included in the armoury at Macleane's command was the right (or so he thought) to tender Hastings' resignation if it was deemed necessary.

By December 1775 the attack on Hastings was at its height within the Company, spearheaded by the unreliable John Johnstone and Nathaniel Smith. Organising the defence were Sulivan and Macleane. Because the Ulsterman had been on the spot in Bengal Sulivan relied upon him. Sulivan witnessed first-hand how hard he worked, saying he 'fought on his stumps'. It was then that Macleane dropped the bombshell news that he had the authority to hand in the Governor-General's resignation. An amazed and disconcerted Sulivan immediately asked to see Hastings' letter. He also wanted to know the background to it. What he saw and heard convinced him; and he shaped his course accordingly. If Hastings must come home, then he would have the best deal and as many honours conferred as possible.

The whole resignation issue was a shadowy business, however. It seems that Hastings had already complained to Lord North that 'the meanest drudge enjoys a condition of happiness compared to mine'. He had begged for immediate recall, or power on an honourable footing to deal with the 'Triumvirate'.[11]

Negotiations between Robinson, Macleane and Sulivan regarding the resignation were going on in May, and these continued into September. In the Commons the issue, stirred up by the Hastings group, attracted much attention. Opposition figures of the stature of Bute, Shelburne, Rockingham and Richmond, fired up by North's relentless drive to oust Hastings, became involved.[12]

Late in 1776 it was obvious that North was making a point of forcing the issue and having the final say. Sulivan and Macleane knew quick action was needed, and were led to believe that they must accept what the ministry deemed right before Parliament met, or Hastings would be squashed. Believing all was lost his supporters agreed that the resignation letter should be handed in. In September, the ministry's terms were accepted and an accord was reached. Macleane then handed in the resignation and this was announced to the public.

However, in the interim Hastings proclaimed that Macleane had gone further than he ought, and revoked the resignation note. The invalidity of the 'Letter of Resignation' sent in by Macleane was based on the non-specific nature of the commands given; and that these had relied entirely upon the discretionary powers given by Hastings to his agents. Although perplexed, Sulivan accepted this 'explanation'.

Ministers were not the only ones upset. Within the Company the issue had created a great furore from the beginning. The hostile Direction had sought corroboration from George Vansittart and others that the Governor-General's intention had been genuine. They had then (by one vote) decided to recall Hastings. However, at a Proprietors' meeting held in late 1776 (where Sulivan was prominent) this was reversed by a majority of 107. This great 'victory' convinced Hastings to stay in India. It helped that the infamous 'Threesome' had also been literally killed off. Clavering was dead by August 1776; Monson died in September. As time went on Hasting continued to resist any implication that he had resigned, and the crisis fizzled out.[13]

The tendering of Hastings' resignation marked the climax to Macleane's employment on Hastings' behalf. From that point onwards he was in Lord North's pocket, and now concentrated upon the Nawab of Arcot's affairs. He died in 1777 while on his way out to India again, on board the *Swallow*, theoretically still acting for Hastings and the Nawab.

Hastings may have survived, but the attacks on him continued. So low did his stock fall, at times Sulivan seemed to be defending him single-handed. However, he had nothing but scorn for the charges that began to appear. A typical one, by Francis, was that due to Hastings' poor administration, at one stage there remained only six *lakhs* in the Bengal treasury. Sulivan wondered if it was possible to find anyone who could 'swallow such insufferable nonsense'.[14] By January 1778 he had 'grown callous' of the abuse directed against his friend. He labelled the language so infamous, 'Mrs. Rudd would have been ashamed to use it.'[15]

Even with all Sulivan was doing for him (that he knew about), the Governor-General seems to have regarded him as having only a limited use. Perhaps he believed his power to actually achieve anything was fatally limited by exclusion from the Direction. With an imperfect grasp of the Irishman's power play in the Proprietors' Court, he would have thought him comparatively toothless. This interpretation could explain some of the long silences from India. It might all have been quite innocent, of course; Hastings had developed the habit of asking that a letter to any one of his friends should be passed on to the others. He did write directly to Sulivan on several occasions, although the flow of mail was frequently interrupted or intercepted.

Given his own predicament at this time, Sulivan's pursuit of reform and better government in the settlements, and Bengal in particular, was remarkable. He spent incalculable hours drafting plans and useful material (all extant and verifiable). Most of his work was based upon real problems and practicalities. He relied on his own experiences in Bombay; his expanded knowledge from years of executive participation; and what he gleaned from reading interminable letters from Bengal, Madras and elsewhere. He possessed an amazing store of accumulated knowledge. All of this information and insight was relayed to Hastings. The Governor-General was expected to use or discard the material as he saw fit. Hastings needed help as he faced quite enormous tasks; but without detracting from the great work he performed, he did owe much to Sulivan.

Yet, Sulivan never sought any plaudits and only ever praised his friend's achievements; although in some instances his own advice, promptings and even draft plans and proposals can be detected in what was accomplished. He preferred to extol Hastings' excellence in transforming words and thoughts into deeds in the midst of the most trying conditions. This attitude can be seen in his own words: 'Happy am I to find that my letters have been of the smallest use.' There is little doubt that they were.[16]

As time went on (and despite the silences) there is no mistaking the high regard in which Hastings held Sulivan, even when quite unaware of how indebted he was to him. The attention he paid to what his mentor said is reflected in a letter to Palk. He believed Sulivan would think him 'wild and chimerical' in the way he was cutting military costs.[17]

It is notable that while a small trickle of advice did reach Hastings from others in London, it was insignificant when compared to the tidal flow from the man in Queen Square. In his private letters home, Hastings always sought after this constant stream of ideas, advice and plans from his friend. A few excerpts suffice as illustration. As early as October 1773 Sulivan was urging him to press on quickly with his intended reforms in the military and revenue branches before the other members of the Council arrived. He urged consolidation of Clive's military gains; the formulation and completion of administrative and justiciary plans; and of any land settlements that were in hand. All the while, he prepared his man against the imminent attacks of the 'Triumvirate'. Much of the correspondence dealt with finance matters, and indicates that the annual Investment would always have first priority in his eyes. He advised Hastings to place an embargo on any trade that hurt the Company; to curtail expenses and correct abuses; recover the Company's credit and generally restore its battered prestige.

Sulivan had been one of the many who believed Clive when he said that £2 million per annum was pouring into the Company's treasury in Bengal. This sum was subsequently upgraded to £4 million. Sulivan did not quite believe, then, that Clive would be so casual over such important claims, upon which so many decisions were to be made. What it led to, unfortunately, was a mad boom in stock, the Parliamentary intervention of 1766-67 and, to some extent, the Company's financial collapse in the 1770-2 period.

In 1775 Sulivan gave Hastings an immensely detailed historical appraisal of how, in his opinion, the Bengal finances had arrived at the terrible state they were in. He covered the years from Plassey to 1775, admitting there were so many areas of mystery he was truly baffled, and urged Hastings to investigate further. In this exhaustive and complicated letter he displayed all his computations yet could not discover the true wealth of Bengal. It was his opinion that nobody could do so: 'The collective wisdom of Leadenhall Street can give no lights.'[18]

He remained perplexed even after using the best and most precise information then available. As he said, 'men believe that in Clive's day there was great and solid revenue'.[19] Since then, he said, they believed the opposite; and Hastings was expected to put things back in a good way. He added a hint of what underlay the need to have precise figures: 'I wish to guard against such for should I return to the Direction, of which I do not despair, our expiring Charter will require deep and serious deliberation. The true value of Bengal will be one of the most important matters for discussion.'[20] It is impossible not to suspect (before he launched into an even more detailed scrutiny of the figures) that a touch of wry humour caused him to add: 'Ill as I have been used by the body of Proprietors, they do give me credit for some little knowledge of their affairs.'[21]

Sulivan enclosed two specific calculations, made by Clive at different times; and he included a particular study of the year 31 January 1766 to 31 January 1767 from figures delivered to him privately by Walsh at Clive's express command. The information stood comparison with Verelst's first year in office. Clive's next statement of account, for 1767 to 1769, showed an expected increase from the revenues of 20 *lakhs* per annum. Sulivan gave him full credit for this and had based his own sums upon his figures. Others did the same.

He then proceeded to give Hastings a comprehensive account (with a breakdown of cash, charges, and expenses) up to 1775. From these figures he calculated surpluses for the Investment each year, which by 1775 reached 'A balance in our favour in Bengal of £1,716,664.'[22] The persons collecting the figures were 'Lord Clive and our auditor – the materials in the period of 1769 taken from the Bengal Books – the account I enclose you…were public papers laid before Parliament by the Company.'[23]

He urged Hastings to give a speedy and complete refutation of these calculations if he found them erroneous, which they obviously were he thought, by the poverty-stricken state of Bengal. The public at home, he asserted, wanted to know why and where everyone was going wrong. He ended: 'Now I no more believe that you have £31,500,000 surplus (in 1775) than I do that you have £15 millions, yet I cannot make out a corrected account.' His last plea to Hastings was that he should be the first to know the truth of the matter.[24]

The Governor-General reported back, giving a 'complete and pleasing picture of our finances in Bengal.'[25] At last Sulivan had a model before him that approximated to the truth; and knew that a proper monetary structure was in place. For this he was unstinting in his praise of Hastings, to all and sundry, in or out of the Company.

Sulivan's mind was forever fertile in schemes for creating and encouraging new trade and accumulating money. The commerce in raw silk, which he initiated, very quickly became a valuable source of income. He first broached the subject in 1770 when writing to Vansittart; and had pressed him to send £100,000 from Bengal to China to invest in this trade because of the great shortage of silk in Britain. In April 1773 Hastings was urged to buy as much as possible. In 1775, Sulivan followed this up, even pleading with him to do so. He exclaimed: 'I KNOW that this is the only article that can restore the Company's credit'; and he then proceeded to outline the commercial approach that Hastings should take.[26]

The opium trade (which was to provide the essential capital for the trade in tea) was another activity Sulivan favoured. He suggested this commerce be stepped up; and in 1775 urged that the Dutch be excluded. The human tragedy lurking in the background was never addressed. He gave instructions on how Hastings should handle delicate matters concerning the native powers; and approved the stoppage of the Nawab of Bengal's allowance in 1774. He was told to pay special attention to the Company's interests on the Coromandel Coast, in particular to Tanjore; and to keep a particular eye on the marauding Marathas.

On the subject of the Bengal revenues he poured out all his (distilled) knowledge. He covered page after page with facts and ideas concerning the regulation of grain; the 'farming out' of Company land; and sent a very detailed land survey of Bengal. This information was tremendously accurate, up-to-date and meticulously planned.[27]

Concern for the situation in Bengal and desire to do something about it was not just directed towards Hastings. In 1772 he and Sir James Stuart had produced several plans, including reforms in the coinage; and proper collection and storage of grain purchases. The specific aim was to avoid repetition of the famine of 1769-70. The criminal neglect by the ministry-controlled Direction (from 1773 onwards) of these and similar attempts at reform is captured in his sardonic phrase, 'All I suppose are grown mouldy at India House.'[28]

He clearly intended Hastings to implement the reforms held in mind for some time; and he was short-circuiting the formal Company machinery, which in the 1773-8 period was out of his control. Hastings was meant to translate Sulivan's words into actions. It will probably never be determined whether in fact the improvements in Bengal owed something to his advice, or were wholly due to Hastings' own genius. However, the impact of his Governorship, which was felt almost immediately, might serve as a pointer, suggesting that they did. Cuts in military and civil expenses in that Presidency alone put the Company back on its feet by 1775.

The Hastings-Sulivan correspondence was vital to both men. It was voluminous, and was deep in content. Perhaps the super-abundance of Sulivan material also reflects best its nature and content. Sulivan never flagged, even though at times Hastings seemed to provide no reply to him directly over periods of a year or more. In May 1777 he wrote, 'Not a single line from you or the dash of a pen from Impey.'[29] However, the proof that Hastings wrote to him at least one long letter per year is seen in the accumulated correspondence of a later date. The packets would seem to have been prevented from reaching him at the time.

2

It would not have been Sulivan if an attempt to re-enter the Direction was not made each year. Yet, he set about preparing for the 1775 election with reluctance and only because of the shipping magnate Sir Charles Raymond's persistence. By February, however, he was making 'another determined effort to get on the House List'.[30] He tried to mend splits in his party, such as the growing enmity between Governor Johnstone and John Macpherson.

Through the Vansittart-Palk connection he influenced Charles Boddam and Captains Richard Hall and Nathaniel Smith, and he hoped to have the support of John Manship. He also attempted to capture the dead Crabb Boulton's lines of interest; and built upon the eleven Directors he reasoned might still be loyal to him from 1774. He was successful in his approach to a long-time friend John Graeme and his relations, Sir William and Robert Mayne.[31] Robert Orme was also contacted in order to secure Frederick Pigou's vote. Macleane's influence was used too.

All this effort was in vain. He had expected North's support, but the Clive group brought political pressure to bear on the minister. Whereas Sulivan still believed in North, Orme and others saw all along that his 'only impediment was the opposition of the ministry'.[32] Later Sulivan said the news that he would stand caused 'Mr. Walsh, at the head of 25 Bengal Proprietors, to form themselves into a canvassing club for opposing me alone. And thus ends this dull history.'[33]

It is amazing, nevertheless, how this battle-hardened warrior could bounce back as optimistic as ever. He considered the prospects for a return to office in 1776 to be very fair 'through the line of Government, for there's an end of Opposition'. He also counted upon Deputy Chairman John Roberts.[34] As usual he was tireless in drumming up support, such as in his cultivation of Sir Gilbert Elliot.[35] At the beginning of December 1776, he was still hopeful, and paid a visit to Mr. Harrison, 'the first I ever made for we were never upon kind terms'. He found little satisfaction there; and by Christmas was having serious misgivings, although John Purling, another influential Proprietor, seemed to be friendly.[36]

Gloomily he told John Stewart in February 1776 that his own avowed attachment to the Governor-General would be one reason for his exclusion. On the eve of the election he had little hope: 'As the friends of Clavering etc. make it a particular point to keep me out.' North remained utterly opposed and he was barred.[37]

For the April 1777 election he was once again disappointed in his expectations of support from North and Robinson, despite a friendlier attitude towards Hastings, Maclean and himself. Robinson's main reason for this relaxation was the aim of reviving ministerial support following a major defeat in the General Court in May 1776. Sulivan maintained afterwards that in order to oblige North, and also to placate Maclean, he did not oppose Purling. He believed he would have won if he had done so.

Following the 1773 Act, it had become customary to re-elect any or all of the four Directors who had been 'out by rotation' for a year, who wished to stand once more. This convention could also be broken by arrangement. Just as he had done in 1758, Sulivan defied any such custom, and this helped his successful comeback in April 1778.

Two versions explaining his triumph were put forward at the time. Sulivan's one was that he stormed the Direction and made it impossible for the Proprietors to deny him. The other was from John Macpherson who insisted that it came about through North's intercession on his behalf. Neither version tells the whole story.[38] John Macpherson had already reflected upon the usefulness of an end to the Sulivan-North stand-off. Tentative efforts towards this had been made over the intervening years, not least by Sulivan himself. In spite of everything, he had never given up hope that North might yet do him justice. It is also possible he had developed cautious solicitations through Maclean. All would depend, he commented, upon North's 'sense of honour'.[39]

His plan in 1778 was to stand against John Pardoe, unpopular in the Company, and being pushed forward by Lord Sandwich. The old maestro's entire support in the shipping interest and elsewhere was brought to bear.[40] Later he said, rather disingenuously, that he had 'tired of waiting for governmental support'; adding that he was 'no longer, since 1766, an object of hatred to the Nabobs'.[41]

However, it is not altogether true, as later claimed, that he carried the day 'with a very high hand against the united and violent efforts of Government and Directors'.[42] For the ministry's own reasons he enjoyed the minimum of opposition, despite complaining to his son before the election that he had been 'positively denied' by Robinson.[43] In fact, North and Robinson (in particular) had been tied by Sandwich's promise to John Pardoe. Sulivan beat this unpopular candidate by 148 votes, and thus qualified as a Director for the next four years. Eighteen of the twenty-four Directors were newcomers, giving him the opportunity to fashion a new party.

No time was lost in broadcasting the news of his success to family and friends; and they were informed of the united efforts of Government and the outgoing Directors to thwart him. He did admit, however, he would be 'happy to believe there would be an agreement between ministry and him', which suggests he knew that the all powerful ministry had been lukewarm in its opposition.[44]

The Chairman and Deputy Chairman were Sir George Wombwell and Sir William James, respectively. His friendship with James dated from Bombay days and through the storms of the 1760s. Although he was (rather unwillingly) in North's pocket, he would eventually swing back to him. Wombwell, a former supporter of Clive and now firmly attached to Sandwich, was unpopular because of his ministry leanings. To Sulivan, such different leanings made it certain he could sit on whichever committee he should choose. There could be no denial, he was back.

3

Three factors now determined Sulivan's approach, and these would continue until 1785. First, his reaction to an incident or circumstance abroad would depend on how he judged it would involve him at India House; and to what extent it would influence his relationship with ministers or their agents. Second, given his impecunious position, he had to read how the situation or event would concern him financially. The third, although feeble from 1774 to 1778, was how far his acceptance and disbursement of patronage would be affected.

Hand in hand with these yardsticks were particular objectives that he never flinched from in the years ahead. He would give unstinting support to Warren Hastings (and to his son Stephen who would go to India in 1778). He also took good care of Sulivan, Owen and Irwin relations, as long as they did not cross his main aims and objectives. To these can be added backing for the Nawab of Arcot, again only if he continued a friend and if his concerns did not cut across other priorities.

Essentially, Sulivan and his fellow Directors wanted the Nawab maintained in his position, with territorial and trading features kept strong and secure. Assistance to the Governor and Council of Madras depended upon those in office remaining friends. He was prepared to ditch everyone concerned should Hastings be crossed; and would confront any faction that was raised in India House against the Governor-General or himself.

He was very concerned, of course, with restoring his fortune. He wanted 'lucrative residencies' and 'commands strung along the rivers of Hindustan' for his family; and their riches were to be remitted to England.[45] He insisted that he would be responsible for the preservation of any bonds, jewels or presents; and that these should be made out to him.

Although out of the Direction until 1778, Sulivan had kept abreast of what was happening in the Carnatic. His relations were there, and the theatre was a cause of increasing anxiety. This would not disappear during the remainder of his life. British disquiet in Southern India was centred on Walajah Muhammad 'Ali Khan, Nawab of Arcot. Company money and men had saved him in the wars of 1757 to 1762; and upon cessation of hostilities he owed a vast sum. The Company required rapid repayment, which was the reason for the *jagir* around Madras being taken. It was rented back to him. He put up a good show in paying off his debts between 1757 and 1776, but this strained his finances and he turned to heavy borrowing from Indian bankers and Madras councillors. The loans carried interest rates of twenty to thirty per cent.

By the late 1770s he was sadly reduced, almost to the role of a Company puppet, his main duty now being to maintain Company troops. His expensive ways had led him to continue indebted; and with the onslaught of new wars with France these debts were to become heavier. On the other hand, his rule was underwritten by the Company and by Sulivan's clause in the final Treaty of Paris of 1763. The years that followed (up to 1785) were particularly confused with the further decline of Mughal control (due to the Anglo-French wars) and the establishment of Company rule. The Nawab's financial embarrassments added to this. Loans to him were like gilt-edged bonds. The 'gentlemen of the coast', councillors and others, invested like mad. The Nawab continued to borrow discreetly, but heavily.

In February 1775 a struggle developed at Leadenhall over who would be the new Governor of Madras. A great deal of malevolence and rancour attended the whole issue – too much in Sulivan's opinion, because it was again giving the Company a bad name. He was sure the office would go to Thomas Rumbold and not Pigot because he was North's choice; and was amazed when Pigot was chosen by ballot at the General Court. In fact, so certain were the Directors of the result, they had already sworn Rumbold in.

George Pigot returned to Madras as Governor in 1775, with an unpopular mandate. He was specifically appointed to restore the state of Tanjore to its rightful Raja. In the early 1770s the Nawab had secured support for an unprovoked invasion and annexation. Its revenues were then regarded as security for even more loans. The Nawab was dismayed, therefore, at Pigot's policy, but was relatively powerless and in the hands of the various European factions in Madras; especially the notorious Paul Benfield.

The proposed restoration of the Raja's territory sparked violent opposition to the Governor. He was faced with Benfield and other creditors, many of them from outside the ranks of the service; others like John Macpherson (then a Factor), he dismissed. Pigot was arrested by a majority of his own councillors, led by General James Stuart and including Benfield. He died in captivity. The facts of his death remain obscure, but the Nawab was implicated. Sulivan noted everything, but said and did nothing. All hinged on what the Governor-General would do.

Hastings showed no sympathy for Pigot, and readily supported his opponents. His stand had little to do with the merits or demerits of the crisis itself and all to do with his own situation. He wanted nothing to disturb the fragile understanding with neighbouring Indian states. His responsibility was for the Company's overall position in the subcontinent; and with a life or death struggle against the Marathas on his hands thought the restoration of the Raja would jeopardise everything.

In his eyes it was essential that the Company's alliance with the Nizam of Hyderbad be maintained to keep him from going over to Haider Ali of Mysore, which would create a united front against the English. Madras, it seemed to him, was going out of its way to antagonise the Nizam; and that Pigot was interfering with the financial terms of the existing alliance by restoring Tanjore to its Raja. To Hastings, the Madras Governor had also sown discord by detaching a chunk of the Northern Circars, which was then leased as security for loans. If he was to face the unthinkable, a triple alliance of the Marathas, the Nizam of Hyderabad and Haider Ali of Mysore, and the French came in with an armada, the Company was done for. To Hastings, the Governor of Madras (despite following direct orders from home) had acted blindly, selfishly and incompetently. He also thought his own supervisory powers were being flaunted.

When news of Pigot's deposition and death reached Leadenhall early in 1777, the Proprietors divided. Sulivan, Macleane, Caillaud and Palk (all friends of Hastings) who were also linked with the 'Arcot interest'* became allies of the Madras Councillors who had perpetrated the 'crime'. Sulivan and his friends joined with this group because foremost in their minds were Hastings' priorities in India. Others, like Macleane, had high expectations from the Nawab.

The Nawab, meanwhile, stoked up further trouble by informing the Company he would not pay his debts to anyone.[46] In December 1777 a meeting was held in London to consider arrangements to ensure he would pay. By then, the whole matter had developed into a Government versus Opposition fight, but one played out in the Company Courts. Pigot's supporters suspected, unfairly, that Hastings had been a party to the overthrow.[47] Ministry, on the other hand, wanted the Company Directors to now state that Tanjore's revenues did belong to the Nawab; Sulivan agreed with this because of Hastings' needs. The Company resisted the ministry, with the backing of the Parliamentary Opposition, with Burke to the fore.

In May 1777 Lord Elibank described the scene and the atmosphere perfectly: 'The affair of Madras gives occasion to much altercation here. I consider it like most other India disputes, as a struggle over who should have the fleecing of the miserable inhabitants.'[48] In the end, the North ministry put an end to it all. Prior to any knowledge of the Madras Governor's deposition and death, John Robinson asked for Pigot's reinstatement, but he was then to be recalled. Robinson's argument was that the Nawab's claims and rights had to be considered as much as the Raja's.

Support for this proposal within the Company was given by the Directors controlled by ministry; by Sulivan's group; Macleane's associates; and friends of the Madras Council majority. As a result, the General Court of 9 May 1777 saw Robinson's solution virtually imposed on both sides. A sort of grudging compromise was reached, one that would last until the expiration of the Company's Charter, due in 1778. It was proposed that Thomas Rumbold would be Governor in Pigot's place, a suggestion that again secured Sulivan's backing. Nonetheless, the struggle left a legacy of animosity. Alas, the situation in the Carnatic became worse with Rumbold's corrupt Governorship; and he returned to England in ignominy in January 1781 to face a storm of criticism. In the end he escaped prosecution, although Sulivan chased him relentlessly for what he termed his 'criminal' actions.

At home the tortuous management system determined by the Regulating Act was seen to be totally unsatisfactory. A pretty negative impression had been created by such unseemly activities in the Carnatic and by war there. Sulivan was alarmed at such public interest, and as a counter, published a memorial on the Nawab of Arcot's debts in the summer of 1778. He continued to stand back from the whole Pigot business, however. The hope of personal financial help via the Nawab and from members of the Madras Council, undoubtedly contributed to his thinking. Nevertheless, the need to support Hastings in everything was the vital factor.

He continued to cling to how things affected Hastings as he viewed unfolding events. As early as March 1777 he considered the threat from the French on the coast made the whole business very serious. In the same vein, he felt Pigot's orders regarding Tanjore should initially have been made subject to the control of the Supreme Council in Bengal as well as that of the Directors. He maintained the view that Hastings, on the spot, with major problems to overcome, should always be brought into any decisions that had to be taken in India. In January 1778, and again in April of that year, he attacked along these lines.[49]

4

The collapse of his father's fortune was a disaster for Stephen Sulivan; the position was made worse by the old warrior's exclusion from the Direction in 1774 and thus from any share of Company patronage. So acute was the Sulivan distress, it was originally thought in 1772 that Stephen would have to accompany the proposed Supervision of that year, acting as Secretary. He had studied Persian for that purpose and was far advanced in his studies when the Commission came to an end. At the time Sulivan asked Hastings to accept a few of 'The Fables of Gulisdan' his son had translated. He also let him know that he was pressing on with his Persian studies, regardless, and was translating the 'Life of Nader Shah'. The Governor-General was asked for more Persian books, 'as no one is more equal than yourself to make a choice'.[50]

Earlier, to keep the family afloat, Stephen had been forced to sell his appointment 'To the Primate in Ireland', for the original purchase money, 7,000 guineas. Then in 1775 he faced a double disappointment with his failure to obtain the post of Under-Secretary of State in the Southern Department, and a seat in Parliament. He was also disenchanted when his application to Sir William Hamilton for the office of Secretary to the Spanish Embassy came to nought. Hamilton failed to take up the assignment. Alas, his other hope, of filling the position of First Secretary to the Lord Lieutenant of Ireland, had Shelburne become Viceroy, also came to nothing. On top of everything else, Stephen had acquired an aversion to practising the law he had been trained for.

Most of the 1770s were miserable for Laurence Sulivan, and he was reduced to the most abject pleading for help. With the assistance of Palk, Dunning, John and Richard Sulivan, who had been despatched to India in the 1760s, he just survived. In March 1777 he also secured permission for the eldest of the Sulivan brothers (Sir) Benjamin, to proceed to Bengal where he would practice as a Barrister-at-Law.

His main hope for financial salvation from 1773 had centred upon Macleane. This had ended with the arrival of the Triumvirate; and with removal of the Ulsterman went the rest of Sulivan's hopes. They perked up slightly with the news in 1775 that he was the agent for the Nawab of Arcot, as well as for Hastings. Memories of promises by the Prince came flooding back. However, the Nawab had changed his mind. He told Richard Sulivan: 'I know Col. Macleane well, he is a snake that if I take him to my bosom he will sting me to death.'[51]

With this warning ringing in his ears, an agitated Sulivan warned his son of Macleane's skill in gaining the confidence of people. He begged him to be wary, 'because there is no defence against his penetration'. He implored Stephen 'to embark with him in no schemes, bonds, bills, engagements or money transactions for any consideration on earth'.[52] He was not wrong to do so. Unknown to him, and even as he wrote, Macleane was embroiled in yet another plot to deliver a petition from the Nawab to the King against the Company.[53] He was lost at sea in 1777/78 while rounding the Cape of Good Hope. He had only negligibly reduced his debt.[54]

There can be no mistaking the extraordinary degree of intimacy and intrigue enjoyed by Sulivan and Macleane. That they shared many secrets is reflected in Sulivan's anxiety that Hastings should get hold of his papers, held by the dead man's attorneys in Bengal. He soon realised, however, that the adventurer had left him out of his plans almost completely, despite salaries of £10,000 from Hastings and £4,300, plus jewels, from the Nawab.

To Hastings he wailed, 'Macleane is a public loss and a mortal stroke to my shattered fortune.'[55] He tried to get his hands on money placed in his account by the Nawab; to no avail. Macleane had also increased his indebtedness to him, from £9,000 to £14,000 in the years 1774 to 1777. His despair echoes in the words, 'Strange fatality in the only vessels lost in their passage for the last fifty years should be the *Aurora* (Vansittart), and the *Swallow* (Macleane).'[56]

He described Macleane's debt as, 'in honour bound (no legal demand for I took none)'. It had 'sprung from generosity, confidence and friendship'. His demise, however, had 'unspeakable dimensions...My own loss is of too great a magnitude and joined to the *Aurora's*, marks me singularly unfortunate.'[57] By June 1778 he was resigned: 'at first I lamented his loss as a heavy misfortune...perhaps his death has saved me an increasing misery'.[58] In December he commented, 'Happy for me if I had never known him, but peace to his ashes.'[59] A few days later, however, he cried out to his son, 'This wicked man has barbarously ruined me and for all that he owes me I am bound to pay for him.'[60]

In February 1778 £7,000 was still owed to Vansittart's estate. However, through Macleane, provision had been made for the Nawab of Arcot to grant a reversion (for life) to Vansittart's widow, of the £1,500 per year originally allowed General Lawrence. This had fallen to Vansittart and Sulivan equally.

When Stephen set off for India in 1778, his father asked him to realise several gifts from the Nawab. He believed the donations might total £23,000, plus interest if allowed. This sum, he said, would clear all debts and allow the Ponsborne estate to be retained.[61] Stephen was to remit the money through 'Mr. Duval's friend at Pondicherry by the Jack and Dick Sulivan channel, by the way of France, by China or by any other safe mode.'[62]

He was in dire trouble, however, and living from day to day. Some time between February and June 1778 he almost landed in prison. As he put it, Sir John Boyd 'behaved with unparalleled barbarity and made a peremptory demand of the money owing by Colebrooke'. He was saved by the chance visit of John Sulivan, newly returned from India, who mortgaged his India stock for the required sum. Laurence Sulivan's gratitude was so great, he implored his son to remember John Sulivan's generosity 'to the last hour of your life'.[63] His desperate straits continued, however; and throughout the autumn of that year he remained in great distress.

14

Restoration
1778-82

1

Sulivan's loss of fortune was not reflected in any fall from grace, and he managed to keep up appearances; he was able to receive friends of the first rank from the political echelons and from society in general. Luckily, major costs associated with his son's education and training in the law were already completed; as was the instruction of his Owen nieces. The income he did have was sufficient to maintain an appropriate facade.

John Dunning, a good friend since the early 1760s when Sulivan gave him a first opportunity to handle Company litigation, remained stalwart in support, as did Robert Palk. His standing, as a London gentleman, had not changed, and his importance within the Company was still recognised. His home continued to be visited by petitioners, because he still had the 'influence of a Prime Minister'.[1]

The happiness of his wife and the bliss of domesticity was high on his agenda. He seldom visited taverns or coffee shops and must have gained all the news he wanted at India House, because he counted perhaps only ten occasions when he was to be found in such public places – and then, mainly when electioneering. Family life, made him 'cheerful and seemingly happy'; and he enjoyed 'domestic felicity'. All this sprang, he said, from leading 'a methodical and regular life'.[2]

All seemed to be well until his wife's health started to deteriorate around 1778. Mrs. 'Betsey' Graeme, a God-daughter, was told that it was 'at best very precarious' and she was not fit to write.[3] From about 1770 his son Stephen was feeling the pinch, and that year begged £500 from Palk, and another £500 in 1774.[4] One of his intimate friends was Sir Horace Mann, famous for being one of Horace Walpole's correspondents. Young Sulivan had borrowed money from him, which displeased his father who had no great liking for Mann. Most of the debt was quickly repaid.

Desperation was reached in 1778 when Stephen was despatched to India. Sulivan spoke of his imminent departure to 'Betsey' Graeme: 'Stee, disappointed in several considerable lines and with an aversion to Law resolves for India. He carries with him a wife, sensible and amiable. The separation affects his poor mother too much.'[5] In February he also wrote to members of the family of Benjamin Sulivan of Cork, who were also resident in Madras, informing them that Stephen and his wife would be arriving. He suggested that they stay with them until settled elsewhere.

This separation was clearly heart-rending. Sulivan's apprehension overflowed on the eve of Stephen's departure, and he held nothing back, fearing that he would never see him again. He appealed to him to 'exercise filial affection and feel for your parents'; to keep good health and make a speedy return.[6]

Sulivan was more than just a father figure to those he considered his responsibility. Apart from flesh and blood, he continued to care for the sons of Benjamin Sulivan. He only ever termed them 'kinsmen', but held them in the highest regard – especially the second son, John. The Irwins, from the maternal branch of this same family were also helped. His wife's family, the Owens, were cared for too; as were sundry godsons and god-daughters. The offspring of close friends and business colleagues were favoured, such as Jack Law, son of Governor Stephen Law. Most depended on him, and owed their start in life and subsequent success to his care.

Why he seldom mentioned actual Sulivan relationships and gave little away in the form of family details remains a mystery. In one of the few times he did so, in February 1778, he said to 'Dick' Sulivan: 'Stee and his mother present their kind compliments and remember us to every relation.' In this particularly rare letter there are one or two other enigmatic remarks and references to people who were obviously intimate family connections.[7]

With his son's transfer abroad, words ordinarily whispered were now put down on paper. They are quite revealing, a fact Sulivan was very conscious of. His son was pressed to let nobody see the particular manuscript, which he described as a 'Letterbook'; and never to show to others anything similarly confidential. He continued to take great pride in his own good name; but depicted his conduct as too unorthodox, embracing 'a nicety of conduct that bordered upon Quixotism, with worldly honesty'.[8] He truly believed he could have been 'as rich and honoured as Clive if not for this, combined with the wish to save an ungrateful Company'.[9]

He enjoyed reasonable health, which can best be attributed to his wife Elizabeth. The change of lifestyle she brought about probably saved him; before marriage he had been disporting himself in a wild manner. He had been unwell in 1762, and again in 1766, when he admitted to pain and a long illness. He followed the fashion and repaired to Bath to take the waters. This he continued to do over the years, to be both fashionable and for his well-being. The deterioration in his eyesight is first mentioned in 1777, although almost certainly troublesome earlier. Things became so bad that he had to dictate his letters to a scribe. It is tempting to say that he was falling to pieces both mentally and physically, such was the strain he was under; and these were the blackest of black times. Yet he possessed amazing resilience. He was not dead yet.

2

The winter of 1777/78, while it marked the death of Lauchlin Macleane, denoted the striking entrance of James, and especially of John Macpherson, into Sulivan's life. Unfortunately for him, he fell into the clutches of two scoundrels equally as cunning and charming as Macleane had been in the life he had just departed. Sulivan had no defence against their combination of flattery and secret design. Now that he was out of the House, his network of informers, operating mainly within the Company, would scarcely reach to backstairs politics at Westminster where they also operated; and this left him vulnerable and gullible. They stalked him carefully, and would linger like vultures to the death.

James Macpherson was the 'author, or translator, or editor, or forger of Fingal and other poems'.[10] He is most remembered for these Ossianic ballads. Through the 'Fragments' he gained entrance to, and instant fame with, the Edinburgh literati; and just as important, in 1761 he secured the patronage of Bute.[11] His direct importance, with regard to Sulivan, does not appear until the 1770s; but through Bute and because of friendships with Company officials, such as Sir Samuel Hannay, 'Fingal' figures in Indian affairs much earlier. He also became a Proprietor.

He resumed an earlier acquaintance with John Macpherson and struck up an association that had one purpose, to make both their fortunes. His efforts to link the ministry and the Company together in pursuit of fortune for John and himself also furthered ministerial control. Ministers were all too eager to become legitimately involved in Company affairs.

John Macpherson met 'Fingal' in 1766; then in 1767, sailed with his uncle, Captain Alexander Macleod, commander of the Indiaman *Lord Mansfield*, for China. At Madras, enroute, he attended the *Durbar* of the Nawab of Arcot, where by dint of boldness, charm and trickery (he gave a magic lantern show) gained the Nawab's confidence. The Scot had introduced himself as an 'interpreter and agent' and the Nawab commissioned him as such, to carry his grievances to the British monarch.

The credit and authority gained from becoming the Nawab's agent was to be immensely important. China was forgotten, and by 1768 he was back in London and plotting with 'Fingal'. They set about gaining the Duke of Grafton's sympathy for the Nawab, and attacked Bute and Shelburne, their former benefactors, because of the Duke's enmity to both. This gained them Grafton's influence with the Company Directors under his control. Both Macphersons tried frightening the Proprietors with the thought of the Nawab throwing his lot in with the French; and argued that he ought to be an ally of the Crown rather than the Company. Their threats failed; but through Grafton's influence John was appointed a Writer to Fort St. George in the Carnatic in 1769.

That same year the Macphersons struck up friendships with Sulivan (newly back in the Direction) and also with Rockingham, Macleane and Andrew Stuart. Before John sailed in 1770, however, Lord North came to power. Their letters of recommendation were now useless, and the agency was lost. As yet, they had no influence with North, but set about switching allegiance to him and Robinson.

Until 1774, John Macpherson concentrated all his attention upon the accumulation of money (as Paymaster to the Army of the Carnatic). He also worked up an understanding with Hastings before the new Governor of Bengal left Madras for Calcutta. Eventually, he won his friendship, through the advocacy of Sulivan and others in London, and managed a transfer to Bengal beside him. This friendship was of the greatest importance later, though he was largely ignored at first. It was only following the arrival of Macleane, and his recommendation, again endorsed by Sulivan, that Hastings took any notice of him.

In 1775 John Macpherson stood in for Macleane at the Nawab's *Durbar* in Madras. As agent for Hastings as well as the Nawab, Macleane had made his way to London on the Governor-General's business. Aided by Benfield, Macpherson again encouraged the Nawab to see the Company as his enemy and the State as his friend – the opposite to what Sulivan preached. Meanwhile, in London 'Fingal' had become useful to Robinson, which brought John Macpherson into the circle as well. Robinson did not like them, but they brought the secrets Sulivan and Hastings had divulged. Everyone in this group felt safe, because Hastings was never a friend of Robinson and vice versa.

From late 1772 onwards, therefore, the Macphersons were backed in Parliament by North and Robinson. In India they had the strongest influence with the Nawab of Arcot; and in Bengal enjoyed the favour of Hastings. At India House Sulivan was in their pocket. The plain truth was that Sulivan and Hastings were duped: first by Macleane; by his friend John Stewart (made Judge Advocate General and Secretary to the Bengal Council by Hastings); then by the Macphersons. Sulivan had no idea of the collaboration with Robinson or that this bureaucrat and Lord North knew all the confidences shared with the Macphersons.

In a letter from John to James Macpherson on 1 October 1772, the lies told, the depth of their intrigue and contempt for those tricked is shown. Moreover, they felt safe, because they usually wrote in Gaelic to each other:

> The wretches are as black as I am, Colebrooke and Sulivan are under my thumb. There is not a year but they receive diamond stones (I have evidence) from my big friend here, the Nawab. And there is not a stone (member) in the King's cabinet who has clean hands.[12]

Meanwhile, John Macpherson convinced Hastings that in himself he had a good 'Company man', and a friend to be trusted. He also made sure of siding with Hastings in his struggles with the 'Triumvirate'; while behind his back, still serving the Nawab of Arcot.

What the two schemers really thought of the Governor-General and his friends is seen in another letter to 'Fingal': 'Impey is in trouble, I know the wretch. He was the manager for Sulivan and for Henry Vansittart, ten years ago. Hastings is altogether without influence.'[13] In the meantime, the flattery, half-truths and lies continued. In June 1775 John Macpherson solemnly informed Hastings, 'I will support old Sulivan and all my friends at any risk.'[14]

In 1777 Pigot sent John Macpherson back to London from Madras in disgrace, because of his part in the revolts centring upon the Nawab's debts. Sulivan and Hastings had no knowledge then of Macpherson's links with Benfield in all this. Once more fortune smiled upon him, however, because the link he had opened (in his own person) between Hastings and the Nawab was useful to both. In helping in Pigot's downfall he found additional favour in the Nawab's eyes; and was now regarded by Hastings and Sulivan as a true friend. He was also re-instated.

The Macphersons took advantage of their improved influence. From positions of trust they mercilessly deceived Sulivan and Hastings. With Macleane's death his agencies (on behalf of both the Nawab and Hastings) fell into their joint control. John Macpherson's wild boasts and half-truths continued. James, he said, had 'laboured with every zeal for his friends, and with an extraordinary effort got Sulivan into the Direction'.[15] He bragged of being the principal instigator of everything done on the Governor-General's behalf; and Hastings believed him implicitly. In 1778 he was told:

> Then I went to old Sulivan who entirely owes his seat in the Direction to my exertions. He went and assured Mr. Dunning – In short, we had our troops in motion over two days. Mr. Sulivan stood calm and ready in the Court of Directors and in that quarter was to secure enough.[16]

This referred to the dispute caused by Hastings' so-called resignation. The letter also showed that Sulivan was squarely in Hastings' corner, fighting for him.

Macpherson returned to familiar themes, the (supposed) importance and reliability of himself and 'Fingal'. He boasted that 'Fingal' was 'Ministry's confidential man' and one of 'Hastings' truest friends and has the secret of all your opponents'.[17] Sulivan was hooked just as securely, gushing, 'our good friend Fingal and I are upon the most cordial terms.'[18] According to him, he and John Macpherson were now:

> in constant habits of intimacy. I have studied his character to pronounce from experience that he is able, honourable, sincere, with a temper and disposition for pleasing and conciliating, that

he is hardly an avowed enemy…His attachment to you [Hastings]
brought us first together…He stood forward boldly at the hazard
of his own prospects in defence of your public character in the
hour when those whom he counted upon found it their interest
to vilify you.[19]

This is a sad letter (as are the others that followed of the same ilk); sad
because of the depth of sorrow and foolishness that would strike when the
deceit was uncovered.

In this particular eulogy Sulivan said, referring to 'Fingal': 'The Minister
and his friends pay attention to him.'[20] This was something he could scarcely
credit, being unaware of the North-Robinson-Macpherson ties. It might even
have warned him. Sulivan concluded with: 'He knows all the secret interior
moves…all have a great affection for him.'[21] He was totally taken in.

Having deceived Sulivan and Hastings so comprehensively, the rewards
for the Macphersons began to appear. In January 1781 Sulivan was ecstatic:
'We have carried John Macpherson into the Supreme Council with a pretty
high hand…he will be to you a second Barwell.'[22] In February he wrote:

Dear Mac, the enclosed (a testimonial) is proof of my regard and
a pledge of my unshaken attachment. Peruse, seal and deliver it.
Should you in any instance forfeit the character given by me I
must solemnly declare I will be the first man to turn against my
friend John Macpherson.[23]

Sulivan and Hastings were cruelly betrayed by the Macphersons. The
deception continued for some years before suspicions were eventually
aroused. Given the cloak of secrecy these impostors worked under, their
victims had little defence.[24]

3

Most of Sulivan's time now was consumed with defending Hastings;
bettering the government of India; and improving the relationship between
Company and State. Politically his position remained shaky; and he thought
in December 1778 he would have little chance at the 1779 election.[25]
Nonetheless, he was going to fight tooth and nail. In the event he was
returned with little real opposition.

From 1778 Britain was again at war with France, and once more he threw
himself wholeheartedly into the war effort. He brought experience, vitality
and insight. His information was drawn from the official (and unofficial)
correspondence of Hastings and the other Governors; and from military
friends serving in India, especially Goddard, Caillaud, Graeme and Coote.

The defeat of the Company's army by the Maratha confederation was a
serious moment; but by May 1779 Hastings had taken steps that would
reverse this blow. Sulivan warned him, however, of bigger threats to follow;

while securing the sinews of war. In an effort to remedy the shortage of fighting men, which had some success, he offered cash incentives to anyone in the Company's service willing to transfer to the Royal Navy.

Renewal of the Company's Charter was due, and Robinson was ready to change the existing system. By February 1779 his list of propositions to serve as the basis for discussion were with the Directors. However, opposition from within Parliament and inside the Company was strong enough to have his proposals (including those for the renewal of the Company's Charter) deferred until the 1780 Parliamentary session. The opposition inside India House was led by General Smith, with backing on the outside from the Rockinghamites, including Edmund Burke.

Towards the end of 1779 Sulivan referred to Robinson's further loss of power within the Company, and of a more conciliatory approach. Evidence for this change was that Dundas (the Lord Advocate) took a part in the new Treasury–Sulivan alliance. In return, Sulivan cared for his friend, Mr. Hay. In effect, the strength of the opposition forces facing Government, within and without Leadenhall, had led to a revolution in alliances. A new coalition, connecting North, Robinson and Sulivan took effect from 1779.

Sulivan was delighted, because Hastings was assured of yet another year in the Indies. By February 1780 he had also prepared a plan, to be placed before the ministry, incorporating proposals for the better government of India. He would not produce it, however, until a promise of power and protection had been secured. That this was indeed the case was shown when at the 1780 election, he was chosen Deputy Chairman. It was a major about-turn.

Later Sulivan put forward reasons for this volte-face by the Ministry. He supposed it was because there was little or no alternative. Those opposed to him at India House had also quarrelled so badly they were split asunder. He believed too that he was backed because a man of business was needed; which meant Hastings had to be included, because they were 'considered…inseparable'.[26] Sulivan recounted to Hastings that North had settled his differences 'upon the most liberal terms, and we are to be supported so long as our actions meet public approbation, and no longer'.[27]

Sulivan lost support because of this coalition, because he had 'betrayed' some of his allies, or at least this is how it was portrayed. Yet, most were tied to him only because it suited their own interests. His financial predicament also dictated that he seize this opportunity. He feigned surprise at the censure he received; but the manner in which he glossed over details suggests otherwise. In the eyes of some, a sacrifice of principles was involved, itself a very strange thing in an era where connection rather than principle counted.

It was only possible for him to return to power by uniting with ministry. At the same time, he was never North's yes-man; and he swallowed years of hostility from the minister to accept his support. Within the Company, dislike of General Smith, whom he detested, made it easier. However, Smith and his ally Edmund Burke, together with the rest of the Parliamentary Opposition, especially the Rockingham group, were furious and never forgot. They were to make life very difficult.

Sulivan's resumption of authority was soon evident. Once more he chaired the Secret Committee, where he unswervingly directed the Company's military and naval might towards the defeat of France. He was soon enmeshed in the dialogue and joint collaboration that had to exist between the ministry and the Company's leaders over direction of the war. Copies of advices from India were presented to North and Robinson.[28] Incredibly, he was heavily censured for this. He in turn was aghast at the abysmal lack of knowledge among his fellow Directors; a total non-comprehension of what was happening in India. Referring to this rabid ignorance, he said to Hastings, 'I am ashamed to go on.'[29] There was also criticism of the so-called 'shameful and unjust practice' of making a private mark upon such letters as he wished should be attended to by the Directors.[30]

Hastings was made aware of the arduous task ahead: 'We are at sea, no renewal of Charters and notice given us by Parliament.' Yet he felt himself equal to the task, 'I feel myself prudently bold.'[31] His friend was reprimanded in the very same letter and told not to break Company orders again: 'There must be obedience or all is anarchy.' On the other hand, he gave his protégé priority in everything.[32]

Soon he was involved in the planning and political trafficking that accompanied the new Charter Bill. Robinson had been actively engaged throughout 1780 in drawing up a constitution. However, it was January 1781 before Indian affairs gained the attention of Parliament. In February Jenkinson drew up a plan based on Robinson's one that had been started in 1778. He did so on the assumption that Parliament must proceed with Indian business with or without the Company's consent.

Sulivan knew in advance every move and every regulation proposed, and was scathing in his comments. The proposals did not give Hastings the near dictatorial powers he judged were needed. He also wanted an extensive administrative system created; and had spread these wishes widely in Parliamentary circles. Few of his ideas were adopted at first, though, as he commented, 'not disproved'. For this he blamed North's easygoing temperament.[33] In an uncharacteristic piece of self-praise he mentioned to Hastings the credit he deserved, and had received for the views he placed before the ministry. The Governor-General was also inundated with lists of regulations for better government. Sulivan considered that these or something similar would have to be agreed to, sooner or later.

He became Chairman once more in April 1781, as was expected. Sir William James was his deputy.[34] On the face of it (if only ministerial influence could be made to disappear) he seemed to have the influence and authority enjoyed throughout the years 1757 to 1764; and his return was without doubt a stimulus to everyone. His enemies again busied themselves spreading accusations that malpractices would flourish. None of this happened: negligence and dishonesty could never be part of Sulivan's design. Yet, he was somewhat compromised in that he had to use the power of his office to help his son. No secret was made of this, it was expected of him.

He had worked tirelessly since re-entering the Direction in 1778. Nevertheless, as he admitted, he had to whip himself even harder following accession to the Deputy Chair and then to the Chair itself. Typically, he tried to create circumstances that would satisfy equally the needs of the Company and himself; and offered proposals to ministers that would serve as the basis for a permanent settlement of East Indian affairs.

Coinciding with his return troubles had grown in number. The war in India increased costs all round; and the general European conflict affected markets. Reform of administration in India had to be postponed. Things became so bad the Directors were forced to approach the ministry for financial help. In view of the twin needs of a new Charter and a loan, Sulivan had to reconcile differences within the Company, considering unity to be vital before an approach was made. He was successful to the extent that North was prevented from gaining 'advantageous pecuniary terms for the renewal of the Charter'.[35]

The main push to settle the form of government for India and the basis of new relations between the State and the Company, took place in the years 1781-4. The year 1781 marked the beginning of both these movements; and it is to Sulivan's credit, and no coincidence, that they were initiated during his period in the Chair. The legislation was to extend the Company's Charter to 1794 at the earliest.

He provided Hastings with a list of the matters his 'poor brain had agitated within these 18 months', that is, from mid-1780 to January 1782.[36] He told Stephen, 'my labours are such and almost without assistance that literally I have not a moment to spare'.[37] His work involved a set of remarkably detailed propositions for prolonging the Company's trade, clearly time-consuming to prepare, which were placed, eventually, before the Government.

Nevertheless, continuous close liaison with ministers over the war was maintained; as well as joint scrutiny of reports from Hastings. He and his Deputy, William James, constituted the Company's Secret Committee, which dealt with war raging mainly in the south and west of the sub-continent. The ongoing conflict with France had pulled in some of the strongest native states in India; and it was quite obvious that help was needed. Once more Sulivan managed to make this understood at national level.

As Chairman it was his duty to keep up-to-date with the course of hostilities, and this he did faithfully. The dire tidings from the East also helped bring about the formation of Dundas' Parliamentary Secret Committee, with Jenkinson and Gregory on board. This was bad news, because the latter was Sulivan's long-standing enemy. He had also been the agent in Britain for Nuncomar (Mahrajah Nanda Kumar). After the Maharajah's execution, Gregory became a rabid enemy. This was to become significant because he became Chairman in April 1782.

4

Protection of Hastings had continued, with more muscle following Sulivan's return to the Direction in 1778. The first problem he faced was that following Clavering's death there was a hint his friend might be accused of murder; although in his eyes this would have been just as absurd as the furore over the death of Pigot. Nevertheless, he warned Hastings to get the proper papers home to Dunning.[38]

In 1778 the North ministry was fully preoccupied with the struggles in America, Europe and elsewhere, and there was no opportunity for resolving India business. The proposed new India settlement, and Hastings' situation, would all have to be attended to later. This, and his fortunate return to the Direction, gave the opportunity to strengthen the protective sheath around his colleague. He was helped in that the Company was left to 'manage' in its own way for a while, so great were the troubles elsewhere. The space and time also allowed enabled him to extend his influence.

With Hastings in mind, he planned to bargain with ministry over continuation of, or changes to, the Regulating Act. With the Company Charter due for renewal, his protégé's future would certainly be the main negotiating piece. His man in Bengal was also made aware of the mood in London. News of the fiasco in 1777, when Clavering had tried to take the chair, had hardened hearts. Hastings was informed that he was to be 'Impeached in Parliament and vengeance was announced by the leaders of this poor country.'[39] It was a chilling and accurate prophecy.

Although he was grudgingly accepted by the ministry in 1778, no such impartiality was granted the Governor-General. Sulivan was beside himself with rage at the vicious campaign waged in the Capital. He termed it 'diabolical with a vengeance'. This 'malignant pressure' as he put it, was maintained, despite 'a full Treasury in Bengal and the Investment cared for'.[40]

It really was an incredible tide of hate, involving despatches that emanated from the Government-controlled Court of Directors. In Parliament as well, efforts were redoubled to make things so uncomfortable that Hastings would resign of his own accord. He appealed to Sulivan for protection against the slurs on his character infiltrating the General Letters.

The many charges were rebutted; and Hastings was assured that his friends remained active on his behalf. However, he was warned in 1778 that he would have only five more years to govern, 'and no longer'. Under a new Charter, Sulivan continued, prophetically, the territories in India would be taken by the State, and a new government there (excluding Hastings and Barwell) would be appointed.[41]

He was certain Philip Francis was telling most of the lies about friend; hence his encouragement to 'go against this incendiary trying to supplant you in government'.[42] He spoke of William Burke spreading the preposterous rumour that he (Sulivan) would be replacing Hastings; and referred to supposed ill-treatment of 'young Fowke' by Hastings and Barwell: 'The flame this has created is not to be conceived.'[43] He finished by saying, 'Oh my friend, I am sick of the world when I reflect upon your treatment.'[44]

In 1779 yet another sustained effort to unseat Hastings was foiled. There were tales of a Hastings-Impey feud; of further enquiries into the Nawab of Arcot's debts; and fall-out from the Pigot scandal. A general impression was deliberately invoked that India was full of intrigues. It was true that a disagreement had flared between Hastings and Elijah Impey; one that was particularly poignant because it was between old friends and schoolmates. They clashed over the powers of the Supreme Court of Judicature in Bengal, headed by Impey, and those of the Governor-General, at the head of the Bengal Supreme Council.

Only personal friendship and long acquaintance with both men enabled Sulivan to pull them together, though he was always on Hastings' side in the argument. Sulivan made a personal appeal to Impey: 'You may have many able and powerful friends but none that exceeds me in zeal and affection.'[45] It took a long time to heal the rift; so much so that in 1781 he grumbled that though his support could be depended upon, 'he grows cool even towards me.'[46]

His becoming Deputy Chairman in 1780 proclaimed that Hastings' position was immensely improved. When in 1781 he occupied the Chair he was secure for at least another year. Even before taking the lead, Sulivan was able to exclude paragraphs in the General Letter to Bengal drawn up by the previous Chairman Devaynes.[47] Once more a stream of useful men were despatched: Lord Macartney to Madras, and John Macpherson to Calcutta were two that he thought (wrongly it was to prove) would be useful to him.[48]

Perhaps Hastings did not realise the enormity of what had happened in 1780; that North was now responsible for the Governor-General's India policy. He either had little conception of the fraught political situation that now existed, or chose to say nothing. The switch to North made Sulivan fully appreciate that everything was now subject to the sway of Parliamentary fortunes. Authority over the Company having been handed to Parliament meant that Company-Westminster relations were susceptible to party warfare at Westminster. The creation of this alliance led to savage assaults on all three men by the Parliamentary Opposition. The attacks, pursued by Francis, Burke and General Smith, inside and outside Leadenhall, were levelled at every aspect of its government at home and abroad.

Sulivan now directed the ministerial faction in the Company, a novel and (to the uninitiated) an alarming situation, although quite in keeping with his early career and the smooth Administration-Company relations that had been the norm. He held the Company firmly to the ministry's point of view – but only as long as Government held fast in support of Hastings, and did not plan to destroy his treasured Company.

He got wind of some deep plotting, which centred in reports emanating from Francis. Hastings was told, 'We can and will be prepared to stem this infamous torrent.'[49] He harnessed North's half-hearted support, and his own supporters in and out of the Company were rallied. He feared that Hastings' conduct of the war in India was leading to threats against him in London. In November 1781 Francis even made repeated efforts to call on him, 'on business of great consequence'.[50] Sulivan had considerable trouble parrying his thrusts. Alex Elliot supplied him with a few facts; but he wondered why his friend did not use the cipher to communicate.

His return to the Direction meant additions to the unfaltering flow of plans, suggestions and criticism sent to Hastings. He reviewed everything his friend attempted, no matter what it might be. In return, Sulivan now received details of nearly every event and decision taken abroad. Typically, these letters were answered promptly. The correspondence became a vital resource in itself.

The Governor-General's political ideas were pored over. He elaborated upon military plans to combat the Marathas; regulations governing trade; and evasions in the Company's Investment. Issues, such as the raw silk trade, saltpetre returns, and relations between the Nizam, Haider Ali, his son Tipu Sahib and the Nawab of Arcot were avidly devoured. Nor did he refrain from passing comment upon the political infighting. Sometimes he exasperated Hastings, who complained to John Macpherson: 'I would only wish Sulivan would drop his plans of making new Establishments when it is as much as we can do to keep the old.'[51]

He also had excellent strategic sense, and Government took up his proposal, made in 1781, of despatching an expedition to take the Cape of Good Hope. This would have effectively ended French and Dutch interest in India. The plan failed, and Sulivan lamented: 'My poor brat is strangled...it was my favourite child.'[52] He also claimed total credit for the seizure and retention of the Nicobar Islands and Achin.[53]

Demonstrating how the Company could be changed and reinvented to meet altered circumstances, he continued to pursue at great length the manner in which the trade in raw silk could be resurrected. He pleaded with Hastings saying, 'It is you that know that with this article and this alone the Company's prosperity in England can be established.'[54] He also set out the method by which this could be done, asking Hastings for an 'option for myself and friends'.[55]

15

Transformation
1780-84

1

In the Carnatic everything was coming to a fine brew and a second war with
Mysore broke out (1780–1784). All problems in India were set against this
backdrop of constant conflict. Some means of paying for it had to be
arranged, and the personnel necessary to ensure survival had to be chosen
and given adequate backup. Sulivan, it might be guessed, was involved up to
his neck. From February 1780 he was voicing deep concern about the
deteriorating situation. As one of the Secret Committee he was ready to pay
troops from an assignment of the Nawab's land revenues,* whether the
Prince liked it or not.[1] In fact he had to stop moves that would have forced
him to turn over all his revenues. Sulivan's main complaint though, was not
being informed of what was going on.

By April he was Deputy Chairman and anxiety had turned to alarm. The
ministry was unhappy as well because things seemed to be getting so out of
hand. They had grounds for apprehension, the Company was in mortal
danger from these wars, which coincided with the end of the American
struggle. Space and time were needed to counteract the French and Dutch.

In February 1781 he attempted to recruit a regiment for the defence of
Madras. Then, with little hope of success, tried to get around 2,000 troops
from an expedition departing for the Cape of Good Hope. In the spring of
1781 he was Chairman, and on a war footing. Reports were invariably bad;
although in April he was pleased that the Cape had been captured. That same
month he advised Hastings to, 'take the bull by the horns', and land Goddard
at Mangalore, from whence he should march to Madras and Seringapatam.[2]

He informed the ministry in May of the need for 'at least 10 sail of the line
and 6,000 troops to secure Madras against the French fleet threatening there'.
But apart from one regiment, the Company fought with little help from
Government.[3] Goddard, who was a particular friend, had already provided
him with information on Haider Ali, the situation in the Carnatic and in
Bombay.[4] By June he was aware the French knew of Company weakness on

the Coromandel Coast. He blamed this on Governor Rumbold and his Council in Madras, while hailing Hastings as a potential saviour.

Although Haider won the opening exchanges, Sulivan thought he would 'play a shy game' with Coote. He was convinced about one thing, however, 'Haider must be destroyed to secure our own power.'[5] This must have been in his mind for some time because he remembered Clive saying: 'Sooner or later it will be found that Hyder Ali must be crushed.'[6] As well as reducing Mysore, Sulivan wanted 'proper bridles on all the native states' because he sensed deadly danger.[7] He feared Haider and his son Tipu, especially in alliance with European enemies. A deal had to be struck with the Marathas as well; and an alliance formed with the Nizam of Hyderabad, regarded as 'dangerous, cunning and deceitful'.[8] Most important of all, the rulers of these native states had to be kept isolated.

Haider Ali and his son had immense revenues, they were great warriors in Sulivan's eyes, and had secret help from France. Nevertheless, he believed neither put much trust in the French. He maintained that Hastings would be lauded in Britain if he prevented a French-Dutch-Mysore combination against the English Company. Even more praise would come if the country powers were ranged against these enemies on a permanent basis. In the end, only the cessation of war with France saved the day. In 1784 the Treaty of Mangalore was signed which Hastings disapproved of because he thought the terms too conciliatory – and he did not like the Nawab being excluded.

2

Sulivan's first public fall-out with the Burkes centred on the dispute between the Nawab of Arcot and the Raja of Tanjore. As per instructions, Pigot, then Governor of Madras, had taken the part of the Raja against the Nawab, over his lands and revenues. In 1777 he was deposed by a majority of his council, who were also creditors of the Nawab. He died in custody. Hastings, who had responsibility for all Company possessions, for strategic reasons had supported the Nawab (and thus the creditors) against Pigot and the Raja. He urged the Madras government to force him to pay the Company. As in everything in these years, Sulivan followed Hastings.

In London, meanwhile, the 'common purse' that Edmund, William and Richard Burke shared was empty. William and Lord Verney (who put up all the money) had suffered financial failure not just in the 'Great Scheme' of 1769, but because of yet another ploy in Amsterdam.[9] William Burke left for Madras in 1777 in search of succour. He returned in 1778 as joint Agent for the Raja, a post that promised the much needed funds. Unluckily for the Burkes these plans were foiled, for which event they blamed Sulivan who was then back in the Direction.

Two of the Burkes became Proprietors: William in July 1778, Edmund in October 1780. In this way they could keep an eye on Tanjore developments. With Sulivan's return to power came the adoption of a number of policies to which they were opposed. One of these appeared in April 1780, when Sulivan drew up orders by which the Raja was to assign revenues from his territory to the Company to pay his (supposed) debts.

Edmund Burke pretended to be scandalised at the Tanjore situation. But his fury was more for private than public reasons – he planned the preferment of his cousin in Tanjore. The reality was that the Burkes and Sulivan were involved in a private war; and the Deputy Chairman was just as determined that William Burke would not succeed through the Raja, at the expense of himself and his son.

Nevertheless, Burke presented the whole business as State interests being placed second to the wishes of individuals. No mention was made of his cousin William's post of agent to the Raja. Burke accused Sulivan and Devaynes of seizing, and delivering over to their servants at Madras, all the revenues of Tanjore. He claimed this action violated a solemn treaty that no Company servants would meddle in its internal government; and referred to a letter of 1775 sent to the Governor and Council of Madras.

The views of Hastings on this subject are interesting. He thought it scarcely deserved serious discussion. The Raja might have been given the title of 'King', but it was a misnomer. The Nawab was his undoubted sovereign. As he understood it, the Raja had refused to contribute during this time of great crisis. Accordingly, he must be compelled to open up his grain store.

Burke's annoyance intensified. On 2 October he more or less accused Sulivan and Devaynes of robbing the Raja. He appealed to Jenkinson 'on public principles', saying that the nation was being placed in a scandalous light. Three days later he encouraged Portland to gather with Proprietors Adair and Crighton, to try and put a stop to everything. Still making no mention of his own interest, he told the Duke that Sulivan had personal designs on the Raja's revenues. Then he appealed again to Jenkinson to do something.

To begin with he seemed to be getting results. Jenkinson consulted Lord Stormont, Secretary of State for the Northern Department; and that same day Stormont asked Sulivan and Devaynes to postpone sending the orders until North came to London. Next day he forwarded Burke's complaint to Devaynes and Sulivan, asking for an answer in writing.[10]

Sulivan was furious. His anger was directed as much against Burke's manoeuvring of Parliamentary allies for personal ends (posing as public interest) as much as everything else. In addition, instead of taking place within the Company, all was being conducted within the Parliamentary arena, from which he was now excluded. To his fellow Director Henry Fletcher, he described Burke's attack as 'violent, indecent and injurious beyond example'.[11]

In the temporary (and suspicious) absence of Fletcher and Gregory, Sulivan had been left to get on with assigning the revenues from the Raja's territory to the Company. He discovered that the Prince had cleared his debt. All orders were then changed, and the Raja informed that the Directors would waive the demand if he agreed to pay two months in advance. Sulivan maintained his colleague Fletcher joined in creating these terms. Crucially, he was thus seen not to be acting alone.

He and Devaynes refused to meet Edmund Burke over the instructions intended for India, upon the correct grounds that it had nothing to do with him. Stormont and Hillsborough also informed Burke that the orders were not what he had thought. In fact the Raja owed little to the Company. The servants in Madras were rebuked by Sulivan and Devaynes for failing to provide information that would have given the correct picture. All was sorted out by the despatch of 18 October.

Understandably these new commands, presented by Sulivan, were of little use to William Burke and Captain William Aldergrove, the Raja's agents. The torment for the Burkes was that Sulivan's son Stephen was to become Resident at Tanjore, with large allowances. He was actually made Judge Advocate General in Bengal before taking up this appointment. Edmund Burke was adamant, and without a doubt correct, that all along Sulivan meant to deliver the Tanjore office to his son; and that the orders were carried through the Direction with this in mind: 'Scarcely was Will's back turned,' he said, 'than Sulivan began his old machinations.' Put another way, he and William Burke had been foiled.[12]

Sulivan then sent 'a relation', Eyles Irwin, to his son (accompanied by a new Writer, Mr. Seton) with an account of the new situation. At exactly the same time, William Burke was taking back an acknowledgement from the monarch of receipt of a letter from the Raja. It was alleged that on the overland route to India, William was deliberately stopped by Benfield and Sulivan's protégé Seton, from boarding a ship in Basra. Seton was given precedence, which meant Stephen Sulivan knew of developments first, and was prepared.

Sulivan became Chairman in April 1781 and though still subject to ministerial whims was all powerful in the Company. It is instructive, therefore, to find that despite Burke's wrath, he still sought the Chairman's help. On 30 August a John Robertson was solicited to approach him on William's behalf. The great statesman was surely conscious of the debt owed; and the request suggests there were still bonds of a sort.

3

While Sulivan vigorously pursued war in the Carnatic theatre, steps were taken to choose a strong man to take charge in Madras. A second disaster hard upon the heels of events in America was dreaded by Government and Company alike. Governor Rumbold's misdeeds had also created a bad press. That is why at the end of 1780 Lord George Macartney was appointed President of Fort St. George, Madras; arriving there in June 1781. He was the first official chosen outwith the ranks of the East India Company's servants.

As virtually executive managing director of the Company, Sulivan had much to do with his selection. Macartney always recognised the fact, stating time and time again how much he owed to him. Sulivan and most of the

Proprietors thought the situation on the Coromandel Coast required someone totally unconnected with India affairs. He also thought Macartney would be quite manageable, and show due deference to the Governor-General. He was to be proved wrong on both counts.

Hastings also favoured his appointment – at first. This was due to Sulivan's influence. He told Hastings that the new Governor was even fit to follow him as Governor-General He emphasised his fellow-Irishman's links with the King and with Bute; and finished by stressing the natural abilities of someone so warmly attached to them.[13]

Macartney was proud and honest. Although he went to India to make a fortune, he would not blacken his character for anyone. Unfortunately he would not stand in an inferior light to Hastings either, which led to much trouble; and he easily fell out with anyone and everyone.[14] His worst feature was his temper, which he tried to keep under control; but in his correspondence he fulminated at length about everything and everybody. Nobody was ever good enough.

The new Governor was convinced there was widespread corruption in India. In his constant carping he also insisted that there must be peace with the Indian states at any price. In this he was going right across all that Hasting had been striving for over many years. Not for anything would the Governor-General compromise the Company's position by a headlong search for peace.

When Macartney arrived in Madras, Haider Ali was almost at the gates. Only the exertions of General Coote and Admiral Hughes, given financial, military and administrative support by Hastings, and backing from Sulivan, saved the day. The Governor's first letter to the Chairman described the wretched condition of the settlement, and he complained of shortages of every kind. He also believed the common saw that the Governor-General was responsible for the struggle with the Marathas, and that this had brought about the Madras tragedy.

He was soon on a collision course with the Supreme Council. By the terms of the Regulating Act all Presidencies were placed subordinate to Bengal. The consent of the Governor-General was required for everything – apart from decisions to be taken during cases of emergency, starting hostilities or concluding treaties. This, of course, led to difficulties of interpretation, and the authority of Bengal could never be really absolute. Such an unsatisfactory arrangement and the disparate characters of the two men led to bitter hostility. Sulivan's dilemma was that he was drawn to both, yet in the end always sided with Hastings – his 'lode star'.

Macartney was also soon on the way to a complete fall out with his fellow Irishman, Sir Eyre Coote. The General had been appointed by Sulivan, and entrusted by Hastings for conduct of the war in the Carnatic – an arrangement that caused even more friction between Bengal and Madras. Macartney despised the General. To Sulivan he growled, 'In God's name how could you send such a man as old Coote here...even persons of his own silly

trade have lost faith in him.'[15] Sulivan certainly had some sympathy, he had
become quite disenchanted with Coote himself.

The General began taking apoplectic fits in 1782, and died the next year.
His successor was General James Stuart, and soon Macartney was arguing
with him. In 1776 Stuart had helped throw Pigot in gaol, where he died. He
had a long acquaintanceship with Madras, and with most of the corrupt
officials. Macartney regarded his behaviour as one of 'systematic
disobedience'. He sent him home under arrest. This almost instigated a
mutiny in Madras; caused uproar in Leadenhall and Parliament; and led to a
duel. The Scottish General had many connections, Sulivan was one of them.
Robinson and Andrew Stuart, the General's brother, also well known to
Sulivan, made approaches to him to do something. It was hoped Stuart
would be cleared at his court martial. It might just be coincidence, or maybe
not, that Sulivan's 'kinsman', Benjamin Sulivan (brother of John, Richard and
Henry Sulivan) was Judge Advocate at the subsequent court martial that
acquitted Stuart.

4

Soon after arriving in Madras, Macartney had gone ahead and assigned the
Nawab's revenues from lands in the Carnatic to the Company for the
duration of the war. This did not please the Nawab's creditors, nor did it go
down well with the Nawab. He had continued to borrow at exorbitant rates
from Indians and Europeans alike, but in particular from Council members.
Many were part of or in alliance with the 'Arcot interest'. Not a lot was
known of the growth within Parliament of this powerful group, numbering
some thirteen MPs, whose attention was firmly fixed upon what was
happening in the south of the subcontinent. This clique also had substantial
support within India House. Sulivan monitored the activities of those he
knew about (in Parliament as well as at Leadenhall).

A commotion was deliberately stimulated in Britain by fellow members of
the so-called 'Arcot interest'. Sulivan had no direct interest in settling the
claims of these creditors; and it was common knowledge, anyway, that many
were both exaggerated and doubtful. Nevertheless, the claimants appealed to
the Governor-General to cancel the assignment, which he did, to capture
their support. Macartney, however, refused to do as instructed and petitioned
his superiors in India House.

Yet at first, Hastings had espoused the assignment; and Stephen Sulivan
had already given him a copy of his father's plans for the liquidation of the
Nawab's debts, based on this tactic; this in turn had been forwarded to
Macartney. Hastings had even commented (before his retraction) that these
were similar to his own in thought and principle.

The Madras Governor had, in the meantime, become wary and suspicious
of John Macpherson and his friends among the 'Arcot interest' who had
recommended Paul Benfield, the leading creditor. He knew well that their
sole aim was to acquire money from the Nawab. However the problem (and

his difficulty) was compounded by the fact that the Prince and his second son had been completely taken in by Macpherson. Every scrap of information they possessed was forwarded to his fellow conspirators in England by 'Johnny McShuffle'.

With Hastings won over to the side of the Nawab and the creditors against Macartney, and overruling the Madras Governor, Sulivan was in a predicament. He knew all the reasons for his friend taking this step: the desire to secure the 'Arcot Interest'; plus dislike of the new Governor, who defied his own authority. What aggravated Sulivan more was that in January 1781, earlier than all these developments now staying his hand, he had proposed that the Nawab's debts should be consolidated. Nothing at all had happened; and now he was impelled to support Hastings (as he did on everything else) upon his change of direction over the assignment.

Throughout the whole affair Sulivan tried to remain cool and uninvolved, particularly with regard to Benfield and the other creditors. His support of Hastings in whatever approach he favoured dictated this. His son Stephen, however, did not like Benfield and could not understand his father's neutrality towards him. He described Benfield as unscrupulous, ambitious and dangerous.[16]

Sulivan was committed to Hastings, and by the end of November 1782 was expressing astonishment at Macartney's entrenched opposition. Hastings was informed that Macartney owed all to him, and that the 'terms' had been a 'confidential union' with the Governor-General. He hoped for a change of conduct, 'if not, we must turn the tables'.[17] His son expressed astonishment at his father's total espousal of Hastings (who he thought too strong in his criticisms) at the expense of Macartney. He believed his father should be promoting liaison and not discord between them; and appreciated Macartney's disgust at the corrupt officials in Madras. In his letter he added, 'I am surprised that you, who are partial to the constitution of the Dutch Government at Batavia, should not have endeavoured at least to remould the Government of Madras.'[18] Stephen was told to keep quiet.[19]

Waging the war now raging in the Carnatic was still Sulivan's first priority. However, he was no longer in the Chair after April 1782, and out of the Direction by rotation. It seemed to him that both the war and Madras affairs were being left untouched. The Chairman would do nothing, and the Direction was growing uneasy. By March 1783 he was also seriously concerned at the size of the Nawab's arrears, now understood to be around £300,000 – and set off against the Company's bonded debt.

There was disquiet as well over whether Macartney was justified, through his interpretation of the orders from the Court of Directors, in refusing to restore the assigned lands to the Nawab. The Deputy Chairman, Nathaniel Smith, one of that earlier Direction, wanted to blame everything on Macartney. Sulivan, probably because of his own involvement at the time, was inclined to acquit him.

In the end, the Nawab was advised that the government and garrisoning of Madras would be in the hands of the Directors, and of the Supreme

Government at Bengal; and that Hastings' projected system of 1783 would be implemented. By this, both the Prince's finances and the Company's demands would be met; as would, to a limited degree, the claims of the most 'justly clamorous creditors'.[20] A letter from a John Cox-Hippisley to General John Caillaud, demonstrates how prickly things had become in Madras by 1783, and how dangerous was the bickering and back-biting. Macartney, he said 'had sorted out' nearly everyone, so the Governor-General was no exception. Hippisley insisted, however, that despite everything, Macartney was still Sulivan's friend.[21]

5

A tremendous flurry of activity had surrounded the despatch of Stephen Sulivan to India in 1778. He was appointed Persian Translator at Madras, effective from 28 November 1777; and was to be Secretary there when Mr. Oakley, retired. Sulivan regarded these offices as of little consequence, however; they were merely vehicles for his son's rapid advancement.

All Stephen's preparation to lead a public life in England was sacrificed in sending him to India, forced by Macleane's death. The only avenue left was succour from friends abroad. Hastings was in the best position to give this aid, but he was kept in reserve; and hopes were centred at first upon the supposed gratitude of those placed in responsible positions in Madras, and upon the Nawab of Arcot.

Sulivan's efforts to solicit help were prodigious. In 1778 he despatched letters of expectation to everyone he thought could influence Stephen's fortunes. It was a bombardment. In addition he began writing a series of letters to his son. Of special importance, was the very remarkable and revealing 'Letterbook.' It was begun when Stephen departed, and was continued while his son was in India. This correspondence and the Letterbook in particular, reveal much about Sulivan's subtle, urbane mind; his knowledge and business acumen. It portrays too what he thought of contemporaries, friends and enemies.

Depicted are plans for his son while in Madras; the dangers to be faced there; and the money troubles that had to be overcome. The young man was to make it his business to enlighten his father of every circumstance: civil, political, military or whatever. He was to observe, analyse and deduce; and come to conclusions on all current affairs. Sulivan was very concerned about the ruthless men his son would meet, far from a father's guiding hand; and he was quite correct in being so solicitous. There was little loyalty or remembrance of past favours, as both discovered. Stephen was sworn to secrecy regarding the contents of the Letterbook. His father even used coded words for names, important items and dangerous material. At the same time, it is evident he intended that this Letterbook should be kept and never destroyed.[22]

Two other exceptional letters to his son were written: one on 27 February 1778, the other on 6 April; and the Letterbook continued to be added to. The first of these, introducing the Letterbook, was important in itself. The first two lines give its tenor and the significance Sulivan attached in it: 'This is my sacred repository which in no events should fall into any hands but yours and more of this, you will ever remember to be careful.'[23]

In these revealing letters, Sulivan introduced his son to his own dealings with individuals from whom he might gain favours and emoluments. A brief history or cursory character sketch of each was included. The letters dwelt particularly upon financial considerations; and he mentioned numerous sources of revenue. All hopes for financial salvation hinged upon Stephen's satisfactory launch in India, so his father bared his soul.[24] His opinion was spelled out on issues, home and abroad. His expectations, fears, disgust, successes, failures and disappointments were all included. The motivation and character of those he had known and whom Stephen would meet were spelled out; as were the dangers.

Sulivan was to be bitterly disappointed. Those he had placed in high office proved to be men of straw. He expected so much from so many, yet in nearly every instance drew a blank: Rumbold was positively hostile, and when Chairman in 1781, this was remembered by 'the old man of Queen Square'. Oakley, supposed to be a friend and advisor, did nothing; likewise John Whitehill.[25] Fortunately, in October Stephen was appointed Secretary to the Civil Department at Fort St. George - the result of scheming by father and son.

It was hoped that salvation would come from the Nawab, and a letter in December seemed to offer gifts, and the promise of Stephen becoming his agent, with a £6,000 salary, paid in London. Sulivan became emotional as he demonstrated on paper all that they could do for the Prince. He produced a veritable tidal wave of advice and instructions.[26] Stephen was to read to him 'in great confidence, the papers I mean to publish in vindication of his honour and interest, but not in my name'.[27] He was to tell the Nawab he expected to be an MP soon, where he would represent him when the Company's Charter was being considered; and would push for his independence. As 'the Under-Secretary in the India Department', he would defend his position; similar, 'to Edmund Burke's support of the American colonists'.

Sulivan specified many ways of making money through the Nawab's good offices.[28] In particular, he expected Stephen to benefit from a £100,000 fund, believed to be held in England, when confirmed as the Nawab's agent alongside Bute's son, Frederick Stuart.[29] In the end, he received nothing; and the agency fell into the hands of the two Macphersons who regarded it as their own.[30]

There was a fund, only it was in the shape of a bond worth 100,000 pagodas in the favour of Macleane, who cashed 73,000 pagodas before his death. Oakley now held it; and Sulivan only heard of it at all because of Macleane's demise. He said, 'I conceived nothing too great for him.'[31] He was right, his erstwhile friend had proved treacherous even beyond death.

He thought he had a right to much of this money, and Stephen was urged to obtain it in such a way that, 'no claim can be made upon us by Macleane's bond creditors'.[32] He worked out that his own adjusted demand was £21,180-15/-; nevertheless, only expected £16,000.[33] Again, he received nothing, yet had been certain his son would receive lucrative offices 'because his father had served the Nawab more than any other...more than all other men put together'.[34] All he held were Macleane's Granada estates, and the reversion to him (in 1775) of a portion of a lot of land measuring 20,000 acres, in Prince Edward Island.

Stephen did not quit his post as Persian Translator until 13 March 1779, thus picking up two salaries, the other was for Secretary to the Madras Council. He was not to be the channel for confidential information, however; and was convinced that neither the Nawab nor John Macpherson was receptive. All the high hopes for great things in Madras were dead. Sulivan was also unsure whether Macleane had died having 'done him well' or sold him out.[35] Everything now depended upon Hastings.

From the mid 1770s plea after plea to the Governor-General had been ignored. These entreaties are typified by that of 15 May 1779: 'Let me conjure you by the affection you bear me, think of my son.'[36] By November, with not a word of reply, Sulivan's anger at this disregard had built up:

> And now my dear friend Warren Hastings, what can I say, what must I think, to question your affection for me is impossible. An only and much beloved son, torn from parents, far advanced, has been recommended by me to your notice, and his very name has no place in your letters. I am deeply wounded by this neglect...Let me again conjure you to promote his prosperity.[37]

Though polite, there was no mistaking how deadly serious he was; and it is difficult to think that Hastings was still blind to all Sulivan was doing in London to promote and safeguard his position.

This letter, expressing deep hurt and anger at being ignored worked; and Stephen began reaping the benefits. In April 1780 he was given a completely unjustified commendation for virtually non-existent services as Secretary to the Madras Council. Then, while accompanying his wife to Bengal in August, carried despatches to Hastings, who immediately appointed him his personal assistant and Judge Advocate General.

It was also 1779 before Hastings made his so-called 'spontaneous effort of generosity' and allowed his creator and mentor to call upon him for up to £10,000. This was shabby treatment, at a time when Sulivan was sick with worry. Still, it would have made the father cringe to know that it took Stephen over twenty-two years to pay back the money.[38]

Remitting these funds proved difficult; and everything had to be kept from prying eyes. Hastings was to think of him using the entire £10,000 loan for the purpose of paying interest, and as a reserve against the time when he might be pressed 'to a state of disgrace.'[39] The help was crucial in maintaining their close relationship. A split would have had severe consequences. Sulivan apologised for doubting 'Hastings' eternal friendship'; the help given he termed 'an affectionate rebuke'; his doubts due to 'a mind tortured by pungent affliction'.[40] As it was, the total ever received was £7,000; and this only arrived in 1783. The whole matter was carried through with great embarrassment on both sides. Stephen reported that Hastings was 'delicate in these matters, as delicate as I feel awkward'.[41]

Now Stephen was in Calcutta he began to benefit from commissions, such as renewing leases for Company lands. At his request and through his father's scheming he was already Resident at Tanjore; and while holding this Residency post, he was given the honorary rank of Councillor in Bengal. Even as this was happening, Sulivan was making him a Senior Merchant, and hoped to place him in the Supreme Council at Calcutta. All this rapid promotion created a mix-up. It was not clear whether he would return to Fort St. George, or would remain in Bengal. In the end, Sulivan had the post in Calcutta confirmed; and secured the Residency of Tanjore for John Sulivan.

The affection Hastings had for Sulivan bore fruit, and expectations turned into reality. He and his agent, Johnson, secured well recompensed positions for Stephen, and so saved the father. However, young Sulivan enjoyed the post of Judge Advocate only until 1781. A 'precipitate slip' was how his father described its loss; it was regretted because it grew 'to be worth £3,000 a year, which no power would have taken from you'.[42] In 1781 Hastings granted Stephen an opium contract, which he sold the following year to a John Burn for over £3,000. Hastings knew nothing of the resale. Apparently, neither did Stephen's father, since in February 1784 Sulivan was advising him to renew it. There was some illegality in the hasty resale; and later Hastings was condemned for it.[43]

Evidence of Stephen's mixed fortunes abound: In 1780 he was money lending, utilising funds belonging to his father at Madras. By 1781 each had a share in bonds based upon the 'New Consolidated Fund of the Nawab of Arcot'.[44] William Burke was to be coerced (or helped) into giving him a bond for half of his £3,939 arrears, because, as Sulivan said, 'my misfortunes call for relief'.[45]

In Queen Square, Sulivan and his wife continued to live frugally. At first there was little left to remit home because of high expenses in India, and the debts there to be erased. He confided that £22,000 was needed to clear everything. Ponsborne would then belong to his son, with no mortgage, 'unless I suffer ultimately by Colebrooke'.[46] His (unfulfilled) financial projections continued to fill the letters and the ongoing Letterbook. When all debts in India were paid, Sulivan stipulated 100,000 pagodas [£30-40,000] would be needed to come home.[47] The minimum he could afford to return with was £20,000; and initially, at least £10,000.[48]

He issued a stream of directions on how to remit funds: such as by 'Star' Pagodas (made of gold); and how diamonds could be conveyed by the commanders of East Indiamen. He planned formation in India of a 'House for receiving monies in cash or kind': accepting diamonds, insurances and remittances of all sorts from Europeans in Madras and in Bengal.[49] Hastings favoured the plan and offered to help in its formation; but it came to nothing.

On return to England, his financial independence secured, Sulivan expected Stephen to do well. He was sure Solicitor-General Thurlow would find him a position; he was to be disappointed. One source of wealth his son was not equal to, lay in what were described as 'the new treasures of the Persian language'. Sulivan referred to Robert Wood, Chatham's Secretary, having made his fortune out of this; and Chatham had even advised Stephen to start a collection.[50]

He made an interesting observation about Sir William Jones: 'I hold Mr. Jones (who is the first in this country of the Persian class) to be a mere superficial smatterer, with this merit, however, that he knows more of the language than any other man and perhaps with such lights and materials as are here within reach he may not be equalled.'[51] Stephen was urged to collect Persian manuscripts and books, 'good stuff, not trash'; and to seek the advice of people like Barwell, Col. Dow and the 'Company's black Persian Translator at Madras'.[52]

16

Personal Loss and Political Revival
1781-83

1

The first half of the 1780s witnessed striking alterations in how Indian affairs would be managed from London. These were the culmination of several developments, all of which involved Sulivan. The most outstanding adjustment was a Board of Control, set up in 1784 and commanded by Henry Dundas. Sulivan's role in all this concerned the evolution of new procedures, their introduction, and the manner in which fresh regulations were achieved. His sincere aim was always better government for India; just as it was that of the ministry and all interested parties. What lay behind this commendable aim, however, meant something different to the protagonists, and is best summed up in their attitudes to Warren Hastings.

Successive ministries wanted rid of him; and, as outlined, colossal effort had already been made to remove him. This persecution was to continue, but had to get past Sulivan. His vigilant defence, long and constant years of service meant that clashes with whichever ministry was in power were unavoidable. The rise and fall of so many Administrations in rapid succession had prohibited coherent planning. It was a sorry state of affairs paralleled by the political jostling at each year's Company election.

From 1778 to 1781 Parliament had tried to make improvements in the government of India. Reorganisation of control, home and abroad, was one objective; a better relationship between Company and State was the other. These goals had come to nothing despite the efforts of Robinson and Jenkinson. An impasse was reached. The whole was attended by public controversy; people were deliberately led to believe that Hastings was the problem, and this criticism included Sulivan and the Hastings party, involved in championing the Governor-General.

The lack of an effective reform settlement had meant renewal of the existing legislation; and it was only with conclusion of the crisis in America that India matters received full attention. Robinson and Jenkinson, meanwhile, with advice from Sulivan, set out to prepare a plan embracing everything to do with the government of India. The basic outline was Robinson's plan of 1778, with additions from Jenkinson's later one. They were then to proceed with a settlement; supposed to be completed with or without the Company's consent.

Consequently, in April 1781 Robinson (helped by Dundas) presented another Bill, which became law in July. This Act did not vary much from his 1778 proposals. Sulivan was not impressed, and hoped for supplementary legislation to rectify things. Yet, this body of work was important. Robinson and Jenkinson also recognised that they were short-circuiting the alliance of interests dominating Company affairs since 1773.

Sulivan had long realised he could not combat the ministry; but was determined to secure the best possible legislation for the organisation he had served so long. He could best achieve this by working with bureaucrats like these two, who he realised genuinely sought better government for India. Long-term control of the Company might be gone forever, but the right to participate in the present and to help form the future remained.

Yet, while attentive and involved in the transformation of the 1780s, Sulivan had a long history of attempted improvements to look back on; so much so that the India Act of 1784 undoubtedly had much of its beginning with him. Working backwards, Pitt's Act is seen to be based on Fox's lost Bill of 1783, which in turn owed its existence to Dundas' earlier one. This in turn had relied almost completely upon the work of Robinson and Jenkinson, discussed above. But in the beginning, long before these two bureaucrats, Sulivan formulated plans and made efforts to place men in India to carry them out: from 1757 to 1763; then 1769 to 1773; and his proposals thereafter.

At every stage of Government interference, and latterly during its attempts at reorganisation, Sulivan had been consulted: through the 1766-7 Inquiry; from 1769 to 1773 and the lead-up to the Regulating Act; and then following his return to power in 1778. His views were widely accepted, then advanced and expanded upon by later Parliamentary administrators. Sulivan said in 1778, 'Necessity dictated that I be consulted by Government upon the new structure because I was the only fit person and only one prepared for it.'[1] He was used again after 1780. Apart from his invaluable knowledge, Robinson and Jenkinson knew that if they wished to make progress within the Company Courts, his political adroitness was just as necessary as his contribution to and agreement with their plans.

Between 1780 and 1783 the ministries of North, Rockingham, Shelburne and the Fox-North Coalition, came and departed against a backdrop of the perennial Indian question. Sulivan found little mutual ground with each new ministry; and was forced to maintain his defence of Hastings against permanently unfriendly Parliamentarians intent on ousting him. Burke-inspired motions polluted the Commons; such as those of May 1782 and October 1783, where the Governor-General's conduct was censured and grounds sought to dismiss him. These were only defeated by the activity of North in the Commons, and the pro-Hastings group in the General Court. Upholding Hastings' integrity impacted harshly on Sulivan's life. He was also going into his twilight years and about to suffer the most severe shock to his system.

2

In January 1782 he was approaching the end of his term as Chairman, and would exit the Direction in April, by rotation, together with five other Government supporters. Sustaining any sort of pro-Hastings group would be a problem; and the new executive was potentially hostile He had warned Lord North, but the minister did nothing. Sulivan's wishful thinking was that 'urged by necessity he will continue me in the Direction'.[2] He believed it was not in Government's best interest to allow supporters who had already 'passed the Chairs', to be excluded by the rotation clause.[3]

The anguish intensified as his exit drew near, because he could see a clear majority of 'malevolent and intriguing enemies in the Direction'. Fletcher he identified as 'a complete fiend'; and General Richard Smith 'a wretch who would hang you (Hastings) me and Impey upon one Gibbet'.[4] He bemoaned the lack of talented individuals; and raged at North's indolence: 'He flies from trouble and yields to his enemies except where they go beyond what he can bear, and then no man is more active or courageous.'[5]

His powers are reflected in the remark that there would be little opposition if he could remain a Director; but how hard he would have to work is revealed in the words: 'the real sentiments of a majority seldom coincide with mine'.[6] The change of ministry to Rockingham in March 1782 sealed his fate. His opponents, headed by General Smith, Fletcher and Gregory formed a majority in the Direction. These men would remain in charge within the Company, despite the fall-out between Rockinghamites and Shelburne's followers, and the early death of Rockingham in July 1782.

Many contemporaries commented upon what they thought was Sulivan's demise: 'I think the reign of Sulivan is over, the reign of Hastings is over,' Burke crowed.[7] A neutral observer, Thomas Allan, thought he had 'been treated with...an infamous regard. He has felt it very severely and, it is said, has been obliged to make his peace on very hard terms and it is a doubtful point if he ever comes into the Direction again.'[8]

His enemy, Robert Gregory, became Chairman in 1782; but Nathaniel Smith, one of his followers, filled the Deputy Chair. Sulivan was instrumental in bringing this about. On 10 April he was thanked by the Court of Directors for all his work. It meant little. 'The truth was,' as Allan reported to Macartney, 'he was sadly broke down by the late attack on him.'[9] He was only partially correct. What really lay behind Sulivan's dejection was his wife's death. He was devastated and inconsolable.

Elizabeth Sulivan died on 4 February and was buried on 12 February 1782. That day,' he informed Warren Hastings, 'put an end to my happiness in this world. And such has been my weakness that it's wonderful I now exist. I struggled with misery.'[10] It was a massive blow to him. The words he used to paint her virtues when she was alive measure out exactly what she had meant to him:

> When I lamented the deceptions I had experienced in my friendships with men I should have marked the peculiar kindness of Providence in giving me your mother, who with every virtue of a Primitive Christian, has been my constant adviser and friend in the solid understanding, unbounded affection, nice and religious honour, with such a share of prudence and discretion as never to divulge a single secret. The loss of character in me   or you I know she could not survive. Experience has often convinced me (I confess it with pleasure) that her judgement surpasses my own; and this has frequently puzzled me to account for, because I do not conceive her abilities are superior to mine, and a greater knowledge of the world must give me an advantage. Perhaps the mind occupied with fewer objects increases the strength of conception. Whatever be the cause, all the capital errors of my life have been committed when I have neglected to consult her. And this testimony I bear to the merit and goodness of the best of women.[11]

His wife was his 'single friend, in her bosom only was deposited my whole confidence and inmost secrets'.[12]

He said to his son, 'The lease of Queen Square house expires in March but if it had not, <u>there I should never go</u>'; and he never did.[13] It was 1785, however, before he sold the lease, when it went to a John Alexander. Such was his loss, Sulivan was wont to proclaim himself helpless. He was no such thing, but certainly much of the spirit had temporarily gone out of him.

At first he stayed with relations of his niece 'Betsy' Wood, at Fordhook House, Ealing. He and the son of his deceased friend Thomas Lane then took a house in George Street, Hanover Square; and another 'in the country, on a lease'. This house was also at Ealing; and Sulivan provides a domestic image: 'Mrs. Hawkins living with us as manager. And to do them both justice (Lane and Mrs. Hawkins) my ease is their study.'[14] At his house in George Street, he employed a William Morris as butler, and an Indian boy called 'Sadi'. After his death they conspired to rob his son; both were caught.

He had been in poor health for a number of years. In April 1780 Hastings was informed: 'A disorder in my eyes disables me from writing much. Excuse me, therefore, to Impey, to Barwell and to Coote.'[15] There were few letters in his hand after this. Without doubt, decades of work had placed strain on his eyes. Yet he was still reading and his sight became worse. In January 1781 he complained: 'My eyes are so bad.'[16] From then he depended upon an amanuensis. His physical condition was undoubtedly made worse by loss of his wife; and he continued in poor health and with troubled eyesight throughout 1782. In November he feared so much for his life that he stated baldly to his son that he was born on 24 April 1713. It appears strange that this had never been mentioned before.

This normally resilient campaigner also began to show signs of hurt and resentment. Towards sworn enemies he carried ideas of revenge and retribution. Stephen voiced much of the disgust and dismay the Sulivans had grown to feel over the years, at what the son termed 'unwarranted ill-treatment':

> With the many examples of ingratitude and treachery which your long and hackneyed experience of the ways of men has afforded you, I should not have wondered if instead of that credulity which has accompanied you through youth and manhood, you had chosen as the companion of age a gloomy and suspicious distrust of mankind. But I perceive you encourage to the last, and will even carry to the very grave, those amiable weaknesses of human nature which, however they may expose us to the artifices of the designing, grow out of the noblest root in the world, universal benevolence.[17]

3

No longer in the Direction from April 1782, Sulivan focussed on his son's affairs, those of Hastings and what was happening in the Carnatic, that is when he was able to concentrate. He also came under quite inordinate pressure from several quarters throughout the year; fortunately, although quite rundown his stamina proved sufficient. He fought back against scurrilous efforts to demean him. His enemies now in control of the Company searched, but found no evidence of any wrong doing; and were disgraced when a motion in the General Court, which implied misdemeanours by him, fell flat on its face.

In Parliament he came under heavy fire. The onslaughts had been building for some time, launched via the Secret and Select Committees. They had actually begun in April 1781, and were levelled at every aspect of the Company's government at home and abroad. Dundas led the Secret Committee; Burke, Francis and General Smith fronted the other.

The Secret Committee had launched a major attack in October 1781, directed primarily at Hastings. Sulivan had been alarmed at the way this Committee pervaded every department at India House, aiming to achieve 'a total revolution in the management of India'.[18] Dundas and his cohorts ranged over problematic events in India, and used them as vehicles for vicious tirades against the Governor-General.[19]

Yet, bad as it was, the Secret Committee was not as loathsome as the Select Committee, chaired and controlled by Burke; much of the information provided by Francis. In April 1782, coincidental with his wife's death and his own exit from the Direction, he was summoned to sit in front of this

Committee, where he was taken to task over alleged inaccuracies, delays and restricting tactics when Chairman. It was an especially heartless examination. Given Burke's displeasure at Sulivan's political 'betrayal' in forming an alliance with Lord North in 1780, and his anger over Tanjore, he was relentless. He tried, without success, to pillory his adversary; and also took the opportunity of censuring Hastings and Elijah Impey. Sulivan deftly avoided the accusations and later referred to them as minor irritations; but that was not true.[20]

He and his fellow Irishman were old antagonists. Burke knew perfectly well that Sulivan's great knowledge would always be placed at the service of 'his' Company, and against the onslaught of a would-be destroyer like himself. Earlier, the great orator had said to a friend, Thomas Lewis O'Byrne: 'Him (Sulivan) I know well.'[21] Now, after subjecting his opponent to the most intense and unpleasant interrogation, he exploded with fury to William Burke: 'That infamous wretch (Sulivan) after shuffling and prevaricating has at length taken refuge, refusing to give answers which may tend to incriminate himself.'[22]

Before this particular grilling was finished, the Select Committee (or rather Burke) had lambasted Sulivan further. He was accused of various 'crimes' and 'neglect of duty', such as failing to send abroad, promptly enough, the Judicature Act of 1781, which he had virtually created.[23] Sulivan thought this charge, 'very feeble'.[24] What incensed him most, however, was the nature of his cross-examination. He detested its viciousness and the sneering, insidious tone in which it was conducted.

He was so angry he sought immediate revenge and asked Dunning to provide a seat in Parliament in order to harass Burke. It was risky, but he wanted to challenge his enemy on his own duelling ground. Not surprisingly, Dunning did not answer. He had to cool his friend down.

The wily old fox had proved too elusive for Burke, but it took time for his anger to subside. The initiative remained with these Parliamentary Committees long after Rockingham's death, and trailed on even beyond the crash of Fox's India Bill in 1783. Yet before that date Sulivan could still express his contempt. In July 1783 he exclaimed: 'The labours of a Secret Committee are done away...and Edmund Burke has become what Richard Smith ever was, a most contemptible wretch.' Burke's 9th Report he described, with some venom, as 'a Dwarf and harmless, though a bitter injustice.'[25] In a tract published on 18 December 1783, signed, 'Detector' he answered the charges. Later, he dismissed the efforts of both Committees as trivial.

4

Until the greatest danger to Hastings was over in December 1783, Sulivan maintained a ferocious defence. Their mutual enemy, Philip Francis spoke of the wonderful support marshalled by 'the Old man of Queen Square'. In June 1781 he had dealt with Rumbold, who had blamed the Maratha war on

Hastings. By November he had faced up to Francis' venomous allegations, difficult to deal with because of his detailed knowledge. Nevertheless, as Sir Charles Lawson put it: 'Sulivan, with infinite ability defeated him.'[26] That he continued to outfox Francis is suggested by the latter's comments: 'The conversation between him and me at my house…was full as curious…A third of the kind is not to be met with in history.'[27]

The Shelburne ministry of July 1782 had shaped an assault because the minister was convinced that Indian reform would secure him votes. Impey was recalled; it was threatened to bring back the whole Bengal council; and the minister toyed with replacing Hastings with Cornwallis. Dundas' accusation that the Governor-General was a warmonger was typical of the odious charges flung about in the Commons.

Within the Company, the ministry-controlled majority followed the party line: Hastings' recall was demanded, amid a plethora of accusations. Sulivan's defence during this Government-inspired onslaught was magnificent; particularly his resistance to the attacks launched between May and October 1782. His objective was to secure terms that would ensure Hastings had an honourable homecoming. When this was not forthcoming, and instead an unconditional return was insisted upon, he fought tooth and nail. The defences he put up were all based on chartered rights and privileges. He maintained the Company had the last word on such an important issue.

Realising the Governorship would be lost if he did not remain firm, he organised a substantial group inside the Company that sided with Hastings. They worked for rejection of Shelburne's (Dundas-inspired) call for his removal. Accordingly, a special meeting of the General Court was held in October 1782 to vote on the recall. At the head of Hastings' supporters Sulivan secured the victory. Despite aches and frailty, 'my frame is shook and I write in pain', he and his group carried all before them by 428 votes to 75. The sheer size of the rout sparked off great celebrations at the *George and Vulture* tavern.[28]

Signs of the intense pressure he faced at this time and of his deepest feelings appeared in a letter written in November. It reflected his brooding frame of mind. He urged Hastings to 'make a speedy retreat, for I am heartily sick of men and measures'; that his friend must not have his fame and honour sullied by staying any longer than he had to.[29] In spite of physical difficulty he was able to add in his own hand:

> Your character is now so universally known and generally admired that we have nothing to fear from the rancour of your active enemies…and the abandoned witch, General R. Smith is (thank God) below contempt. Nor is the sublime and beautiful [Edmund Burke] in much greater estimation.[30]

Yet, he understood nothing had been settled, that his protégé could be removed. He also knew others were ferreting for a 'person of distinguished rank, tried abilities and unsullied honour' to succeed him. Sulivan believed that person would be Lord Cornwallis, with whom Major Scott, Hastings' appointee, had already opened discussions.[31]

Major John Scott was a problem on his own. Hastings had appointed him to care for his interests in Parliament and in the Company. Scott arrived in late 1781, and immediately joined with Sulivan; and at first he seemed to take advice. It was soon found out, however, he was rather 'volatile', had a headstrong attitude and poor grasp of essentials. Sulivan's dilemma was that because the Governor-General listened to the man, he was constrained to maintain confidentiality and an understanding, regardless of Scott's nonsense.

Hastings was incredibly naive to expect such a man, straight from service in India, to deal successfully on his behalf in England. The Major would have to work within a milieu of amazing complexity in the Company's Courts; and do the same within the equally intricate field of national politics in the 1780s. Sulivan and the Governor-General's other friends became convinced of his mistake in even appointing a representative, regardless of capabilities. As it was, Scott could be called before the Parliamentary Committees, where he would be no match for Dundas, Burke and Francis.

When this was pointed out to Hastings, he wrote to the effect that Scott had been despatched in order to save him some work; that no malice was intended. This was ironic indeed. To Sulivan it was then almost unbelievable that Hastings saw fit to be piqued. He sensed it in their correspondence during 1782 and defended himself vigorously, maintaining his friend was being poisoned against him. His suspicions were correct; the culprits being Major Scott, ruffled at his own helplessness and negativity, and the treacherous John Macpherson, whose cover had not yet been blown. It was fortunate that no umbrage was taken.

5

Having come to terms, somewhat, with the death of his wife, Sulivan's appetite for Company politics returned; and he offered himself for re-election in April 1783. He saw no real obstacles to gaining a share of power. A return to the Direction was also imperative. Stephen and kinsmen: Benjamin, John, and Richard Sulivan, were all in India; as were Eyles Irwin and others he favoured. All of them relied on the backing he could give; and of course Warren Hastings was never far from his thoughts.

The fall of North's ministry in March 1782 was speedily followed by the demise of Rockingham's in July of the same year. Sulivan's expectations rose with the end of this ministry. Among its ranks, in Parliament and at Leadenhall, were some of his most vicious opponents. It is not surprising that their hopes fell in equal amount to the rise in his.

Shelburne, his friend of earlier years, formed a ministry; but Sulivan's dreams of a reunion were doomed. Although the minister's supporters were inclined towards Hastings and himself almost to a man, the minister's need for political support among their enemies in the Commons decided matters. There was also a coolness between them that can be dated to the 1769 crash and to the machinations of Macleane. They met, uncomfortably, at a dinner on 1 November 1782. Shelburne kept 'a princely distance', and Sulivan's pride would not allow the required courting.[32]

Despite Shelburne being 'lost to remembrance', Sulivan was sure he would regain office, though he would have to share with people he disliked intensely.[33] His support in the Company came principally from the Johnstones and Lord North's connections, who had ties with John Macpherson and John Stables. It was a bitter reversal of roles for Sulivan when Shelburne urged Hastings' recall. In December Francis was confident that Sulivan would not be a Director; adding that he would be 'grievously mistaken if he ever gets in again'.[34] Passing judgement on the Irishman, he supposed that 'in Europe there is not so wicked and abandoned a villain'.[35] It was a view that more truly reflected his own depraved nature.

The fall of Shelburne in February 1783 and the appearance of the remarkable, and utterly unstable, Fox-North Coalition, opened the way for yet another attack on Hastings by the Select Committee. In a series of reports, Hastings was severely criticised for his handling of problems in India. These placed Sulivan in deep defensive mode.

With the conclusion of the European war that accompanied and overlapped the American struggle, there was now time for Company business to be debated in the House. Through 'Indian' friends in the Commons Sulivan thought he could fight for the monopoly; but they struggled to maintain its position in the discussions. The problem was these friends supported different groups. Six were deemed to be followers of Pitt the Younger; eight others supported Charles Fox; another three, Sir James Cockburn, Sir Hector Munro and James 'Fingal' Macpherson, would switch to Pitt in 1783.

But even though Sulivan kept up his exertions within Parliament through these men, it was to be of no avail. In the end his contribution was a legacy of past efforts at reform and the massive injection he gave to discussions with ministers and their officials. He also put hard work into getting the shareholders to accept such defined regulations for the better government of India.

6

During the lead-up to the 1783 contest, Sulivan and Sir William James were placed together on the 'Proprietors' list. However, at a meeting held near the end of March, an alternative and rival list of six candidates was proposed and accepted; this one put these two in opposition to one another. It was an anti-Sulivan move. Putting in his shilling's worth, Burke deliberately timed publication of the 7th Report (so hostile to Sulivan) to coincide with the election.

This set the scene, but how the election would turn out would depend upon Lord North. Even though his strange alliance with Charles Fox made the minister appear untrustworthy to all candidates, both sets of supporters,

Burke's through Sir William James and Sulivan's via Woodhouse, beseeched him for assistance. Fortunately for Sulivan, the combination of North's hedging and the appearance of the Select Committee Report, all shortly before the ballot, suggested that an attempt was being made to exclude him. It led to a deputation, headed by Governor Johnstone, forcing North to support him. The minister gave Burke no support for his alternative list and called upon him to prove Sulivan was the criminal he declared him to be.

The success that followed left Sulivan highly elated. There was even a possibility he would accept one of the Chairs. Apart from gratitude for North's crucial backing, he was overflowing with praise for the Johnstones. He launched a public attack upon his enemies and, 'offered a reward in the public papers of 100 guineas for the discovery of the person that wrote the ministerial letters circulated to the Proprietors against me.'[36]

Parliamentary interest in Indian affairs, during and following the Fox-North Coalition of 1783, was stimulated by the Company's financial trouble. It was fed all the way through by the Select Committee Reports stemming from the vitriolic pen of Burke and by proposals in Dundas' Bill. Sulivan was requested to be present at a joint committee of the Company's Treasury and Accounts departments to look into what all this might mean. It was part of Charles Fox's grand pan. A report of September 1783 was to be examined, which recommended that the Chairs inform the ministry that the Company could not pay its bills without Government aid.

Meanwhile, Fox's plan to transfer all Company patronage to Parliament was being drafted into his Bill. Further approaches were made to Sulivan to help smooth their acceptance at Leadenhall. To secure his support and that of Hastings' other friends a compromise over the terms for the Governor-General's return from Bengal was offered. It was unsuccessful. Sulivan's unblinkered understanding of the political reality and his implacable hostility to all that was implied made such a deceit impossible. Although George III hated everything about this ministry, it staggered on. Only when Fox's India Bill appeared on 18 November did things begin to happen. The Bill stimulated reaction in the Company and in Parliament. It forced joint action from disparate groups such as: Hastings' supporters; the 'Arcot interest'; and various factions in the City, and among the shippers.

Sulivan was at the forefront in everything that now happened. After the failed attempts to entangle him during the introduction of Fox's India Bill, he was totally involved with its defeat and the consequences. Only on 18 November were its terms known, but active, organised opposition from within the Company had already commenced. Sulivan, alongside Edward Becher and Hastings' agent, Major Scott, had been collecting materials for the defence. Only the Company Chairman, Henry Fletcher, together with Gregory and seven other Directors joined with Fox.

On 22 November a 'Committee of Nine Proprietors' was set up, whose remit was to defend the Company against the attack on chartered rights inherent in the Bill. Sulivan was its leading light. His presence produced sufficient agreement at Leadenhall; and he had been working closely with

Atkinson and Robinson. Defeat of the Fox Bill also suggested support for Hastings might be attracted among those opposed to it.

Parliamentary Opposition seized the opportunity opening up. In December 1783 Pitt, Thurlow, Dundas, Jenkinson and Robinson pushed the monarch into expressing his disapproval of the Bill. This was enough to kill it. Thurlow kept alive the impression that Fox was destroying the Constitution and reserving all Company's patronage for himself. Thereafter, Sulivan (considered a Northite by everyone but himself) said that he was 'lost to all remembrance by Lord North and his friends' because of his organisation of Company hostility to the Bill.[37] He went on to say that the minister 'and all his connections abandoned me in this hour as they had before done in Parliament; and peace be with them all to Eternity'.[38]

He now controlled the 'Committee of Nine Proprietors', appointed in November 1783 by the General Court to watch over rights and privileges. It had co-ordinated the combined Parliamentary and Company opposition to the Bill and was to hold the initiative in Company matters until June 1784. He made sure the 'Committee of Nine Proprietors' now backed Hastings to the hilt.

Throughout the winter of 1783-4, he was alert, negotiating the best terms for the Governor-General's return. A softer attitude towards Hastings had been presented by the Fox-North Government; a line dictated by the problems it faced, but nobody was fooled. Eventually, however, a signal did arrive that confirmed Sulivan's protection had been successful. At the General Court of 7 November 1783, called by Sulivan and friends to congratulate Hastings on the ending of the Maratha war, the Proprietors thanked the Governor-General for all he had done. Sulivan believed the end of war had brought this turnabout. He became emotional:

> Instead of the Company being, annihilated past redemption, with my advice to return as soon as possible…Genius (so says Lord Mansfield) has brought about a wonderful and sudden revolution and you have the principal merit of saving the Company in England as you have done in India. Can man rise higher?[39]

Sulivan was usually self-effacing, never mentioning his own input. He would endlessly praise Hastings' achievements. This time, however, he could not restrain himself: 'And it is a pleasant reflection to your friend, which he will enjoy in his latest moments that we have fought back to back in this glorious conflict.'[40] Later he added the significant comment that the removal of the Fox-North ministry had probably saved the day. He still advised Hastings to prepare to come home; then, sensing the initiative lay with his friend, urged him (in the immediate term) to stay a little longer.

17

Closing of an Era
1782-86

1

In December 1783 the Fox-North Coalition was replaced by the ministry of William Pitt the Younger. He was pledged to bring about change in the field of Indian administration, introduced by the now departed Fox and North. He was forced, therefore, to deal with Hastings, with Sulivan's defence of the Governor-General's position, and with public concern.

Directors and Proprietors alike were now conscious of the threat to the organisation's existence; of the need for reform in its government, home and abroad. There was some understanding that a better relationship with the State must be forged. Others were now as determined as Sulivan to protect privileges and hang on to the last vestiges of independence.

The able Parliamentarian Richard Atkinson served as the main contact with Sulivan and an aroused, prickly Company. He was particularly friendly with Francis Baring and his friends in the Direction, who together formed the 'City' interest. This group had joined with Sulivan and the Hastings party in the struggle against Charles Fox. Progress pivoted around Atkinson winning support within the Company for the young Pitt. Sulivan worked with him for the good of the Company, for Hastings, and for himself. Atkinson laboured for his own (secret) aims, as well as for Pitt. Together, they had disproved Fox's allegations of the Company's financial instability.

Pitt soon displayed his political adroitness. Recognising Sulivan's strength, he was secretly adamant from the start that he would not be allowed to dominate the Company; or bring about the much-needed reforms from within. Sulivan was completely in the dark to these views at this point. He, meanwhile, was using the 'Committee of Nine Proprietors' to re-establish the ascendancy of his own, or what was sometimes termed, the 'Indian' or 'Old' interest.

By January 1784 the Direction and the General Court had been brought around to accepting a resolution supporting the Pitt-Dundas scheme for reform. Sulivan, working with Atkinson and James Macpherson, was certainly the instigator in these moves since the 'Committee of Nine', which he led, pushed this action. He was also asked to occupy the Chair whenever this Committee was asked to wait upon His Majesty's ministers. The alliance with Government was cemented, therefore, just as Pitt desired. The Company agreed to work with the minister upon whatever terms for reform in India he should produce.

These were not long in preparation; and although some clauses were ambiguous, he obtained a general agreement. The minister then listened to any modifications. Yet even while he was suggesting some of these adjustments, Sulivan was pushing Pitt's main proposals through the two Company Courts. Almost immediately afterwards, on 12 January, the Bill was introduced into the Commons. It failed on the 23rd, and Indian reform was delayed.

Thus, prior to the April 1784 national election (where he was certainly helped by Sulivan) Pitt had tried to act decisively. The time had also been appropriate because the Company was more relaxed after the defeat of Fox's Bill and pre-occupied with its financial worries. The Court of Directors too was disorganised following the forced resignation of Chairman Fletcher. Now, following the failure to push the India Bill through the House, Pitt was faced with the problem of how to manage the Company while the Act was in abeyance.

He was thrown back upon the system of patronage used so successfully by North. The agents were to be Atkinson and Baring. Their proposals boiled down to the minister nominating the Chairmen annually, thus effectually managing the course of business. Pitt refused to do this; so Atkinson and Baring then suggested he should make Sulivan all-powerful. Pitt turned this down too.

Sulivan was well aware that he was being backed by Atkinson and Baring. He also knew about their partnership 'in contracts'; of Atkinson's links with North, Robinson and James Macpherson; and of Baring's ties with Shelburne. The worst part was that he also believed (until shortly before his election to the Direction in April 1784) that they were friends of his and of Hastings, as well as now being true to Pitt.

It was during the lead-up and course of this 1784 election that the full extent of the duplicity emanating from Westminster, from within the Company, and from so-called friends was laid bare. Sulivan's hesitation as events unfolded reflects the difficulty he had in accepting these deceptions.

Within the Company it was now obvious that he was the real power. He was helped in that from December 1783 to January 1784 there was unexpected harmony among the Directors. However, the uncertain political climate at Westminster meant, as he knew all too well, there could be no permanent alignments at Leadenhall. When he was offered the post of Deputy Chair, his reasons for turning it down were vague: that 'he had secret notice of the impending storm that was to annihilate the Company'; that his 'mind and body required some tranquillity'.[1] These excuses reflect the disturbing information he was receiving.

Until March he held firm: 'I will take a respectable line on the new Direction but I will fill no Chair.'[2] Then he relented and admitted to Hastings that 'the pressing wish of my friends may possibly force me back if (as is suggested) Mr. Pitt should make the request'.[3] It was then that he found out how base his supposed friends were. Not only would there be great opposition from his enemies Burke and Fox, his 'friends' Atkinson, Baring, Robinson and James Macpherson would challenge him as well.

Pitt also played him false; while secretly instructing Atkinson and Baring that he did not want Sulivan in either Chair, he received the old Company man most handsomely. At this private meeting Pitt said (deceitfully) how much he wished to see him occupy the premier executive position. He also spoke of how he expected Sulivan to hold his own against the imminent attack by Fox and Burke.

Sulivan accepted Pitt's observations with good grace, saying that he was more concerned that his honour had not been sullied than anything else. The fact was he already knew the truth. It came from many mouths: from John Robinson, who had added that the minister would not protect him from an attack; and from 'Fingal' Macpherson.[4]

The Scot's treachery now showed, when he advised Sulivan that he should 'submit to place Messrs. Baring and Atkinson in the Chairs for this year only, but reserving real power to himself'.[5] Sulivan deduced by 'Fingal's' pleading for men he now knew to be enemies and in the Pitt camp, that he was being duped. He made it public knowledge that though he would not solicit a Chair, neither would he now decline one.

The further activities of James Macpherson and John Robinson in pushing every interest in favour of Baring and Atkinson galvanised him into action; and before the election seventeen Directors had pledged him the Chair, with the nomination of his Deputy.[6] He knew he and Hastings were secure, which suggested the best approach was to take the position. This roused Pitt to interfere once more, and he was just able to convince Sulivan that 'an inferior situation this year would best answer every purpose'.[7]

In that all future dealings would be with the Pitt ministry, Sulivan probably thought he had little choice. Yet, even as late as 18 April, it was proposed by others that he should occupy the top post. This might indicate he was still mulling things over. It is a view substantiated by Richard Sulivan; and Atkinson seemed to suggest the same thing: 'He could not be prevailed upon to wait a year out of the Chair.'[8] What probably sealed things was Dundas' decided negative; which was enough to destroy any grand plan of his to take control regardless.

He then firmly brought forward Devaynes and Smith. The former was generally in support of Hastings, thus had credit. Nathaniel Smith was one of his own followers.[9] Through the 'Committee of Nine Proprietors' he also carried the selection of Governor Johnstone, Richard Atkinson (for private reasons) and Woodhouse. Fox's six nominees were defeated. Sulivan's comment to his son summed up his mastery: 'Thus Messrs. Robinson, Macpherson, Atkinson and Baring have been smothered in their own Pit – and instead of sharing power with me, which they might have, they are now of no consequence whatever.'[10]

When all was done and dusted, although Pitt could do nothing about Sulivan's entrenched position within the Company, he had managed, by negotiation, flattery and pure artifice to clear the way inside the organisation for his Bill. Only Sulivan's genuine wish to see the reform proposals inherent in the proposed Act implemented explains his complacency; especially in the face of Pitt's double-dealing. The first minister then gained a majority in Parliament following the national election success of April 1784, again with help from the Company. The new India Bill was finally enacted in July of that year.

Sulivan was involved to the very end: smoothing the way within India House; ensuring acceptance of the Pitt ministry there; pushing for the Dundas-Pitt proposals; and afterwards, working tirelessly for acceptance of the Act within the Company. He could also maintain he had some share in its original conception; could lay particular claim to the clauses that strengthened the powers of the Governor-General in Bengal; and to ensuring that everyone in charge abroad was answerable to the Government in London.

2

During Hastings' final years in India, Sulivan knew there were traitors working against both their interests. He had spoken of his suspicions as early as June 1781. But it took a long time to discover that John Macpherson and John Stables, both in Bengal, and James Macpherson in London were their worst enemies. They had relied upon these men and their associate, John Stewart.

The old Irishman had even chosen John Macpherson to be Richard Barwell's replacement in the Supreme Council; and had then forwarded a glowing character reference. Hastings too was totally deceived. In the case of 'Fingal', Sulivan had always been impressed by his confidential relationship with North and Robinson. That this connection did not waken danger signals was probably because of the subsequent support given by both Macphersons to the Hastings cause. In 1781, he had chosen Stables to fill Francis' vacancy in the Supreme Council, thinking he would consolidate the Governor-General's position. Unknown to Hastings and himself, he was Robinson's man and in league with John Macpherson.

From 1778 the two Scotsmen had played their double-cross with finesse, maintaining a close relationship with the ministry, pursuing their own ends; and all the while keeping the face of friendship turned towards Sulivan and Hastings. It was unknown at first, that Atkinson, 'Fingal' and John Macpherson were all members of the 'Arcot interest' and discreetly tied to Benfield and others at Madras.

Since it was the aim of the 'Arcot interest' to line their own pockets, they wanted cancellation of the assignment of the Carnatic revenues. Atkinson and the Macphersons were after full settlement of the Nawab's private debts, by which they would benefit. What is more, they wanted it done without investigation into the validity of the amounts. Sulivan shared these sentiments, not because of the aims of the 'Arcot interest' or because of his own pecuniary difficulties, but rather to buttress Hastings. The Governor-General had annulled Macartney's Carnatic assignment in order to have his authority over Madras recognised; and to fit with his view of affairs from his seat in Calcutta. Sulivan always backed Hastings.

Doubts about the trustworthiness of 'Fingal' began to trouble Sulivan from October 1781; but he had no proof and could only advise Hastings to be cautious. Then he more or less negated this advice by expressing his belief that 'Fingal's' friend John Macpherson was spotless. In 1782 he wallowed in the thought of how firmly Hastings was being supported by Stables and John Macpherson, saying things like, 'Stables has been always yours.'[11] Only in March 1783 did Hastings discover the duplicity of both. Sulivan did not know until April 1784. In fact, in December 1783 he was still writing 'My dear Mac', quite freely, and was appalled when all was made clear:

> Oh my friend, what has availed my labours, my influence? I have sent snakes to your bosom and have been the dupe of Macpherson and Stables, they acting under their General here…but you and I very lately have blown up a deep plan that would have thrown the patronage of Asia into the hands of 3 persons, couple this with the history of the Chairs that Scot[t] gives you, and I will be understood.[12]

By November 1784, having had time to reflect upon things and gain more facts, he was able to state (to his son) what he thought had been finally exposed. Presumably, the plot would have placed 'the patronage of Asia' into the hands of Robinson (the General), Atkinson and John Macpherson. He was 'happy for this country that their power was at an end'.[13]

3

Because of Sulivan's support for him, in or out of the Direction, Macartney kept in touch. When, in September 1782 he heard of the ministerial changes in London, he paid Sulivan a handsome compliment. He was not sure how the revolutions at national level would affect India affairs, but was sure of one thing:

> whoever took the lead in Leadenhall…will find the task very difficult and laborious…and will soon greatly regret the want of our good friend from Queen Square. In truth, I consider him from his

experience and assiduous attention to our affairs, as absolutely necessary to carry them on.[14]

At the end of March 1783 his affection was just as strong; and John Sulivan had informed him: 'Our old friend in Queen Square would certainly be in the Chair next April (1783). I fear much that he will not accept it.[15] Macartney hoped Sulivan would continue 'to lend (his) able hand to calm and compose...the troubled sea of Indian Affairs.'[16]

Although at this stage Sulivan was still seen as fair and fresh, Macartney continued his litany of criticism and condemnation of what was around him. Hastings was severely censured, repetitively blamed for the Maratha war and the collapse of Madras. He also maintained, 'The whole system on the Coast is wrong. It was well suited to a commercial factory, but now totally inadequate to the management of your present possessions.'[17] He went on to say that he did not possess sufficient powers to maintain discipline: that he needed full military authority and the sole power of appointment. No councillor should have any other employment. There should be only one army, the King's or the Company's, and they must obey the Governor. These were views strikingly similar to Sulivan's own.

Macartney continued to counter Hastings by believing that nothing but immediate peace would save the day. Only this and the policies he suggested would do. If not, 'they (the territories) will assuredly slip away from you in a few years, and your Asiatic Empire will be lost like your American.'[18] He repeated his conviction that the whole future of the Carnatic was based on the assignment; that all would be anarchy and distress if this was changed. This Irish Lord then complained once more of Hastings' antagonism and spoke of leaving, finishing with the words that he had 'acted upon great public principles, as an honest man and a good Englishman'.[19]

Sulivan was on the receiving end from both Hastings and Macartney. In the Supreme Council, Macartney's suspension was called for over alleged ill-treatment of the Nawab. Hastings was fed up with his sarcasm; opposition to the policy of keeping the Nizam of Hyderabad and the Marathas apart; and hostility to the cancellation of the assignment. Macartney would not change anything, and a stalemate was reached. When in 1784 the Supreme Council would not oblige the Governor-General, all the issues went to India House to be resolved; and, as far as Macartney was concerned, to seek redress.

Although he was largely responsible for Macartney becoming Governor of Madras, Sulivan never deviated in his support for Hastings. The upshot was that when Macartney realised he would always take Hastings' side, all correspondence ceased. Stephen Sulivan received a vivid account of what then happened in London:

> At an interview with his lady, which she earnestly solicited, the decency and good sense she possesses forsook her. The expressions she used against Mr. Hastings and me were too strong for your father to bear and I parted with observing that

when her Ladyship became cool and temperate I might renew my
visit; which is, however, what I never mean. Neither Lord nor
Lady Macartney gave just cause for their behaviour. But I am
warranted in charging him with ingratitude, for he alone knows
what he owes to me.[20]

He finished by expressing his exasperation, 'after this detail be you not
surprised that I am still an infidel'.[21]

4

In 1784 Richard Atkinson wished to cancel the assignment of the Carnatic
Revenues* and liquidate the creditors' claims. Self-interest lay behind this
proposal. He was the agent for Paul Benfield, the most notorious creditor,
and both were part of the 'Arcot interest'.* Despite his suspicions, Sulivan
was ready to support Atkinson, on condition that he would publicly join
forces; and that the cancellation of the assignment would be to the benefit of
the Company. This, however, was not in the 'Arcot Interest' plans. The
Macphersons, also members of this group, were working hand in glove with
Atkinson. Consequently, John Macpherson, the Nawab's influential agent, in
collusion with his other creditors, stirred the Prince to deliberately play off
their claims against those of the Company.

Atkinson and Macpherson had already swung over to Pitt the Younger in
national politics; a move at least partly influenced by their interest in ensuring
the assignment was cancelled and the creditors paid. However, for many
reasons Sulivan did not want the creditors claims investigated and paid:
foremost was his suspicion that the Company was to be left out; bad
publicity; and enhanced suspicions that the Board was dancing to the wishes
of Atkinson and others in the 'Arcot Interest'.

This drove him to influence fellow Directors to object on the grounds
that: 'whilst the Nawab continues to declare that all his debts are just…to
enquire into the grounds of his debts appears therefore wholly useless.'[22] He
wanted the clause cancelling the assignment and liquidating the creditors'
claims excluded from Pitt's Bill. Nevertheless, the paragraph remained, due
to Pitt's fear of a Burke and Fox attack.

John Call, of the 'Arcot interest', put new pressure on Pitt and Dundas to
validate the creditors' claims, and pushed for cancellation of the assignment.
However, Nathaniel Smith, the Company Chairman, was now as resolutely
opposed as Sulivan; he disliked the 'Arcot interest' and he too wanted
Company claims to come first. He proposed an annulment of the assignment
(that is, declaring it invalid). This secured Sulivan's support and that of others
uneasy with the 'Arcot interest'. The Chairman next queried the activities of
Benfield and John Macpherson; and the Madras Government was ordered to
pay only those claims that were obviously legal. Sulivan and all his interest
again supported Chairman Smith's proposals, and Atkinson was abandoned.

By late October 1784 control of the Direction had fallen into Sulivan's hands; Dundas, reported that 'a determined faction in the India House' was operating against the ministry.[23] As far as Sulivan was concerned, since an annulment of the assignment satisfied the Governor-General's requirements, then that was enough for him. He felt no qualms about discarding Atkinson, now known to have been intriguing against him at the April 1784 election. By then the opposition of the 'Arcot interest' to himself and Hastings was also known; and the deceit of the Macphersons uncovered.

Following the passage of the India Bill, the India Board began studying the debts.[24] Political weight was brought to bear on Dundas and the Board of Control to settle the creditors' demands; and Dundas hoped the Directors would yield to its suggestions. Sulivan, however, seized upon what he saw as an opportunity (perhaps even contrived at by him) of putting Dundas and Atkinson in a predicament. He made certain the majority of the Directors stood firm on a particular point: that the origin of the Consolidated Loan of 1777 was obscure. Dundas had to agree, but skated around everything by saying the Nawab had recognised all his debts.

The Directors did not reply. There was no need to; Sulivan's aim had been achieved, he had brought the matter to the public's notice. On 28 February 1785 Fox and Burke moved for papers on the Arcot debts; and they subsequently charged Dundas with malpractice in conducting negotiations through the 'Arcot interest', by using Atkinson.[25] By bringing the whole issue of the Nawab's debts into the open, the creditors' wish to secure the money with no questions asked was foiled; and there was better chance of the Company being paid, which was Sulivan's main wish.

5

Macartney's original action of procuring the assignment of the Carnatic revenues was annulled in June 1785. He then resigned. At Leadenhall Sulivan had already taken steps in case the Governor stood down. In December 1784 he had moved for Mr. Hollond to succeed as Governor. Undoubtedly this was because the choice of Macartney as Hastings' successor would have placed him in an impossible situation.

The enmity of the two Governors loomed large. Nor had he forgotten his own distasteful scene with Macartney's wife. Yet what bothered him most was that the contest was to be between Macartney and George Vansittart, brother of his deceased friend, Henry Vansittart. Sulivan did not vote; the Directors split, 10:10, and the issue was decided by drawing a ball. Macartney was the lucky one. He, meanwhile, had gone to Calcutta, and it was there that he was offered the post of Governor-General. Hastings had already left for home.

In a letter of explanation to Macartney in March 1785, Sulivan tried, ineffectually, to justify why he did not vote for him. He maintained that he had been given the impression that all intercourse was at an end. He added that since his own 'conduct…has been seemingly hostile', he would explain

things and also put a stop to the lies of his enemies. He then accused
Macartney, among other things of reducing the Nawab to a mere cipher; and
not taking care of captives left in Tipu's hands. He listed the prejudices and
opposition he had stirred in India.[26]

Despite these criticisms, he concluded, if Macartney should accept the
position of Governor-General, he could expect his full support. But this
would be done only 'in all instances where your conduct shall (in my own
judgement) coincide with the Company's and the National interest.'[27] But
Macartney declined to become the next Governor-General of India, because
he wanted and was refused, absolute control over the army.[28]

6

In 1782, through his father's exertions, and aided and abetted by Hastings,
Stephen was nominated for one of two vacancies in the Supreme Council at
Calcutta. The choice of Charles Stuart and Sulivan's son caused ripples in the
Company.[29] George Cuming, of the shipping interest, charged that Sulivan
had gone too far; and that he was turning senile. Stephen had maintained that
by getting him a seat in the Supreme Council his father would unite 'Power
with Profit'. If not, he would have the 'mortification to find that the
Chairman of the East India Company has not carried the seat...for his only
son'. He warned also that 'if a Minister should prevent it' he would return to
England.[30]

In a postscript to this letter, he scribbled that he had just learned of his
appointment, and gushed: 'I scruple not therefore, to thank you a thousand
and a thousand times.' He was also placed upon the 'supernumerary service'
list, which pleased Sulivan because he could be accumulating money without
the ties of office. It was a letter that carried even greater news, his wife
expected their child to be born around the middle of December 1782.[31]

A hint that Stephen might become Hastings' agent did not materialize.
Nevertheless, the emoluments already granted considerably fattened his
official annual salary of 2,000 rupees (approximately £200). Stephen was also
given the agency for supplying the Royal fleet in India, then under command
of Admiral Sir Edward Hughes. The Admiral helped because of friendship
with Robert Palk. By 1784, however, Sulivan senior was concerned, because
by virtue of this contract, Admiral Hughes was cut off from his own
emoluments; and in order to gain the agency for himself had landed Stephen
in trouble with naval superiors. Sulivan pleaded with Hastings to shield his
son.

It was not until 1782 that Stephen was in a position to remit money home.
Some funds arrived via a scaled down version of Sulivan's consortium idea.
Friends like Pechell, Caillaud and Motteux used this conglomerate to receive
remittances. Stephen, John Sulivan and his brother Henry Boyle Sulivan,
together with John Cox-Hippisley used this channel. In India everything was
controlled by John Sulivan. In London, Sulivan was then able to free his son
from 'every other person to whom you stand indebted.'[32]

Stephen had disappointments to face as well as successes. He was prevented from gaining two posts in Oudh: that of Paymaster, the other a 'Commissarship'. His letters began to reflect weariness with India, and a longing to resume the life his father had prepared him for. Remitting money proved difficult, despite his father's alternate channels; but it was absolutely vital that he persevere. Sulivan wanted his son home, but not until he had put together a moderate fortune.

Early in 1784 Sulivan was 'still distressed for shirts', that is, short of cash. He could not even use two Lottery tickets that had brought a prize of £20 each. Stephen's Bengal bills, worth £16,900, were unobtainable, because the Company was paying them out only optionally over three years. By 1784 the situation had turned even worse, if that was possible. It was doubly frustrating because he could not touch a fund now standing at £26,000. However, by December 1784 'young Thomas Lane' had been repaid; and Stephen had remitted sufficient funds to satisfy Mr. Jeckyll and some others. Some outstanding debts due to his son were difficult to recover, such as the one owed by a Mr. Livins.[33]

Until 1784 the Sulivan family had lived in a state very close to penury. Disaster was averted, but only because of the kindness of friends. From the moment Stephen arrived upon Indian soil, he was urged to remit money home. Sulivan called upon all his own channels for this, as well as those provided by others. John Sulivan in particular, made strenuous efforts on his namesake's behalf.

Sulivan came up with the novel idea of having funds remitted through the 'new' trade in raw silk that he had been encouraging. Yet another route was via Navy and Victualling bills from one or all of the Presidencies. A word of warning was added: 'you should find out some (certainly safe) channel…because the Company will hardly be able, for some years to come, to pay their Bills but at long credit'.[34]

If the note of June 1786 entitled: 'Debts of Laurence Sulivan undischarged at the time of his death' is used as a yardstick, then he failed to remedy the disaster that began in 1769. He still owed £23,000: £6,000 to Vansittart's estate; £4,000 to Palk; £7,000 to Hastings; and £6,000 to John Sulivan. Stephen later added a few lines to this note: 'John Sulivan made it easier to pay by accepting what he was due from the paper…in India.' Vansittart's estate was repaid in £1,000 instalments.[35]

However, this gives a wrong image; it does not tell what Sulivan had really done. The father had not left his son hopelessly encumbered. He had procured offices for Stephen by which the Sulivan fortunes were revived before his death. As early as 1784 enough to clear all debts were en route from India. He had located channels for remittance of these funds; and it was only a matter of time before the transfers were completed. In many respects too, it suited the Sulivans to owe this money in England while their security for it remained in India.

The complications involved in securing a great deal of Sulivan's own money in India is exemplified by a bond for 37,000 pagodas (worth about

£15,000) which the Nawab of Arcot granted in February 1785 to John Stewart, in trust for him. The whole issue cropped up in Parliament in May 1806.[36]

In his address to the Commons John Sulivan said: 'The bond to Mr. Stuart (John Stewart) in trust for Mr. Sulivan...is dated 5 February 1785. Mr. Sulivan was informed of this transaction in the summer of 1785.' Sulivan asked to have the bond cancelled because, although honourable and above board, he was a public figure, which made it open to misconstruction.

Following Sulivan's death in February 1786 Stephen (who inherited the bond) found that his father's assets did not equal his liabilities and was obliged to use it to settle with his creditors. It was eventually examined in 1788 at Madras, admitted to be just, and was to be paid with interest accruing from February 1785.[37]

Before he died, Sulivan had secured everything of importance to himself and his son; meaning that Ponsborne estate and the house in Hanover Square, were safe. In February 1785 he held sufficient India stock to retain qualification as a Director. £4,000 cash became Stephen's on 2 May 1786, by virtue of his father's Administration. Stephen also inherited potentially lucrative land holdings in Prince Edward Island. There were five lots, each lot amounting to 20,000 acres; all were in part payment of the debts owed him by Lauchlin Macleane.[38] Sulivan had won back for himself and his family the independence and self-respect they craved.

18

Endings
1784-86

1

In June 1784 Atkinson supposed Sulivan would never again be allowed to take the lead in the Company. He gauged that his attitude towards Pitt, to Dundas and to himself would remain forever hostile and this would exclude him. Sulivan had a somewhat different view, he saw no great obstacles in his way to the Chair in April 1785 and if his health held good, meant to take it.

He was helped by the Commutation Act of August 1784, which brought down the duty on tea, made an impact upon tea smuggling and established a monopoly of its importation by the Company. This increased sales and thus the demand for tonnage. The 'Old' shippers, many of them already his friends, who knew of his involvement were very pleased and assured him of their support. They could quickly produce the necessary ships, unlike the 'New' shippers.

By January 1785 Atkinson had changed his views. In a remarkable assessment, expressed in two letters to Dundas, he concluded that there was little hope of reducing Sulivan's power in the Direction. He even suggested that his Chairmanship might be the best choice open to Government in order to proceed with further reforms. He knew that Sulivan shared this desire. Ministerial support, he argued, would be a means of keeping some control over him. Before the April 1785 election, however, the ministry had managed to woo Devaynes with the promise of backing for his re-election to the Chair.

As late as March 1785, Sulivan toyed with the idea of taking the post himself. The need to support his son and kinsmen drove him on; and Hastings' return from India was imminent. He wanted the best deal for his friend so shrugged off his own advanced years and Pitt's constant veto. He was still a force to be reckoned with.

He was up against stiff ministerial opposition, however. Dundas had worked to deprive the Company of its remaining powers and to establish himself as the supreme authority. Atkinson, on the other hand, was concerned with reform and with his 'Arcot interest'. He was convinced restructuring could only be achieved with Sulivan's help. To succeed, he saw that either Parliament appointed the monopoly's leaders, in so doing taking power from Sulivan, or Pitt, Dundas and Sulivan would have to come to terms.

Pitt refused point-blank to entertain the latter course of action and prevented Atkinson from making a bargain with Sulivan. Dundas preferred to think he could gain control at the 1785 election. Not to be deterred, Atkinson pressed ahead and he and Sulivan struck a private deal. Sulivan promised to join with ministerial intentions if his friends Darell, Townson and Major John Scott were supported. Pitt and Dundas refused to contemplate this. Accordingly, although at the election Sulivan was not selected for the Deputy Chair, and Dundas gained control over the new Chairman Devaynes and his Deputy, Smith, Sulivan and his interest commanded the Direction.

Atkinson had correctly foreseen there would be total frustration of ministerial desires, no matter how it acted. Gone now were sarcastic terms like 'dotage', 'veteran' and 'senility' to describe this able man. In his second (extraordinarily objective) scrutiny, shortly before his own unexpected death in May 1785, he measured the other members of the Direction against him, testing ability and skill in building relationships against the old Irishman. He was filled with reluctant admiration as his analyses revealed the quicksilver mind and political adroitness of his adversary.

Since the Pitt ministry's inception in December 1783, while still maintaining a defensive shield, Sulivan had sought the best terms for Hastings should he be forced to return. Everything was so unresolved and uncertain throughout January and February 1784 he could not say whether the Company would continue or not. To Hastings he said ruefully, it all depended upon, 'A Pitt or a Fox...Poor old England.'[1]

By March 1784, however, he was fairly certain his friend was safe; and in April urged him to stay another year, because Pitt's Act would only be effective after supplementary legislation in 1786. Then, sometime before July 1784, after the Act was passed, he changed his views again. He sensed further danger stemming from the Pitt ministry. In September he nominated Edward Wheler to succeed Hastings; but this was not acceptable to others in the Company or to the Board of Control where Dundas favoured Macartney. After he refused the post, Pitt, not the Company, then appealed successfully to Cornwallis.

Sulivan had to be satisfied with securing a sound financial settlement for the outgoing Governor-General, and proposed that he should have '10 lakhs quartered upon Clive's jaghire'.[2] At first there was little objection to this, although no honours would be entertained. By October, however, he was aware of new hostility; and within the Direction he had a struggle to even get a vote of thanks for Hastings.

He continued his opposition to the Board of Control's plans for the Nawab of Arcot's debts; but in November, while these were being discussed, the ministry's coolness to him and the askance view it took of Hastings were made public.[3] The unfriendliness stemmed from Dundas in particular. He began to criticise the power of the Directors over appointments to the various governments in India; and manoeuvred to place this solely with the Board. He also continued to work for Hastings' speedy removal. Sulivan replied in kind, such as by proposing John Hollond as successor to Macartney, in opposition to Dundas' favourite, General Sir Archibald Campbell. He also called for Hastings to be continued for a year after his successor had been appointed. Dundas, of course, objected to both suggestions.

Alas, despite all Sulivan's manoeuvres, the critical moment had arrived, marking the end of the Company executive's prerogative of making appointments. Transfer of power was taking place, despite his best efforts to the contrary, and the Board of Control had in effect become the supreme decision-making authority. Sulivan's guardianship of the Company's chartered rights was nearly at an end. After a long rearguard defence, power had finally slipped away to Westminster.

His protection of Hastings was very nearly ended too. He urged his friend's speedy return; his wife Marion was already home. Hastings resigned and left Calcutta in February, arriving in June 1785, never ever having contemplated (as has been suggested) an American style 'Declaration of Independence' from the Company or from the British Government. In London he was feted and thanked by the Directors for his work in India. It is not difficult to see Sulivan's hand here as well.

After his return Hastings understood better all that Sulivan had done for him, and never forgot his benefactor. Sulivan's portrait was to hang in a place of honour in Daylesford House. The ties remained strong: in 1795, nine years after his father had passed away, Stephen Sulivan was at Hastings' post-impeachment victory dinner.

The Governor-General's return also marked the end of a decade and a half of Sulivan-Hastings correspondence. It is an extraordinary testimony to their coalition; and forms one of the clearest and most continuous discussions upon Indian affairs and associated topics from 1770 to 1786. Sulivan's observations show understanding and acute analysis of ongoing changes in his own environment. He had unique insight, perceiving the real springs of action when hidden from most. This reached as far as India. These private letters dealt with much of public life. Sulivan toyed with the idea of turning his own epistles into a diary; then changed his mind, believing that this would try his time and Hastings' patience.

He was probably right, but posterity owes a large debt to both. Probably inescapably, it has been the Hastings end of the correspondence that has been dwelt upon by writers without number. It seems incredible that

Sulivan's contribution has been so overlooked. Surely it must have struck someone that he had been writing to a useful and probably extraordinary man if he continued such a long conversation with him.

Without this alliance the Governor-General could not have remained in office. In every sense he owed his public career and its continuance to his friend in India House. Sulivan's support was sustained for a variety of reasons, some altruistic, some not. Partly it was because Hastings was so able, thus about natural justice. At the same time his protégé served as a channel for his own ideas, even if only indirectly applied. He also hoped the powerful Governor-General would be stimulated by his faithful support, to help him and his son. Last but not least, Hastings was his personal choice, and that was always important to Laurence Sulivan.

2

Sulivan took things a bit easier following the April 1785 election. He still had a year to run in the Direction; and the firm support he enjoyed among his fellow Directors was vouchsafed far beyond his exit by rotation the next April. There was also renewed respect for him as a politician and fighter. Throughout 1785 he remained in command of his 'troops', but made little effort to lay the foundations for future political management. This is readily explained by the return of Hastings, by his age and the fact that the future welfare of Stephen, his wife and the precious baby grandson, Laurence, was assured.

He divined the direction of Dundas' further expansionist ideas at the Board of Control; and his ready presence was a deterrent to any over-zealous activity. He remained a barrier, an object of dislike and irritation to both the Pitt Government and to its opponents in Parliament, like Edmund Burke. This formidable foe said: 'I know hardly any of the Directors except enemies, by sight, the enemy (he referred to Sulivan of course) I know very well.'[4]

Not unnaturally, chartered rights, defence of Hastings, retrieval of his financial independence through Stephen, and furtherance of the careers of his immediate kinsmen had occupied most of Sulivan's thoughts. However, he had spent time and effort in bringing his plans to fruition, many of which had been germinating for a long time

He also perceived that it could only be through ideas apparently formulated within, and emanating from the Company (and not seen as his alone) that any of the reforms he held precious had a hope of being realised. They would then have to be channelled upwards into ministerial hands. It was fortunate that Dundas directed a favourable eye on most suggestions, though not on Sulivan himself. It was doubly fortunate that Sulivan was able to ensure that Atkinson (before his death) and Dundas understood his proposals. The shrewd campaigner knew the future lay with the Board of Control but hoped to influence the shape of things to come.

His blueprints dealt with the future nature and purpose of the Company's Committees; and the way patronage was to be organised at home and abroad.

His ideas were laid before the Directors in March 1785. A letter from Atkinson to Dundas on 31 January makes it evident that Sulivan had previously aired them with that writer, and he in turn with Dundas. Before his own death in May, Atkinson had gained Dundas' support for these reforms.

Sulivan recommended that the system be simplified by regrouping the existing twelve committees into three divisions: political, military and commercial. Corresponding groups of committees were to come into existence at Calcutta, Madras and Bombay. He also pointed out there had been no change in the Company's rules since 1707, which had led to a lack of accurate accounting and only a 'conjectural estimate'. Although brilliantly conceived, his scheme was doomed to failure because of the patronage factors involved.

He made yet a further attempt to achieve the improvements sought. This was based on a scheme brought forward by the Chairman, Nathaniel Smith, though clearly owing its existence to Sulivan's prototype. In this, the twelve Committees were to be grouped into three classes. Sulivan proposed that the Committees of Correspondence and Warehouses should be the most important. The first of these was to confine itself to political matters and have nothing to do with commerce; that would be handled by the Committee of Warehouses.[5] Eventually, the Direction (with Dundas' blessing) allowed the plans to be promoted in India, as Sulivan had suggested; and division into Boards went ahead there.

These plans, dealing with the Company's organisation, began to be overlapped by his earlier ones. Meanwhile, the Directors faced the problem of Company debts abroad now amounting to £8 million, which had to be funded. Sulivan's proposal was one among many put forward for establishing credit in India.[6] In June 1785 Dundas accepted Sulivan's figures; and agreed with his argument that the charges in India should be transferred to London and formed into a permanent debt at a fixed interest.

Dundas' plan followed in September 1785, based on those of Sulivan and his fellow Directors; and in turn was accepted by the Company's Secret Committee (which included Sulivan). Sulivan replied to heated opposition within the Company by affirming that his own ideas, and those of the Secret Committee, were almost exactly the ones being promulgated by Dundas. In his rebuttal, he fumed that the very poverty of understanding shown, in itself emphasised what was needed; and that their feeble views only strengthened his views.

In October 1785 he opposed Dundas' proposal to allow the French East India Company to trade once more in India. In this he was ably helped by Hastings. Both feared French political and military encroachment. Hastings continued to oppose Dundas on this issue after Sulivan was gone; but the minister became too powerful and a commercial treaty with France was eventually established.

3

The last duty Sulivan embarked upon was Hastings' defence against possible Impeachment. Sulivan's words to his friend in 1778 had been prophetic: 'Pray bring home every material that may be of future use to justify your public conduct (for that day must certainly come) in support of your own honour and condemnation of your enemies.'[7]

He worked alongside Hastings, after his arrival, creating a shield against the looming attack by Francis and Burke. If he had lived, Sulivan's defence would have stated the charges were motivated by rank hatred, not principle. The arraignment gives all the appearance of a deliberate act of savagery. This is how a great number of contemporaries saw it. Half the kingdom, as Thurlow, the Lord Chancellor put it, considered Burke little better than 'an ingenious madman'. In an epigram the poet Robert Burns exhibited how far and wide such revulsion had spread: 'Oft I have wonder'd that on Irish ground/No poisonous Reptile ever has been found:/Revealed the secret stands of great Nature's work:/She preserved her poison to create a Burke!'[8]

The great orator's earlier attack on Sulivan through the Select Committee was only the precursor. That interrogation too was personal and vindictive; but Sulivan only played a John the Baptist to the role Hastings was to fill. He was to be struck down. Frustration and pent-up malice, made worse by Sulivan's scorn, seem to have unbalanced him. Hastings was to be the ultimate victim and the sublime gratification.

Glorification of it all in the spectacle at Westminster Hall spells this out. It was never about 'man's inhumanity to man', other than that perpetrated by Edmund Burke from the safety of the Commons. The Impeachment of Hastings was a premeditated act of revenge. The Clive-Sulivan struggles of 1758 to 1774; the Hastings-Francis feud in Calcutta of 1773 to 1780; and the Burke family's frustration and rage at Sulivan were transferred to Burke and Francis to prosecute. The Governor-General was viewed as incorporating all the 'sins' of his mentor Sulivan.

In his attack on Hastings, Burke was assailing the man who symbolised all he detested about the Company, which in turn was the symbol of all the injustices he saw in so many spheres of life, but couldn't touch. It is summed up in his wonderful, though cruel imagery. Hastings was: 'An Indian Rajah with a white face – the most terrible animal in God's creation', representing avarice and untrammelled power.[9]

Burke began his attack in the Commons on 17 February 1786, launched with appalling viciousness, excess of language and invective. Its enormity at once thrusts the reader's sympathies towards Hastings. Two days later, on 19 February, and just two days before his death, Sulivan called at Hastings' home to discuss the issues involved. It was a duty that he was more than willing to perform; and followed on from those he had cheerfully shouldered for the previous twelve years.

After the Governor-General was found not guilty, Burke reflected that the trial and its result had been the 'glory and the shame' of his public life. Rather than Burke's meaning that it was appalling Hastings had been acquitted, generations have dwelt more on the shame that attaches to the whole Impeachment; one that might be seen to have besmirched Burke's own glorious career.

4

There seemed nothing unusual about Sulivan's physical condition during what proved to be his final months. The general pattern had remained the same for some time. It merely suggested that old age was encroaching with its customary aches and pains.[10] The fact that before the end of 1783 he and Hastings had finally beaten the opposition, both in India and in London, had cheered him. This is reflected in his tribute that year: 'my feeble abilities have been constantly, and ever shall be, exerted with unremitting zeal in support of the highest character that ever shewed in India. You must bear this from me because I am too honest and too old to commence a flatterer.'[11]

His health had fluctuated from that point: he was much better from August 1783 to February 1784, then the cold weather took its toll; however, by November he was in fine spirits again and strong enough to produce 'a veritable book' for his son.[12] He let him know that 'with a wonderful share of health (for which I cannot be sufficiently thankful) I have been very active in this Direction'.[13] Yet, he did admit, 'the winters begin to shake me and I must study warmth. In my former letters, I desired you would send me some shawl wastecoats…and pray add a shawl night-gown if procurable.'[14] While the birth of his grandson had cheered him enormously, the actual sight of the child in the summer of 1785, not to mention the safe arrival of Stephen and his wife, was an occasion of great joy. He was surrounded by those closest to him.

When death came, it was quick and without prior indication that something was seriously wrong. In his diary Hastings provides probably the most appropriate record of his passing. They were in constant contact, either at his home or at Sulivan's, where they attended each other on alternate days. They supped together, and scrutinized whatever intelligence was to hand. Tactics and strategy were organised, opinions exchanged and letters studied.

On 11 December 1785 he wrote to Sulivan from Bath; and soon after arriving back in town they were again deep in discussion. On 19 February 1786, a Sunday, he called at Sulivan's house 'by appointment' to 'talk on the first enquiry' into his affairs.[15] At midnight on Monday he scribbled in his diary, 'Mr. Sulivan seized with a disorder in his bowels'. On Tuesday 21 February he 'Called at Mrs. H. and Mr. Sulivan's. Not admitted – Evening at the opera. The Sulivans called there to give me the afflicting news of Mr. Sulivan's death. It happened at 4, suddenly and without pain.'[16]

On the day Sulivan died, out of respect, the Directors postponed the appointment of a Governor-General to fill Hastings' place. The papers carried the news all week.[17] His passing had significant political repercussions. A man of first class abilities and drive, active until the last, was now gone.

His party disintegrated because it had no bond or union after his passing. Over the years he had provided leadership and backbone.

In the *Morning Chronicle and Advertiser* for Friday 24 February there was a letter from a John Travers who intended to fill the vacancy in the Direction. He was unsuccessful and Sulivan's place was taken by Abraham Roberts. Major John Scott broadcast that but for the forthcoming impeachment, he would have asked Sulivan's friends to vote for him. It would have been a poor substitution.

The burial was on Monday 27 February at the church of St. George the Martyr, Queen Square, where he was interred beside his wife. Hastings commented, 'Continued heavy snow. Called on Sir Robert Palk at 1 and went with him to Mr. Sulivan's funeral. Returned after 3.'[18] John Caillaud penned a fine tribute, addressed to Stephen Sulivan:

> Were I to give way to all my heart dictates, I could dwell long on the great abilities and many virtues which composed the character of your much respected father. To these the voice of the public, which he so long, eminently and faithfully served, will do justice. And the pen of some more able friend record, and transmit them to posterity. But of those among the many he left behind, none was more warmly attached to him, more grateful for his kindness. Nor any who honoured and loved him more while living. Nor can more bewail his loss, or feel for yours than...John Caillaud.[19]

5

Laurence Sulivan was consumed with a never-ending desire to be known and accepted as the undisputed leader of the East India Company. He was ever ready to protect this goal. Along with this, he always wanted to be one of that powerful coterie found in the innermost sanctums, making major decisions affecting public life. His career, the power-play, everything was geared to these objectives.

This led to a form of obsession with authority and command. For a time, when in full control, debasing symptoms accompanied this, and an overweening vanity. However, the terrible financial losses he suffered can be said to have returned him to a degree of humility; and there was always some restraint. He was conscious too of a 'general good' that had to be supported. This said, he never trusted anyone with authority over him.

His special abilities were perfectly suited to an organisation like the East India Company, because the mixture of commerce, money and politics at its core were the fields in which he excelled. It became imperative to him that he operate there, after having learned the ropes in Bombay. He was a living, talking authority on the Company. In this he found contentment.

The fights and feuds arose when these ambitions were tampered with; when attempts were made to oust him, or even just denigrate his managerial abilities and exploits. It marked the quarrel with Clive; and underlay the long losing struggle against ministerial interference and Parliamentary encroachment. It was to the fore in later years and especially in the clashes with Edmund Burke.

He had the amazing ability to handle a multiplicity of interactions simultaneously, and deal competently with all of them: home life; private business; affairs at India House and abroad; and Parliamentary relations. He was a truly clever man and invariably managed to uncover what lay behind the manoeuvres of others. His son Stephen referred to his great persistence. He marvelled at his 'indefatigable perusal of the records', and ability to scour through endless material in order to 'sift things through to the bottom'.[20]

He would never face losing the respect of family and friends; and he seldom gave the game away. Playing card imagery was constantly used in his correspondence, and perhaps this echoed his nature. He had good manners and even in the worst situation never lost his comportment. This politeness endorsed a genuinely benevolent but determined temperament. His disposition was tempered by the needs of someone who led such a public life to always appear gracious and courteous.

His public reputation was very important, which his opponents understood and did their best to destroy by slander and belittling him. It was part and parcel of the political 'game'. They wanted him out and so he was described in as many demeaning terms as could be conjured up. Friends said he was quicksilver in thought and speedy of action; prompt with a response; and capable of rapid summaries and assessments. He was also described candidly by them as emotional, a gambler, and someone who made a virtue out of honesty.

Although opinionated, often biased and able to nurse a grudge for a long time, he seldom displayed real ferocity towards adversaries. This absence of viciousness was most obvious in his struggle with Clive. Sulivan's general absence of gut-hatred appears the more striking when he did express severe dislike, such as for Edmund Burke. His friends pointed to his positive qualities: proud, courageous and defiant; an astute, unflagging realist; the sort of man who, in private or in public, searched, probed and thoroughly tested all alternatives before making a decision. They applauded him as a wonderful raconteur; someone with a warm human nature, who was vigorous and alive.

The utmost personal satisfaction, even exultation, came with command. Only in exercising himself in this manner did life become full. He wanted to be considered indispensable. From 1757 to 1786 he was ever-present, whether a Proprietor, occupying a Chair, or sitting as a Director; and it was seldom he was not on the main committees. He was almost never off the Committee of Secrecy. It must have seemed to contemporaries that he was always there, at the very centre of all that was going on.

What emerges is that for some thirty years he was the Company's brain and the driving force within the executive; operating at a time when (despite itself) the Company was forming the nucleus of an empire. The times demanded a greater degree of managerial dexterity than was ever needed before; and Sulivan fitted the bill. He provided the dynamic energy required during these momentous years. The roots of this dynamism can be traced to the years spent in Bombay; or perhaps to dark events in his native Ireland. However, Sulivan remains a man of mystery in this respect.

Throughout the whole era of his pre-eminence in the Company, he was more occupied with the task of preserving its credibility than he was with any other issue. Determined efforts to balance the books were major features of his career. In his efforts to reform the organisation, he was faced with ignorance among colleagues and national figures alike. Nevertheless, he never gave up. It was part and parcel of saving his precious Company.

The evidence is overwhelming that most of his plans, reviews and abstracts can be accepted as sound, some were exceptional. Many of his ideas were turned down, sometimes justifiably because they were unworkable. Others were implemented successfully by himself when he had the power, or by his protégés. Latterly they were used by Jenkinson, Robinson, Atkinson, Dundas and Pitt the Younger. His account of things can be accepted too.[21]

Throughout his career his soul belonged to nobody; and he was certainly never controlled by any minister or Parliamentarian. It was his independence that Chatham, Shelburne, North, Burke and others did not like. What also made him so unusual and effective was his ability to persuade and mollify many different interest groups and yet maintain clear profit goals and pro-business objectives. He succeeded in grafting together politics and commerce.

He fought for the Company's existence, and nullified the efforts of any European power to get rid of it. He thwarted the endeavours of Indian Princes to scupper the organisation and expel the British from the subcontinent. Strict control through a strong official, following policies, objectives and methods initiated at India House was his favoured approach. He tried to impose his will upon those he picked to govern. This was quite legitimate in his eyes, and he relied on them to mark the boundaries if they felt he was interloping.

Sulivan was a leader, an astute and persuasive man; throughout his career he personified ability, hard work and drive. Yet despite all this, his position was founded upon the patronage he controlled. It was this that produced the authority that was recognised and understood all over the globe. Great influence and pre-eminence went together; and the process was self-perpetuating because his favours were the means by which he ensured his continued support.

Thus he found positions for friends, fellow Directors, Proprietors, ministers in office and various MPs, even some landed gentry. Important figures who could respond in kind were provided for; or anyone who could help (or hurt) him. Nepotism was rampant, and he was no different from others. He was forever being harassed to give lines of introduction, and always the degree of favour depended upon intimacy and importance, as measured by him. In 1773 he summed it up in a letter to Hastings:

> Many are the recommendations I am obliged to trouble you with.
> India voters expect it of me or they are affronted. Therefore,
> these must be understood to extend to common civilities only, by
> no means to burden you. And when I wish to solicit particular
> favours, such will always be mentioned in my private letters.[22]

From a notional list of Sulivan's patronage recommendations from 1757 to
1786, culled from numerous sources, the following emerges: At the very
least, he patronised around 200 people, though there might have been double
that number. Of these, five were women. Between 1757 and 1765 some 40
odd were provided with posts; from 1769 to 1777 the figure was between 80
and 90. In the years 1778 to 1786 this fell to around 50.

120 of those identified were civil servants; 23 were military; 12 nautical. Six
favoured were judges or lawyers. The numbers also included an artist, an
engineer, a surgeon and a labourer. 54, but almost certainly more, were
suggested to Hastings as worthy of help. A minimum of 18 Scots asked for
special treatment for friends and relations; 37 were endorsed, and probably
more. The Irish enjoyed patronage from their fellow-countryman as well – at
least 12 were helped to posts. Some individuals were approved for office
several times. Yet despite being the possessor of such enormous largesse,
Sulivan always claimed that his hands were clean:

> Such has been my conduct...without fee or reward, resisting all
> temptation and some very extraordinary, one in particular of a
> lady offering me her person, a seat in Parliament and £10,000 for
> a capital Government for her son. Many other bribes of equal
> magnitude, but in no instance of my life can a single blot stain
> my character.[23]

Defence of the Company's chartered rights was never far from his thoughts;
he was dedicated to preserving its independence and monopoly. That is why
he baulked at the thought of such a commerce-based institution being
transmuted into a territorial and imperial power – he foresaw danger. After
Plassey he could not put the clock back, yet until 1765 at least, was able to
keep the Company from becoming totally burdened by territorial
responsibilities and the costs entailed.

The new aspirations led, as he saw clearly, to complicated questions. Could
the Company manage the territorial, financial, judicial and political
responsibilities that accompanied such a role? Would recognition and
toleration of cultural and other differences be maintained? He did not think
so. Most crucial of all, in the blink of an eye, Parliament was questioning the
Company's right to its subordinate powers; and in 1766-67, then later,
Government intervention could not be countered by argument based on
chartered right. There was none, as Sulivan knew.

After the Regulating Act of 1773 he envisaged the Company's continued
existence as utterly reliant upon the power of the Governors in each

Presidency and upon the Governor-General in particular. By that date he had also accepted that commercial priorities had to give way to territorial ones; and recognised the suzerainty of the state. The new breed of administrators working for ministers also ensured that the awkward features of the Company's hierarchical system were avoided as much as possible.

By the third quarter of the century, a general feeling had spread in Britain that it was not proper that a private concern should monopolise all that India had now come to represent; it was much more than a trading matter. Alterations to the Company's set-up were required to deal with a changed situation; and such reform could only be imposed from outwith its confines.

The loss of the American colonies deepened the general anxiety, with fears of similar losses in the east; thus the Company's affairs and the administration of its settlements were no longer viewed as being its own business. Nor was the old mercantilist system, followed so faithfully by Sulivan, regarded as sustainable. Surely, it was argued, the spiralling, seemingly uncontrollable chain of events in India was proof of this.

A mark of his contribution, however, was that long after his death the Company survived with many of its commercial features intact. To some extent the flag continued to follow the dictates of commerce.[24] The organisation still exhibited many of the original trading characteristics, especially those of barter with other peoples on a fair and level surface. What he had done was to combine and enshrine a 'rigorous tradition of administrative accountancy' and 'an ideology of transcendent law and sovereignty'.[25]

However, continual and increasing military expense called for fresh demands that could not be paid out of strictly commercial profit. He recognised this in 1761 with regard to the Carnatic. The double-edged nature of Hastings' military campaign did not help either; but on the whole, the acquisition of more territory was largely resisted until the 1780s. Repeated demands thereafter, backed by force, destroyed the balance in India. What followed his demise was the principle of 'trusteeship' for Indians and their lands. It was to replace the limited sovereignty and strict trading principles so sacred to him; and seemed to accompany the shift from trade to tax collection.

Through no fault of their own, indigenous peoples were adjudged to have become increasingly dependent upon the British. It was a development with an inbuilt disposition towards racial superiority that Sulivan would have recoiled from. He never would impose British manners upon the Indian peoples. He had a great and lasting interest in the culture of the subcontinent; and was not responsible for the racial discrimination that developed with the later British Empire.

He partly determined the nature and course of the British domain in India for something like half a century; and it remained largely non-racist for many years after his death. This more harmonious form of co-existence, and the 'benevolent despotism' form of rule using Governor-Generals was favoured by the British Government until 1815. Both threads can be traced back to Sulivan.[26]

It might be argued that in his attitude, as in nearly all else, it was his wife's moral rectitude that directed Sulivan. After all, it was she who pushed him initially towards what was a careful, domesticated and sober life. Perhaps much of the caution he exhibited in Company business was deliberately fostered and encouraged by her. All indications are that his personal inclinations were towards a more riotous form of existence.

The course of his life reflected a belief in material progress; and he worked for this in the world he knew. The pursuit of happiness was for him encapsulated in the East India Company, but he was intrigued with the condition of his fellows, and with their hopes and aspirations. But as he came more and more into contact with greed, envy and deceit, he was increasingly sickened. The irony was that he could not live without human contact.

In some ways he possessed a different kind of honesty or set of values from most contemporaries, in or out of service. His integrity was portrayed through a sort of fearlessness and astuteness. While most thought that Company and native alike were fair game, he would have none of it. Some forms of commercial advantage he agreed with – but not at the expense of decency. He would admit to no stain on his record.

When, as here, focus is placed upon the endeavours of the merchant executives to make the Honourable Company work, Sulivan stands out. He was the central figure in all that happened during what were probably the most eventful and dangerous years in its history. Without his contribution at critical junctures, it might possibly have fractured and fallen apart, or been vanquished at home and in the east. With no Indian settlements it is doubtful if there would have been a second British Empire; one expanded by preservation of the routes there, and the accumulation of territories on the way.

There is no doubt either that Sulivan was aware of his astonishing role; indeed at first he seemed content to luxuriate in the knowledge; but after having suffered the 'slings and arrows' of life he portrayed things differently. He depicted himself having traversed the classic route from saviour to sacrifice and latterly martyrdom – all for his treasured Company. Before his death, however, he seems to have reached a plateau of contentment; probably because the future of his family was secured, his service to Hastings and the Company ended.

Two mysteries still cling to Sulivan. One is that apart from some connection with Benjamin Sulivan of Cork and the Irwin family, his origins remain unknown. He never made any reference to either his father or mother. Even the names of his children broke with tradition. Nothing in writing was allowed to come down through the ages.

The final intriguing question is whether before his death he realised some form of personal fulfilment, his own epiphany. In a life that was so full and varied, beset by conflicts and vengeful interludes, it is very possible that satisfaction eluded him. On the other hand, perhaps he did experience contentment, despite the financial wreckage of his later life. One of his rewards was certainly a lengthy, happy marriage.

Yet it remains uncertain whether he ever did quench the desire for those 'lights' that would give him understanding; or an end to the constant curiosity and activity that was the outward manifestation of his restless spirit. To be involved was everything to Laurence Sulivan. It must have pleased him, therefore, that to the very last breath of his long life he was still thoroughly embroiled in matters of consequence.

Short Titles and Abbreviations

Add.MSS. –	Additional manuscripts kept in the Department of Manuscripts in the British Library, London.
Bodl. -	Manuscripts kept in the Bodleian Library, Oxford
B.L.	British Library, London
Bute MSS. -	The papers of John Stuart, 3rd Earl of Bute, kept at Mountstuart, Isle of Bute.
Cal.H.O.Papers -	Calendar of Home Office Papers in the Reign of George 111 (1760-5), J. Redington & R. Roberts (eds.), London 1878.
De Bertodano Papers	Papers belonging to Mr. Martin De Bertodano
E.P.L. -	Edinburgh Public Libraries. George 1V Bridge, Edinburgh
E.U.L. -	Edinburgh University Library.
G.M. -	*Gentleman's Magazine.*
Hansard -	*The Parliamentary History of England from the Earliest Period to the year 1803,* T. C. Hansard, W. Cobbett (Eds.), (London, 1813/4).
H.M.S.C. -	Historical Manuscripts Commission Reports.
I.O.L. MSS. -	Manuscripts in the Asia, Pacific & Africa Collections in the British Library, London.
I.O.R. -	Records of the East India Company kept in the Asia, Pacific & Africa Collections in the British Library, London.
N.L.S. -	National Library of Scotland, George 1V Bridge, Edinburgh.
N.L.W. -	National Library of Wales, Aberystwyth.
n.p. –	No pagination.
P.A. -	*Public Advertiser.*
P.R.O. (Ireland) -	Public Record Office, Four Courts, Dublin.
P.R.O. (London) -	Public Record Office, London.
P.R.O. ((N. Ireland)	Belfast, Northern Ireland.
S.R.O. -	Scottish Record Office, Register House, Edinburgh.

Chapter Notes and References

Preface

1. McGilvary [1].
2. See Sutherland [1]; Feiling; Philips, C.H. [4]; Davies, A.M. [1].

1. Bombay and Origins 1713–52

1. I.O.R. Range 341, Bombay Public Consultations, vol. 10, p.357, J. Horne to S. Law, 30 August 1739.
2. Bodl. Sulivan MSS. Eng. Hist. c.269, L. Sulivan's Letterbook to Stephen Sulivan, April 1778. [Note: De Bertodano Papers, Laurence Sulivan's 'Letterbook to his son', April 1778, is an exact copy].
3. Quoted in, Dodwell [3], p.4.
4. Bodl. Sulivan MSS. Eng. Hist. c.269, L. Sulivan's Letterbook to Stephen Sulivan, April 1778.
5. *Ibid.*
6. *Ibid.*
7. *Ibid.*
8. Commander John O'Sullivan, of Cork City; son of Philip O'Sullivan and his wife Elizabeth Irwin; brother of Benjamin Sulivan. Born 1716, died 1780; buried at St. Mary's Shandon, Cork. Married Susannah O'Sullivan, City of Cork, born 1726, died 1792. He had one son, Captain Philip O'Sullivan.
9. Commander James Irwin was from Roscommon and Cork City.
10. He was a free merchant and inhabitant of Calcutta by 1730; also appearing in Madras in February 1730 and May 1732.
11. S.R.O. GD/Sect.1/464/(c), ff. 25-27. In the 1720s, a Philip Roche from Cork, named the ship he stole, *Mary*. See also Hayward, pp.95, 337; *Analecta Hibernica*, vol.20, p.64, Doneraile Papers; vol.23, p.250; P.R.O. (Ireland) m.6282.
12. Born at Calcutta in 1728, died at St. Helena in 1792. She was the daughter of Mary Beale of St. Helena.
13. Eyles Irwin was born in 1751. Through Sulivan he was chosen to be a Writer at Madras in 1767.
14. Possibly also a connection with an Andrew Galwey (alias Andrew Gardiner).
15. Laurence might have been an illegitimate older brother. Benjamin Sulivan was born in the Parish of St. Paul, Cork City, in 1720, died 1767. In 1733 admitted to Kings Inns: 'Mother (Elizabeth Irwin) a Presbyterian.' In 1740 appointed Attorney. [Kings Inns Admissions Papers, pp.458-69, 468-69]. From 1752: Barrister at Law and Clerk of the Crown and Clerk of the Peace, by letters patent, for Counties Cork and Waterford; renewed in 1758 and 1761. He married in 1742, Bridget, daughter of Rev. Paul Limerick, D.D. from Scull, County Cork.
16. See Exeter Record Office, Palk MSS. no. 169, L. Sulivan to R. Palk, 27 May 1772; *Grants of Arms*, vol.22, pp.212-213; and McGilvary [1], pp.1-2.
17. Add. MSS. 29143, f.334, Francis Sykes to W. Hastings, 16 May 1779. He referred to the youngest son as, 'Mr. Sullivan's nephew'.
18. John and Richard Joseph Sulivan paid for research by G. Beltz in 1801. Laurence Sulivan is not mentioned. Nor did Beltz seem to know that his son Stephen was alive.

19. Bodl. Sulivan MSS. Eng. Hist. c. 472, f.2, L. Sulivan to John Sulivan, 6 February 1775. Col. Wood and Mr. Darvall were married, respectively, to Laurence Sulivan's nieces, 'Betsy' and 'Nancy' Owen.

20. De Bertodano Papers, n.p. Laurence Sulivan's Letterbook to his son, April, 1778. He died in Madras, unmarried and with no issue, on 9 October 1793.

21. His first name is clearly from the Irish *Labhras*. 'Sulivane' was the form then in use among maritime members of the *O'Suileabhan Beara* Sept.

22. A Laurence Sulivan was convicted of high treason in February 1680 for being part of the Earl of Tyrone's 'Popish' uprising. [See H.M.S.C. Ormonde MSS., vol.36, p.510; and p.580, 12 February 1681].

23. De Bertodano Papers, n.p. Laurence Sulivan's 'Letterbook to his son', April 1778.

24. I.O.R. Bombay Public Consultations, vol. 2, n.p. 17 March 1740.

25. See Sutherland [1], p.53, and Dodwell [3], p.31, for a description of what would have been his daily work.

26. De Bertodano Papers, n.p. Laurence Sulivan's 'Letterbook to his son', April 1778.

27. I.O.L. MSS. Eur. E. 302/2, 'Letterbook of Mrs. Adriana Spencer', *passim.*

28. Later, he became Superintendent of the Bombay marine. In 1749 he was Mayor of Bombay. [Low, vol.1, p.120].

29. He was a Senior Merchant in Bombay in 1747, Marine Paymaster in 1748 and third in Council by 1749.

30. At least twenty-five trusted close friends can be picked out.

31. I.O.L. ORB 50/15, 12 December 1752.

32. I.O.R., Bombay Public Consultations, vol. 16, p. 162.

33. *Ibid.* p. 347. This was payment for 'passing notes and seeing it be exported in no undue manner but in the proportions which the Honourable Company usually allowed'.

34. I.O.R. Bombay Public Consultations, vol. 18, f.435.

35. I.O.R., Surat Factory Records, vol.37, f.1; ff. 16-18, The Committee to the Board, 8 January 1752.

36. *Ibid.* ff. 18-19.

37. *Ibid.* ff.25-27.

38. *Ibid.* ff.39-46.

39. *Ibid.*

40. In January 1750 he used the accounts and the estates of Nathaniel Whitwelf, Henry Talbot, William Binnel and Anthony Upton for bills totalling £230.13.9.

41. De Bertodano Papers, n.p. Laurence Sulivan's 'Letterbook to his son', April 1778.

42. *Ibid.*

43. *Ibid.*

44. *Ibid.*

45. *Ibid.*

46. *Ibid.*

47. *Ibid.*

48. *Ibid.*

49. *Ibid.*

50. *Ibid.*

51. *Ibid.*

52. *Ibid.*

53. *Ibid.*

2. London and India House 1753–63

1. Bodl. Sulivan MSS. Eng. Hist. c.472, f.40, et seq. [See also Sutherland [1], p.62].
Edward Owen's widow Ann, was paid an annual allowance of £40; a house was
rented for her in Great Russell Street. Nothing more is then heard of her.
2. *Ibid.* Purchased in 1741 by the Chandlers from Edward Randolph. In 1763 sold to a
distiller, Isaac Lefevre. Formerly owned by Sir John Gayer, ex-Governor of Bombay.
[Morris [1], p.10; and pp.45-47. My thanks to Derek Morris for his information].
3. See Morris [1], pp.45-47 *et passim*; and Jucker, pp.25-2].
4. For additional material on Captain Thomas Lane see: Morris [2], pp.20-27. See also
Morris [1], pp.46-47, 70, *et passim*.. Note: In 1711 a Mr. Lane was present at India
House. [Jucker, p.25].
5. Morris [2], pp.23 and 26 *et passim*.
6. Bodl. Sulivan MSS. Eng. Hist. c.472, f.40, et seq. He laid out £200 for repairs;
stumped up law fees; paid his 'share of the dinner to the steward and jury' of the
Court granting possession; paid a 'fine' at a special 'Court Baron' held at the *Angel and
Crown*, Whitechapel. [See Morris [1], p.10; pp.45-47].
7. *Ibid.* Everything on the outside was painted twice. The house, in magnificent
condition, survives to this day as 37, Stepney Green.
8. *Ibid.* The estimate for painting the staircase was £49.8.7; the total bill: £193.11.4.
9. *Ibid.* The cost of wine was also itemised.
10. *Ibid.* [Additional information, courtesy of Derek Morris].
11. *Ibid.* The obligations shouldered were many. Mrs. Lane's nurse was paid for. Gifts
were made.
12. *Ibid.*
13. *Ibid.* He itemised: suits, coats, waistcoats, breeches, garters, wadding, lining, lacing,
stockings, buttons, buckles, wigs, hats and shoes – in every conceivable material:
Velvets, satins, silks, cotton, worsteds, in a dazzling riot of colours: black, brown,
blue, orange, scarlet, crimson – and, above all, gold.
14. *Ibid.* Strict book-keeping allowed little room for manoeuvre; six footmen and eight
coachmen came and went before November 1763. Everything was modelled on the
Stephen Law household.
15. *Ibid.*
16. De Bertodano Papers, n.p. Sulivan to his son Stephen, 24 February 1784; *et passim*.
See also Bodl. Sulivan MSS. Eng. Hist. c.269, f.7. Laurence Sulivan's 'Letterbook to
his son', April 1778; and c.472, f.40, *et seq*.
17. Sutherland [3] p.47 *et. passim*; and Dickson, *passim*.
18. De Bertodano Papers, n.p. L. Sulivan to his son, April 1778.
19. *Ibid.*
20. See N.L.W. Powis MSS. Clive Papers, Letterbook No, 10, f.92, Clive to Orme, 1
August 1758; and 'Journal' for December 1757 to December 1758.
21. My thanks to Derek Morris for information on Clive's visit to Sulivan.
22. Bodl. L. Sulivan MSS. Eng. Hist. c.472, f. 40 *et seq*. 'Accounts.' These shares
amounted to 27,399 rupees in 1761, that is, approximately £3,500 (at two shilling to the
rupee). The 8 ships noted were: *Hardwicke, Lively, Prince Edward, Neptune, Doddington,
Cauder, Pastorinho* and *Fatty Salem*.
23. I.O.L. MSS. Eur.E. 302/1, 'Letterbook of John Spencer', f.79.
24. De Bertodano Papers, n.p. Laurence Sulivan's 'Letterbook to his son', April 1778.
In 1757 Thomas Lane subscribed £5000 to the £3 million loan raised by the City.
This, or part, was probably Sulivan's money. [See Sutherland [7], p.110. See also
Morris, [1], p.50].

25. The *Royal Exchange Company* had Captain James Saunders, James Tierney and James Savage (all ex-Company servants) among its directors. The *Amicable Society for Perpetual Assurance* had Elijah Impey, a Jeremiah Bentham and Thomas Manningham.
26. De Bertodano Papers, n.p. Laurence Sulivan's 'Letterbook to his son', April 1778.
27. *Ibid.*
28. See Sutherland [3], p.14.
29. P.R.O. London, Will of Samuel Hough, 15 July 1762. Sulivan also received a diamond ring.
30. *The Petition and Appeal of Rawson Hart Boddam and Nathaniel Stackhouse Esquires, Executors in India of John Spencer, Esquire, deceased, complaining of certain parts of a decree or decretal order of the Court of Chancery, of 31st October 1785, and praying that the same may be reversed or varied.* Also: 'Journal of the House of Lords', 7 February 1786. [Judicial Records of the House of Lords, House of Lords Record Office, London.]
31. *Ibid.*
32. *Ibid.*
33. See I.O.R. Correspondence Memoranda, vol.15 (1756), n.p. Item dated 12 November 1756. 'A list of interest notes claimed at Bengal and tendered to be registered and attested copies given.'
34. East Suffolk Record Office, Martin family of Hemingstone Papers, HA 13/A/1-15.
35. Bodl. L. Sulivan MSS. Eng. Hist. c.472, f. 40 *et seq.* 'Accounts.'
36. See Joslin, p.342.
37. For definitions of the shipping interest, see Philips, C.H. [2], p.462; also Glossary.
38. N.L.W. Powis MSS. Clive Papers, 'Letterbook dated May 1764 to September 1766', ff.43-40, John Walsh to Clive, 22 November 1764.
39. *Ibid.* Later in life Captain Thomas Lane was listed as owner or 'husband' of the *Ponsborne.* Captain Samuel Hough (son of Sulivan's late friend) was in charge
40. Namier & Brooke [1], vol.11, p.267.
41. Perhaps it is only coincidence, but a Peter Godfrey bought land in County Kerry between 1754-8, from a Cornelius Sullivan, an uncle of Benjamin Sulivan. [See Register of Deeds, Henrietta Street, Dublin, Memorial 189, *et passim.*]
42. Chaudhuri, K.N [1], pp.82-83.
43. There were at least sixteen in the group.
44. Sutherland [3], p.88.
45. Holwell, pp.62.
46. See Chaudhuri, K. N. [1], p.86.
47. See also Sutherland [1], p.51.

3. The Court of Directors 1755-58
1. The Society included public figures, like Chatham, Cavendish, and Grafton. Prominent individuals like Wilkes; and bankers, such as George Colebrooke.
2. Clive to Sulivan, 30 December 1758. See also Forrest [2], vol.2, p.65.
3. Quoted in Furber [2], p.483, R. Atkinson to H. Dundas, 22 July 1784.
4. Davies, A.M. [2], p.52.
5. Sutherland [1], p.54.
6. S.R.O. Buccleuch MSS. GD/ 224/45/38. Item 75.
7. See I.O.L. Orme MSS. O.V. 147. 8, ff. 35-36; O.V. 158.2, ff. 4-5; O.V. 32.1; and McGilvary [1], pp.45, 50, 74.
8. They were: Godfrey, Plant, Dudley, Savage, Tullie, Gough, Phipps and Rous. [For Peter Godfrey and Charles Gough, See Parker, pp. 118-122].
9. For example he dealt with the buying in one committee; in another decided upon issues involving farms, duties, *Zamindari* powers and disputes between castes.

10. See I.O.R. Committee of Correspondence Memoranda, vol.16 (1757), n.p.
11. Sinha p.xxx.
12 *Ibid.,* pp.xxxviii and xxxix.
13. Dodwell [2], p.16.
14. *Ibid.*
15. I.O.R. Correspondence Memoranda, vol.16 1757, (in Sulivan's handwriting). See also I.O.L. Orme MSS. O.V., 32.1.
16. See I.O.L. Orme MSS. O.V. 147. 8, ff. 35-36; O.V. 158.2, ff. 4-5; O.V. 32.1; and McGilvary [1], pp.45, 50, 74.
17. Sutherland [1], p.63.
18. De Bertodano Papers, n.p. Laurence Sulivan's 'Letterbook to his son', April 1778.
19. Sutherland [1], p.71. See pp.66-73 *passim*, for this first contested election; and McGilvary [1], pp. 54-61.
20. See also McGilvary [2], pp.217-222 *et seq*. This patronage found other uses.
21. Sutherland [l] p.66. See also Holwell, pp.155-6.
22. He had fourteen supporters.
23. Holwell, p.156.
24. *Ibid.* See p.157.
25. *Ibid.*
26. *P.A.* for 13 March 1758.
27 Holwell, p.165.
28. N.L.W., Powis MSS., Clive Papers. 'Letterbook', January 1764 to September 1765, f.53, John Walsh to Clive, 5 February 1765.
29. Chaudhuri, K.N. [1], p.82.

4. Priorities 1757-65

1. De Bertodano Papers, n.p. Laurence Sulivan to Stephen Sulivan, 27 February 1778.
2. Davies, A.M. [1], p.52.
3. I.O.R., Court Book 70, pp. 34, 107-8.
4. Davies, A.M. [1], p.52.
5. Forrest [1], vol.2, p.180, citing a letter from Clive to Henry Vansittart, 3 February 1762. Volume 32 of Robert Orme's 'History' is based on papers given to him by Sulivan, on war theatres, 1756-62; naval intelligence, battle lines, treaty proposals, and articles; maps and plans on all theatres. [See I.O.L., Orme MSS .O.V., 32.l, n.p. See also Orme MSS. O.V., 147.8, ff.35-36].
6. N.L.S. MSS. E.F.P. 41. 10/3. Item entitled 'Account of the Numbers in the Establishment of the Company's European Officers and Soldiers in the East Indies, from 1747 to 1770.'
7. P.R.O., Chatham MSS. 30/8/60. Sulivan to Pitt, 5 February 1761.
8. Quoted in Dodwell [2], p.194.
9. De Bertodano MSS., n.p. L. Sulivan to S. Sulivan, 27 February 1778.
10. Peters, p.102.
11. Williams, vol.1, p.27
12. *Ibid.,* vol.1, p.28.
13. De Bertodano Papers, n.p. Laurence Sulivan to Stephen Sulivan, 27 February 1778.
14. I.O.R., Home Miscellaneous Series, vol.808, f.186, Sulivan to Pitt, 27 July 1761.
15. P.R.O. (London), Chatham MSS. 30/8/60, ff.169. From internal evidence c.1760.
16. I.O.L., Orme MSS. O.V. 63.26,217.
17. Dodwell [2], pp.287-8. Also I.O.L., Orme MSS. O.V. 63.26,217.
18. See I.O.R. Committee of Correspondence Memoranda, vol.18, n.p.

19. I.O.R. Home Miscellaneous Series, vol.96, ff.427-433, November 1761, Bute to the Directors.

20. *Ibid.*

21. Entitled: *A Defence of the United Company of Merchants of England trading to the East Indies and their Servants (particularly those of Bengal) against the Complaints of the Dutch East India Company, being a Memorial from the English East India Company to his Majesty on that subject.* Published in April 1762.

22. I.O.R. Correspondence Reports, vol.6, See Letters from Jenkinson to Sulivan of 10, 11, 19 March 1762.

23. Malcolm, vol.2, p.128.

24. Cushner, p.11. *et passim* (Quotes Court Minutes for 30 December 1761 on p.251).

25. P.R.O. 30/47/20/3, ff. 1-3.

26. Quoted in Cushner, p.201

27. One of his final measures was to plan the downfall of Yusuf Khan's rebellion at Madura, which lay to the south of the Carnatic.

28. S.R.O., Buccleuch MSS. GD 24/Box 45/Bundle 38, Item 53. 'Extract from Mr. Scrafton's Book of Transactions in the East Indies.' See also Hotblack, pp.56-96.

29. Lenman & Lawson, p.807.

30. Philips, C.H. [2], p.461.

31. Already Clive had despatched bills totalling £39,000. Sulivan, in partnership with Thomas Manningham, Richard Baker and Dr. John Munro had remitted bills worth £31,602.

32. I.O.R. Committee of Correspondence Memoranda, vol.18, Sulivan's reply to the Bengal General Letter, dated 5 March 1759.

33. Edwardes, p.178.

34. Quoted in Dodwell [2], p.182.

35. *Ibid.*, p.187.

36. Sutherland[1] p.75.

37. In their own words, the Directors were: 'Seldom in a position to meet large drafts at a short date.' [Quoted in Dodwell [2], p.188].

38. De Bertodano Papers, Laurence Sulivan to Stephen Sulivan, 27 February 1778.

39. *Ibid.*

40. I.O.R., General Ledgers, July 1756-June 1763. L/AG/14/5/3-12 *et passim*; L/AG/14/7/1.

41. Sulivan to Chatham, 27 July 1761. Quoted in Williams [1], vol.1, pp.28-9.

42. I.O.R., Committee of Correspondence Memoranda, vol.18, n.p. Sulivan's reply to the Bengal General Letter of 29 December 1759.

43. S.R.O. Buccleuch MSS. GD 224/45/38/Items 40-114, *passim.* [See also Sutherland [l], pp. 26, 138-9].

44. Dodwell [2], pp.118, 324, 415. See also I.O.R. Committee of Correspondence Memoranda, vol.17, n.p. Sulivan's reply to the Bengal General Letter of 31 December 1758.

45. S.R.O. Buccleuch MSS. GD 224/45/38/Items 4O-114, *passim.*

46. *Ibid.*

47. I.O.R., Home Miscellaneous Series, vol. 808, f.141, Sulivan to Coote, 16 March 1761.

48. I.O.R. Committee of Correspondence Memoranda, vol. 18, Sulivan's reply to the Bengal General Letter of 26 August 1758.

49. Sinha, p.51. The 4th head.

50. *Ibid.*, p. 187 (1759).

51. *Ibid.*

52. *Ibid.*

53. *Ibid.*
54. Dodwell [2], p.185. Company to Pigot, 1 November 1758.
55. I.O.R. Committee of Correspondence Memoranda, vol.17. n.p. Sulivan's answer to clause 143 of the 'infamous' General Letter from Bengal.
56. Quoted in Dodwell [2], p.182.
57. Add MSS. 29136, ff.104–108, L. Sulivan to W. Hastings, no date, but circa 1 March 1775.
58. *Ibid.*
59. I.O.R. Home Miscellaneous Series, vol.808, f.189, L. Sulivan to Clive, 29 September 1761.

5. India: Developments and Plans 1757-65

1. See Keay, pp. 319-27, 369-371.
2. Marshall [2], pp.40-1.
3. *Ibid.,* pp.39-40.
4. See I.O.R. Home Miscellaneous Series, vol.809, f.364 et seq. Clive to Sulivan, 30 December 1758.
5. Mir Jafar (privately) promised the army and navy £400,000; the Select Committee of the Bengal Council £120,000, and later £150,000; Clive £160,000.
6. Marshall [2], p.38.
7. Malcolm, vol.2, p.142.
8. Edwardes [1], p.175.
9. *Ibid.,* p.176.
10. See Malcolm, vol.2, p.192.
11. I.O.R. Home Miscellaneous vol.96, f.179, Sulivan to Robert Wood, 17 June 1761. See also Malcolm, vol.1, p.255.
12. See Bodl. Sulivan MSS. Eng. Hist. b.191, f.71. Vansittart to Sulivan, 17 April 1762.
13. I.O.R. Home Miscellaneous Series, vol.808, ff.189-90, Sulivan to Clive, 29 September 1761.
14. Bodl. Sulivan MSS. Eng. Hist. b.191, f.99, H. Vansittart to L. Sulivan, 22 September 1762.
15. *Ibid.*, ff.107-114, Palk to Sulivan, Madras 5 November 1762.
16. Bodl. Sulivan MSS. Eng. Hist. b.191, ff.181-187, Vansittart to Sulivan, 24 December 1763. Gave details of the slaughter.
17. See Bodl. Sulivan MSS. Eng. Hist. b.191, f.209. Vansittart to Palk, 25 June 1764.
18. I.O.L. MSS. Eur. 302/1 'Letterbook of John Spencer', f.28. Spencer to Sulivan, Calcutta 27 September 1764.
19. Quoted by Namier and Brooke [1], vol.1, p.156.
20. See I.O.L. MSS. Eur. 302/1 'Letterbook of John Spencer', f.44. Spencer to Sulivan, 21 December 1765.
21. See Marshall [3], pp.234-242; *et passim*
22. Quoted in Dodwell [2], p.257.
23. Dodwell [2], p.335.
24. *Ibid.* p.217.
25. *Ibid.* p.193 *et passim.*
26. *Ibid.* p.217.
27. B.L. Pamphlet 100.n.20. It was claimed that only Pigot's fine character had stemmed the just resentment.
28. I.O.R. Home Miscellaneous Series, vol.808, n.p. Sulivan to Chatham, 27 July 1761.
29. *Ibid.*
30. Bodl. Sulivan MSS. Eng. Hist. b.191, f.25, Palk to Sulivan, 9 January 1761.

31. The Governor also cared for Sulivan's two nieces now in India, Nancy and Betsy Owen; and also young Eyles Irwin (a kinsman). See also B.L. Pamphlet 100.n.20.
32. Dodwell [2], p.288.
33. *Ibid.*
34. *Ibid.* p.301.
35. I.O.L. Eur. MSS. 302/1. 'Letterbook of John Spencer', f.4, Spencer to Sulivan, 24 January 1764; and f.15 Spencer to Sulivan, 2 February 1764.
36. See B.L. Pamphlet 100.n.20.
37. Dodwell [2], p.301, 8 April 1762.
38. *Ibid.*, p.415. Company to Palk, 21 November 1764.
39. I.O.R. Court Book 69, p.43.
40. I.O.R. Committee of Correspondence Memoranda vol.18, n.p. Sulivan's clauses for Fort Marlborough, 30 October 1760.
41. S.R.O. Douglas MSS. vol. 2, pp.499-501, entry 499/22. Letter from Alex. Hall to his brother, Sir John Hall of Dunglass (near Berwick), 4 December 1762.
42. P.R.O. (London), Chatham MSS. 30/8/60, ff.109-10. Sulivan to Robert Wood (Secretary to Pitt), 5 February 176]. Chatham's order to use the Royal Navy was not heeded.
43. Due to shortage of pepper the best commercial use was made of the treaty and a Resident (Dalrymple) was installed.
44. Sir John Murray's MSS. Cabinet Minute No.30 (s.p. 84/504), quoted in Spencer, F (ed.), pp. 133-4.
45. See I.O.R. Committee of Correspondence Memoranda, vol.16 (1757), n.p. Sulivan's 'Observations on the Bengal Establishment with such Alterations and Amendments as Appear absolutely Necessary.' dated 1757.
46. Quoted Davies, A.M. [1], p.344.
47. See also Marshall [1], pp. 24-27.
48. P.R.O. (London) Chatham MSS. 30/8/60, Sulivan to Pitt, 27 July 1761.
49. *Ibid.*
50. See I.O.R. 'Abstracts Coast & Bay', vol. l, p.237, Despatch from the Calcutta Board to the Court of Directors, 9 October 1759.
51. I.O.R. Committee of Correspondence Memoranda, vol.18 n.p. Sulivan's reply to the Bengal General Letter of 5 July 1759.
52. P.R.O. (London) Chatham MSS. 30/8/60, Sulivan to Pitt, 27 July 1761.
53. Foster, pp.303-4; see also Barun Dé, *passim.*
54. Barun Dé, *passim.*
55. I.O.L. MSS. Eur. 302/1 'Letterbook of John Spencer', f.28. Spencer to Sulivan, Calcutta 27 September 1764.
56. I.O.R. Committee of Correspondence Memoranda, vols.1 and 18 (1757-1760), n.d. (All in Sulivan's writing).
57. N.L.W. Powis MSS. Clive Papers, 'Letterbook No.10'. Letters from Col. Clive, from 8 January 1757 to 11 October 1759. ff.160-1, Clive to Vansittart, Calcutta 25 December 1758.
58. Sulivan to Sir Eyre Coote, 16 Mar. 176l. Quoted in Forrest [1], vol.2, p. 112.
59. Quoted in Sutherland [1], p.74.
60. Bodl. Sulivan MSS. Eng. Hist. b.191, f.191, Vansittart to Sulivan, 3 March 1764.
61. Davies, A.M. [1], p.314.

6. Feuds and Peace Treaties 1757-63

1. Davies, A.M. [1], p.286.
2. *Ibid.* Quoted on p.175.

3. This idea of a Secret Committee caught the eye of Government, and in particular, that of John Robinson. They were also set up in the Presidencies.
4. B.L. Pamphlet, 100.n.20.
5. I.O.R. Home Miscellaneous Series, vol. 808, f. 118, Sulivan to Clive, 20 February 1758.
6. On 29 December 1758 he wrote to his father, and to Messrs. Law, Belchier, Smyth King and Mabbot. Clive had nothing to do with Sulivan's success in 1758.
7. See N.L.W. Powis MSS. Clive Papers, ff.172-78.
8. I.O.R. Home Miscellaneous Series, vol. 809, f.364, Clive to Sulivan, 30 December 1758.
9. Quoted in Malcolm, vol.2, pp.141-42.
10. I.O.R. Home Miscellaneous Series, vol. 809, f.364, Clive to Sulivan, 30 December 1758.
11. Clive to Stephen Law, 29 December 1758. [Quoted in Malcolm, vol.3, pp.140-3].
12. See Davies, A.M. [1], p.313.
13. I.O.L. MSS. Eur. D.546/iii-vii, ff. 99-100, Clive to Walsh, 14 October 1764.
14. I.O.R. Bengal Despatches, vol.1, p.898. General Letter to Bengal of 23 March 1759.
15. Quoted in Gleig [1], p.123.
16. See Forrest [1], vol.2, p.181.
17. B.L. Pamphlet 100.n.20. 'No man of merit escaped – (not) even Lord Clive.'
18. The signatories were Clive, Holwell, Playdell, Sumner and McGuire. [Quoted in Gleig [1], p.127].
19. Quoted in Malcolm, vol.2, p.133.
20. *Ibid.*, vol.2, p.197. Letter dated 22 November 1762
21. I.O.R. Home Miscellaneous Series, vol.808, f.141, Sulivan to Sir Eyre Coote, 16 March 1761. 1761.
22. I.O.R. Court Book, vol.69, ff.106-107; also General Court Minutes, vol.2, f.266.
23. *Ibid.* pp.362-3, 18 March 1761.
24. *Ibid.*
25. I.O.R. Home Miscellaneous Series, vol.808, f.191, Sulivan to Clive, 18 November 1761.
26. Malcolm, vol.2, p.195. Quotes Clive to Pybus, Madras on 27 February 1762.
27. *Ibid.*
28. I.O.R. Home Miscellaneous Series, vol.192, ff.280-281, Sulivan to Thomas Nuttal (Company solicitor), 29 July 1762.
29. Forde demanded £5,000 as compensation for losing his commission and rank in the King's service. [Dodwell [2], p.188, Company to Pigot, 1 November 1758].
30. I.O.R. Home Miscellaneous Series, vol. 808, f.189, Sulivan to Clive, 29 September 1761.
31. *Ibid.*
32. Quoted in Forrest [1], vol.2, p.191.
33. P.R.O. (London), 30/8/60, Sulivan to Robert Wood (Chatham's secretary) on 5 February 1761.
34. N.L.W. Powis MSS. Clive Papers, Letterbook, no.10, ff.192-5, Clive to Forde, 24 August 1759.
35. See De Bertodano, n.p., Laurence Sulivan to Stephen Sulivan, 27 February 1778. [See also Bodl. Sulivan MSS. Eng. Hist. c.269, f.22, Laurence Sulivan's Letterbook to his son, April 1778].
36. P.R.O. (London), Chatham MSS.30/8/60, ff.116-9, n.d. By Sulivan, though no author or addressee. It is included among a bundle of letters.
37. I.O.R. Home Miscellaneous Series, vol.808, ff.186-8, Sulivan to Pitt, 27 July 1761.

38. *Ibid.* Sulivan thought this approach was only in line with 'honour, justice and good policy'.

39. Cal. H.O. Papers, p.150, no.473, Charles Jenkinson to Mr. Sulivan, 25 January 1762.

40. Sutherland [2], p.184.

41. The terms the Secret Committee recommended were noticeably similar to those placed before Pitt by Sulivan on 27 January 1761.

42. Bute MSS. ff.522-4. Sulivan to Shelburne, 12 October 1762.

43. Bodl. Sulivan MSS. Eng. Hist. c.471, f.5, Shelburne to Sulivan, 13 October 1762.

44. Sutherland [1], p.93.

45. *Ibid.* This effectively excluded Dupleix's gains in the Coromandel during that year.

46. *Ibid.* Referred to on p.96.

47. Add. MSS. 32944, f.30v, 3 October 1762.

48. Davies, A.M. [1], p.338.

49. De Bertodano Papers, n.p. Laurence Sulivan to Stephen Sulivan, 27 February 1778.

50. Bodl. Sulivan MSS. Eng. Hist .c.269, f.22, Laurence Sulivan's Letterbook to his son, April 1778.

51. De Bertodano Papers, n.p., Laurence Sulivan to Stephen Sulivan, 27 February 1778.

52. See Bodl. Sulivan MSS. Eng. Hist. c.269, f.22, Laurence Sulivan's Letterbook to his son, April 1778.

53. N.L.S. Pamphlets, Entitled, 'East India Company 1764-1771.' No. 3/637, 'A Letter to the Proprietors of East India Stock.' Lord Clive 1764. [See also Malcolm, pp.205-9].

54. See Gleig [1], pp.135-6; Malcolm, vol.2, pp.205-9; and Forrest [1], pp.192-4.

55. See Malcolm, vol.2, p.205-9. Also Forrest [1], pp.192-4. Bute would never be influenced to do this by Wood, Sulivan's great friend.

56. I.O.L. Orme MSS. J, f.248. See also B.L. Pamphlet 100.n.20, *passim.*.

57. *P.A.* for 28 March 1763.

58. See also Dodwell [2], pp.333-4, Company to Pigot, 9 March 1763.

59. Quoted in Gleig [1], p.138.

60. Quoted in Sutherland [1], p.88.

61. See Malcolm, vol.2, pp.190-191.

62. *Ibid.*, p.195-196.

63. *P.A.* for 3 April 1765. See also I.O.R.. Committee of Correspondence Reports of 3 and 8 December 1767.

64. B.L.Pamph. 100.n.20.

65. I.O.L. Orme MSS. vol.124, pp.247-50; and also B.L. Pamphlet 100.n.20. *passim.*

66. N.L.S. Pamphlet no, 3/637, East India Company 1762-1771. *A Letter to the Proprietors of India Stock, from Lord Clive.* Lord Clive (1764).

67. *Ibid.*

68. Bute MSS. ff.186-8, Sulivan to Shelburne, 24 February 1763.

69. Quoted in Gleig [1], p.138.

7. Activities: Public and Private 1757-63

1. Sutherland [3], p.76.

2. Bramwell, 176l, 1st George 111, 64. Strode, William.

3. Sulivan might have been reliving a landed position once held by his own family in Ireland.

4. *The Cosmopolitan Magazine,* vol.3, [1889] pp.28-32.

5. See De Bertodano Papers, n. p. 'Particulars of Ponsborne Park, from Laurence Sulivan's A/C Book.' Also Noble, p.189, *et passim.*

6. Hertford County Records, Session Books, 1752-1799 in 'Presentation Book', vol. l, p. 216.

7. Sutherland [1], pp.51-52.

8. P.R.O. (London), Chatham MSS. 30/8/60, Part l. Sulivan to Chatham, 22 October 1761; f.120, Sulivan to Lady Hester Chatham, 29 October 1761.

9. *Ibid.*, Sulivan to Chatham, 6 June 1762.

10. See Anson, p.36.

11. At that time these included: Sergeant Glyn, Alderman Townshend, Pratt, Francis, Calcraft, Nugent and George Dempster, as well as Dunning and Barré.

12. Bute MSS. f.175. Sulivan to the Earl of Bute, 7 July 1762.

13. De Bertodano Papers, n.p. MSS. entitled 'Ashburton Election'. See also Hanham, *passim.*

14. *Ibid.*

15. *Ibid.* See also Bodl. Sulivan MSS. Eng. Hist. c.471, f.1, Jas. Eyre to Sulivan, June 1761.

16. P.R.O. (London), Chatham MSS. 30/8/60, f.111, Sulivan to Chatham, Ashburton 5 April 1761.

17. De Bertodano Papers, MSS. on the 'Ashburton Election'.

18. I.O.R. Home Miscellaneous Series, vol.808, f.189-90, Sulivan to Col. Clive, 29 September 1761.

19. De Bertodano Papers, 'Ashburton Election'.

20. *Ibid.* See also Jucker, pp.25-27.

21. *Ibid.*

22. See Devon and County Records, D. of Bedford's MSS. 'Mr. Sulivan's Case'. Also Devon Record Office, 'Brief for the Honourable John Harris Esqr. and the Honourable Thomas Walpole Esq.'

23. De Bertodano, Papers, 'Ashburton Election'. Also, B.L. Add. MSS. 38337, ff.271-24, Quoted in Jucker, pp.25-27.

24. *Ibid.*

25. Lewis, vol.23, p.288.

26. N.L.W. Powis MSS. Clive Papers, 'Letterbook.'.

27. I.O.R. Court Book no. 69, pp.362-3. Sulivan was in the Chair.

28. I.O.R. Court Book 69, p.362, for 18 March 1761.

29. Bodl. Sulivan MSS. Eng. Hist. b.191, f.13, H. Vansittart to Sulivan, 2 July 1760.

30. *Ibid.* f.206, Henry Vansittart to Sulivan, 24 March 1764.

31. See Dodwell [2], p.337, Company to Governor Pigot, 6 April, 1763.

32. The Rev. Neville Maskelyne, Mr. Robert Waddington and a Charles Mason were to proceed to Bencoolen to observe the transit of Venus over the sun on 6 June 1761.

33. Dodwell [2], p.239, Governor Pigot to the Company, 8 March 1761.

34. Bute MSS. ff.186-188, Sulivan to Shelburne, 24 February 1763.

35. Quoted in Forrest [1], p.196.

36. See N.L.S. Pamphlet No, 3/637. *The East India Company 1764-1771, A Letter to the Proprietors of India Stock,* by Lord Clive.

37. Macaulay, p.61.

38. Browne was an ex-Bombay Free Merchant. Tullie had been in Madras. William Barwell was a Director between 1753 and 1759; and then from 1761 to 1764.

39. See McGilvary [2], *passim.*

40. Bute MSS. ff.186-188, Sulivan to Shelburne, 24 February 1763.

41. *Ibid.*

42. Bowen [1], pp.39-53, quoting William L. Clements Library, Ann Arbour, Michigan, Lansdowne MSS. 90, f.84, 'Views incorporated in a plan submitted to Lord Shelburne in January 1767.'

43. Bute MSS. ff.186-188, Sulivan to Shelburne, 24 February 1763.

44. *Ibid.*

45. *Ibid.*

46. Newcastle, Rockingham, Grenville, Portland and Middleton were all involved, although Grenville did not really want any part of Clive's feud with Sulivan.

47. Bute MSS. ff.186-188, Sulivan to Shelburne, 24 February 1763.

48. *Ibid.*

49. Stuart was rewarded in return with posts for his friends. The group also included George Dempster, Sir Adam Fergusson and Alex Wedderburn

50. I.O.L. Eur. MSS. 63. 'Letters of George and John Johnstone, 1757- 1773.' Taken from the Pultney Papers in the Henry E. Huntingdon Library, California), f.468, George to William Johnstone, 3 February 1763.

51. J. West to Newcastle, 14 April 1763. Cited in Namier & Brooke [1], vol.2, p.356.

52. *P.A.* for 21 April 1763.

53. J. West to Newcastle, 14 April 1763. Cited in Namier & Brooke [1], vol.2, p.356. The splitting machinery created about 380 votes: 220 for Clive and about 160 for Sulivan.

54. Cited in Namier & Brooke [1], vol.2, p.356.

55. Built about 1707 by a Mr. Chapman; sold to a George Watson; then in 1751 to a John Mason; to a Richard Bootle; to Sulivan. It is now part of the Great Ormonde Street Hospital for Sick Children.

56. See P.R.O. Chatham Papers. 30/8/60, f.124, Sulivan to W. Pitt, Mile End Green, 22 October 1761.

57. Bodl. Sulivan MSS. Eng. Hist. b.191, f. 141. H. Vansittart to Sulivan, 27 February 1763; and f.200, H. Vansittart to Sulivan, 24 March 1764.

58. *Ibid.*, ff.25, 59, R. Palk to L. Sulivan on 26 January 1761; and 26 February 1762.

59. He was in remittance-type partnerships with Peter Godfrey, Thomas Manningham, Richard Baker and Dr. John Munro.

60. Bodl. L. Sulivan MSS. Eng. Hist. b.191, f. 140, Vansittart to Sulivan, 24 March 1763.

61. *Ibid.* f.199. Vansittart to Sulivan, 24 March 1764.

62. See I.O.R. L/AG/14/5/3-12 general Stock Ledgers for 1763 to 1766. *passim.*

63. Bodl. L. Sulivan MSS. Eng. Hist. b.191, f.170, Palk to Sulivan, 5 September 1763. This referred to land in St. Johns, Newfoundland.

64. *Ibid.* f.217, Palk to Sulivan, 24 August 1765. This might refer to Sulivan (secretly) being involved in buying back estates in Counties Cork and Kerry, once belonging to his family.

8. Challenge: Defeat: and Reflection 1757-65

1. De Bertodano, n.p. Laurence Sulivan to Stephen Sulivan, 27 February 1778.

2. I.O.L. Orme MSS. vol. J, ff.247-250; and B. L. Pamphlet 100.n.20, *passim.* From internal evidence this was dated March/April 1764.

3. B.L. Pamphlet. 100.n.20.

4. I.O.L. Orme MSS. vol. J, ff.247-250. Signed 'A Proprietor'.

5. B.L. Pamphlet 100.n.20. *passim;* also I.O.L., Orme MSS. vol. J, ff.247-50.

6. *Ibid.*

7. Quoted in Malcolm, vol.2, p.225.

8. *Ibid.* p.228. The opinion of Clive's counsel, the Attorney-General, Charles Yorke, and the Solicitor-General, Sir Fletcher Norton, was that the Directors had no case.

9. I.O.R. Home Miscellaneous Series, vol.808, ff.219-223, 30 December 1763.

10. *Ibid.*

11. See Malcolm, vol.2, p.220.

12. E.P.L. *A Letter to the Proprietors of East India Stock on the subject of Lord Clive's Jaghire, occasioned by His Lordship's Letter on that Subject.* By John Dunning, Baron Ashburton, 28 April 1764.

13. Tomlinson, p.72, Letter no.65, Grenville to Clive, December 1763.

14. I.O.L. Ormathwaite MSS, D.546, Clive to Walsh, 12 December 1763.

15. I.O.R. Bengal Despatches, vol.2, 9 February 1764.

16. See Add. MSS. 29135, f.401, Sulivan to Hastings, 20 December 1774.

17. N.L.S. MSS. 1006. 'Small Collection', f. 11, Alexander Johnstone [brother of George, John, James, Gideon and William (Pultney) Johnstone], to an unknown recipient, 11 February 1764.

18. Bodl. Sulivan MSS. Eng. Hist. b.190, Sulivan to Palk, 22 May 1764. He added, enigmatically, that for £360,000 he could have 'bought over' Clive and won handsomely.

19. *Ibid.*

20. *G.M.* vol.34 (1764), p.192.

21. I.O.L. MSS. Eur. E.302/1, 'John Spencer's Letterbook', f.43 Spencer to Sulivan 6 February 1765. See also Bodl. Sulivan MSS. Eng. Hist. b.190, f.1, Sulivan to Palk, 22 May 1764.

22. Quoted in Jucker, p.286.

23. I.O.R. Court Books, vol.73, p.88, 1 June 1764. He was supported in this by George Dempster and Governor George Johnstone.

24. Quoted in Forrest [1], p.203.

25. N.L.W. Powis MSS. Clive Papers, 'Letters from England to Lord Clive', ff.42-6, Walsh to Clive, 22 November 1764.

26. N.L.W. Powis MSS. Clive Papers, f.53, Walsh to Clive, 5 February 1765.

27. *Ibid.* ff.148-49, Scrafton to Clive, 20 January 1765. He might have referred to Mary Barwell, a very persuasive lady.

28. I.O.L. Orme MSS. O.V. 222, f.111, Orme to Clive, 19 November 1764.

29. N.L.W. Powis MSS. Clive Papers, 'Letters from May 1764 – September 1766', f.41, Walsh to Clive, 3 July 1764.

30. *Ibid.* f.42, Walsh to Clive, 22 November 1764.

31. I.O.R. Homes Miscellaneous Series, vol.808, ff.225-27, Walsh to Clive, 20 November 1764.

32. N.L.W. Powis MSS. Clive Papers, 'Letters from May 1764 - September 1766', f.96, Walsh to Clive, 17 May 1766. Vansittart's attack on Scrafton and Clive really brought this change.

33. *Ibid.* ff.13-14, Henry Clive to Robert Clive, 13 February 1765.

34. *Ibid.* 'Letters from England to Ld. Clive', 14 May 1764 to 30 December 1766, f.53, Walsh to Clive, 5 February 1765

35. I.O.R. Home Miscellaneous Series, ff.231-5, Walsh to Clive, 5 April 1765. Walsh said: 'Sulivan conceived it to be a piece of extraordinary jockeyship on our side.'

36. N.L.W. Powis MSS. Clive Papers, 'Letters from England to Ld. Clive', 14 May 1764 to 30 December 1766, ff.231-35, Walsh to Clive, 5 April 1765.

37. *Ibid.* ff. 148-149, Scrafton to Clive, 21 January 1765.

38. *G.M.* vol.35 (1765), p.108.

39. N.L.W. Powis MSS. Clive Papers, 'Letters from England to Ld. Clive', 14 May 1764 to 30 December 1766, f.135, Scrafton to Clive, 8 April 1765.

40. See also I.O.L. Orme MSS. 22, f.118, Orme to Clive, 27 April 1765.

41. N.L.W. 'Letterbook', c.11 (Letters to England from Clive), n. p., Clive to Fowke, 25 September 1765.

42. The Bill was finally passed in 1767, and stipulated that the stock was not only to be owned by the Proprietor, but that he had held it for at least half a year.

43. N.L.W. Powis MSS. Clive Papers, 'Letters from England to Ld. Clive', 14 May 1764 to 30 Dec.1766, f.150, Scrafton to Clive, 12 February 1766.

44. Quoted in Davies, A.M. [1], p.317.

45. I.O.R. Committee of Correspondence Memoranda, vol.18, n.p.

46. I.O.L. MSS. Eur. 302/1, 'Letterbook of John Spencer', Spencer to Sulivan, 24 January 1764, quoting Sulivan.

47. Quoted in Davies, A.M. [1], p.317.

48. De Bertodano Papers, n. p. Laurence Sulivan to Stephen Sulivan, 5 May 1778.

49. Grierson, p.77. *et passim.*

50. See Davies, A.M. [1], p.344

51. See *P.A.* for 8 April 1768.

52. I.O.R. Home Miscellaneous Series, vol.808, f.225, Walsh to Clive, 20 November 1765.

53. See *G. M.* vol.34 (1764) p.288.

54. Spencer had already recognized the Vizier in exchange for £200,000 and confirmation of duty-free trading rights.

55. See Edwardes, *passim;* and Davies A.M., [1], *passim.*

56. I.O.L. Eur. MSS. 302/1, 'Letterbook of John Spencer,' f.70, Spencer to Sulivan, 25 September 1765.

9. Fresh Start and New Game 1765-67

1. See I.O.R. Court Book 74, p.52, 31 May 1765

2. The structure was organised along the lines laid out in his *'Observations on the Bengal Establishment....'* [See I.O.R. Committee of Correspondence Memoranda, vol.16 (1757), n.p].

3. Quoted in Dodwell [1], p.182.

4. See Sutherland, L.S. & Woods, J. *passim*

5. Clive to Walsh, February 1766. Cited in Davies, A.M. [1], p.466.

6. Sutherland [1], p.151.

7 . S.R.O. GD224/Box 46/Bundle 46.

8. *Ibid.*

9. See Sutherland [1], pp.159-60.

10. Taylor and Pringle [eds.], vol.3, pp.189-90, Chatham to Shelburne, 3 February 1767.

11. P.R.O. Chatham MSS.30/8/56, ff.76-83. Included in a paper from Shelburne to Chatham, n.d. (from internal evidence can be firmly dated as 14 March 1767).

12. P.R.O. Chatham MSS.30/8/56, ff.76-83. 'Mr. Sullivan's Propositions to serve as the Basis of a negotiation with the Government', 16 March 1767.

13. Add. MSS. 32980, f.296, Rockingham to Newcastle, 15 March 1767

14. I.O.R. General Court Minutes, vol.3, f.53, 2 April 1767

15. It was noted then (as well as now) that the sum of £400,000 was almost the same as the loss to Government created by reduction of the land tax.

16. Spear [1], pp.178.

10. Great Designs and Personal Struggles 1768-72

1. See I.O.R. General Stock Ledgers L/AG/14/5/3-12.

2. Exeter Record Office, Kennoway Documents, 58/9, Box 104, Item 6. Sulivan to R. Palk, 13 September 1767.

3. *Ibid.*
4. Kaye & Johnstone, Section 16, p.62, ff.97-100, Lord Clive's letter to Harry Verelst, 9 March 1768.
5. H.M.S.C. Palk MSS. p.91, Letter 62, Palk to William Goodlad, 1 November 1768.
6. *Ibid.*
7. I.O.L. Eur, Photo. MSS. 63, 'George and John Johnstone Letters', *passim.*
8. Sulivan and Duncan Clerk stood security for this sum.
9. This settlement was eventually contracted in January 1769, and in fact was to last five years.
10. *P.A.* of 4 April 1769.
11. *G.M.* vol.39 (1769), p.211.
12. Royal Society of Arts, Subscription Book, 1754-63, *passim.*
13. It was not for nothing that the Company was known as 'The biggest multinational Corporation of all time.'
14. De Bertodano Papers, n.p. Sulivan to Stephen Sulivan, 6 April 1778.
15. *Ibid.*
16. Quoted in Sutherland [1], p.192.
17. De Bertodano Papers, n.p. Sulivan to Vansittart, 28 May 1770.
18. Add. MSS. 29194, f.97, Sulivan to Warren Hastings, n.d. (from internal evidence c. April 1773).
19. H.M.S.C. Palk MSS. pp.126-8, Letter 97, L. Sulivan to R. Palk, c. May-September 1770.
20. De Bertodano Papers, n.p. Sulivan to Vansittart, 24 January 1770. This surprised him because Scrafton, Clive's friend, was badly affected.
21. *Ibid.*, n.p. Sulivan to Vansittart, 28 May 1770.
22. *Ibid.*
23. Add. MSS. 29194, Sulivan to Hastings, (from internal evidence, April 1774).
24. De Bertodano Papers, Laurence Sulivan to Stephen Sulivan, c. 6 April 1778.
25. *Ibid.*
26. De Bertodano Papers, n.p. Sulivan to Vansittart, 28 May 1770. He described himself as the 'victim' of 'dreadful treachery' and 'base behaviour' at the hands of the Johnstones.
27. *Ibid.*
28. H.M.S.C. Palk MSS. p.148, Letter 119, R. Palk to W. M. Goodlad, 7 December 1770.
29. Sutherland [1], p.204.
30. H.M.S.C. Palk MSS. p.157, Letter no.134, R. Palk to W. M. Goodlad, 2 April 1771.
31. Add. MSS. 29132, f.465v, R. Leycester to Hastings, 1 December 1771. By February 1772 Colebrooke was traversing the same downhill road taken by many of his fellow jobbers.
32. I.O.L. MSS. Eur. D.535, R. Barwell's Letterbook, f.53, Richard Barwell to Roger Barwell, n.d. (but c.1772).
33. Add. MSS. 29133, ff.533-6, L. Sulivan to W. Hastings, 28 April 1773.
34. Davies, A.M. [1], p.472.
35. H.M.S.C. Palk MSS. p.123, Letter No.93, Palk to Wm. Goodlad, 15 March 1770.

11. Defences Breached 1769-73

1. See Shearer, pp. 210-222
2. A deal done in 1767 resulted in the Indemnity Act (7 Geo III, c.56) lasting for five years and ending in July 1772. See also Bowen [3], *passim.*
3. The £400,000 annual payment continued, but if the dividend went to six per cent it would not be paid. It would then be allowed to increase at one per cent per annum.

4. Add. MSS. 29133, f.535, L. Sulivan to W. Hastings, 28 April 1773.

5. Colebrooke, vol.1, p.219. He said that Sulivan and 'Tookey' (the Company Accountant) went over the figures 'minutely' and thought them correct.

6. Add. MSS. 29133, f.533-6, L. Sulivan to W. Hastings, 28 April 1773.

7. Hansard, vol.17, pp. 361-377.

8. *Ibid.,* vol. 17, pp.469-70.

9. H.M.S.C. Palk MSS. p.189, letter no. 170, Sulivan to R. Palk, no date (but early July 1772).

10. Add.MSS. 29133, ff.533-6, Sulivan to W. Hastings, 28 April 1773.

11. Copeland, vol.2, p.321, George Dempster to Edmund Burke, 4 August 1772. Some of those asked were: Cornwall, Amherst, Burke, Col. Barré, Sir Richard Sutton and Andrew Stuart.

12. Nor had he ever insinuated any such policy to anyone else.

13. I.O.R. General Court Minutes, vol.4, 3 December 1772.

14. Add. MSS. 29133, ff.533-8, Sulivan to W. Hastings, 28 April. 1773.

15. N.L.S. Minto MSS. E.F.P. 41/41/3c. Laurence Sulivan's printed election manifesto, Queen Square, 3 April 1773.

16. Add. MSS. 29133, ff.533-6, L. Sulivan to W. Hastings, 28 April 1773.

17. *Ibid.* 29194, f.96, L. Sulivan to W. Hastings, n.d. (but April 1773 from internal evidence).

18. De Bertodano Papers, n.p. L. Sulivan to Col. Wood, n.d. (but April 1773 from internal evidence).

19. Add. MSS. 29133, f.389, L. Sulivan to W. Hastings, 12 February 1773.

20. *Ibid.*, f.69, L. Sulivan to W. Hastings, 13 October 1773.

21. Exeter Record Office, Kennoway Documents, 58/9, Box. 104, Item 6, L. Sulivan to R. Palk, 13 September 1767.

22. Quoted in Feiling, p.185.

23. Add. MSS. 29126, f.94, W. Hastings to L. Sulivan, 30 January 1772.

24. *Ibid.*

25. Davies, A.M. [1], pp.472-3.

26. Feiling, p.106.

27. Add. MSS. 29133, f.97, Sulivan to W. Hastings, n.d. (but from internal evidence, April 1773).

28. *Ibid.* f.561, Sulivan to R. Barwell, 20 May 1773.

29. *Ibid.* 29134, ff.69-70, L. Sulivan to Hastings, 13 October 1773.

30. *Ibid.*, ff.84–91; (and see also ff.96-9) n.d., L. Sulivan to Hastings.

31. *Ibid*, from ff.69 onwards; the start date is 13 October 1773. These papers constitute a 'history' of the Regulating Act, going on to 28 March 1774.

32. *Ibid.*

33. *Ibid.*

34. *Ibid.*

35. Add. MSS. 29133, ff.84-98, L. Sulivan to Hastings, commencing in October 1773, ending on 28 March 1774.

36. *Ibid.*

37. *Ibid.*, 24 April 1774.

38. *Ibid.*

39. *Ibid.*

40. *Ibid.*

41. *Ibid.*

42. *Ibid.*

43. The attack on 'rights' illuminates changes taking place in society. *Laissez faire* ideas were penetrating old business cultures.

12. Desperation and Defiance 1774-78

1. Add. MSS. 29194, ff.97-8. L. Sulivan to W. Hastings, n.d. From internal evidence, April 1773.
2. See Feiling, p.89.
3. Greene, *passim.*
4. It is possible he already owned or rented this property, it was occupied by a Mary Irwin, a name that suggests she was one of his relations.
5. Quoted in Hamilton, p.77.
6. *Ibid.,* p.33.
7. The cemetery was part of 'Lamb's Conduit Fields'. Jacobites who died on Kennington Common in 1746 were buried in there with heads exposed.
8. Add. MSS. 29133, ff.533-6, L. Sulivan to W. Hastings, 28 April l773.
9. *Ibid.* 29194, f.84-91, Sulivan to Hastings, 13 October 1773.
10. *Ibid.*
11. *Ibid.* ff.84-89, L. Sulivan to W. Hastings, 7 January 1774.
12. *Ibid.*, ff.96-98, L. Sulivan to W. Hastings, 28 March 1774.
13. *Ibid.*, ff. 251-2, L. Sulivan to W. Hastings, 7 January 1774.
14. *Ibid.* ff.84-91, 96-8, L. Sulivan to W. Hastings, 28 March 1774.
15. H.M.S.C. Palk MSS. pp.240-1, Letters, 238, 240, Stephen Sulivan to R. Palk, both on 3 April 1774.
16. Add. MSS. 29134, f.335v, R. Palk to W. Hastings, 22 March 1774.
17. *Ibid.* 29194, ff.84-91, 96-8, L. Sulivan to W. Hastings, 28 March 1774.
18. *Ibid.*
19. *Ibid.*
20. See E.U.L. Strachey MSS. Strachey to Clive, April 1774.
21. Add. MSS. 29134, f.407, L. Sulivan to W. Hastings, 15 April 1774.
22. *Ibid.*
23. E.U.L. Strachey MSS., Strachey to Clive, April 1774.
24. Quoted in Bence-Jones, p.281.
25. *Ibid.*
26. H.M.S.C. Palk MSS. pp.242, 246, Sulivan to Palk, 23 August and 30 September 1774.
27. Add. MSS. 29131, f.171, Sulivan to Hastings, 14 April l775.

13. Fight for Survival 1774-78

1. Add. MSS. 29135, f.401, L. Sulivan to W. Hastings, 20 December 1774. [Much of Sulivan's correspondence with Warren Hastings from 1766 to 1785 can be traced in the Hastings Papers, Add. MSS. 29132-29194; and in Gleig [2], vols. 1-3.]
2. Some identified were: Macleane, the Macphersons, the Johnstones, Caillaud, Sykes, Pechell, Du Pré, Graham, the Barwells, Gilbert Elliot, Colebrooke, James Cockburn, Major Scott.
3. See Maclean [2], for James and John Macpherson.
4. Add. MSS. 29194, ff.186-7, L. Sulivan to W. Hastings, 3 October 1773.
5. Sulivan was an old friend of the Barwells. To him Mary Barwell was 'philosophy in petticoats'.
6. N.L.W. Powis MSS. 'Clive Letterbook 1767-74,' n.p. Clive to Hastings, 14 October 1773.
7. E.U.L. Strachey MSS., n. p. P. Francis to H. Strachey, 13 September 1775.
8. Add MSS. 29136, ff. 19-20, L. Sulivan to W. Hastings, 15 January 1775.
9. *Ibid.*
10. See Sutherland [6], *passim.*

11. Quoted in Feiling, pp.145-46.

12. See E.U.L. Strachey MSS. n. p. P. Francis to H. Strachey, 16 September 1776.

13. Hastings believed his friends betrayed him over the resignation affair. To Sulivan it was one of the most difficult decisions of his life.

14. Add. MSS. 29138, f.54, L. Sulivan to W. Hastings, 23 December 1776.

15. *Ibid.* 29140, ff.23-4, L. Sulivan to W. Hastings, 15 January 1778.

16. *Ibid.* 29194, ff.86, L. Sulivan to Hastings, 3 October 1773.

17. Exeter Record Office, Kennoway Documents, Palk MSS. (Haldon Trust), f.3, W. Hastings to R. Palk, 5 October 1771.

18. Add. MSS. 29136, ff.104-107, L. Sulivan to W. Hastings, 27 February 1775.

19. *Ibid.*

20. *Ibid.*

21. *Ibid.*

22. *Ibid.*

23. *Ibid.*

24. *Ibid.*

25. *Ibid.* 29138, f.409, L. Sulivan to W. Hastings, 14 May 1777.

26. Add. MSS. 29136, ff.19-20, L. Sulivan to W. Hastings, 15 January 1775. John Delamar, a silk merchant, backed-up Sulivan's claims for making Bengal silk after the Italian method.

27. *Ibid.* He suggested an organised structure: Districts, a District Collector of Revenues, the office of Collector-General at Calcutta; and a Board of Revenues to supervise.

28. *Ibid.*, ff.59-61, L. Sulivan to W. Hastings, 20 February 1775.

29. Add. MSS. 29138, f.235, L. Sulivan to W. Hastings, 12 May 1777.

30. Add. MSS. 29131, f.171, Sulivan to Hastings, 14 April l775.

31. S.R.O. GD 29/2122/4, Robert Mayne to his nephew John Graham, 11 January 1775.

32. I.O.L. Orme MSS, O.V. 202, f.43, R. Orme to L. Macleane, 28 March 1775.

33. Add. MSS. 29136, f.171, L. Sulivan to W. Hastings, 14 April 1775.

34. *Ibid.*

35. N.L.S. Minto MSS. E.F.P. 10, n.p. L. Sulivan to Sir Gilbert Elliot, 15 July 1775; also Alex. Elliot to Sir Gilbert Elliot, 30 November 1774.

36. Add. MSS. 29136, f.381, L. Sulivan to W. Hastings 7 December 1775; also ff.44-5, L. Sulivan to W. Hastings, 23 December 1775.

37. *Ibid.* 29137, f.58, L. Sulivan to John Stuart, 1 February 1776; also f.137, L. Sulivan to W. Hastings, 1 April 1776.

38. Later Macpherson put forward an unverifiable claim that he had been responsible for Sulivan's come-back.

39. De Bertodano Papers, n. p. L. Sulivan to Stephen Sulivan, 6 April 1778.

40. *Ibid.* The Bishop of Carlisle helped: 'He even carried a Book of Proprietors (unasked) to canvass for me.' He was the son off Edmund Law.

41. *Ibid*

42. Add. MSS. 29140, ff.286-87, L. Sulivan to W. Hastings, 20 April 1778.

43. De Bertodano Papers, n. p. L. Sulivan to Stephen Sulivan, 6 April 1778.

44. Add. MSS. 29140, f.287, L. Sulivan to W. Hastings, 20 April 1778.

45. Feiling, p.173.

46. Exeter Record Office, Palk MSS. Box 104, Item 15, 17 December 1777.

47. They included the Rockingham Opposition (notably Edmund Burke).

48. S.R.O. GD 32/24/34-57, William Young Correspondence, 1767-1814, Elibank to his son, William Young, 3 May 1777.

49. Add. MSS. 29140, f.24, Sulivan to Hastings, 15 January 1778.

50. *Ibid.* 29136, ff.171-72, Sulivan to Hastings, 14 April 1775.
51. De Bertodano Papers, n. p. L. Sulivan to S. Sulivan, 27 February 1778.
52. *Ibid.*
53. *Ibid.*
54. H.M.S.C. Palk MSS. p.241, L. Sulivan to Palk, 23 August 1774. Enough had been sent back to repay Dunning for India stock mortgaged to him.
55. Add. MSS. 29140, f.287, L. Sulivan to Hastings, 20 April 1778.
56. De Bertodano Papers, n. p. L. Sulivan to S. Sulivan, 5 May 1778.
57. *Ibid.*
58. De Bertodano Papers n. p. L. Sulivan to W. Hastings, 10 June 1778.
59. Add. MSS. 29142, f.29, L. Sulivan to Hastings, 21 December 1778.
60. De Bertodano Papers, n. p. L. Sulivan to S. Sulivan, 28 December 1778.
61. *Ibid.* 27 February 1778. Before his death Macleane had arranged a tribute for Sulivan from the Nawab.
62. *Ibid.*
63. *Ibid.*, n. p. L. Sulivan to S. Sulivan, 12 June 1778.

14. Restoration 1778-82
1. Colebrooke, vol.1 p.196.
2. De Bertodano Papers, n. p. Laurence Sulivan's Letterbook, April 1778. He still gave to charity. Ten guineas went to Fielding's plan for the support of distressed boys.
3. *Ibid.*, n.p. L. Sulivan to Mrs. Graeme, 15 January 1778.
4. H.M.S.C. Palk MSS., no. 189, Stephen Sulivan to Robert Palk, n.d., but 1774.
5. De Bertodano Papers, n. p. L. Sulivan to Mrs. Graeme, 15 January 1778.
6. *Ibid.*, n.p. L. Sulivan to S. Sulivan, on 6 April and 13 April 1778.
7. *Ibid.*, n.p. L. Sulivan to R.J. Sulivan, circa. February 1778.
8. *Ibid.*, n.p. L. Sulivan to S. Sulivan, 27 January 1778.
9. *Ibid.*
10. Trevor-Roper, *passim.*
11. Maclean [2], *passim.*
12. *Ibid.*
13. *Ibid.*, quoting Macpherson MSS. 4/28, James to John Macpherson 5 April 1776.
14. *Ibid. passim.*
15. Add. MSS. 29140, ff.279-80, John Macpherson to Hastings, 17 April 1778.
16. Maclean [2], *passim.*
17. *Ibid.*
18. *Ibid.*
19. *Ibid.* Quotes Macpherson MSS. 41/10.
20. *Ibid.*
21. *Ibid.*
22. *Ibid.*
23. *Ibid.*
24. See also I.O.L. MSS. Eur. 64. Loose Papers 61, No.1, John Bristow to P. Francis, 29 February 1788 for a pen-portrait of John Macpherson.
25. De Bertodano Papers, n. p. L. Sulivan to S. Sulivan, 28 December 1778.
26. Add. MSS. 29145, ff.18-19, L. Sulivan to W. Hastings, 14 April 1780.
27. *Ibid.*
28. In 1780 he proposed to Hillsborough (Secretary of State for the Southern Department) that islands in the Celebes and Mindanao chain should have Company settlements.
29. Add. MSS. 29147, ff.12-15, L. Sulivan to W, Hastings, 6 February 1781.
30. *Ibid.*

31. Add. MSS. 29145, ff.18-19, L. Sulivan to W. Hastings, 14 April 1780.
32. *Ibid.*
33. *Ibid.* 29149, ff.98-101, Sulivan to Hastings, 2 June 1781.
34. *Ibid.* 29146, ff.175-7, L. Sulivan to W. Hastings, 23 October 1980.
35. I.O.R. General Court Minutes, vol. 6, p.124, 17 June 1781.
36. Add. MSS. 29152, ff.429-41, L. Sulivan to W. Hastings, 20 January 1782.
37. De Bertodano Papers, n.p., L. Sulivan to Stephen Sulivan, 20 January 1782.
38. A 'bargain' was concluded with the Clavering family. If they kept quiet, the Hastings group would not oppose any settlement made. It was accepted.
39. De Bertodano Papers, n. p. L. Sulivan to W. Hastings, 10 June 1778.
40. *Ibid.*
41. Add. MSS. 29143, ff.245-6, L. Sulivan to W. Hastings, 15 May 1779.
42. *Ibid.*
43. *Ibid.*
44. *Ibid.*
45. De Bertodano Papers, n.p. Sulivan to Sir Elijah Impey, 15 January 1778.
46. Add. MSS. 29147, f.300. L. Sulivan to W. Hastings, 6 February 1781.
47. *Ibid.* He gave Hastings free reign 'to win against the Poona Marathas'.
48. *Ibid.* 29149, ff.242-9, L. Sulivan to W. Hastings, 8 June 1781.
49. *Ibid.* 29150, ff.100-101, L. Sulivan to W. Hastings, 15 August 1781.
50. *Ibid.* 29151, f.424. Copy of P. Francis to L. Sulivan, 12 November 1781.
51. Dodwell [5], p.143, 9 July 1782.
52. B.L. Add. MSS. 29149, f.176-7, L. Sulivan to W. Hastings, 2 June 1781.
53. *Ibid.*
54. *Ibid.* ff.242-9, L. Sulivan to W. Hastings, 8 June 1781.
55. *Ibid.* John Motteux was his middleman. The scheme proved successful.

15. *Transformation 1780-84*

1. Add. MSS. 29144, ff.33-4, Sulivan to Hastings, 5 February 1780.
2. *Ibid.* 29147, f.246. L. Sulivan to W. Hastings, 11 April 1781.
3. I.O.R. General Court Minutes, vol. 6, ff.56-71, 15 May 1781. Army suspicions forced old recruitment methods; only 1,000 men were allowed on standby; double when at war.
4. E.U.L. Laing MSS, La 11, 624, Col. Goddard to Sulivan, Bombay, 20 November 1781. He said Sulivan was 'a person whose whole life has been devoted to promote the interests of the public, and who has himself rendered such eminent services to the Company and his country'.
5. Add. MSS. 29149, ff.175-6, Sulivan to Hastings, 2 June 1781.
6. *Ibid.*
7. *Ibid.*
8. N.L.S. Minto MSS. Hippisley Papers. I.E. 93 n. p. J. Coxe-Hippisley to Caillaud, 1 September 1782.
9. See Sutherland, L.S. & Woods, J. *passim.* In 1769 William Burke and Verney faced a loss of £53,000 (£23,000 each on this deal alone) which ruined them.
10. Nottingham University, Portland MSS. L. Sulivan to Fletcher 9 October 1780; enclosed in Fletcher's letter to Portland, 14 October 1780. Portland made a revealing comment: 'The original author of this illuminating report [Laurence Sulivan] possesses great talents, but he presumes too much.'
11. *Ibid.*
12. Copeland, vol.4, p.316, Edmund Burke to Hillsborough and Stormont, 19 October 1780.
13. See Sutherland [5], *passim.*

14. *Ibid.; and* Fraser, pp.154-215 *passim.*
15. Quoted in Feiling, p.297.
16. De Bertodano Papers, n. p. Stephen Sulivan to L. Sulivan, 1 December 1782.
17. Add. MSS. 29156, ff.449-453, L. Sulivan to W. Hastings, 28 November 1782.
18. De Bertodano Papers, Stephen Sulivan to L. Sulivan, 1 December 1782.
19. Sulivan was also being misled and corrupted by the Macphersons, whose deceit had not yet been uncovered.
20. Add. MSS. 29162, ff.291-5, L. Sulivan to W. Hastings, 1 March 1784.
21. N.L.S. Minto MSS. Hippisley Papers. I.E. 93, n.p. J. Coxe-Hippisley to J. Caillaud, 1 September 1782.
22. Bodl. Sulivan MSS. Eng. Hist. c.269, L. Sulivan's 'Letterbook' to S. Sulivan, April 1778.
23 De Bertodano Papers, n.p. L. Sulivan to S. Sulivan, 27 February 1778.
24 *Ibid.*, n.p. L. Sulivan to S. Sulivan, 27 February 1778 and 6 April 1778.
25. *Ibid.*
26. Bodl. Sulivan MSS. Eng. Hist. c.269, L. Sulivan's 'Letterbook' to S. Sulivan, April 1778.
27. *Ibid.* The Nawab was to understand that this publication really would be his father's own work.
28. *Ibid.*
29. *Ibid.* Stephen was to ensure his position 'should at least equal that of (the untrustworthy) Mr. Frederick Stuart'.
30. Agents from 1771 to 1793 were: Lindsay, Harland, Macleane & Johnson, Frederick Stuart, Jas. & John Macpherson, Jas. Macpherson & Nathaniel Wraxall, Jas. & John Macpherson.
31. De Bertodano Papers, n. p., L. Sulivan to S. Sulivan, 28 December 1778.
32. Bodl. Sulivan MSS. Eng. Hist. c.269, L. Sulivan's 'Letterbook' to S. Sulivan, April 1778.
33. *Ibid*
34. *Ibid.*
35. De Bertodano Papers, n. p., L. Sulivan to S. Sulivan, 12 June 1778.
36. Add. MSS. 29143, f. 246, Sulivan to Hastings, 15 May 1779.
37. *Ibid.* 29144, f.152, L. Sulivan to W. Hastings, 6 November 1779.
38. The long delay in repayment might be tied to the split between Mrs. Hastings and Mrs. Stephen Sulivan late in 1781.
39. *Ibid.* 29194, ff.98-100, L. Sulivan to W. Hastings, June 1781.
40. *Ibid.*
41. De Bertodano MSS. n.p. S. Sulivan to L. Sulivan, 1 December 1782.
42. Bodl. Eng. Hist. Sulivan MSS, c.471, L. Sulivan to S. Sulivan, 28 February 1784. Copy of Stephen Sulivan's appointment as Judge Advocate, 30 October 1780. [See also B.L. Add. MSS. 29149, ff.244-49, Sulivan to Hastings, 8 June 1781].
43. Hastings suffered a reprimand in 1782; and it was also brought up at his Impeachment (charges 9 and 10).
44. Even after Sulivan's death in 1786 the money from these bonds had not been realised.
45. De Bertodano Papers, n. p. L. Sulivan to S. Sulivan, 27 February 1778. Stephen was to demand immediate payment, but to give him time to pay if needed.
46. *Ibid.*
47. £10,000 of this would go towards paying Stephen's debts in Britain.
48. De Bertodano Papers, n. p. L. Sulivan to S. Sulivan, 27 February 1778.
49. *Ibid.*

50. Bodl. Sulivan MSS. Eng. Hist. c.269, f.29, L. Sulivan's 'Letterbook' to Stephen Sulivan, April 1778.
51. *Ibid.*
52. *Ibid.*

16. Personal Loss and Political Revival 1781-83

1. Bodl. Sulivan MSS. Eng. Hist. c.269, ff.39-42, L. Sulivan's Letterbook to his son, April 1778.
2. Add. MSS. 29152, f.456. Excerpt from a letter of L. Sulivan, 5 June 1781, contained in a letter from Richard Joseph Sulivan to W. Hastings, 22 January 1782.
3. *Ibid.* 29149, ff.174-8, L. Sulivan to W. Hastings, 2 June 1781.
4. *Ibid.* 29152, ff.429-41, L. Sulivan to W. Hastings, 20 January 1782.
5. *Ibid.*
6. *Ibid.*
7. Magnus, p.126.
8. P.R.O. (N. Ireland), D.O.D. 572/19/84, Thos. Allan to Ld. Macartney, 8 June 1782.
9. *Ibid.*
10. Add. MSS. 29156, ff.449-53, L. Sulivan to W. Hastings, 28 November 1782. A portrait was painted by Tilly Kettle in 1767, a miniature by Richard Crosse in 1778. She left an Owen family bible, which went to Stephen's wife.
11. Bodl. Sulivan MSS. Eng. Hist. c.269, f.30, Laurence Sulivan's Letterbook to Stephen Sulivan, April 1778.
12. *Ibid.*
13. De Bertodano Papers, n. p. L. Sulivan to S. Sulivan 10 November 1784. He allowed Major Scott to live there, though nothing was to be moved.
14. *Ibid.*
15. Add. MSS. 29145, f.18, L. Sulivan to W. Hastings, 14 April 1780.
16. *Ibid.* 29147, L. Sulivan to W. Hastings, 5 January 1781.
17. De Bertodano Papers, n. p. S. Sulivan to L. Sulivan, 1 December 1782.
18. Add. MSS. 29147, ff. 143-4, L. Sulivan to W. Hastings, 21 August 1781.
19. *Ibid.*
20. Accusations made were of: restoring John Macpherson; screening Impey; delaying a despatch (affecting Patna prisoners); maltreatment of Maratha agents in London.
21. Copeland, vol.5, p.334, E. Burke to T. L. O'Byrne, 30 January 1781.
22. *Ibid.*, vol.5, p.447, E. Burke to W. Burke, 25 April 1782.
23. See also Cone, pp.111-118.
24. De Bertodano Papers, n. p., L. Sulivan to W. Hastings, 20 July 1783.
25. *Ibid.*
26. Lawson, Sir C, p.80.
27. Parkes & Merivale, vol.2, p.216.
28. Add. MSS. 29156, ff.449-453, L. Sulivan to W. Hastings, 12 to 28 November 1782.
29. *Ibid.*
30. *Ibid.*
31. *Ibid.*
32. Add. MSS. 29156, ff.449-453, L. Sulivan to W. Hastings, 28 November 1782.
33. *Ibid.*
34. I.O.L. Eur. MSS. E.19, Francis MSS. 54, 'Letters from Francis 1781-2', f.42, Francis to Ducarel, 7 December 1782.
35. *Ibid.*
36. De Bertodano Papers, n. p., L. Sulivan to W. Hastings, 20 July 1783.
37. *Ibid.*, n. p. L. Sulivan to W. Hastings, 26 December 1783.

38. *Ibid.*, n.p. L. Sulivan to John Macpherson, 26 December 1783.
39. *Ibid.,* n. p. L. Sulivan to W. Hastings, 26 December 1783.
40. *Ibid.*

17. Closing of an Era 1782-86

1. De Bertodano Papers, n. p. L. Sulivan to Wheler, 26 December 1783.
2. *Ibid.*, n. p., L. Sulivan to Stephen Sulivan, 10 November 1784.
3. Add. MSS. 29162, f.294, L. Sulivan to W. Hastings, 1 March 1784.
4. De Bertodano Papers, n.p., L. Sulivan to Stephen Sulivan, 11 October 1784.
5. *Ibid.*
6. *Ibid.*
7. *Ibid.*
8. Furber [2], p.483, Atkinson to Dundas, 22 July 1784.
9. Add. MSS. 29163, John Scott to Hastings, 24 April 1784.
10. De Bertodano Papers, n. p., L. Sulivan to Stephen Sulivan, 11 October 1784.
11. Add. MSS. 29156, ff.449-453, L. Sulivan to W. Hastings, 28 November 1782.
12. *Ibid.* 29163, f.230, L. Sulivan to W. Hastings, 27 April 1784.
13. De Bertodano Papers, n. p. L. Sulivan to Stephen Sulivan, 10 November 1784.
14. Bodl. MSS. Eng. Hist. C.111, f.43, Lord Macartney to L. Sulivan, 27 September 1782.
15. *Ibid.*, ff.60-3, Lord Macartney to John Sulivan, 30 March 1783.
16. *Ibid.*
17. De Bertodano Papers, n. p. Lord Macartney to L. Sulivan, 10 August 1783.
18. *Ibid.*
19. *Ibid.*, n.p. Lord Macartney to L. Sulivan, 14 October 1783. .
20. De Bertodano Papers, n. p., L. Sulivan to S. Sulivan, 10 November 1784.
21. *Ibid.*
22. P.R.O. (London), Chatham Papers, vol.356. Quoted in Philips, C.H. [4], sub-section, 'The Opposition of the Indian Interest, 1784-88', p.37.
23. *Ibid.*
24. See Philips, C.H. [4], pp. 38-41. Three categories were formed: the Consolidated Loan of 1767; the Cavalry Loan of 1777; and the Consolidated Loan of 1777.
25. *Ibid.* pp. 40-41. See especially p.40, footnote 1: that Sulivan secretly gave the papers to Debrett, who published them.
26. P.R.O. (N. Ireland), DS 572/10, Sulivan to Macartney, Hanover Square, 16 March 1785.
27. *Ibid.*
28. Add. MSS. 29168, ff.223-4, L. Sulivan to W. Hastings, 16 March 1785.
29. Stuart, Bute's protégé, filled the first vacancy. Also, Dundas' dependant Edward Hay and Stephen being friendly resulted in Hay being made Secretary at Bengal, via Sulivan.
30. De Bertodano Papers, S. Sulivan to L. Sulivan, 1 December 1782.
31. *Ibid.* This grandson, named Laurence, was to marry Elizabeth Temple, Palmerston's sister. He was to become the Prime Minister's great friend and an Under Secretary of War.
32. *Ibid.*, n.p., L. Sulivan to S. Stephen Sulivan, 20 January 1782. Stephen owed money: to Sir Horace Mann (£1, 800 was already paid); Thomas Lane (Younger); Mr. Jekyll; & Mary Barwell.
33. *Ibid.*, n.p., L. Sulivan to S. Sulivan, 28 February 1784.
34. *Ibid.*, n.p., L. Sulivan to S. Sulivan, 10 November 1784.
35. Add. MSS. 29170, ff.121-2, John Sulivan to S. Sulivan, 9 July 1786.
36. Hansard, vol.7, pp.366-414, 30 May 1806. Speech by John Sulivan.
37. *Ibid.*

38. In 1772 he received £1,375, based on this land; in 1775 he received portion of another (shared) lot. Title to the remainder came in 1783. 66,000 acres were expropriated (with compensation) by the Prince Edward Island legislature in the mid-1870s. The money was paid to his Great grand-daughter, Charlotte Antonia Sulivan.

18. Endings 1784-86

1. Add. MSS. 29162, f.131, L. Sulivan to W. Hastings, 12 February 1784.

2. *Ibid.* 29166, f.123, L. Sulivan to W. Hastings, 15 September 1784.

3. See also Philips, C.H. [4], pp. 41-44.

4. Copeland, vol.5, p.208. Edmund Burke to G. L. Staunton, 7 April 1785. See also Philips, C.H. [4], p.49.

5. See also Philips, C.H. [4], pp. 44-45.

6. Among various others were: the 'Bombay Plan'; 'B's' plan; 'Townson's'; and 'Call's'. [See also Philips [4], pp. 46-47].

7. De Bertodano Papers, n.p. L. Sulivan to W. Hastings, 10 January 1778.

8. Mackay, p.534.

9. Quoted in Lawson & Philips, p.239.

10. De Bertodano Papers, n.p., L. Sulivan to W. Hastings, 20 July 1783. 'Rooted affliction and the weakness of my eyes has for some time rendered me tardy'.

11. *Ibid.*

12. De Bertodano Papers, n.p. Lord Macartney to Stephen Sulivan, 3 August 1783. In August 1783 a Mr. Toone informed Macartney that he was recovering.

13. *Ibid.*, n.p. L. Sulivan to S. Sulivan, 10 November 1784

14. *Ibid.*

15. Add. MSS. 39880, vol.x, (8 September 1785–31 December 1787), W. Hastings' Diary, ff.6–18.

16. *Ibid.*

17. *The London Chronicle,* vol.33, Tuesday, 21 February 1786; the *Public Advertiser,* Wed. 22 February 1786; *The Morning Chronicle and London Advertiser* for Friday 24 February 1786.

18. Add. MSS. 39880, vol.x, (8 Sept. 1785 – 31 Dec.1787), W. Hastings' Diary, f.19.

19. De Bertodano Papers, n. p. John Caillaud to Stephen Sulivan, 26 February 1786. [See also John Sulivan's tribute made in the Commons in 1806].

20. De Bertodano Papers, n. p. S. Sulivan to L. Sulivan, 1 December 1782.

21. The 'Letterbook' to his son is true in what it says; as were his published pamphlets dealing with the public domain, such as his: *History of the Administration of the Leader.*

22. Add.MSS. 29194, f.89, L. Sulivan to W. Hastings, no date, but 1773.

23. I.O.R. Home Miscellaneous Series, vol.808, f.141, Sulivan to Eyre Coote, 16 March 1761.

24. Philips, C.H. [2], p.462. 'He (Sulivan) emerges with credit, standing firm in defence of the Company as an independent trading concern against the incursions… of the state.'

25. Bayley, p.198 and 199-234 *passim.*

26. See James, p.219. He makes almost the same point – without reference to Sulivan.

Bibliography

Primary Manuscript Sources

Bodleian Library, University of Oxford.
Papers of Laurence Sulivan: Eng. Hist. b.190; b.191; c.237; c.269; c.270; c.271; c.471; c.472. Macartney MSS. Eng. Hist. c.82; c.111. Vansittart MSS. f.78.

British Library London.
Add. MSS: 5143, 5147, 16260, 18409, 18464, 24611, 28211, 29126, 29128, 29131 to 29156, 29159 to 29163, 29165 to 29168, 29170, 29172, 29173, 29175, 29178, 29193, 29194, 32892, 32896, 32929, 32934, 32935, 32944, 32948, 32980, 34686, 35636, 38198, 38201, 38309, 38337, 38458. Warren Hastings: Diary: 39879 to 39891, 39903. Clive Papers – 44061. Papers of Henry Fox, Lord Holland (Holland House): 51378, 51379, 51388, 51398, 51431 to 51434. Pamphlets: 100.n.20; 101.n.25.

Bury St. Edmunds & West Suffolk Record Office.
Folios 423, and 446 to 448.

Bute Manuscripts Mountstuart Isle of Bute.
Correspondence of John Stuart, 3rd Earl of Bute: folios 139-40, 175, 186-8, 205, 276-7, 522-524, 633-634, 642, 643.

De Bertodano (Private Collection).
Papers belonging to Mr. Martin De Bertodano (These are authentic transcripts of the correspondence of Laurence Sulivan. The original manuscripts of most are now held in the Bodleian Library, Oxford and the British Library, London; but for many the originals have disappeared).

Devon County Record Office.
Bedford MSS.; Burgage Records of Ashburton; 'Brief for the Honourable John Harris Esqr. and the Honourable Thomas Walpole Esq.'

Devon and Exeter Institutions Library, Exeter.
Petition of the Freeholders of Ashburton, 1761.

Dublin Castle Record Office.
Betham Will Abstracts - MSS. G.O. 278(Ball); Professor Wardell's Correspondence with the Chief Herald, Dublin Castle.

Dublin City Library.
Gilbert Collection - Beltz MSS. Manuscript collection of evidence relating to the family of O'Sullivan More, the result of an expedition to Ireland by the genealogist G. Beltz in 1802.

East Suffolk Record Office.
Martin family of Hemingstone Papers, HA 13/A/1-15.

Edinburgh University Library.
Laing MSS. La. 11,73,77, 77 Div.2, 105,111,364,477; Strachey MSS. (Copies from the Principal of Lady Margaret Hall, Oxford): letters to Clive 1765 - 1775; letters to H. Strachey 1764 – 1770.

Exeter Record Office.
Manuscripts of Mark Kennaway (solicitor), Kennaway Documents, 58/9, Box 104, Item 6; Haldon Trust: Palk MSS. boxes 2, 104, 159, 169, 239, 242, 246.

Greater London Record Office, Westminster.
Records of St. Mary, Whitechapel.

Guildhall Library.
'The St. James' Register'.
Hertford (County) Record Office.
Carlisle MSS. - D/Ex 2-7. Session Books, 1752-1799 ['Presentation Book,' Vol. l].
Historical Manuscripts Commission
Abergavenny MSS. ; Charlemont MSS. ; Laing MSS. ; Ormonde MSS. ; Palk MSS. ;
Portland MSS.
Holborn Public Library, London.
Original Rate Books for St. Andrew Holborn and St. George the Martyr; Rates
(Holborn); 'Highway Rate'.
House of Lords Record Office, London.
Journals of the House of Lords. 'The Petition and Appeal of Rawson Hart Boddam
and Stackhouse', dated 7 February 1786. Judicial Records of the House of Lords.
India Office Library, London.
Manuscripts:
Eur. 6.4. Loose Papers 61, No.1; Eur. Eng MSS. Photographs: 63, 162, 638 *et passim* -
Johnstone letters. (From Pultney Papers in the Henry L. Huntingdon Library,
California); Eur. 302/1 - Letterbook of John Spencer; Eur. 302/2 - Letterbook of
Mrs. Adriana Spencer; Eur. D.535 - Letterbook of Robert Barwell; Eur. D/546.
Ormathwaite Collection; MSS. Eur. E.13A, Philip Francis Papers: MSS. Eur. E.15,
MSS. Eur. E.16, Eur. MSS. E.19, 'Letters from Francis 1781-2'; Eur. E.23, No.66, P.
Francis' Journal; Eur. MSS. 54 Francis MSS, Eur.E.379/4, Eur.E.379/8.
Microfilm, reel 1542 - Macartney Papers; (Microfilm) Eur. MSS. reel 625.
O.V. – (Orme Various) vols. 1.7, 21, 22, 28, 32.1, 37, 40.l, 63.26, 124, 147.8, 158.2,
159, 202, 214, 217, 222, 271.1, 293; vols. J, J.28, X. 202-64.
Powis MSS. Box 3.
Records:
Abstracts Coast & Bay, vol. l. Bengal Abstracts, vols. l & 2. Bengal Baptisms 1713 -
1800. Bengal Births, Marriages, Burials 1713-54. Bengal Civilians - 0/6/21 to 0/6/29.
Bengal Despatches, *passim.* Bombay Abstract Letters Received 1723-32, and 1751-62.
Bombay Baptisms 1709-1800. Bombay Burials 1709-1800. Bombay Civil Servants
1712-52. Bombay Civilians - 0/6/32 to 0/6/35. Bombay, Copies of Wills registered in
the Mayor's Court 1738-45. Bombay Despatches, vols.1 to 6; Bombay Diary. Bombay
Ecclesiastical Returns 1709-57. Bombay European Inhabitants 1719-22. Bombay
Journal 1739-41. Bombay Letters Received 1709-25, 1735-58. Bombay Marriages
1709-1800. Bombay Proceedings 1729-32. Bombay Public Consultations 1730-52.
Bombay, Register of Proceedings of the Mayor's Court. Bond Book of Company
Servants Abroad. Committee of Correspondence Memoranda, vols. 15 to 23.
Committee of Correspondence Reports, vols. 6 to 8. Court Books, vols.45 to 78, 80,
81, 86, 89 to 94. Despatches from England. European Inhabitants Bombay, 1719-92.
European Inhabitants Madras, 1702-1780. General Court Minutes, vols. 2 to 7.
General Court Minutes - Elections of Directors 1702-1846. Haileybury Records -
Writer's Petitions 1763-4. Home Miscellaneous Series, vols: 82, 96, 118, 153, 154, 191,
192, 208, 214, 322, 369A, 462, 614, 764, 788, 808, 809. Madras Civil Servants, 1702-
75. Madras Civilians. Madras Despatches, *passim.* Madras Register of Baptisms and
Burials, vol. l. Madras Marriages 1698-1800. Marine Records-L/Mar/B;
L/Mar./C/605H; L/Mar./C/644; L/Mar./C/651. Register of Commands 1737-1832.
Miscellaneous Letters Received, vol. 29. ORB 50/15, dated 12 December 1752.
Personal Records, *passim.* Petitions, *passim.* Press List of the Ancient Records of the
Government of India, 'Fort William Minutes of Consultations', vol.4. Records of the
Accountant General's Department. Stock holders and Stock purchased 1718 to 1761.

Records of Fort St. George, Madras; Diary and Consultation Books. Stock and Bonds, Stock Transfer Books (1753-1786), General Stock Ledgers L/AG/14/5/3-12 *et passim*; L/AG/14/7/l. Sumatra Records, vol. 8. Surat Factory Records, vols. 23,33,34,37,38. Tracts (Bound), no.487. Writers Petitions. J/1/1-15. Microfilms: George and John Johnstone Letters, MSS. Eur. Photo. 63. Verelst's Europe Letter Books, MSS. Eur. Photo.606.

National Library of Ireland
Doneraile Papers; vol.23; Kings Inns Admissions Papers, pp.458-69, 468-69

National Library of Scotland.
Minto Papers: MSS. EFP 3, 10, 15-17, 41 *et passim*; MSS. 11001 to 11005, 11018, 11027, 11041 *et passi*; Minto MSS. Hippisley Papers. I.E. 93. Small Collections - MSS. 1006, 1026; Andrew Stuart Papers–Stuart Stevenson Papers: Castlemilk and Torrance Muniments: MSS. 5330, 5381 to 5386, 5346, 5388, 5391, 5400, 8250, 8251, 8256, 8278, 8280, 8326, 8327, 8352, 8404, 9246; C/959, Tracts on India Affairs; Pamphlets: no.2/133; no.3/637; MSS. 1694.

National Library of Wales Aberystwyth.
Powis MSS. (Papers deposited by the late George Charles 4th Earl of Powis); Clive Papers.

National Register of Archives.
The Bute Papers, Nos. 29, 64, 65; The Shelburne/Henry Fox Correspondence, Nos. 56, 57, held in West Register House, Edinburgh.

North Riding Record Office.
Affidavit by Robert and Duncan Clerk, London 10 May 1769.

Nottingham University
Portland MSS: P.W.F. MSS. PWF l0359; 10360; 10364.

Public Record Office (Ireland), Dublin.
Betham Genealogical Abstracts, Prerogative Admonitions, Marriages, Wills; Calendar of Converts; Diocese Bonds and Wills for Cork; Groves Abstracts; Indexes to Cork and Ross Wills, Prerogative Grants, Diocese Bonds; Philips MSS, vols.46,62,63. m.6282.

Public Record Office, London.
Chatham MSS. – 30/8/56; 30/8/60. Egremont MSS–30/47/20/2-3; 30/47/29. Treasury Papers - T.49, documents 1-9. Ewan Law Papers - 30/12/17. Herbert MSS. 30/53. DS 572/10. Original Wills proved in the Prerogative Court of Canterbury: - John Home, Captain Samuel Hough, Stephen Law, John Spencer, Benjamin Sullivan; Administrations of Laurence Sulivan and Stephen Sulivan.

Public Record Office (Northern Ireland) Belfast.
Macartney Papers – D.O.D. D572/10; D.O.D. 572/19/21; D.O.D. 572/19/84.

Registry of Deeds, Dublin.
Memorials in vols. 167, 170, 175,189,201,211,242,248,301.

Royal Irish Academy Dublin.
O'Gorman MSS 'A History of Kerry'; MSS 'Distribution of Forfeited Land in the Counties of Cork and Kerry' - Returned by the Downe Survey.

Royal Society of Arts, London.
Minutes of the Society, vol.1; vol.15. Transactions by Dr. Templeman, vol.l. Guard Books, vol. l, f.17, nos.124, 127. Subscription Book, 1754-63, *passim*.

John Rylands Library, Manchester.
Eng. MSS. 152,153,162.

Scottish Record Office, Edinburgh.
Buccleuch MSS GD224; Clerk of Penicuik Muniments: GD18; Douglas MSS. vol. 2, Entry 499/22; Elibank Papers: 'William Young Correspondence, 1767-1814' GD32;

Graham Papers (Kinross House MSS) GD29; Melville Castle Muniments: GD32;
Macpherson of Cluny Papers: GD80; Also: GD 110; GD156; GD 240
Sheffield City Library.
FitzWilliam MSS. Correspondence of the 2nd Marquess of Rockingham and
Correspondence of Edmund Burke deposited by the Trustees of the Wentworth-
Woodhouse Estates: R.1-1443. [Especially R. 66, R.67, R.81, R. 86, R. 207, R.208].
Shropshire County Record Office
Powis MSS. 552/1/c.6.

Select List of Laurence Sulivan Publications
Address to the East India Proprietors respecting questions for ballot. (no date)
A Defence of the United Company of Merchants of England trading to the East Indies and their servants, against the Complaints of the Dutch East India Company. (1762)
A Defence of the Leader. (1765)
A Defence of Mr. Sulivan's Propositions with an answer to the objections against them, in a letter to the Proprietors of East India Stock. (1767)
Plan for Augmenting the capital and extinguishing the debts of the East India Company. (1772)
Letters to the Proprietors. (1773)
An Analysis of the Political History of India. (1779)
On Martial Law. (1779)
A Letter to the Directors of the East India Company. (1784)
Laurence Sulivan was also responsible for a great deal of *The East India Examiner.*

Selected Printed Works
[All books below are cited by author's surname. If an author has more than one work quoted, then the surname is followed by a number [in sequence] distinguishing each particular work. Authors with the same surname are differentiated by their initials.]

Allan, D.C.C., 'The Contest for the Secretaryship 1769-70', (Studies in the Society's Archives XXXVI-XXXVIX). In *Journal of the Royal Society of Arts.* vols. 112-113. (August-December 1964).
Analecta Hibernica, Irish Manuscripts Commission. (1930)
Anson, Sir W. R., *The Autobiography and Political Correspondence of Augustus Henry, 3rd Duke of Grafton, K.G.* (1898)
Arrowsmith, R. L., *Charterhouse Register 1769–1872.* (1974)
Bayley, C.A., 'The British Military-Fiscal State and Indigenous Resistance: India 1750-1820', in Patrick Tuck, *The East India Company 1600-1858.* vol.5. (1998)
Bedford, E. C., *St. George the Martyr, Queen Square.* (1910)
Bence-Jones, M., *Clive of India.* (1974)
Bengal Past and Present, *Journal of the Calcutta Historical Society.* vol. 2, part 2; vol. 10; vol.11.
Bolts, W., 'Considerations on Indian Affairs', in Patrick Tuck, *The East India Company 1600-1858.* vol.3. (1998)
Bowen, H.W. [1], ' "Dipped in the Traffic." East India Stockholders in the House of Commons 1768-1774', in, *Parliamentary History*, vol.5. (1986)
_____ [2], *Revenue and Reform: The Indian Problem in British Politics 1757-1773.* (1991)
_____ [3], 'Teas, Tribute and the East India Company c.1750-1775', in S. Taylor, R. Connors, C. Jones, *Hanoverian Britain and Empire.* (1998)
Bramwell, G., *Table of Private Statutes, 1727-1812.* (1813)

Brooke, J., *The Chatham Administration*. (1956)
Bryant G.J. [1], 'The East India Company and its Army 1600–1778.' (Ph.D. thesis, London 1975)
_____ [2], 'Officers of the East India Company's Army in the Days of Clive and Hastings', in Patrick Tuck, *The East India Company 1600-1858*. vol.5. (1998)
Buist, N.G., *At Spes Non Fracta: Hope & Co. 1770-1815*. (1974)
Cannon, J., *The Whig Ascendancy*. (1981)
Chandra, P., 'The Relations Between the Court of Directors and the Board of Commissioners for the Affairs of India 1784-1816.' (Thesis submitted for the degree of Ph.D., London School of Economics and Political Science. London 1932)
Chaudhuri, K.N. [1], 'The English East India Company in the 17th and 18th Centuries: A Pre-Modern Multinational Organisation', in Patrick Tuck, *The East India Company 1600-1858*. vol.4. (1998)
_____ [2], 'The English East India Company and its Decision Making', in Ballhatchet, K. & Harrison, J. [eds.], *East India Company Studies. Papers presented to Professor Sir Cyril Philips*. (1986)
Chaudhuri, N. C., *Clive of India: A Political and Psychological Essay*.(1975)
Cheung, H. & Mu, L.H., 'William Pitt and the Enforcement of the Commutation Act 1784-1788', in *English Historical Review*, vol. lxxvi. (1961)
Christie, I.R., *The Fall of North's Ministry 1780-1782*. (1958)
Clark, F.P., *Edmund Burke*. vol.1 1730-1784. (1998)
Colebrooke, Sir G., *'Retrospection' or Reminiscences Addressed to my son Henry Thomas Colebrooke Esquire*, 2 vols. (1898)
Colley, L., *Britons, Forging the Nation 1707-1837*. (1992)
Cone, C.B., *Burke and the Nature of Politics: The Age of the American Revolution*. (1957)
Copeland, T.W. (ed.), *The Correspondence of Edmund Burke*. vols.1, 4, 5. (1958)
Cork Historical and Archaeological Society, Journal. (1898)
(The) Cosmopolitan Magazine, vol.3. (1889)
Cranmer-Byng, J.L., *An Embassy to China*. (1962)
Crowe, C.E., 'Sir Philip Francis 1740 1818 - A Biography.' (Ph.D. Dissertation, University of Georgia, 1971)
Cushner, N.P. (ed.), *Documents Illustrating the British Conquest of Manila, 1762-1763*. Camden Fourth Series, vol.8. (1971)
Cussans, J.E., *History of Hertfordshire, Broadwater volume*. (1878)
Dagliesh, W.H., *The Company of the Indies in the Days of Dupleix*. (1933)
Dasgupta, A., 'Trade and Politics in 18th Century India', in Patrick Tuck, *The East India Company 1600-1858*. vol.4. (1998)
Datta, K.K., *Fort William-India House Correspondence*. vol. 1 (1748- 1756). (1958)
Davies, A.M., [1], *Clive of Plassey*. (1939)
_____ [2], *Warren Hastings*. (1935)
Davies, C.C., [1], "The Private Correspondence of Lord Macartney, Governor of Madras (1781-85)", *Royal Historical Society, Camden, Third Series*. (lxxiii)
_____ [2], 'Warren Hastings and Pitt the Younger', in *English Historical Review*, vol.70. (1955)
Dé, B., 'Henry Dundas and the Government of India (1773-1801). A Study in Constitutional Ideas'. (Oxford University D.Phil. thesis, 1961)
Dickson, P.G.M., *The Financial Revolution in England*. (1967)
(The Oxford) Dictionary of National Biography, vol.53. (2004)
Dodwell, H. [1], *The Cambridge History of India*. vol. 5. (1929)

_____[2], *Calendar of the Madras Despatches, 1754-1765.* (1930)
_____[3], *The Nabobs of Madras.* (1926)
_____[4], *Dupleix and Clive.* (1949)
_____[5], *Warren Hastings' Letters to Sir John Macpherson.* (mcmxxii)
_____[6], 'Warren Hastings and the Assignment of the Carnatic', in *English Historical Review.* vol. xl. (1975)
Douglas, J., *Bombay and Western India, 2 vols.* (1893)
Drew, B., *The London Assurance.* (1949)
Edwardes, M., *Plassey, The Founding of an Empire.* (1969)
Farrington, A., *A Catalogue of the East India Ships' Journals and Logs, 1600-1834.* (2000)
Fawcett, Sir C. (ed.), *East Indiamen: The East India Company's Maritime Service, by Sir Evan Cotton.* (1949)
Feiling, K., *Warren Hastings.* (1954)
Fitmaurice, Lord E., *Life of William Earl of Shelburne, afterwards Marquess of Lansdowne, with Extracts from his Papers and Correspondence.* 3 vols. (1875)
Fitzroy-jones, I., 'The Sulivans of India.' In, *The Genealogists Magazine*, vol.6, no.11. September 1934.
Forrest, Sir G.W. [1], *Life of Lord Clive.* 2 vols. (1918)
_____[2], *Selections from the Letters Despatches and other State Papers preserved in the Bombay Secretariat, Home Series.* 2 vols. (1887)
_____[3], *The Administration of Warren Hastings 1772-1785.* (1892)
Foster, W., *The Embassy of Sir Thomas Roe to India 1615-19.* (1926)
Fraser, T.G., 'India 1780-86', in P. Roebuck [ed.], *Macartney of Lisanoure 1737-1806.* (1983)
Furber, H. [1], *Bombay Presidency in the Mid-Eighteenth Century.* (1965)
_____ [2], 'The East India Directors in 1784', in, *Journal of Modern History.* vol.5. 1933)
_____ _[3], *John Company at Work.* (1948)
_____ __[4], 'The United Company of Merchants trading to the East Indies, 1783-96,' in *English Historical Review,* vol.10.
_____ _[5], 'Edmund Burke and India', in *Bengal Past and Present,* vol.lxxxvl. (1757)
Gentlemans Magazine (New Series)
Gleig. G.R. [1], *The Life of Robert 1st Lord Clive.* (1848)
_____[2], Memoirs of the Life of the Rt. Hon. Warren Hastings, 3 vols. (1841)
Greene, R., *The Forty Eight Laws of Power.* (2000)
Grier, S.C., *The Letters of Warren Hastings to his Wife.* (1905)
Grierson, E., *The Imperial Dream. British Commonwealth & Empire: 1775-1969.* (1972)
Gurney, J.D. [1], The Debts of the Nawab of Arcot, 1763-1776. (Oxford University D.Phil. thesis 1968)
_____ [2], 'Fresh Light on the Character of the Nawab of Arcot', in, Whiteman, A., Bromley, J.S. & Dickson, P.G.M. (eds.), *Statesmen, Scholars and Merchants. Essays in Eighteenth Century History. Presented to Dame Lucy Sutherland.* (1973)
Hamilton, G. H., *Queen Square, its Neighbourhood and Its Institutions.* (1926)
Hanham, H.J., 'Ashburton as a Parliamentary Borough.' *The Devonshire Association. Report on Transactions.* vol. xcviii.
Hansard, T.C., & Cobbett, W. (eds.) *The Parliamentary History of England from the Earliest Period to the year 1803.* vols.14-17. (1813/4)
Hardy, C., *Register of the East India Company's Shipping.* (1799)
Hayward, A. L. (ed.), *A General History of the Robberies and Murders of the most notorious Pirates, by Capt. Charles Johnson.* (1955)

Hill, A.H., 'Three Centuries of the Island', a Historical Geography of Settlement and Agriculture in Prince Edward Island, Canada. Appendix B. (1959)

Hill, S. C, Catalogue of Manuscripts in European Languages in the India Office Library, vol.11, part 1, the Orme Collection. (1916)

Hodson, Major V.C.P., List of the Officers of the Bengal Army, 1758-1834. (1927)

Holwell, J. Z., Important Facts Regarding the East India Company's Affairs in Bengal. (1764)

Holzman, J. M., The Nabobs in England: A Study of the Returned Anglo-Indian 1760-85. (1926)

Hotblack, K., Chatham's Colonial Policy: A study in the Fiscal and Economic Implications of the Colonial Policy of the Elder Pitt. (1917)

James, L., The Rise and Fall of the British Empire. (1998)

John, A. H., 'Insurance Investment and the London Money Market of the Eighteenth Century.' In Economica, new series, xx. (1953)

Johnstone, C.L., History of the Johnstones, 1191-1909. (1909)

Joslin, D.M., 'London Private Bankers: 1720-1785,' in Essays in Economic History, vol.2, edited by E. M. Carus-Wilson. (1966).

Journals of the House of Commons. vol. xxix.

Jucker, N. S. (ed.), The Jenkinson Papers, 1760-1766. (1949)

Judd, G.P., Members of Parliament 1734-1832. (1955)

Kaye & Johnstone, European MSS. in the India Office Library. vol.2, part 2, Minor Collections and Miscellaneous MSS. (1937)

Keay, J., The Honourable Company, A History of the English East India Company. (1991)

Khan, A. M., 'Muhammed Reza Khan, Naib Nazim and Naib Diwan of Bengal, 1756-1775'. (London University Ph.D. thesis 1966)

Laprade, W.T. (ed.), Parliamentary Papers of John Robinson 1774-1784. Camden 3rd Series, vol.xxxliii. (1922)

Lawson, Sir C., The Private Life of Warren Hastings. (1905)

Lawson, P. [1], The East India Company: A History. (1993)

_____[2], 'Parliament and the First East India Inquiry 1767', in Parliamentary History, vol.1 (1982)

Lawson, P. & Philips, J., 'Our Execrable Banditti', in Albion, vol.16, no.3.

Lenman, B. & Lawson, P., 'Robert Clive, the "Black Jagir" and British Politics', in The Historical Journal, vol. 26, no. 4. (1983)

Lewis, W. (ed.), The Yale Edition of Horace Walpole's Correspondence. (1961)

(The) London Assurance, Minutes of the Court of Directors; Minute Books; Copy of Letters 1751-1805.

Love, H. D., Vestiges of Old Madras 1640-1800. 4 vols. (1913)

Low, C. R., History of the Indian Navy. 2 vols. (1877)

Macaulay, T. B., Lord Clive. (1898)

McGilvary, G.K. [1], 'The Early Life and Career of Laurence Sulivan, 1713-1765'. (M. Litt. thesis, Edinburgh University, 1978)

_____ [2], 'East India Patronage and the Political Management of Scotland, 1720-1774'. (Ph.D. thesis, Open University (1989)

Mackay, J.A. (ed.), The Complete Works of Robert Burns. (1988)

Maclean, J.N.M. [1], Reward is Secondary: The Life of a Political Adventurer and an Inquiry into the Mystery of "Junius". (1963)

_____ [2], 'The Early Political Careers of James 'Fingal' Macpherson (1736-1796) and Sir John Macpherson, Bart. (1744-1821)'. (Edinburgh University Ph.D. thesis, 1967)

Magnus, Sir P., Edmund Burke, A Life. (1939)

Malcolm, Sir J., The Life of Robert Lord Clive. 3 vols. (1836)

Marshall, P.J. [1], *Problems of Empire: Britain and India, 1757-1813.* (1968)
_____ [2], 'British Expansion in India in the Eighteenth Century;' A Historical
                  Revision, in, *History*, vol.60. (1975)
_____ [3], *East Indian Fortunes, The British in Bengal in the Eighteenth Century.*
                  (1976)
_____ [4], *The Impeachment of Warren Hastings.* (1965)
_____[5], [ed.], 'The Eighteenth Century', in *The Oxford History of the British
                  Empire,* vol.2. (1998)
_____[6], 'Burke and India', in Crowe, I, [ed.], *Edmund Burke, His Life and
                  Legacy.* (1997)
Miller, J. L., *The History of the Rise and Progress of the Church and Parish of St. George the
Martyr, Holborn.* (1881)
Monckton-Jones, M. E., *Warren Hastings in Bengal 1772-4.* (1918)
Morris, D.B. [1], *Mile End Old Town 1740-1780.* (2002)
_____ [2], 'Mile End Old Town and the East India Company', in *East London
                  Record,* no.9. (1986)
Namier, Sir L. [1], *The Structure of Politics at the Accession of George III.* 2nd edition.
                  (1965)
_____ [2], *England in the Age of the American Revolution.* (1966)
Namier, Sir L. & Brooke, J., *The History of Parliament. 1754-1790.* 3 vols. (1964)
Nightingale, P., *Trade and Empire in Western India 1784-1806.* (1970)
Noble, W.F., *History of the Manors of Ponsbourne and Newgate Street alias Tolmers Bedwell -
alias Bedwell Louth - in the Parishes of Hertford and Essendon Hertfordshire. (1879)*
Norris, J., *Shelburne and Reform.* (1963)
O'Brien, C.C., *The Great Melody: A Thematic Biography and Commented Anthology of
Edmund Burke.* (1994)
O'Hart, J., *Irish Pedigrees.* vol. l. (1915)
Page, W. (ed.), *Victoria History of England.* (1907)
Pandy, B. N., 'Sir Elijah Impey in India 1774-1783'. (Thesis submitted for the degree
of Doctor of Philosophy in the University of London. S.O.A.S. 1958)
Parker, J.G., 'The Directors of the East India Company, 1754-1790'. (Ph.D. thesis,
University of Edinburgh, 1977)
Parkes, J. & Merivale, H., *Memoirs of Sir Philip Francis with Correspondence and Journals.* 2
vols. (1867)
Paurvels, L. & Bergier, J., *The Dawn of Magic.* (1963)
Peters, M, *The Elder Pitt.* (1998)
Philips, C.H. [1], *Handbook of Oriental History.* (1963)
_____ [2], Review of L. S. Sutherland, 'East India Company in Eighteenth
                  Century Politics,' in *English Historical Review,* no.70. (July, 1955)
_____ [3], 'The Secret Committee of the East India Company,' in *Bulletin of
                  the School of Oriental and African Studies,* vol.l0, part 2. (1940)
_____ [4], *The East India Company 1784-1834.* (1961)
_____ [5], 'The East India Company Interest and the English Government
                  1783-4,' *Transactions of the Royal Historical Society,* 4th Series, vol.XX.
                  (1937)
Philips, J., 'A Successor to the Moguls: The Nawab of the Carnatic and the East India
Company, 1763-1785', in Patrick Tuck, *The East India Company 1600-1858.* vol.4.
(1998)
Prendergast, J., 'History of the O'Sullivans', in *Cork Historical and Archaeological Society
Journal,* vols. 4 (1898); 5 (1899); 6. (1900)
Prinivasachari, C.S. (ed.), *Fort William–India House Correspondence.* vol.4. (1764-66)

Prinsep, C.C., *Record of the Services of the Honourable East India Company's Civil Servants 1741-1858*. (1885)

Records of Fort St.George, Madras, *'Diary and Consultation Books'*. (1932)

Register of Admissions to the Honourable Society of the Middle Temple', vol.1. (1501-1781)

Register of Burials, Cemetery of St. George the Martyr, Queen Square.

Reports from Committees of the House of Commons. vols.5 and 6. (1782-83)

Riddy, J., 'Warren Hastings: Scotland's Benefactor', in G. Carnall & C. Nicholson (eds.), *The Impeachment of Warren Hastings*. (1989)

Saunders, T.B., *The Life and Letters of James MacPherson*. (1895)

Sethi, R.R., *Fort William–India House Correspondence*. vol.3. (1760-63)

Shearer, T., 'Crisis and Change in the Development of the East India Company's Affairs, 1760-1773'. (Ph.D. thesis. University of Oxford, 1976).

Sinha, H.N., *Fort William-India House Correspondence*. vol.2 (1757-1759). (1957)

Spear, P. [1], *Master of Bengal: Clive and his India*. (1975)

_____ [2], *The Nabobs*. (1932)

Spencer, A., (ed.), *Memoirs of William Hickey*. 4 vols. (1913)

Spencer, F., (ed.), *The Fourth Earl of Sandwich: Diplomatic Correspondence 1763-1765*. (1961)

Supple, B., *The Royal Exchange Insurance: a History of British Insurance 1720–1970*. (1970)

Sutherland, L.S, [1], *The East India Company in Eighteenth-Century Politics*. 2nd edition. (1962)

_____ [2], 'The East India Company and the Peace of Paris', in *English Historical Review*, vol.62. (1947)

_____ [3], *A London Merchant 1695-1774*. (1933)

_____ [4], 'Lord Shelburne and East India Company Politics', 1766-69, in *English Historical Review*, vol.49. (1934)

_____ [5], 'Lord Macartney's Appointment as Governor of Madras, 1780: The Treasury in East India Company Elections', in *English Historical Review*, vol. xc. (July 1975)

_____ [6], 'The Resignation on Behalf of Warren Hastings, 1776: George Vansittart's Evidence', in A. Newman (ed.), *Politics and Finance in the Eighteenth Century*. (1984)

_____ [7], 'The City of London and the Devonshire-Pitt Administration, 1756-7', in A. Newman (ed.), *Politics and Finance in the Eighteenth Century*. (1984)

Sutherland, L.S. & Woods, J., 'The East India Speculations of William Burke', in A. Newman (ed.), *Politics and Finance in the Eighteenth Century*. (1984)

Sutton, J, *Lords of the East: The East India Company and its ships (1600-1874)*. (2000)

Srinivasachari, K.D., *Fort William–India House Correspondence*, vols. 1-6. (1957 to 1960)

Taylor, W.S. & Pringle, J.H. (eds.), *Correspondence of William Pitt, Earl of Chatham*. 4 vol. (mdcccxl)

Tomlinson, J. (ed.), *Additional Grenville Papers, 1763-1765*. (1962)

Trevor-Roper, H., 'The Ossian Forgeries', in *The Spectator*. (16 March 1985)

Weitzman, S., *Warren Hastings and Philip Francis*. (1929)

Williams, B., *Life of William Pitt, Earl of Chatham*. 2 vols. (1913)

Wylly, Col. H.C., *A Life of Lt. Gen. Sir Eyre Coote K. B.* (1922)

Yapp, M.E., 'The Brightest Jewel', in Ballhatchet, K. & Harrison, J.[eds.], *East India Company Studies. Papers presented to Professor Sir Cyril Philips*. (1986)

Glossary

'Arcot Interest': Madras Councillors and their associates in Parliament and in the Company benefiting from involvement in the Nawab of Arcot's debts.

Assignment of the Carnatic Revenues: This was the annual sum due from four of the Nawab of Arcot's districts, assigned to the debt-ridden Madras government in October 1781.

Batta was an allowance given to officers in the field, but was generally applied to all ranks. The officers obtained the revenues from the cultivation of land reserved for that use.

A begah approximated to one third of an acre.

Bills of exchange: Rupees were paid into a settlement's treasury in India; the equivalent sum, in sterling, was recovered by an agent in London after the sales.

Charter parties were the signatories (ship's owners as well as master) who agreed with the Company to the terms of the hire of a ship.

Comptoirs: This alluded to factories or trading settlements during the peace negotiations with France between 1761 and 1763.

Country trade (Coastal trade): The term used to signify European commerce with Indian peoples and merchants throughout the East Indies. The normal commerce was in peppers and spices, silks and betel nut, indigo, cotton and saltpetre. This exchange was distinct from the traffic of goods to and from India and Europe carried by EastIndiamen.

Dastak: The passport or permit granted to the Company to trade.

Directors: Proprietors who owned £2,000 of Company stock chosen by ballot at Company election in April each year (until 1774).

Diwani: The right to receive the revenue-collections of Bengal, Bihar and Orissa.

Durbar: The term used to describe a Nawab's court.

EastIndiamen: Company registered ships that had the monopoly of sailing from London to the East Indies and return.

Factor: The second appointment in the Company's civil service in the settlements abroad.

Firman: The imperial grant confirming the right to trade.

Free Merchant (Free trader): European (usually British) merchants involved in the country (or coastal) trade along the coasts of India and in the Indies in general. No commerce was allowed with Europe.

General Letters: Official communications from the Directors in London to the Presidencies; and the same from the Governor and Council of each Presidency to India House.

Investment: Funds required that were gathered by each settlement in order to purchase goods that were later sold in London.

Jagir: This was a quit-rent paid for territory. It was 'A tenure common under Mughal rule, in which the revenues of a given tract of land along with the power of government were made over to a servant of the state. The assignment was either conditional or unconditional, usually for life, lapsing, on the holder's death, to the state.'

Lakh: A sum of rupees worth approximately £12,500.

Leadenhall (Street): Location of India House, Company headquarters.

Mayor's Courts were established at Bombay, Madras and Calcutta in 1726. Each Court consisted of a Mayor and nine Aldermen, seven of whom were to be natural born British subjects.

Pagoda: The gold coin formerly minted at Madras, named thus because of the temple device on its face.

Pargana: Sub-division of a district, including many villages.

Permanent Bottoms: came to mean a vested right by owners and/or commanders to have a ship in the Company's service.

Perpetuity of Command: came to mean a vested right by a commander to a right of command. It became a 'property' to sell, with control over appointments, a monopoly.

Phirmaund: letters patent. Mughal authorisation.

Proprietors: Owners of East India stock.

Rupees: In the mid-eighteenth century a rupee was worth between two and three shillings sterling.

Sepoys: The name given to Indian troops.

Ship's Husband: For purposes of organisation one of the owners chosen as managing-owner, agent, or, as he was usually called, 'ship's husband'. He was responsible for supervising the building, fitting and sailing of the ship and had to keep complete accounts. These were incorporated into those kept by the master and purser during the voyage and presented by the ship's husband at a meeting of the owners when the ship returned.

Shipping interest: A body whose main concern was to perpetuate the Company as a trading monopoly; and also held strong views on state intervention. It took a decisive part, especially under the ship's husband in the election of directors.

Subadari: Military government of a Province. This meant ownership and administration of the area as well as military overlordship.

Supercargo: He looked after the ship's manifest, handling freight charges and the purchasing and sale of goods on board. Although not one of the crew, he would have appeared on the ship's muster.

Writer: This was the lowest rank in the Company's civil service in the Presidencies abroad.

Zamindari: Revenue collecting powers.

Index